AAA Identity Management Security

Vivek Santuka, CCIE #17621

Premdeep Banga, CCIE #21713

Brandon J. Carroll, CCIE #23837

D1224886

Cisco Press

800 East 96th Street

Indianapolis, IN 46240

AAA Identity Management Security

Vivek Santuka, Premdeep Banga, Brandon J. Carroll

Copyright © 2011 Cisco Systems, Inc.

Published by:
Cisco Press
800 East 96th Street
Indianapolis, IN 46240 USA

All rights reserved. No part of this book may be reproduced or transmitted in any form or by any means, electronic or mechanical, including photocopying, recording, or by any information storage and retrieval system, without written permission from the publisher, except for the inclusion of brief quotations in a review.

Printed in the United States of America

First Printing November 2010

Library of Congress Cataloging-in-Publication data is on file.

ISBN-13: 978-1-58714-144-7

ISBN-10: 1-58714-144-2

Warning and Disclaimer

This book is designed to provide information about AAA Identity Management Security. Every effort has been made to make this book as complete and as accurate as possible, but no warranty or fitness is implied.

The information is provided on an "as is" basis. The authors, Cisco Press, and Cisco Systems, Inc. shall have neither liability nor responsibility to any person or entity with respect to any loss or damages arising from the information contained in this book or from the use of the discs or programs that may accompany it.

The opinions expressed in this book belong to the author and are not necessarily those of Cisco Systems, Inc.

Trademark Acknowledgments

All terms mentioned in this book that are known to be trademarks or service marks have been appropriately capitalized. Cisco Press or Cisco Systems, Inc., cannot attest to the accuracy of this information. Use of a term in this book should not be regarded as affecting the validity of any trademark or service mark.

Corporate and Government Sales

The publisher offers excellent discounts on this book when ordered in quantity for bulk purchases or special sales, which may include electronic versions and/or custom covers and content particular to your business, training goals, marketing focus, and branding interests. For more information, please contact:

U.S. Corporate and Government Sales   1-800-382-3419   corpsales@pearsontechgroup.com

For sales outside the United States please contact: **International Sales**   international@pearsoned.com

Feedback Information

At Cisco Press, our goal is to create in-depth technical books of the highest quality and value. Each book is crafted with care and precision, undergoing rigorous development that involves the unique expertise of members from the professional technical community.

Readers' feedback is a natural continuation of this process. If you have any comments regarding how we could improve the quality of this book, or otherwise alter it to better suit your needs, you can contact us through email at feedback@ciscopress.com. Please make sure to include the book title and ISBN in your message.

We greatly appreciate your assistance.

Publisher: Paul Boger	**Cisco Representative:** Erik Ullanderson
Associate Publisher: Dave Dusthimer	**Cisco Press Program Manager:** Anand Sundaram
Executive Editor: Brett Bartow	**Senior Development Editor:** Christopher Cleveland
Managing Editor: Sandra Schroeder	**Technical Editors:** Rohit Chopra, JesseDubois, Chris Murray
Project Editor: Seth Kerney	**Proofreader:** Leslie Joseph
Editorial Assistant: Vanessa Evans	**Copy Editor:** Mike Henry
Book and Cover Designer: Louisa Adair	**Indexer:** Tim Wright
Composition: Mark Shirar	

Americas Headquarters	**Asia Pacific Headquarters**	**Europe Headquarters**
Cisco Systems, Inc.	Cisco Systems (USA) Pte. Ltd.	Cisco Systems International BV
San Jose, CA	Singapore	Amsterdam, The Netherlands

Cisco has more than 200 offices worldwide. Addresses, phone numbers, and fax numbers are listed on the Cisco Website at **www.cisco.com/go/offices**.

CCDE, CCENT, Cisco Eos, Cisco HealthPresence, the Cisco logo, Cisco Lumin, Cisco Nexus, Cisco StadiumVision, Cisco TelePresence, Cisco WebEx, DCE, and Welcome to the Human Network are trademarks; Changing the Way We Work, Live, Play, and Learn and Cisco Store are service marks; and Access Registrar, Aironet, AsyncOS, Bringing the Meeting To You, Catalyst, CCDA, CCDP, CCIE, CCIP, CCNA, CCNP, CCSP, CCVP, Cisco, the Cisco Certified Internetwork Expert logo, Cisco IOS, Cisco Press, Cisco Systems, Cisco Systems Capital, the Cisco Systems logo, Cisco Unity, Collaboration Without Limitation, EtherFast, EtherSwitch, Event Center, Fast Step, Follow Me Browsing, FormShare, GigaDrive, HomeLink, Internet Quotient, IOS, iPhone, iQuick Study, IronPort, the IronPort logo, LightStream, Linksys, MediaTone, MeetingPlace, MeetingPlace Chime Sound, MGX, Networkers, Networking Academy, Network Registrar, PCNow, PIX, PowerPanels, ProConnect, ScriptShare, SenderBase, SMARTnet, Spectrum Expert, StackWise, The Fastest Way to Increase Your Internet Quotient, TransPath, WebEx, and the WebEx logo are registered trademarks of Cisco Systems, Inc. and/or its affiliates in the United States and certain other countries.

All other trademarks mentioned in this document or website are the property of their respective owners. The use of the word partner does not imply a partnership relationship between Cisco and any other company. (0812R)

About the Authors

Vivek Santuka, CCIE No. 17621, joined Cisco TAC - Global Partner Delivery Management five years ago as a Customer Support Engineer in the AAA team. He then moved to a Technical Lead role and led a team of 15 engineers in resolving complicated AAA cases. He is currently working in the IPS signature development team. He holds two CCIEs, one in Security and the other in Routing and Switching. In addition to that, he holds a RHCE certification.

Premdeep Banga, CCIE No. 21713, joined Cisco TAC - Global Partner Delivery Management five years ago as a Customer Support Engineer in the AAA team where he was instrumental in training and mentoring of many new engineers. Prem has extensive knowledge of AAA technology and experience in real-life customer deployments. He is currently working in the IPS signature development team. He holds a CCIE in Security. In addition to that, he holds a SSCP certification.

Brandon J Carroll, CCIE No. 23837, is a Senior Technical Instructor and has been training in Cisco Related Technologies for more than nine years. Brandon has consulted on large enterprise and service provider networks. Brandon is the author of other Cisco Press titles and has attended St. Leo University. He holds a CCIE in Security.

About the Technical Reviewers

Rohit Chopra, CCIE No. 20325 (Security), is one of the Lead Engineers in High Touch Technical Support (HTTS) based in Bangalore, India, where he has been working as a Security Technologies Engineer for the last year. In his current role, he is involved in troubleshooting security/VPN/AAA issues in some of the biggest and most critical networks in the industry around the world. Before joining HTTS, Rohit was Security Lead with Advanced Services Virtual Team where he collaborated between teams to contribute towards rule creation and leading practice document creation and also helped virtual teams with security technologies. He has also handled diverse projects at the capacity of Project Manager with Cisco Advanced Services. Prior to that Rohit was an Escalation Engineer in the Cisco Technical Assistance Center (TAC) based in Gurgaon, India, for four years. Rohit routinely provided escalation support to his immediate team and other security support teams within Cisco. He imparts training as well as answers customer questions on the Networking Professionals Connection e-community. His areas of expertise are configuring and troubleshooting all forms of security technologies such as identity management, IPS, Firewall, NAC, and VPN. Rohit holds a bachelor's degree in Electronics and Telecommunication Engineering, is MCSE Certified, and holds total experience of more than nine years in the networking domain.

Jesse Dubois is a customer support engineer working in the Technical Assistance Center (TAC) for Cisco, and he has been focusing on the Security/AAA team since 2005. Jesse works with customers from around the world, assisting with Security/AAA products from the Cisco portfolio. Jesse graduated with a bachelor's degree in applied networking and system administration from the Rochester Institute of Technology in 2005.

Chris Murray is the tech lead in the ACS sustaining team at Cisco, where he supports and enhances both the 4.x and 5.x products. He was one of the original developers of ACS, and he has been developing and supporting ACS ever since. He has been working in the software and networking fields since the early 1980s.

Dedications

I would like to dedicate this book to my best friend and wife Sweta, Mom, and Dad. Thank you for being there for me.

—Vivek

I would like to dedicate this book to my family, Mom, Dad, Sis, and my friend for life, my wife Aastha; and to my colleagues and friends. Thank you for limitless love and support.

—Prem

This book is dedicated to my wife Celeste, who continues to put up with me. She is always understanding when it comes to the things I love, such as the technologies seen in this book. Also I would like to say thanks to my sons, Weston and Logan, who give me something to turn to when the technology doesn't go my way. I love you guys and thank you for your patience with me.

—Brandon

Acknowledgments

From Vivek:

First, I want to thank Nirav Sheth, whose support and encouragement has made this book possible. Sir, you truly are a gem of a person and it is an honor to work with you.

I also want to thank the Cisco Press Program Manager Anand Sundaram, Brett Barrow, Christopher Cleveland and the rest of the team at Cisco Press for their hard work.

Thank you to Prem and Brandon for agreeing to be a part of this book and giving those countless hours.

Finally to the person who makes my life complete—my lovely wife Sweta—for supporting me through everything.

From Prem:

There are so many people that are behind completion of this book. To start with, Nirav Sheth, for helping initiate this book, holding us through wherever and in whatever way possible, without whom this book or me being an author couldn't be a reality; also many thanks to Anand Sundaram. I also want to thank Brett Bartow, Christopher Cleveland, and the rest of the team for being there for any query that we had.

I wasn't aware of what goes into writing a book, especially where to start, so thank you Brandon for sharing your experience with us, it really helped and meant a lot. I can never forget Vivek for his help, input, directions, and the list goes on. Words are not enough to cover what you have contributed; therefore I am only going to say a big thank you to you.

I would also like to thank the members of the TAC family here, especially the AAA team. Special thanks to my managers for being supportive.

This book, being my first book as an author, means a lot to me, and there are many more people to thank. To everyone who contributed in the completion of this book, thank you so much!

From Brandon:

I'd like to give special recognition to my coauthors Vivek and Prem. These guys have had a ton of patience with me in the process of writing this book. They have provided loads of support and without them I would have had a very difficult time.

I also want to recognize the team at Cisco Press who make this all come together. They are such a professional team that I must thank them for all the support.

I want to thank Tyson Scott for being a technical mentor to me and teaching me a lot.

I also want to thank Ascolta Training and Ted Wagner, Irene Kinoshita, Kevin Mars, and all the instructors there as well as the support guys—especially Kevin Masui. Ascolta gave me my start in Cisco training and it was there that I grew to love teaching about technology.

Contents at a Glance

Contents

Icons Used in This Book

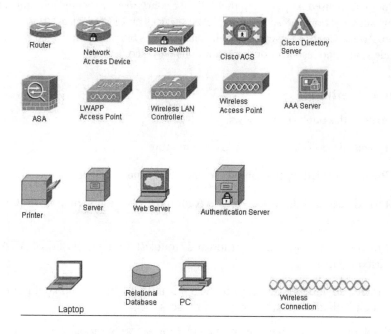

Command Syntax Conventions

The conventions used to present command syntax in this book are the same conventions used in the IOS Command Reference. The Command Reference describes these conventions as follows:

- Boldface indicates commands and keywords that are entered literally as shown. In actual configuration examples and output (not general command syntax), boldface indicates commands that are manually input by the user (such as a **show** command).

- *Italic* indicates arguments for which you supply actual values.

- Vertical bars (|) separate alternative, mutually exclusive elements.

- Square brackets ([ ]) indicate an optional element.

- Braces ({ }) indicate a required choice.

- Braces within brackets ([{ }]) indicate a required choice within an optional element.

Introduction

This book is focused on providing the skills necessary to successfully configure authentication, authorization, and accounting (AAA) services on Cisco devices using Cisco Secure Access Control Server/System 4.2 and 5.1. This book was motivated by a desire to provide a one-stop resource for AAA solutions on Cisco devices.

Goals and Methods

The goals of this book are as follows:

■ Provide an overview of the AAA architecture

■ Provide detailed discussion on the TACACS+ and RADIUS protocols

■ Provide detailed discussion on AAA for most common scenarios of network access

■ Provide an in depth configuration and troubleshooting overview of AAA on Cisco devices

■ Provide an in-depth overview of ACS 4.2 and 5.1 features and configuration to match with configuration on Cisco devices

This book discusses different means to control the access to various network resources. This is followed by configuration and troubleshooting on Cisco devices and ACS. In the end, you are given a lab scenario to reinforce the learning.

Who Should Read This Book?

This book is targeted toward the following people:

■ Network security professionals tasked with the implementation and management of access control and identity management using Cisco devices and/or Cisco ACS.

■ Those who are pursuing different Cisco certifications requiring knowledge of AAA, such as CCSP and CCIE.

How This Book Is Organized

This book is separated into the following six logical parts.

■ Part I, "AAA and CiscoSecure ACS"—This part is designed to introduce AAA and ACS. Chapters 1 and 2 provide an overview of AAA and ACS. Chapters 3 and 4 provide an in-depth understanding of ACS 4.2 and ACS 5.1. Chapter 5 builds on the previous two chapters and dicusses various user databases which can be configured with ACS.

■ Part II, "Administrative AAA"—This part is designed to discuss AAA for administrative sessions on Cisco IOS and Cisco PIX/ASA. This part is also the foundation of establishing and troubleshooting connectivity between devices and ACS. It contains two chapters and five lab scenarios.

■ Part III, "802.1x"—This part is designed to discuss the IEEE 802.1x protcol and its implementation on Cisco Catalyst Switches and Cisco Access Points. In this part you will learn about different EAP types, their advantages and disadvantages, and how to configure Cisco devices, ACS, and clients running Windows XP. This part contains two chapters and five lab scenarios.

■ Part IV, "Pass-Through Traffic"—This part discusses access control on traffic passing through a device running Cisco IOS and through Cisco ASA/PIX. This part contains two chapters and three lab scenarios.

■ Part V, "Remote Access"—This part discusses access control on Remote Access sessions such as VPN and PPP on Cisco IOS and Cisco PIX/ASA. This part contains two chapters and three lab scenarios.

■ Part VI, "ACS Advanced Configuration"—The final part of the book looks at advanced topics of ACS management such as backup, restore, remote logging, and replication. This part contains two chapters.

Chapter 1

Authentication, Authorization, Accounting (AAA)

This chapter covers the following topics:

- **Overview of Authentication, Authorization, and Accounting (AAA):** This section provides a brief overview of the AAA concept.

- **Authentication:** This section provides the fundamental concepts behind authentication.

- **Authorization:** This section provides the fundamental concepts behind authorization.

- **Accounting:** This section provides the fundamental concepts behind accounting.

- **Overview of RADIUS:** This section discusses the RADIUS protocol and its role in AAA.

- **Overview of TACACS+:** This section discusses the TACACS+ protocol and its role in AAA.

It has always been interesting to me that different aspects of networking can relate so closely to the things that we do in real life. If you would have asked me to explain authentication, authorization, and accounting (AAA) seven years ago, you would have probably received a different answer. If I were to sum it all up in simple terms today, I would say that AAA is the process of verifying who you are (authentication), what you can do (authorization), and what you did while you were here (accounting). Of course that's perhaps oversimplifying it, but you at least get the point. There are multiple actions involved in AAA because AAA is a framework that provides three independent functions.

The goal of this chapter is to put AAA into perspective so that when the time comes to configure and verify you will be well equipped to do so and should the need arise, understanding the differences of each process will strengthen your skills at troubleshooting. In the following sections you'll learn what authentication, authorization, and accounting is, put in terms that relate to everyday life. Finally you'll learn about two common protocols used in AAA: Remote Authentication Dial-In User Service (RADIUS) and Terminal Access Controller Access Control System Plus (TACACS+).

Tip   AAA is discussed in a number of Requests for Comments (RFCs). RFC 2903 discusses the general AAA architecture. This is an experimental RFC. Since then, AAA has been more clearly defined in other RFCs. Other RFCs include RFC 2924, Accounting Attributes and Record Formats; RFC 2975, Introduction to Accounting Management; RFC 2989, Criteria for Evaluating AAA Protocols for Network Access; and RFC 3127, Authentication, Authorization, and Accounting: Protocol Evaluation. A great deal of information on AAA can be obtained at http://www.ietf.org/html.charters/aaa-charter.html. You can also find information on RADIUS in RFC 2865. It's also mentionable that TACACS+ never made it as an RFC; however it is available as a draft.

Authentication Overview

As was mentioned in the introduction paragraph, I now see things in a relationship with common activities in day-to-day life. I have come to compare common networking scenarios to scenarios that happen outside of networking and see many parallels. Take for instance a night at the movies. You buy a ticket to see a new release and are excited about seeing it. You walk through the entry of the theatre and are asked to show your ticket. You are being authenticated. Authentication can take place based on something you have. In this case, you have a ticket, so you are admitted.

In another scenario, you are invited to a secret society meeting—spies only! Upon arrival, you are asked for the "*secret password*." You reply "*JumpinJackFlash*" and are admitted to the meeting. Again you were authenticated, only this time, it was not something you had that you used to authenticate; it was something you know.

For a third example, you were so wrapped up in that secret spy movie that you saw you have decided to join the ranks and become a spy (this is why you infiltrated the secret society). After your spy training, you are given the location to a secret spy hangout. When you arrive at the door, you see a retinal scanner and a fingerprint scanner. You present your eye and your index finger and the big metal door slides open allowing entrance. In this situation, you were again authenticated, only this time it wasn't based on something you had (although having your index finger and eye is a good thing), and it wasn't something you knew. This time it was something you are.

In short, authentication can be based on:

- Something you have

- Something you know

- Something you are

When you relate this to a Cisco environment, you will see that various scenarios would call for different types of authentication. For example, using 802.1x (discussed in Chapter 8, "IOS Switches") you might choose to authenticate users on a wireless network using Extensible Authentication Protocol-Transport Layer Security (EAP-TLS). This would involve the use of a client certificate (something you have) to authenticate to the authentication server. In another scenario, you would like to use the Secure Shell (SSH) protocol to manage a router on your network. Upon connecting to your router, you are presented with a prompt to enter a username followed by a prompt to enter a password (something you know)

Just as many types of authentication processes take place in today's world, many types of authentication methods can be performed on a Cisco device. An example of an authentication method might be a state-issued driver license or a boarding pass for a specific airline. When the airline attendants request identification for the use of their services, you are prepared with the proper identification. This is the most basic process of AAA.

Authentication provides a method for identifying users and includes login and password prompting, challenge and response functions, messaging support, and quite possibly encryption as well. Authentication usually takes place prior to a user being allowed access to any of the network resources.

Note   Authentication can take place as an individual process or can be combined with authorization and accounting.

When you configure a Cisco device for authentication, you need to complete three basic steps:

Step 1.   Enable the AAA process. Although AAA is a common protocol that is seen in most enterprise networks, the protocol is not enabled by default.

Step 2.   Define the location, protocol, and secret key for the server communication.

Step 3.   Define a method list and protocols for authentication.

A method list defines the type of authentication to be performed and in which sequence to perform it. You must apply the method list to an interface before the authentication methods are used; however, one exception to this rule of application exists. A default list exists and believe it or not, it's named "default." This default method list is applied to any interface, line, or service, if a specific list is not configured or specified already. In a nutshell, the default method list does whatever you tell it to. You are responsible for defining the methods used by the default method list.

Auth-Proxy is a method by which users can be authenticated when accessing a network service. As users attempt to access a network service, they are presented with an authentication prompt. The users can then prove that they are who they say they are. In your network environment, this prompt can be presented in a Telnet application, File Transfer Protocol (FTP) application, or web application. You can also use virtual authentication methods such as virtual Hypertext Transfer Protocol (HTTP) and virtual Telnet. If users need access to other resources, one of the previously mentioned methods of access must be performed first or an alternative method such as *virtual Telnet* must be used because other protocols can't be used to present the user with a prompt.

Authentication Example

In this example, your user "local-admin" is attempting to Telnet to a Cisco router. The Cisco router is configured to request authentication from anyone that attempts to access it via Telnet. As the user enters a password, it is sent as clear text to the router. The router then takes that username and password and if authenticating to an external server, places it in a packet that is sent to an AAA server, such as Access Control Server (ACS), or it could keep the credentials local and compare them to a locally configured username and password.

Here is a step-by-step look at the process as illustrated in Figure 1-1:

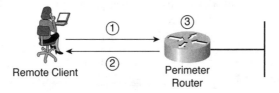

Figure 1-1   *A Simple Authentication Example*

Step 1.   The client establishes connection with the router.

Step 2.   The router prompts the user for her username and password.

Step 3.   The router authenticates the username and password in the local database. The user is authorized to access the network based on information in the local database.

Of course, Telnet is not the recommended type of connectivity in which to perform authentication because anyone that has access to the network and the data path can see the username and password by using an application such as Wireshark. In fact, most protocols don't encrypt the password and yes, although some claim encryption, it's often a weak cipher and can be susceptible to brute force attacks. More secure methods might include protocols such as the Challenge Handshake Authentication Protocol (CHAP), or even the use of one-time passwords or the use of smart tokens such as RSA SecurID or CRYPTOCard. The point is that you should really understand the type of traffic you are allowing users to authenticate within.

Authorization Overview

To take AAA a step further, imagine that you are about to take a vacation. You are going to take a commercial airline to your vacation hotspot. The airplane has a couple of rows in the front that are very nice, leather, wide, and comfortable. You would prefer to sit here instead of the seats that are farther back because those are stiff, uncomfortable, and do not offer much leg room. Unfortunately, if you purchased a coach class ticket, you cannot sit in the first-class seat in the front of the plane. Similar to this process is the authorization function of AAA. If you have a coach-authorized ticket, you cannot access first-class resources. This information is all kept in the airline's database and can easily be veri-fied by looking up your identity (name) in the computer and referencing the seat assign-ment. That's the basic process of authorization.

Authorization is a method of providing certain privileges or rights to remote users for services requested. It's likely that you are going to see EXEC authorization, where one user is allowed access to an EXEC shell and another is allowed access to a privilege shell. This can be configured for a group that a user belongs to, or it can be configured on an individual user basis, depending on your goal. User authorization overrides group author-ization. Authorization can be configured locally in some cases or kept on a remote AAA server. The remote server might be easier for administration depending on your network environment. Authorization is the second module of the AAA framework.

The following steps are needed for authorization to take place:

Step 1.   AAA assembles a set of attributes based on the services that a user is request-ing authorization to perform.

Step 2.   These attributes are compared against a database that contains the user's actual permissions.

Step 3.   After a user's authorization is verified or not verified, the result is returned to the AAA process.

Step 4.   After the preceding step sequence, the AAA process is then able to impose the proper restrictions to the user data.

Step 5.   If the user's authorizations are located on a remote server, they are usually determined by comparing to Attribute-Value (AV) pairs, which are discussed in Chapter 13, "Authentication, Authorization, and Accounting of VPN on ASA."

As seen in the "Authentication Overview" section of this chapter, a method list config-ures authentication. A method list is also used to define the method of authorization. One thing to keep in mind though is that you'll need to authenticate a user before you can determine what that user is authorized to do. Therefore, authorization requires authentication.

Authorization Example

Figure 1-2 demonstrates a basic authorization process that can take place; that is, after the authentication process shown in the previous example. One difference you might note here is that with the previous authentication example, only a local authentication was discussed. In this authorization example, the AAA server is added to give you an idea of the process when an external server is used. This server can be used for authorizations, as seen in Figure 1-2, but it can, and usually is, also used to authenticate users.

In this situation, the following steps take place:

Step 1.   After authentication has been completed, a session is established with an AAA server.

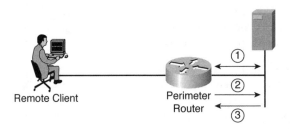

Figure 1-2   *Basic Authorization of FTP*

Step 2.   The router requests authorization for the requested service from the AAA server.

Step 3.   The AAA server returns a PASS/FAIL for authorization.

As already seen with authentication, a method list is also used here. This method list, however, does not define a method of authentication; rather, this method list defines what authorization is to be performed. The configuration of a method list for authorization is very similar to the method list configuration for authentication that was already discussed. It is nearly the same as a method list that would define accounting, although there will be slight differences.

Accounting Overview

The final portion of AAA is the accounting module. Accounting can also be explained using an example of the airline industry as seen in the "Authorization Overview" section. As you enter or board the plane, you hand a boarding pass to the agent, and it is scanned through a machine. This accounts for you boarding the plane. As far as the airline is concerned, you were there and you were on the airplane. AAA accounting is similar. When you access the network, AAA can begin to track any actions you take. After you authenticate, you were there, as far as the AAA process is concerned.

Accounting in a Cisco environment enables you to track the amount of network resources your users are accessing and the types of services they are using. For example, system administrators might need to bill departments or customers for connection time or resources used on the network (for example, total time connected). AAA accounting enables you to track this activity, as well as suspicious connection attempts into the network.

When using AAA accounting, the router can send messages either to the AAA server or to a remote SYSLOG server, depending on your configuration. You then have the ability to import the accounting records into a spreadsheet or accounting program for viewing. The Access Control Server (ACS) can be used to store these accounting messages, and you can also download these accounting statements in .CSV format or use Open Database Connectivity (ODBC) logging, which is supported in ACS. You can even install a Log agent and forward log information to a Cisco Secure-Monitoring Analysis and Response System (CS-MARS) for mitigation monitoring and correlation.

The accounting records sent by a Cisco device to the accounting server are sent in the form of an AV pair. An AV pair is an attribute and a value. Some of these attribute value (AV) pairs contain information such as username, address, the service being requested, or the Cisco device that this request is going through, also known as the access server or AAA client.

AAA supports multiple types of accounting including the following:

- **Network accounting:** Network accounting provides information for all Point-to-Point Protocol (PPP), Serial Line Internet Protocol (SLIP), or Apple Remote Access Protocol (ARAP) sessions, including packet and byte counts.

- **Connection accounting:** Connection accounting provides information about all outbound connections made from the AAA client, such as Telnet, local area transport (LAT), TN3270, packet assembler/disassembler (PAD), and rlogin.

- **EXEC accounting:** EXEC accounting provides information about user EXEC terminal sessions (user shells) on the network access server, including username, date, start and stop times, the access server IP address, and (for dial-in users) the telephone number the call originated from.

- **System accounting:** System accounting provides information about all system-level events (for example, when the system reboots or when accounting is turned on or off).

- **Command accounting:** Command accounting provides information about the EXEC shell commands for a specified privilege level that are being executed on a network access server. Each command accounting record includes a list of the commands executed for that privilege level, as well as the date and time each command was executed, and the user who executed it.

- **Resource accounting:** The Cisco implementation of AAA accounting provides start and stop record support for calls that have passed user authentication. The additional feature of generating stop records for calls that fail to authenticate as part of user authentication is also supported. Such records are necessary for users employing accounting records to manage and monitor their networks.

Accounting Example

Back once again to our sample network, you can now use AAA accounting to perform one of the previously mentioned types of accounting. In this example, you pick up after authentication and authorization have taken place. Here resource accounting performs start stop accounting for FTP on the network. See Figure 1-3.

In this example, the following process is performed. Note that once again authentication must take place.

Step 1.   After a user has been authenticated, the AAA accounting process on the AAA client generates a start message to signify the beginning of the session.

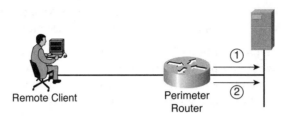

Remote Client   Perimeter
                                    Router

Figure 1-3   *Basic Accounting of Resources*

Step 2.   When the user finishes his session and disconnects, a stop message is sent by
              the AAA client to signify the end of the session.

Again, a method list determines what type of accounting is to be performed.

Now that you have the core knowledge of the AAA process, there is still another element
of AAA that needs to be addressed. That element is the actual communication protocol
between the AAA server and the AAA client. That communication can be done using
either RADIUS or TACACS+. The remainder of this chapter explains these protocols and
how they differ.

Overview of RADIUS

RADIUS is a protocol that supports each of the three modules of AAA. Cisco Systems
introduced support for RADIUS in Cisco IOS Software Release 11.1 and it has gained
more and more support over the years. The RADIUS authentication protocol is docu-
mented separately from the accounting protocol; however, the two can be used together.

Note   RADIUS can be referenced in RFC 2865 and 2866. These RFCs supersede RFC
2138 and RFC 2139.

RADIUS was developed by Livingston Enterprises, Inc. Even though Livingston is no
longer around, after being subject to acquisition, RADIUS has lasted and is covered in
RFC 2865 as an open standard, which differs from its alternative, the TACACS+ protocol
that is implemented by Cisco. RADIUS is an IP-based protocol that uses UDP as its transport, an AAA client, and an AAA server.

Imagine a user attempting to access a resource that requires AAA authentication. The
device that is configured to authenticate the user is the AAA client. This client then
prompts the user for credentials, sends those credentials to the AAA server, and waits for
a response, PASS/FAIL, from the AAA server. The AAA server returns a result to the
AAA client based on the compared credentials in a local or external database. In addition, the AAA server might return other attributes to the AAA client, which might
include access-control filters, locks to a group, and so on. This information that the AAA
server returns to the client can be located on the AAA server or on an external device

that the server communicates with directly, such as LDAP, Active Directory, Token Card Servers, and so on. When this is the case, the requesting user does not have any knowledge of the communication that is conveyed between the AAA client and the AAA server. While the client is using some network protocol such as TCP to access the resource that it is being authenticated for, the communication between the AAA client and the AAA server is sent via RADIUS.

Additionally, RADIUS performs authentication and authorization at the same time and accounting separately, unlike the alternative TACACS+, which separates each process.

RADIUS in Detail

RADIUS is an Internet Engineering Task Force (IETF) standard that is used for AAA. It is also a client/server model. This means the AAA client sends user information to the AAA server, in this case via the RADIUS protocol, and the RADIUS server responds with all the information that is needed for the AAA client to provide connectivity and service to the end user. The AAA client acts in response to the reply it receives from the RADIUS server.

For network authentication, a shared secret key authenticates and encrypts certain parts of the payload between the AAA/RADIUS server and the AAA client. The shared secret key is never actually sent across the wire, so the integrity of the key is maintained.

When RADIUS authenticates users, numerous authentication methods can be used. RADIUS supports authentication via Point-to-Point Protocol Challenge Handshake Authentication Protocol (PPP CHAP) and PPP Password Authentication Protocol (PAP), as well as others.

In addition to these features, RADIUS is an extensible protocol that provides vendors with the capability to add new attribute values without creating a problem for existing attribute values.

A major difference between TACACS+ and RADIUS is that RADIUS does not separate authentication and authorization. RADIUS also provides for better accounting. In this section, you see the operation and functionality of RADIUS.

RADIUS operates under the UDP protocol. RADIUS uses ports 1645 and 1812 for authentication and 1646 and 1813 for accounting. The ports 1812 and 1813 are seen in newer RADIUS implementations. The use of RADIUS port 1645 in early implementations conflicts with the datametrics service. Therefore, the officially assigned ports are 1812 and 1813.

Generally, the RADIUS protocol is considered a connectionless service. Issues related to server availability, retransmission, and timeouts are handled by the RADIUS-enabled devices rather than the transmission protocol.

RADIUS Operation

The following is the process used in a RADIUS-managed login:

Step 1.   A user login generates a query (Access-Request) from the AAA client to the RADIUS server.

Step 2.   A corresponding response (Access-Challenge, Access-Accept, or Access-Reject) is returned by the server.

The Access-Request packet contains the username, encrypted password, IP address of the AAA client, and port. The format of the request also provides information on the type of session that the user wants to initiate. Optionally, if the RADIUS server needs more information, it can send an Access-Challenge.

Figure 1-4 shows the format of the RADIUS packet.

Code	Identifier	Length
Request Authenticator		
Attributes		

Figure 1-4   *RADIUS Packet Format*

Each RADIUS packet contains the following information:

- **Code:** The code field is one octet; it identifies one of the following types of RADIUS packets:
    - Access-Request (1)
    - Access-Accept (2)
    - Access-Reject (3)
    - Accounting-Request (4)
    - Accounting-Response (5)
    - Access-Challenge (11)
    - Status-Server (12)
    - Status-Client (13)
    - Reserved (255)

Note   Status-Server and Status-Client are experimental.

- **Identifier:** The identifier field is one octet; it helps the RADIUS server match requests and responses and detect duplicate requests.

- **Length:** The length field is two octets; it specifies the length of the entire packet.

- **Request Authenticator:** The authenticator field is 16 octets. The most significant octet is transmitted first; it authenticates the reply from the RADIUS server. Two types of authenticators are as follows:

  - **Request-Authenticator:** Available in Access-Request and Accounting-Request packets.

  - **Response-Authenticator:** Available in Access-Accept, Access-Reject, Access-Challenge and Accounting-Response packets.

The attributes that are seen in Figure 1-4 are RADIUS AV pairs.

RADIUS Encryption

Encryption in RADIUS differs from that of TACACS+ because RADIUS encrypts only the password and the rest is sent in clear text.

The process of encrypting the password in RADIUS is as follows:

Step 1.   A RADIUS packet includes an Authenticator field, as seen in Figure 1-4. This is a field that contains a 16-octet random number called the Request Authenticator.

Step 2.   The Request Authenticator is combined with the preshared key value and runs through an MD5 hash algorithm. This derives a 16-octet hash. For this example, this is called HASH_A. Therefore, HASH_A is equal to the MD5 request authentication plus the preshared key.

Step 3.   The user-provided password is padded in the message with a null value so that it reaches a 16-octet value.

Step 4.   HASH_A is then XORed with the padded password from step 3, and that generates the cipher text that is transmitted to the AAA server running RADIUS.

Step 5.   The AAA server calculates HASH_A on its own and XORs it with the received cipher text to get the padded user-provided password back to clear text.

RADIUS Authentication and Authorization

When an AAA server running RADIUS receives the Access-Request from the AAA client, it searches its configured databases for the username listed. If the username does not exist in the database, either a default profile is loaded or the RADIUS server immediately sends an Access-Reject message. This Access-Reject message can be accompanied by an optional text message, which could indicate the reason for the refusal.

If the username is found and the password is correct, the RADIUS server returns an Access-Accept response, including a list of AV pairs that describe the parameters to be used for this session. Typical parameters include service type (shell or framed), protocol type, IP address to assign the user (static or dynamic), access list to apply, or a static route to install in the AAA client's routing table. The configuration information in the RADIUS server defines what is installed on the AAA client.

Optionally, the AAA server can send an Access-Challenge request to the AAA client to request a new password.

Figure 1-5 demonstrates a RADIUS exchange between an AAA client and AAA server.

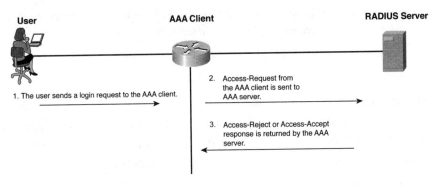

Figure 1-5   *A RADIUS Exchange*

Authorization within RADIUS is done in conjunction with authentication. As a server returns an Access-Accept message, it also includes the list of AV pairs that the user is authorized for.

RADIUS Accounting

RADIUS accounting is performed by sending messages at the start and the stop of a session. These messages include information about the session. Information that might be included includes time, packets, bytes, and so on. These messages are sent using UDP port 1813. The accounting process for RADIUS is seen in RFC 2866. The messages sent between the AAA server and the AAA client are Accounting-Request and Accounting-Response. Figure 1-6 illustrates the basic process of RADIUS accounting.

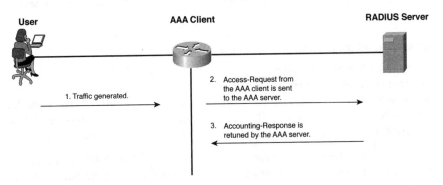

Figure 1-6   *RADIUS Accounting*

During this process, the accounting information is also sent via AV pairs. You can find a list of RADIUS AV pairs in the Cisco.com document, *RADIUS Attributes Overview and RADIUS IETF Attributes* at http://www.cisco.com/en/US/docs/ios/sec_user_services/configuration/guide/sec_rad_ov _ietf_attr_ps6441_TSD_Products_Configuration_Guide_Chapter.html.

Overview of TACACS+

TACACS+ is a relatively recent protocol providing detailed accounting information and flexible administrative control over authentication and authorization processes. TACACS+ is facilitated through AAA and can be enabled only through AAA commands. In a situation where TACACS+ is used, a server runs the TACACS+ daemon and uses this to communicate and build packets destined for AAA clients. Again, TACACS+ is a Cisco-proprietary implementation. It is however, described in Internet Draft versions 1.77 and 1.78. TACACS+ uses the TCP protocol to provide reliable delivery of AAA requests. A shared secret key is also used between the AAA client and the AAA server running the TACACS+ protocol. Each portion of AAA is performed separately with TACACS+. Each one of these services, authentication, authorization, or accounting, can be tied to its own database on the AAA server to take advantage of other services available on that server or on the network, depending on the capabilities of the daemon.

Note   The TACACS+ Draft can be found at http://tools.ietf.org/html/draft-grant-tacacs02.

TACACS+ is the result of the evolution of TACACS and extended TACACS (XTACACS). Cisco IOS supports all three of these protocols. Note the following details:

TACACS is an older access protocol, incompatible with the newer TACACS+ protocol. It provides password checking and authentication, and notification of user actions for security and accounting purposes. TACACS uses User Datagram Protocol (UDP) as its communication protocol.

XTACACS is an extension to the older TACACS protocol, supplying additional functionality to TACACS. XTACACS provides information about protocol translator and router use. This information is used in UNIX auditing trails and accounting files. XTACACS is incompatible with TACACS+. XTACACS also uses UDP.

TACACS+ in Detail

This section provides information about the architecture of TACACS+. TACACS+ performs reliable communication between the AAA server and AAA client. This communication, as well as the TACACS+ format, is reviewed in the following sections. In addition to this reliable format, TACACS+ optionally performs encryption and authentication of the entire message between the AAA server and AAA client. Although it's not recommended, you could have a blank secret in which the payload would not be encrypted. Finally, this section wraps up with the actual operation of the protocol.

TACACS+ Communication

TACACS+ communication between the network access server (NAS) and AAA client is based on TCP and provides a reliable delivery mechanism to AAA messaging. TACACS+ uses TCP port 49 and creates a session to facilitate the messaging in an AAA exchange. Many benefits exist in using TCP for session control in TACACS+. Among these benefits is the fact that TACACS+ uses TCP to provide an acknowledgment of requests made by a NAS or an AAA client.

In addition to the acknowledgments provided within TCP, TACACS+ also has the capability, through inherent functionality of TCP, to adapt to congestion and bandwidth. An example of this functionality is the utilization of TCP windowing.

TACACS+ Format and Header Values

The TACACS+ ID defines a 12-byte header that appears in all TACACS+ packets. This header is always sent in clear text format. The following defines the TACACS+ ID fields:

- **Major_version:** This is the major version number of TACACS+. The value appears in the header as TAC_PLUS_MAJOR_VER=0xc.

- **Minor_version:** This field provides the revision number for the TACACS+ protocol. It also provides for backward compatibility of the protocol. A default value, as well as a version one, is defined for some commands. These values appear in the TACACS+ header as TAC_PLUS_MINOR_VER_DEFAULT=0x0 and TAC_PLUS_MINOR_VER_ONE=0x1. Should an AAA server running the TACACS+ daemon receive a TACACS+ packet defining a minor version other than one of the ones just listed, it sends an error status back and sets the minor_version to the closest version supported.

- **Type:** This distinguishes the packet type. Only certain types are legal. The legal packet types are as follows:

  TAC_PLUS_AUTHEN=0x01—This is the packet type that signifies authentication.

  TAC_PLUS_AUTHOR-0x02—This is the packet type that signifies authorization.

  TAC_PLUS_ACCT=0x03—This is the packet type that signifies accounting.

Note   The significance of these possible message types is that TACACS+ has the capability to perform authentication, authorization, and accounting as separate functions. RADIUS does not have this capability.

- **Seq_no:** This determines the sequence number for the current session. TACACS+ has the capability to perform multiple TACACS+ sessions or to use one TACACS+ session per AAA client. The beginning packet of a session is identified by the sequence number 1. All subsequent packets are an increment from that initial number. Because the AAA client sends the first packet to the AAA server running the TACACS+ daemon, it is always the number 1, and all subsequent packets from the AAA client are identified with odd sequence numbers. In addition to this sequencing scheme, the highest sequence number that can be reached is 28-1. After this value is reached, the session that is established between the AAA client and the AAA server is reset, and a new session is started. When the session restarts, it begins, once again, with a sequence number of 1.

- **Flags:** In this section, the field can contain various flags. These flags can be TAC_PLUS_UNENCRYPTED_FLAG and TAC_PLUS_SINGLE_CONNECT_FLAG. The TAC_PLUS_UNENCRYPTED_FLAG flag specifies whether encryption is being performed on the body of the TACACS+ packet. If this flag is set, meaning that the value is set to 1, encryption is not being performed and likewise, if the value of this flag is set to 0, the packet is, in fact, being encrypted. The ability to disable TACACS+ encryption should be used primarily for debugging purposes. This functionality is nice when you need to see all the information in the body of the packet. Keep in mind that the header is always sent clear text. The TAC_PLUS_SINGLE_CONNECT_FLAG determines whether multiplexing multiple TACACS+ sessions over one TCP session is supported. This is determined in the first two TACACS+ messages of a session. When determined, this does not change. It is important to note here that multiple versions of IOS don't support that bit correctly; that is, they try to do single-connect and don't set this bit when they should have. ACS works around this by basically following the TCP connection, not this bit, so if an AAA client keeps its TCP connection open and keeps sending new requests on it, that is single connect more, ACS will stay connected with it and work, even if the single connect bit is not set on the device.

- **Session_id:** This is a random value that designates the current session between the AAA client and the AAA server running the TACACS+ daemon. This value remains the same for the duration of a session.

- **Length:** This field states the total length of the TACACS+ packet, not to include the 12-byte header.

Encrypting TACACS+

One feature that provides more security under TACACS+, as opposed to its alternative RADIUS, is the encryption of the entire packet. This encryption is sent between the AAA client and the AAA server running the TACACS+ daemon. This is not to be confused with encryption of user data. This is not an encryption such as 3DES-IPsec or RSA encryption, but is rather a combination of a hashing algorithm and an XOR function. TACACS+ uses MD5 to hash using a secret key provided on both ends.

The process of TACACS+ encryption is as follows:

Step 1.   Information is taken from the packet header, and the preshared key calculates a series of hashes. The first is a hash that is calculated on a concatenation of the session_id, the version, the seq_no, and the preshared key value. Each hash created has the previous hash in it as well. This is done a number of times that is dependent on the particular implementation of TACACS+.

Step 2.   The calculated hash is concatenated and then truncated to the length of the data being encrypted. Each hash has the previous hash concatenated to its input values. The result is called the *pseudo_pad*.

Step 3. The cipher text is produced by doing a bytewise XOR on the pseudo_pad with the data that is being encrypted.

Step 4. The receiving device uses its preshared key to calculate the pseudo_pad, and then an XOR of the newly created pseudo_pad results in the original data in clear text.

TACACS+ Operation

Three possible activities can be performed during TACACS+ operation:

- The first operation performed is authentication. This is done to clearly identify the user.

- The second operation is authorization and is possible only after a user has been identified. Therefore, you must authenticate prior to authorizing.

- The third operation is accounting. The accounting process keeps track of actions performed.

- The three processes are each independent of the other. Figure 1-7 shows one possible instance of the messaging that is involved with TACACS+. This messaging process is discussed in the sections that follow.

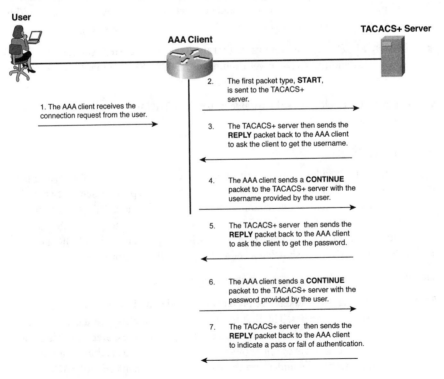

Figure 1-7 *TACACS+ Messaging*

The section that follows covers the authentication portion of TACACS+.

TACACS+ and Authentication

When authentication is performed in TACACS+, three distinct packet exchanges take place. The three types of packets are as follows:

- **START:** This packet is used initially when the user attempts to connect.
- **REPLY:** Sent by the AAA server during the authentication process.
- **CONTINUE:** Used by the AAA client to return the username and password to the AAA server.

When a user initiates a connection which requires authentication, the following process occurs:

Step 1. The AAA client receives the connection request from the user.

Step 2. The first packet type, START, is sent to the AAA server that is running the TACACS+ daemon. This START message contains information about the type of authentication.

Step 3. The TACACS+ server then sends the REPLY packet back to the AAA client. At this point, the server requests the username.

Step 4. The AAA client sends a CONTINUE packet to the TACACS+ server with the username provided by the user.

Step 5. The TACACS+ server then sends the REPLY packet back to the AAA client to ask the client to get the password.

Step 6. The AAA client sends a CONTINUE packet to the TACACS+ server with the password provided by the user.

Step 7. The TACACS+ server then sends the REPLY packet back to the AAA client to indicate a pass/fail of authentication. The possible returned values can be these:

- **ACCEPT:** The user is authenticated and service can begin. If the NAS is configured to require authorization, authorization begins at this time.
- **REJECT:** The user has failed to authenticate. The user can be denied further access, placed in an "auth-fail" vlan, or possibly prompted to retry the login sequence, depending on the TACACS+ daemon.
- **ERROR:** An error occurred at some time during authentication. This can be either at the daemon or in the network connection between the daemon and the NAS. If an ERROR response is received, the NAS typically tries to use an alternative method for authenticating the user.
- **CONTINUE:** The user is prompted for additional authentication information.

Note   START and CONTINUE packets are always sent by the AAA client, and REPLY packets are always sent by the TACACS+ server.

TACACS+ and Authorization

In the previous section, you learned the authentication process of TACACS+. This section discusses the authorization process.

To facilitate authorization in TACACS+, two message types are used. The first message is an authorization REQUEST, and the second is the authorization RESPONSE. The REQUEST sources from the AAA client, and the RESPONSE sources from the AAA server.

Figure 1-8 shows a basic authorization attempt.

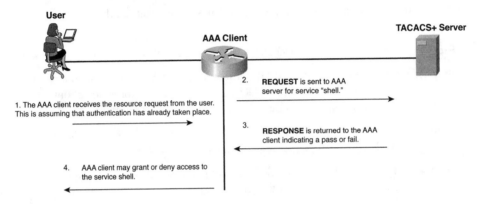

User

AAA Client

TACACS+ Server

2.   **REQUEST** is sent to AAA server for service "shell."

1. The AAA client receives the resource request from the user. This is assuming that authentication has already taken place.

3.   **RESPONSE** is returned to the AAA client indicating a pass or fail.

4.   AAA client may grant or deny access to the service shell.

Figure 1-8   *Simple TACACS+ Authorization*

The RESPONSE message (in step 3 in Figure 1-8) contains one of the following replies:

A FAIL response from the server indicates that the services requested for authorization are not granted.

If the server responds with a PASS_ADD, the request is authorized and the information returned in the RESPONSE is used in addition to the requested information. If no additional arguments are returned by the AAA server in the RESPONSE, the request is authorized.

In some cases, a PASS_REPL might be returned to the AAA client. In this case, the server is choosing to ignore the REQUEST and is replacing it with the information returned in the RESPONSE.

If the status is set to FOLLOW, this indicates that the AAA server that is sending the RESPONSE wants to have the authorization take place on another server, and this server information is listed in the RESPONSE packet. The AAA client has the option of using this server or simply can treat it as a FAIL.

If the status returned is ERROR, this indicates an error on the AAA server. This is commonly a preshared key mismatch; however, it can be a number of issues and further troubleshooting needs to take place.

In authorization, Attribute-Values (AV) can determine authorized services. You can find more information about TACACS+ AV pairs in the Cisco.com document, *TACACS+*

Attribute-Value Pairs at http://www.cisco.com/en/US/docs/ios/sec_user_services/ configuration/guide/sec_tacacs_attr_vp_ps6441_TSD_Products_Configuration_Guide_ Chapter.html.

TACACS+ Accounting

The functionality of accounting in TACACS+ is similar to that of authorization. Accounting takes place by sending a record to the AAA server. Each of these records includes an AV pair for accounting. The three types of records that can be sent to the AAA server are as follows:

- The Start record indicates when a service begins and contains the information that was included in the authorization process, as well as information specific to the account.

- A Stop record indicates when a service is about to stop or is terminated and includes information that was included in the authorization process, as well as information specific to the account.

- A Continue record is also called a Watchdog or UPDATE record. This is sent when a service is still in progress and allows the AAA client to provide updated information to the AAA server. As seen in the previous records, this also includes information that was included in the authorization process, as well as information specific to the account.

Note   A record can be sent as both a Start record and a Continue record. This indicates that the Continue record is a duplicate of the Start record.

Accounting also uses the two message types that authorization uses, a REQUEST and a RESPONSE. The AAA server has the capability to send the following in a RESPONSE:

- SUCCESS indicates that the server received the record that was sent by the AAA client.

- ERROR indicates that the server failed to commit the record to its database.

- FOLLOW is similar to that of a FOLLOW in authorization. This indicates that the server wants the AAA client to send the record to another AAA server, and the AAA server information is included in the RESPONSE.

Figure 1-9 shows a basic example of the accounting process between the AAA client and the AAA server.

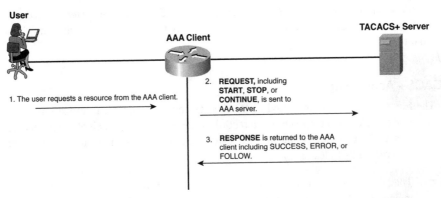

Figure 1-9 *Basic Accounting*

Summary

AAA is a framework for authentication, authorization, and accounting in a Cisco environment. To perform these processes, a Cisco device uses a method list, along with other configuration tasks to designate the server and protocol. At this point, you should have a basic understanding of what the AAA framework is, what it provides in your network, and the most basic process of configuration.

The TACACS+ and RADIUS protocols are used to communicate between the AAA server and the AAA client.

Now that you have had an opportunity to explore the AAA framework and protocols involved it's time to begin working with the devices that make this possible. In Chapter 2, "Cisco Secure ACS," you will take a look at two versions of Cisco Secure ACS, version 4.2 and version 5.1. In this chapter you will get a great comparison of the version that possibly has the largest install base along with the version being offered by Cisco at the time this book was being written.

Cisco Secure ACS

This chapter covers the following subjects:

Introduction to ACS: This section familiarizes you with the Cisco AAA server.

Cisco Secure Access Control Server 4.2: This section provides you with an overview of the features available in Cisco Secure Access Control Server 4.2, installing Cisco Secure Access Control Server 4.2, and common installation issues.

Cisco Secure Access Control System 5.1: This section provides you with an overview of the features available in Cisco Secure Access Control System 5.1, the difference between 4.2 and 5.1, and the initial setup and licensing of Cisco Secure Access Control System 5.1.

Numerous enterprise-level authentication servers are available in the market today. Popular among these are the Cisco Secure Access Control Server/System (ACS), Juniper's Steel-Belted radius server, and Microsoft's Network Policy Server. Among these, only Cisco Secure ACS is a one-stop solution for authentication, authorization, and accounting (AAA) via both Terminal Access Controller Access Control System Plus (TACACS+) and Remote Authentication Dial-In User Service (RADIUS). Getting familiar with Cisco Secure ACS is the focus of this chapter.

Introduction to ACS

For access control and identity management, Cisco has a wide variety of product range available. The following are among some of the identity management solutions provided by Cisco:

- Cisco Access Registrar

- Cisco Secure Global Roaming Server (GRS)

- Cisco Secure Access Control Server Express

- Cisco Secure Access Control Server Solution Engine

■   Cisco Secure Access Control Server for Windows

■   Cisco Secure Access Control System

This chapter focuses on Cisco Secure Access Control Server for Solution Engine, Cisco Secure Access Control Server for Windows, and Cisco Secure Access Control System.

Overview

As networks grow large and cross campus boundaries, network security gains much more importance than ever before. With the increase in the importance of network security, the administrative tasks associated with maintaining network security increase proportionately.

Addressing this complex requirement calls for a policy-based identity management solution. Cisco Secure Access Control Server and Cisco Secure Access Control System both follow a policy-based model. A policy-based model provides granular approach towards identity management and access control in a network. Along with providing a granular approach towards security, it also provides administrative ease by providing centralized management through Cisco Secure ACS products.

Cisco Secure ACS products combines AAA architecture with policy-based control to provide centralized access control management, increased network security with scalability, and flexibility with user productivity gain.

Figure 2-1 shows a simple AAA scenario using ACS.

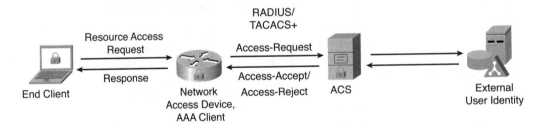

Figure 2-1   *Simple AAA Scenario Using ACS*

AAA Client-Server Framework

AAA server is based on a framework that consists of two components:

■   AAA client

■   AAA server

Cisco Secure ACS server plays the role of the server side (AAA server) in the AAA model by providing authentication, authorization, and accounting services to the network devices that compose the client end (AAA client) in the AAA model. The client end

(AAA client) is also referred to as Network Access Server (NAS) or Network Access Device (NAD). The NAS/NAD can be any Cisco device, such as router, switch, firewall, or access point. The NAS/NAD can also be any non-Cisco device that complies with RADIUS or TACACS+ standards and that is supported by the AAA server.

In an AAA scenario, the AAA client acts as a gateway and forwards all access requests to AAA server on behalf of the end client. The end client, also known as the supplicant, is an entity at one endpoint of a network segment that seeks to be authenticated by the AAA client. After the AAA server receives the request, it verifies it according to the policy configured. After evaluating the policies, the result is either authentication successful or authentication failure. If it is authentication successful, depending on the protocol used (RADIUS/TACACS+), authorization attributes might be sent back to the AAA client. After locally evaluating the result returned by the AAA server, the AAA client allows access to the end client with the authorization level permitted or denies access. Further AAA clients can be configured to account for the activity of the end client who was authenticated and authorized.

Cisco Secure Access Control Server Release 4.2 Characteristics and Features

This section provides a more product-specific and familiarity focus of Cisco Secure Access Control Server covering Release 4.2.

As discussed in the previous section, Cisco Secure ACS is based on a policy-based model to provide granular control and centralized access control management over security by consolidating the authentication, authorization, and accounting (AAA) model.

Policy Model

Cisco Secure Access Control Server is based on a *group-based* policy model. In a group-based policy model, all the policies are defined on a group. A group further ties together different types of information, such as identity information, restrictions/conditions, and permissions.

Identity information is based on one of the following:

External database and external database group membership; for example, users in Active Directory or a Lightweight Directory Access Protocol (LDAP) database and their group membership in these external databases

A user in ACS internal database and its group membership on ACS

Restrictions or conditions compose access control, such as time of day or day of week access specification, restriction of access to network devices, and so on.

Permissions comprise information such as privilege level on IOS devices permitted to a group, VLAN information after a user authenticates successfully using 802.1x, and so on.

In Cisco Secure Access Control Server, you can define most of the restrictions or conditions and permissions at a user level, as well as at a group level. If any such policy is applied at the user level, it always takes precedence over the conditions and permissions configured at the group level. For instance, you might configure a group to have Cisco IOS privilege level of 1 except for one of the users in the group, where you configure privilege level at the user level configuration as 7. During AAA authorization, that particular user will be granted privilege level 7 on Cisco IOS rather than 1. The remaining users in the group will get the privilege level 1 as specified for the group.

Platform

Cisco Secure Access Control Server is available on two platforms:

- Cisco Secure Access Control Server for Windows
- Cisco Secure Access Control Server Solution Engine

Cisco Secure Access Control Server for Windows is a software platform that can be installed on Windows 2000, Windows 2003, or the Windows 2008 server platform. If a user database exists on Windows AD, ACS for Windows can be installed on a member server or on a domain controller.

For further detail on supported operating systems and other requirements, please refer to the installation guide for Cisco Secure Access Control Server for Windows release 4.2:

> http://www.cisco.com/en/US/docs/net_mgmt/cisco_secure_access_control_server_
> for_windows/4.2.1/Installation_Guide/windows/igwn421.html

Cisco Secure Access Control Server Solution Engine is a network appliance. It is both a hardware and a software platform. The operating system of the Cisco Secure ACS SE for release 4.2 is a customized and minimized version of Windows 2003. On ACS SE, all unused ports are blocked, all extraneous services are removed and do not provide you access to the ACS SE as in a normal Windows server. ACS SE can be accessed only through the serial console (before/after installation) and web interface (after installation). Running only the required components necessary to run ACS SE increases the security posture of the device. For further detail on ACS SE, refer to the installation guide for ACS SE release 4.2:

> http://www.cisco.com/en/US/docs/net_mgmt/cisco_secure_access_control_server_
> for_solution_engine/4.2.1/Installation_Guide/solution_engine/se421.html

Both platforms are identical in terms of functionality. The only difference is that support for ODBC databases and the *CSUtil.exe* database utility are available only on ACS for Windows.

Protocol Compliance

Cisco Secure Access Control Server supports and conforms to the TACACS+ AAA security protocols as defined by Cisco Systems in draft 1.78.

Additionally, Cisco Secure Access Control Server supports and conforms to the RADIUS protocol as defined in following RFCs:

- RFC 2138
- RFC 2139
- RFC 2284
- RFC 2865
- RFC 2866
- RFC 2867
- RFC 2868
- RFC 2869

As per the RFCs, RADIUS ports have been changed for authentication and accounting. ACS supports both old and new RFC-defined ports for RADIUS authentication and accounting. For authentication, ACS accepts requests on UDP port 1645 (old) and UDP port 1812 (new). For accounting, ACS accepts accounting packets on UDP port 1646 (old) and UDP port 1813 (new).

Along with IETF RADIUS attribute support, Cisco Secure Access Control Server also includes RADIUS vendor-specific attributes (VSAs). The following are the predefined RADIUS VSAs on ACS:

- Cisco Airespace
- Cisco Aironet
- Cisco Building Broadband Service Manager (BBSM)
- RADIUS (3COMUSR)
- Cisco IOS/PIX 6.0
- Cisco VPN 3000/ASA/PIX 7.x+
- Cisco VPN 5000
- RADIUS IETF
- RADIUS Ascend
- RADIUS Juniper
- RADIUS Nortel
- RADIUS iPass

If there still exists a need to add some more RADIUS VSAs for other vendors, ACS supports up to 10 RADIUS VSAs that can be defined in addition to the predefined RADIUS VSAs.

ACS has a pretty decent list of password protocols that it supports. The following are the common password protocols supported by ACS server:

- ASCII
- Password Authentication Protocol (PAP)
- Challenge Handshake Authentication Protocol (CHAP)
- MS-CHAP v1
- MS-CHAP v2
- Lightweight Extensible Authentication Protocol (LEAP)
- AppleTalk Remote Access Protocol (ARAP)
- Extensible Authentication Protocol Message Digest 5 (EAP-MD5)
- Extensible Authentication Protocol Transport Layer Security (EAP-TLS)
- Protected Extensible Authentication Protocol (PEAP)
    - PEAP (EAP-GTC)
    - PEAP (EAP-MSCHAPv2)
    - PEAP (EAP-TLS)
- Extensible Authentication Protocol Flexible Authentication via Secure Tunneling (EAP-FAST)

Implementation of the aforementioned password protocols depends on the external database that you intend to use. The listed password protocols are supported by the ACS internal database; however, the same is not the case for the rest of the available external database available. Table 2-1 lists the protocol database compatibility.

Note   ACS Internal DB does supports MSCHAP, but it does not support change password by MSCHAP.

Features Available

Cisco Secure Access Control Server offers many features for authentication, authorization, and accounting, including the following:

- **Advance Password Configuration:** Provision for configuring inbound password, outbound password, and token caching.
- **Password Aging:** For password security, password aging can be configured on ACS to force users to change passwords after a specified date or number of login attempts.
- **User Changeable Password:** This is a separate web-based application available that can be integrated with Cisco ACS to enable users to change their password.
- **Max Sessions:** For limiting the concurrent sessions available to a group or a user.
- **Dynamic Usage Quotas:** To limit network access of each user in group or a user.

Table 2-1 *Protocol-Database Compatibility*

Database	ASCII/ PAP	CHAP	MS-CHAPv1	MS-CHAPv2	LEAP	ARAP	EAP-MD5	EAP-TLS	PEAP (EAP-GTC)	PEAP(EAP-MSCHAPv2)	PEAP (EAP-TLS)	EAP-FAST (Phase Zero)	EAP-FAST (Phase Two)
ACS	Yes	Yes	Yes	Yes	Yes	Yes	Yes	Yes	Yes	Yes	Yes	Yes	Yes
Windows SAM	Yes	No	Yes	Yes	Yes	No	No	No	Yes	Yes	No	Yes	Yes
Windows AD	Yes	No	Yes	Yes	Yes	No	No	Yes	Yes	Yes	Yes	Yes	Yes
LDAP	Yes	No	No	No	No	No	No	Yes	No	No	Yes	No	Yes
ODBC	Yes	Yes	Yes	Yes	Yes	Yes	Yes	Yes	Yes	Yes	Yes	Yes	Yes
LEAP Proxy RADIUS Server	Yes	Yes	Yes	Yes	Yes				Yes	Yes		Yes	Yes
Token Server	Yes	No	No	No	No	No	No	No	Yes	No	No	No	No

- **Shared Profile Component:** Under the Shared Profile section on ACS you can configure authorization profiles, which can be applied to multiple groups or users later on. This helps you save time and effort in creating the same authorization policies on every group or user.

- **Default Time-of-Day Access**

- **Network Access Restriction (NAR)**

- **Downloadable ACL**

- **Network Access Filter**

- **Network Access Profile**

- **IP Pools for IP address assignment**

- **Accounting logs accumulation in CSV log file, syslog file, or in an ODBC database**

For a full list of features, refer to the Cisco documentation.

Cisco Secure Access Control System Release 5.1 Characteristics and Features

After going through a Cisco Secure Access Control Server overview, this section focuses on Cisco Secure Access Control System Release 5.1. Both Cisco Secure Access Control Server and Access Control System work on a policy-based model; however, there is a difference in the approach of how this policy is applied. The sections that follow will attempt to highlight the differences between Cisco Secure Access Control *Server* and Cisco Secure Access Control *System* to see how Cisco Secure Access Control System provides granular control and centralized management over security by incorporating the AAA model into one.

Policy Model

Cisco Secure Access Control System is based on a *rule-based* policy model, which provides more powerful and flexible access control that is not available in group-based policy model.

In Cisco Secure Access Control System, you create both condition and result.

The conditions and results are defined as global shared objects, which means you define them once and then you can use them later on anywhere. Based on conditions and rules created globally, you create *rules*. In Cisco Secure Access Control System terminology, conditions and results are known as *policy elements* and they are the building blocks for rule creation.

The difference between the rule-based and group-based policy models can be summarized as follows:

Cisco Secure Access Control System is based on rule-based policy of the form:

If condition, then result

Cisco Secure Access Control Server is based on group-based policy of the form:

If identity-condition, restriction-condition, then authorization-profile

The "Policy Elements and Access Services" section in Chapter 4, "Getting Familiar with ACS 5.1," covers the type of policies that can be configured on Cisco Secure Access Control System in greater detail.

Platform

Cisco Secure Access Control System is available in two platforms:

- Cisco Secure Access Control System appliance
- Cisco Secure Access Control System on a VMware server

Cisco Secure Access Control System appliance runs on a standard Cisco Linux-based platform. It comes with Cisco Secure Access Control System software already installed. After this appliance is placed in network, it just needs to be configured with basic initial configuration parameters.

For more information on installation of Cisco Secure Access Control System appliance in network, please refer to the "Installation and Upgrade Guide for the Cisco Secure Access Control System 5.1" guide:

> http://www.cisco.com/en/US/docs/net_mgmt/cisco_secure_access_control_system/
> 5.1/installation/guide/acs5_1_install_guide.html

Cisco Secure Access Control System on a VMware server is virtualization of the Cisco Secure Access Control System appliance. Hardware configuration of the virtual machine must be similar to the Cisco Secure Access Control System appliance. For more detail on the minimum hardware configuration requirement for the virtual machine, please refer to "Installing ACS in a VMware Virtual Machine" in the "Installation and Upgrade Guide for the Cisco Secure Access Control System 5.1" guide:

> http://www.cisco.com/en/US/docs/net_mgmt/cisco_secure_access_control_system/
> 5.1/installation/guide/csacs_vmware.html

Protocol Compliance

Cisco Secure Access Control System interoperates with RADIUS and TACACS+ client devices, similar to how Cisco Secure Access Control Server interoperates with these protocols.

For TACACS+, Cisco Secure Access Control System conforms to the TACACS+ protocol as defined in draft 1.78.

For RADIUS, Cisco Secure Access Control System conforms to following Request for Comments (RFC):

- RFC 2138
- RFC 2139
- RFC 2865
- RFC 2866

- RFC 2867
- RFC 2868
- RFC 2869

Cisco Secure Access Control System accepts RADIUS authentication requests on UDP port 1645 and UDP port 1812. For accounting, it accepts RADIUS accounting packets on UDP port 1646 and UDP port 1813. This is done to support both old and new RADIUS RFCs.

As Cisco Secure Access Control System conforms to RADIUS RFC, it supports IETF RADIUS attributes. Along with IETF RADIUS attributes, it also supports RADIUS Vendor Specific Attributes (VSAs). The following is the list of predefined RADIUS VSA on Cisco Secure Access Control System:

- Cisco
- Cisco VPN 3000
- Microsoft
- US Robotics
- Ascend
- Nortel (Bay Networks)
- RedCreek
- Juniper
- Cisco VPN 3000
- Cisco Business Service Management(BSM)
- Cisco Aironet
- Cisco Airespace

Cisco Secure Access Control System provides an option to modify these predefined RADIUS VSAs and allows defining new RADIUS VSAs, if required.

To control access of user and host machines in the network, Cisco Secure Access Control System supports the following authentication protocols:

- Password Authentication Protocol (PAP)
- ASCII
- Challenge Handshake Authentication Protocol (CHAP)
- MSCHAPv1
- MSCHAPv2
- Extensible Authentication Protocol Message Digest 5 (EAP-MD5)
- Protected Extensible Authentication Protocol (PEAP)
  - PEAP (EAP-GTC)
  - PEAP (EAP-MSCHAPv2)

- Extensible Authentication Protocol Flexible Authentication via Secure Tunneling (EAP-FAST)

    - EAP-FAST (EAP-GTC)

    - EAP-FAST (EAP-MSCHAPv2)

- Lightweight Extensible Authentication Protocol (LEAP)

- Extensible Authentication Protocol Transport Layer Security (EAP-TLS)

Functions and Features

Cisco Secure Access Control System provides numerous and granular functions and features for access control. With the help of access services, policy elements, authorization profiles, and many more components available, a rule can be defined to satisfy the network security policy of a network.

Table 2-2 provides an overview of the menu options available and a brief description about each option.

Table 2-2 *Cisco Secure Access Control System Menu Options*

Menu Option	Description
My Workspace	Section provides access to task guide and shortcuts to common tasks.
Network Resources	AAA clients, network devices, and network device group are configured under this section, which can later on be used as elements for a policy.
User and Identity Stores	Internal user and external databases such as LDAP, Active Directory, RSA SecurID Token Server. In this section, certificate-related configuration is also done. This section provides an option to a sequence in which users must be searched in identity store.
Policy Elements	Various policy conditions can be created with a result. This section contains time-of-day access configuration, end station filters, device filters, device port filters, RADIUS authorization profiles, shell profiles, command set, and downloadable ACL.
Access Policies	Rules are created in this section by selecting policy elements, identity store, and authorization profiles from previous sections. Access requests are processed through the ACS server based on rules configured under this section.
Monitoring and Reports	All authentication- and authorization-related success and failures, all accounting-related logs, all system-related debug logs, detailed reports, and troubleshooting tools are available in this section.
System Administration	This section handles all ACS system-related configuration. ACS administrators and their access level are created in this section. RADIUS VSA and TACACS+ attributes are configured under this section. Certificates are loaded on the server from this section. Licensing and migration from Cisco Secure Access Control Server is also handled through this section.

The preceding overview of Cisco Secure Access Control Server and Cisco Secure Access Control System should have familiarized you with common and distinct features available in both products. You will see in more detail how you can use the features available in both products for everyday security for wired and wireless network access, along with network administration to provide more secure and robust network security architecture. The sections that follow delve into the installation of Cisco Secure Access Control Server and Cisco Secure Access Control System.

Installing Cisco Secure Access Control Server 4.2

As discussed previously, Cisco Secure Access Control Server is available in two platforms:

- Cisco Secure Access Control Server for Windows
- Cisco Secure Access Control Server Solution Engine

The sections that follow look at the installation steps for both Windows and Solution Engine as well as cover a few common problems encountered during installation or upgrade, and the best practices to avoid them.

Installing Cisco Secure Access Control Server for Windows 4.2

Cisco Secure Access Control Server for Windows 4.2 is installed on Windows Operating system and can be installed on a member server or a domain controller. Cisco Secure Access Control Server for Windows 4.2 is installed on the Windows 2000, Windows 2003, and Windows 2008 server platform, and can also be installed on a VMware instance. For details on Windows server requirements and VMWare platform specifications, please refer to the "System Requirements" section in the "Installation Guide for Cisco Secure Access Control Server for Windows 4.2" guide:

> http://www.cisco.com/en/US/docs/net_mgmt/cisco_secure_access_control_server_
> for_windows/4.2.1/Installation_Guide/windows/install.html#wp1041324

This section first looks at installing Cisco Secure Access Control Server for Windows 4.2 as a fresh install. Later on you will see how to reinstall and/or upgrade it. The steps for fresh install, reinstall, and upgrade do not vary much.

During a fresh install of ACS software, you are required to provide initial configuration information. After a platform has been decided as per the supported hardware and software for ACS install, you are ready to move ahead.

As you begin installing ACS, it will guide you through what information is required to complete the installation. To have a better understanding, you can have all this information prepared in advance for a smooth installation process.

The installation of the server software is as follows:

Step 1.   Log in as a local administrator on the Windows server where you want to install ACS.

Note ACS should not be installed over Remote Desktop (RDP). RDP provides different file system permission than being on the local console of the server. Installation of ACS has been tested successfully with Virtual Network Computing (VNC).

Step 2. If you have ACS installation media on CD, you can insert it into the CD-ROM drive. The Windows *autorun* feature will launch the installation process. In case it does not launch, search for *Setup.exe* on the drive and launch it. If you have obtained software in a zipped format, unzip it and launch the *Setup.exe* program.

If auto launch starts, click on **Install**.

Step 3. Setup will show you the software license agreement as shown in Figure 2-2. Read the software agreement and if you accept it, click ACCEPT.

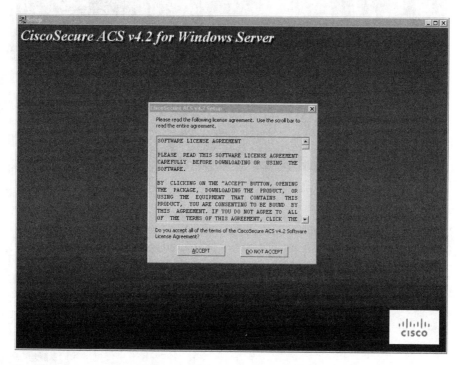

Figure 2-2 *License Agreement During Installation*

Step 4. Setup will launch the Welcome dialog as shown in Figure 2-3. This section will contain information about the setup. After the information has been read, click **Next**.

Step 5. The next screen will be the IMPORTANT NOTICE dialog, which provides information about the process running on the system that might affect ACS installation, as shown in Figure 2-4. When you have read the information, click **Next**.

Note   Ensure that there are no other database processes running on the server, as they might interfere with ACS installation. Especially SQL based databases.

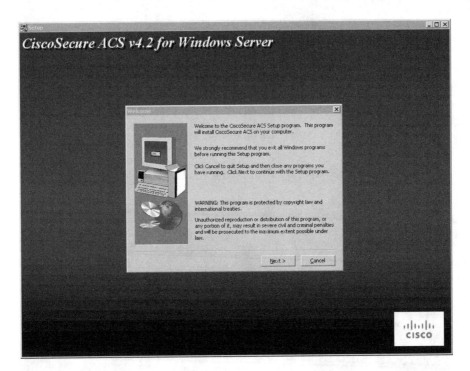

Figure 2-3   *Welcome Dialog*

Step 6.   Setup utility will now provide a Before You Begin dialog that will have a checklist for ACS installation before you can proceed further, as shown in Figure 2-5. Ensure that you have satisfied the entire list of requirement, and then check the appropriate requirement check box and proceed further until all the check boxes are checked. When checked, you'll have the option to click on **Next.** If you need explanation about the checklist, you can click on **Explain** before clicking on Next.

Tip   Press Alt-A to select all checkboxes simultaneously.

Step 7.   In this step, the setup utility will ask you to provide information about the install folder for ACS as shown in Figure 2-6. Once specified, click on **Next.**

Note   System logging for the ACS services will be stored under the mentioned installation location and cannot be changed once ACS is installed.

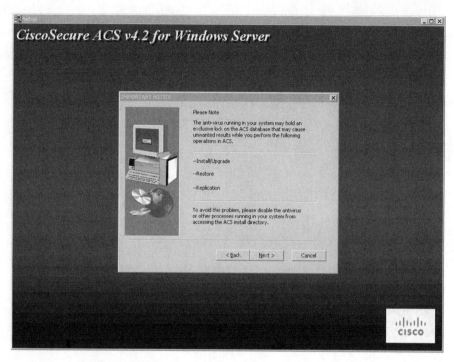

Figure 2-4   *Important Notice*

Step 8.   This step is database related. During setup, you have a choice to specify whether you want to extend the user database to the Windows database as shown in Figure 2-7. You can choose the ACS Internal Database if you do not have an already existent database on Windows Active Directory. If you do have a database on Windows Active Directory, choose Windows User Database to configure it during installation. When you have decided what you need to choose, select it and click on **Next**.

Step 9.   Now that you have provided the ACS setup utility with the basic information, it will begin installing software on the Windows operating system as shown in Figure 2-8. When the core components have been installed, setup will provide you with an Advanced Option dialog to specify what option needs to be displayed after installation completes as shown in Figure 2-9. You can configure this section later, after installation completes, if you so desire. If you check the options available in Advanced configuration, those options will be visible in ACS GUI when installation finishes. If you skip these options during installation, these options/features can be turned on/off from the Interface Configuration section after installation completes. It is better to configure these options later, as and when it is required. Interface Configuration is covered in the "Interface Configuration" section in Chapter 3, "Getting Familiar with ACS 4.2."

Step 10.   The setup utility now provides you with the option for Active Service Monitoring as shown in Figure 2-10. In this section during setup, you can

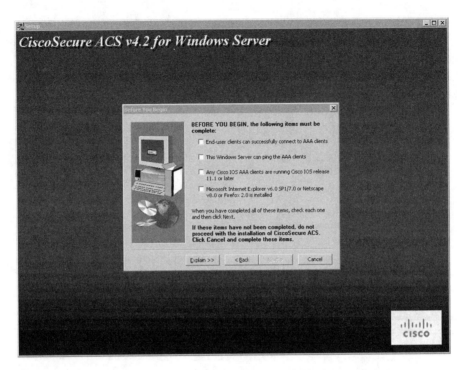

Figure 2-5 *Before You Begin*

specify an action that needs to be taken if there is any failure with the core
ACS services. This can be further changed after installation completes, if
required. This section also provides an option for mail notification, in case of
service failure. You do not have to complete the mail notification during
installation because it can be configured later on; however, recommended
practice dictates that you should at some point configure this option so that
you can get proactive alerts in case there is some issue with the ACS services.

Step 11.   In this step, you will be asked to provide a password for ACS Internal
Database encryption as shown in Figure 2-11. Please keep a note of this password because it might be required for troubleshooting by Cisco TAC. After
the password has been provided click **Next**.

Step 12.   In this step, the setup utility asks to start the ACS core services; launch the
ACS administrative interface using the browser and an option to view the
Readme file as shown in Figure 2-12. Clicking on **Next** will take you to the
Setup Complete dialog.

Step 13.   The Setup Complete dialog provides you with the ACS administrative interface as shown in Figure 2-13. After you select the **Finish** option, the setup
utility will launch the ACS administrative browser along with the Readme file
as shown in Figure 2-14.

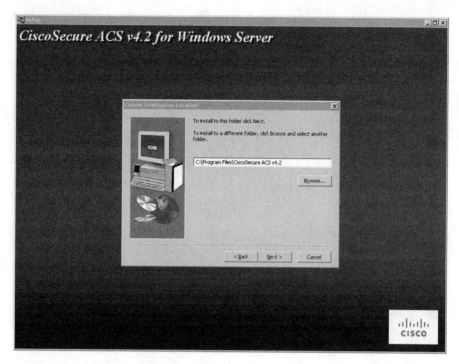

Figure 2-6 *Destination Location*

In case of reinstallation or upgrade, ensure that you have completed a proper database backup. On ACS, database backup is performed through the System Configuration and ACS Backup section. Initiate one manual backup process. This process will create a backup file with the extension *.dmp*. Keep this database backup file for restoration in case of reinstallation or upgrade failure.

Tip   In my tenure while supporting AAA technology, I have found database backup to be a life saver in some instances. I would recommend configuring a periodic automatic database backup on ACS.

The difference among first time installs and upgrades occurs after Step 6 in the installation process. After step 6, the setup utility will detect the already installed ACS software and ask you to import the configuration setting from the existing installation. Check the check box that says **Yes, import the existing configuration**, as shown in Figure 2-15, and click **Next** and follow the setup utility instructions.

A reinstallation might be required if upgrade or install fails and leaves it in a state where it cannot be uninstalled. The ACS CD contains a utility called ACS clean utility (*clean.exe*) that can be used to remove all trace of ACS.

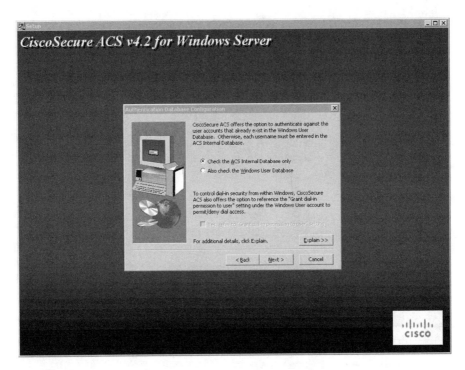

Figure 2-7   *Authentication Database Configuration*

Tip   During upgrade, ensure that you take a latest ACS database backup first and then follow the proper upgrade path. The complete upgrade path is available in the Installation Guide for Cisco Secure ACS for Windows 4.2 guide. Following an unsupported upgrade path might corrupt your database.

Installing Cisco Secure Access Control Server Solution Engine

Cisco Secure Access Control Server Solution Engine, as discussed in previous sections, is a network appliance with a customized and minimized version of Windows 2003 operating system. Before installation, the only way to access Cisco Secure ACS SE is through the serial console.

For more information, refer to the section "Installing and Configuring Cisco Secure ACS SE 4.2" in the "*Installation Guide for Cisco Secure ACS Solution Engine 4.2*" guide.

Initial configuration of Cisco Secure ACS SE is as follows:

Step 1.   Establish a serial console connection to Cisco Secure ACS SE using two DB-9 to RJ-45 adapters, an RJ-45 cable, and terminal emulation software. For more detail refer to the section "Establishing a Serial Console Connection" in the "Installation Guide for Cisco Secure ACS Solution Engine 4.2" guide.

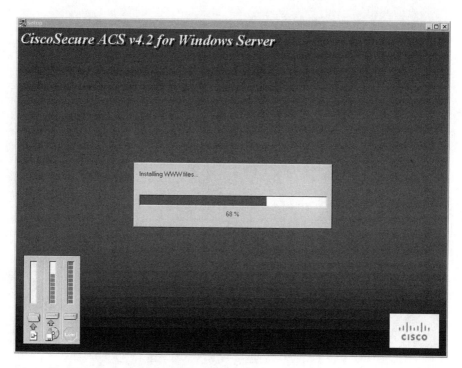

Figure 2-8 *ACS Software Installation*

Note ACS SE ships with a Cisco blue cale which already has on DB-9 and a second DB-9 for the other end. The cable used is a roll over (null modem) cable. Ensure that adaptor is not missing any pins; all pins are required to establish a serial console connection.

Step 2. Power up the ACS SE with an active connection to serial console connection as described in step 1 with terminal emulation software.

Step 3. Set the terminal emulation software to operate on following settings:

- Baud = 115200

- Databits = 8

- Stops = 1

- Flow Control = None

- Terminal emulation type = ANSI

If the connection and terminal settings are correct, the login: prompt should appear.

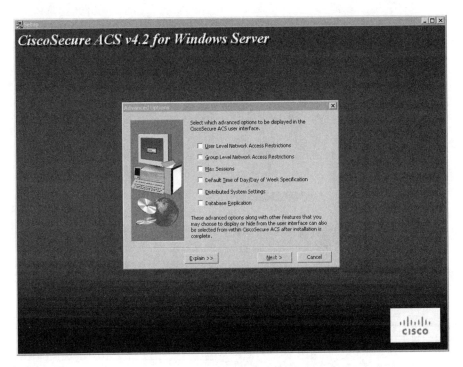

Figure 2-9 *Advanced Options*

If the ACS SE is being configured for the first time or has been reimaged, as soon as the system initializes, it displays the system information along with software version as demonstrated in the following output:

```
Cisco Secure ACS: [version number]
Appliance Management Software: [version number]
Appliance Base Image: [version number]
CSA build [version number]: (Patch: [version number])
Status: Appliance is functioning properly
The ACS Appliance has not been configured.
Logon as "Administrator" with password "setup" to configure appliance.
```

If this information is not available, reboot Cisco Secure ACS SE and this information should appear after system initialization.

Step 4.   At the login prompt, as instructed, enter **Administrator** as the username and **setup** as the password. After providing default initial login, Solution Engine displays the following message:

```
Initialize Appliance.
Machine will be rebooted after initialization.
Entering Ctrl-C before setting appliance name will shutdown the
appliance
```

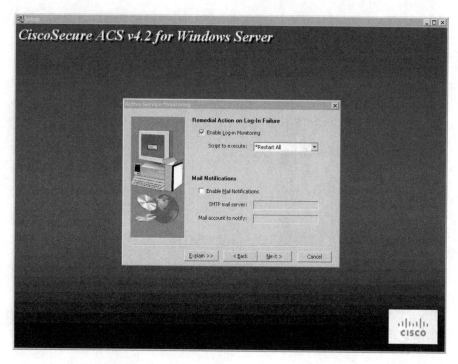

Figure 2-10   *Active Service Monitoring*

Step 5.   At this stage, initial configuration of Solution Engine begins. Appliance prompts with **[deliverance1]:** prompt. *deliverance1* is the default appliance name. The new appliance name has to be specified in this step. The appliance name can be up to 15 characters without spaces.

After the appliance name has been set successfully, the appliance displays the following message:

```
ACS Appliance name is set to appliance name
```

Step 6.   At this step, Solution Engine prompts you to configure the DNS domain. Specify the domain name and press **Enter**.

After the DNS domain is set, Solution Engine will display the following console message:

```
DNS name is set to domain name
You need to set the administrator account name and password.
```

Step 7.   In this step, you change the default serial console login username and password. The appliance prompts you to choose a new username and password. After specifying the password, the appliance requests that you retype the

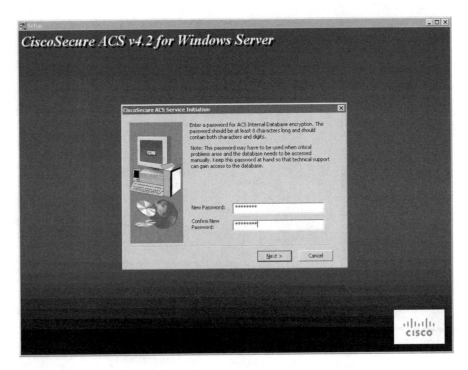

Figure 2-11   *ACS Internal Database Encryption*

password. After the provided password matches in both fields, the appliance displays confirmation message:

```
Password is set successfully.
Administrator name is set to serial username
```

This username password combination is used to log in to Solution Engine from the serial console Solution Engine CLI.

Note   You can also establish an SSH session into the solution engine. The username password used to log into solution engine through SSH is the same that is used for the serial console. SSH to solution engine is used only for invoking RDBMS synchronization. It does not provide CLI functionality that is available through serial console.

Step 8.   The appliance next prompts you to provide the encryption password to encrypt ACS database:

Please enter the Encryption Password for the Configuration Store.

Please note this is different from the administrator account, it is used to encrypt the Database.

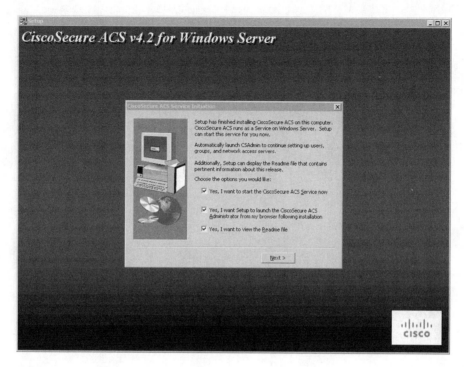

Figure 2-12 *ACS Service Initiation*

Type the new encryption password and retype it for confirmation when prompted by Solution Engine. After the encryption password is set, the appliance will display confirmation message on console:

```
Password is set successfully.
```

Step 9.   In Solution Engine, there are two administrative accounts. One provides access via the serial console or through SSH, whereas the other provides access to the ACS GUI. At this step, the appliance prompts you to create a new GUI administrative account, although this account can be created later on using the **add guiadmin** command. Type **y** to create a GUI administrative account and specify the new GUI administrative account name and account password. Retype the account password to confirm. After the account is created, the console will display the confirmation message:

```
GUI Administrator added successfully
```

Step 10.   Next, the appliance will prompt you to provide basic network connectivity configuration:

```
Use Static IP Address [Yes]:
```

To specify a static IP address, type **yes**; else type **no** to pick an IP address from DHCP server in the network.

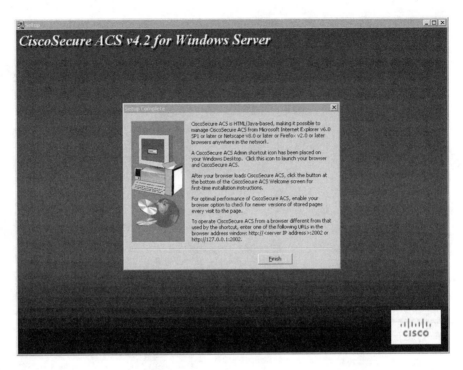

Figure 2-13   *Setup Complete*

Note   Ensure that before specifying an IP address on the solution engine, the NIC is connected to a working Ethernet connection. In addition, ensure that only one Ethernet connection is active, only to Ethernet 0 port (NIC 1). Please refer to "Connecting Cables" section of the *Installation Guide for Cisco Secure ACS Solution Engine 4.2.*

If you choose to assign a static IP address, setup will prompt you to provide a static IP address, subnet mask, default gateway, and DNS servers.

After accepting the network IP settings, the console will display the confirmation message:

```
New ip address is set.
Default gateway is set to xx.xx.xx.xx
DNS servers are set to: xx.xx.xx.xx xx.xx.xx.xx
```

Accept the network settings by typing **y** or pressing the **Enter** key. The appliance will also provide an option to test network connectivity using **ping** to ensure the appliance is able to communicate.

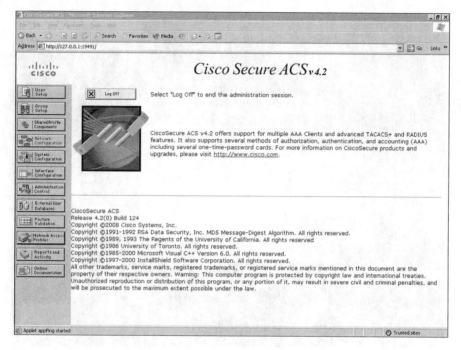

Figure 2-14   *ACS 4.2 GUI*

Step 11.   The appliance will now prompt you to set the system date/time and time zone
setting. The console will display following message:

```
Current Date Time Setting:
Time Zone: (GMT -xx:xx) XXX Time
Date and Time: mm/dd/yyyy
NTP Server(s): NTP Synchronization Disabled.
```

To set the system date/time and time zone settings, type **y** or press **Enter**.

Tip   NTP configuration is recommended as it ensures correctly time-stamped log data,
which is helpful in log auditing later on.

After applying the date/time and time zone settings successfully, the console
will display following message:

Initial configuration is successful. Appliance will now reboot.

The system reboots.

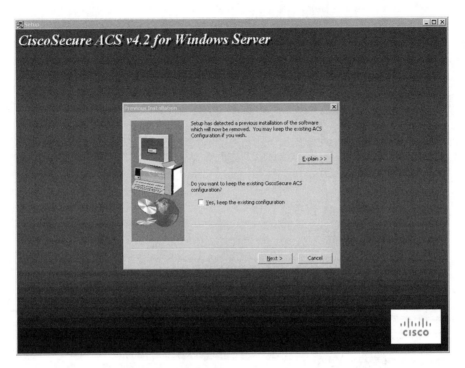

Figure 2-15   *ACS Reinstall or Upgrade*

Step 12.   When the appliance comes back up after reboot, log in to the serial console
connection using the newly set serial console appliance administrator user-
name/password combination. Execute the command **show** to ensure that all
the settings are correct as demonstrated in the output that follows:

```
acs01.cisco.com
Cisco Secure ACS: 4.2.0.124
Appliance Management Software: 4.2.0.124
Appliance Base Image: 4.2.0.107
Session Timeout: 10
Last Reboot Time: Tue Oct 06 16:17:07 2009
Current Date & Time: 10/7/2009 13:14:07
Time Zone: (GMT-08:00) Pacific Time (US & Canada)
NTP Server(s): time.cisco.com
Appliance IP Configuration


        CPU Load    Free Disk    Free Physical
                                 Memory
        0.00%       54.8 GB      802 MB
```

```
DHCP Enabled. . . . . . . . . .: No
IP Address. . . . . . . . . . .: 192.168.10.11
Subnet Mask . . . . . . . . . .: 255.255.255.0
Default Gateway . . . . . . . .: 192.168.10.1
DNS Servers . . . . . . . . . .: 192.168.10.15


        CSAdmin              running

        CSAuth               running
        CSDbSync             running
        CSLog                running
        CSMon                running
        CSRadius             running
        CSTacacs             running
        CSAgent              running
```

Now the appliance can also be accessed through the GUI using the GUI administrative username password combination. To access the ACS Solution Engine GUI, launch a HTTP connection to the IP of the appliance on port 2002. For example:

http://192.168.10.11:2002

To be able to log in to the ACS Solution Engine from a web browser, ensure that your browser supports Java and that Java is installed. For more detail on supported web browsers for GUI access, please refer to the "Web Browsers" section in the "Supported Interoperable Devices and Software Table for Cisco Secure ACS Release 4.2" document:

http://www.cisco.com/en/US/docs/net_mgmt/cisco_secure_access_control_server_ for_windows/4.2/device/guide/sdt42.html#wpxref57460

Initial Setup of Cisco Secure Access Control System 5.1

As discussed in previous sections, Cisco Secure Access Control System is available in two platforms:

- Cisco Secure Access Control System appliance
- Cisco Secure Access Control System on a VMware server

Initial setup for both Cisco Secure Access Control System platforms is identical. The only prerequisite difference is that you must create a VMware instance for the Cisco Secure Access Control System on VMware server. After a VMware instance is created for Cisco Secure Access Control System, there is no difference in initial setup.

Installation of Cisco Secure Access Control System 5.1 is supported on VMwareESX 3.5 and 4.0. For details on hardware requirements, configuring VMware ESX and the virtual machine for Cisco Secure Access Control System 5.1, please refer to the "Installing the ACS Server with VMware ESX" section in the "Installation and Upgrade Guide for the Cisco Secure Access Control System 5.1."

Cisco Secure Access Control System Appliance 5.1

After the appliance has been placed in the rack, the network cable and appliance console have been connected, and the appliance has been powered on, you are ready for initial setup and installation of ACS.

For details on network and console connection and powering the appliance up, please refer to the section "Installing the Cisco 1121 Secure Access Control System Hardware" in the "Installation and Upgrade Guide for the Cisco Secure Access Control System 5.1."

Note   Cisco Secure Access Control System 5.1 also has two Gigabit Ethernet ports. Only Gigabit Ethernet 0 is supported for configuring Cisco Secure Access Control System 5.1.

There are two options available to connect to appliance 5.1 for initial configuration:

■   Connecting through the console

■   Connecting using keyboard and video monitor

To connect using the console, configure terminal or terminal emulation software for 9600 baud, 8 data bits, no parity, 1 stop bit, and no hardware flow control. To connect a PC running terminal-emulation software to the console port, use a DB-9 female to DB-9 female straight-through cable. To connect an ASCII terminal to the console port, use a DB-9 female to DB-25 male straight-through cable with a DB-25 female to DB-25 female gender changer.

Tip   You can use Cisco blue cable with one DB-9 as in case of Cisco Secure Access Control Server 4.2. The cable is a roll over (null modem) cable.

To connect using a keyboard and video monitor, there are ports available at the back panel of the appliance for connecting the keyboard and video monitor.

Installing Cisco Secure Access Control System 5.1

Step 1. When everything is in place and the appliance is powered up. You should see following prompt appear on the console/monitor:

```
Please type 'setup' to configure the appliance
localhost login:
```

Type **setup** and press **Enter**.

Setup is a one-time configuration task. After this process is initiated, it requires some basic information to configure the appliance. After settings have been committed, the next time you are allowed to log in normally into the appliance CLI.

Step 2. The appliance will request basic information for appliance network connectivity, including hostname, IP address, netmask, default gateway, DNS domain, name server, and appliance CLI administrative account detail as demonstrated in the example that follows. After the basic required information has been provided, the appliance installs and configures the application and reboots.

```
localhost login: setup

Enter hostname[]: acs-server-1
Enter IP address[]: 209.165.200.225
Enter IP default netmask[]: 255.255.255.0
Enter IP default gateway[]: 209.165.200.1
Enter default DNS domain[]: mycompany.com
Enter Primary nameserver[]: 209.165.200.254
Add/Edit another nameserver? Y/N: n
Enter username [admin]: admin
Enter password:
Enter password again:
Pinging the gateway...
Pinging the primary nameserver...
Do not use 'Ctrl-C' from this point on...
Appliance is configured
Installing applications...
Installing acs...
Generating configuration...
Rebooting...
```

After reboot, appliance can be accessed through console/monitor or remotely using SSH.

Step 3. Accessing ACS 5.1 GUI is different from accessing ACS 5.1 CLI. To log in to ACS 5.1 GUI, enter the following ACS URL:

https://<acs 5.1 IP>/acsadmin

Log in to ACS GUI using default username **ACSAdmin** and default password **default**. Username is not case sensitive, but password is case sensitive. The appliance will prompt you to change the default password from **default** to a user-configured password. When done, it will prompt to install a valid license. Only after a valid license has been installed is the ACS GUI fully functional. The next section discusses licensing in more detail.

Note You will get a warning message from the browser about the self-signed certificate. Please ignore this warning or add the self-signed certificate to exception list on your browser.

Installing Cisco Secure Access Control System 5.1 on VMware

Installing Cisco Secure Access Control System 5.1 on VMware is the same as installing it on Cisco Secure Access Control System 5.1 Appliance. The only difference is in the initial steps.

After a VM has been created as per the "Installation and Upgrade Guide for the Cisco Secure Access Control System 5.1," you need to use ACS 5.1 recovery disk and perform a system install:

Step 1.   Log in to the VM infrastructure client created.

Step 2.   Insert the ACS 5.1 install disk into VMware ESX host CD/DVD drive and power on the VM.

During the boot up process, you must see the following on the console:

```
Welcome to Cisco Secure ACS 5.1 Recovery
To boot from the hard disk press <Enter>
Available boot options:
[1] Cisco Secure ACS 5.1 Installation (Monitor/Keyboard)
[2] Cisco Secure ACS 5.1 Installation (Serial Console)
[3] Reset Administrator Password (Keyboard/Monitor)
[4] Reset Administrator Password (Serial Console)
<Enter> Boot from hard disk
Please enter boot option and press <Enter>.
boot: 1
```

Step 3.   Choose either option **1** or option **2**. Connect accordingly to the VM.

Step 4.   After approximately 20 minutes, the installation process will end and the VM will reboot. Take out the install disk.

From this step onwards, all the steps are identical to installing Cisco Secure Access Control System 5.1. That is, at the system prompt after reboot, you type **setup** and follow the setup process.

Licensing Model of Cisco Secure Access Control System 5.1

As opposed to Cisco Secure Access Control Server 4.2, with Cisco Secure Access Control System 5.1, you must have a valid license. If you do not have a valid license, ACS 5.1 will not provide full feature support.

> **Note**   Each Cisco Secure Access Control System instance requires a unique base license. If you have Primary and Secondary Cisco Secure Access Control System deployed, each must have its own and unique base license to operate in a distributed deployment.

Type of License

There are four types of license available on Cisco Secure Access Control System:

- Base License
- Add-on Licenses
- Evaluation License
- Not-For-Resale (NFR) License

Base License

The base license is required for all software instances deployed, as well as for all appliances. The base license enables you to use all the ACS functionality except license controlled features, and it enables standard centralized reporting features.

The base license does not have any expiration date. If you have deployed ACS in a distributed environment (that is, a primary and secondary ACS instance), the base license is required for each instance.

The base license supports deployment up to 500 managed devices.

> **Note**   The number of devices is determined by the number of unique IP addresses that you configure. This includes the subnet masks that you configure. For example, a subnet mask of 255.255.255.0 implies 256 unique IP addresses and hence the number of devices is 256.

Three types of base license exist:

- **Permanent:** Supports up to 500 managed devices
- **Eval:** Supports up to 50 managed devices and expires in 90 days.
- **Not-For-Sale (NFR):** Supports up to 50 managed device and expires in 365 days.

Add-on License

The types of add-on licenses available are as follows:

- **TrustSec Access Control License:** This add-on license requires an existing ACS base license and enables Cisco TrustSec (CTS) management functionality. The TrustSec feature licenses are of three types: Permanent, Eval, and NFR; however, the permanent TrustSec feature license can be used only with a permanent base license.
- **Large Deployment License:** This add-on license requires an existing ACS permanent base license and supports an unlimited number of managed devices. This add-on license can be used only with a permanent base license.

Evaluation License

The evaluation license can support up to 50 managed devices and expires in 90 days from the time license is installed. If your evaluation license expires or is about to expire, you cannot use another evaluation license or extend your current license. Before your evaluation license expires, you must upgrade to either an NFR or a permanent license.

Not-For-Resale (NFR) License

The NFR license is sold to distribution partners for demonstration and training purposes. NFR supports up to 50 managed devices and expires in 365 days from the time the license is installed. ACS accepts multiple unique NFR licenses. If an NFR license is about to expire, it can be extended by installing another NFR license before the current one expires.

Common Problems After Installation

This section covers a few common problems encountered after ACS installation.

ACS Solution Engine Does Not Respond to Pings

This is among most common problem encountered by customer. In reality, this is not a problem, but an expected behavior. The Cisco Secure ACS Solution Engine, also known as the Cisco Secure ACS Appliance, is based on Microsoft Windows, and therefore is vulnerable to Path Maximum Transmission Unit Discovery (PMTUD) attacks and to attacks based on Internet Control Message Protocol (ICMP) "hard" error messages. The

Cisco Secure ACS Solution Engine ships with Cisco Security Agent (CSA), which is configured to block all incoming ICMP messages. This ensures that Cisco Secure ACS Solution Engine is not vulnerable to ICMP-based attacks.

Some organizations use tools based on ICMP to check the status of their network devices. For their monitoring tool to report the correct status of the device, the only solution earlier was to stop CSAgent completely. In the case of ACS SE 4.2, you can have both CSAgent running as well as the capability to allow or stop ICMP responses from the ACS SE.

Cisco.com provides two patches: one to turn ping on and another to turn ping off:

- **applAcs_4.x-PingTurnOn_CSCtb62656.zip:** ACS SE patch for turning ping on. This patch is suitable also for ACS SE 4.0 and 4.1. This patch is suitable for all ACS SE platforms including ADE 1120.

- **applAcs_4.x-PingTurnOff_CSCtb62656.zip:** ACS SE patch for turning ping off. This patch is suitable also for ACS SE 4.0 and 4.1. This patch is suitable for all ACS SE platforms including ADE 1120.

Refer to the readme files included for instruction on patch application on ACS SE.

Note   This is specific to ACS 4.2 and is not an issue in ACS 5.x

No Proper Cisco Secure Access Control Server GUI Access

This is in case of Cisco Secure Access Control Server or Solution Engine. If, after installation, you try to open the administrative interface of the ACS server using the following URL:

   http://IP-of-ACS:2002

You might encounter a GUI with error and some cross marks, where the browser was not able to load some images. In the case of Solution Engine, you won't be prompted for a username/password combination. In the case of ACS for Windows, you'll get incomplete or browser loading sections with errors.

The only common cause for this is that the client machine from where browser is being launched does not have Java installed. Java installation and support is required for ACS 4.2 GUI to work properly. Please ensure to install Java as instructed in the Installation guide for Cisco Secure Access Control Server 4.2.

Remote Administration Access to Cisco Secure Access Control Server

This is observed in the case of Cisco Secure Access Control Server for Windows. After finishing installation on Windows server, you might try to access to ACS GUI interface remotely. When doing so, you are prompted for a username and password in the GUI. Your first reaction is, "what is the default username and password?" Actually, none exists.

To access ACS remotely, you must ensure that you have created an administrative account. This can be done from Administration Control section on ACS. To create this account, you need to log in to the server locally where ACS is installed, and launch the browser as

http://127.0.0.1:2002

ACS Folder Is Locked During Upgrade or Uninstall

While upgrading or uninstalling Cisco Secure Access Control Server for Windows, you might get the following error message:

```
The CiscoSecure ACS folder appears to be locked by another application....
Please close any applications that are using any files or directories and re-run
Uninstall.
```

This is among the most common issues and occurs due to the accumulation of service logs, which the setup utility is not able to remove.

To fix this, go to **System Configuration > Service Control**.

In the Services Log File Configuration, check Manage Directory, and choose Keep only the last <n> files. Set <n> to 3. These logs can also be removed manually from the ACS installation directory.

If *PNLogAgent* is running, stop that service to release any locks that the service might have on the folder. If you have any files inside the ACS installation folder opened in the browser or editor, close them to release any lock.

TACACS+/RADIUS Attributes Do Not Appear Under User/Group Setup

When you want to configure certain attributes for TACACS+/RADIUS and those attributes do not appear for some reason under User/Group setup, ensure that those attributes have already been configured to be visible under User/Group setup from the Interface Configuration section. You can control what attributes should be visible from this section. It makes sense to have only those attributes available for configuration under User/Group setup that are being used. Also, for the attribute to show up, at least one network device (AAA client) must be configured for that authentication type.

Key Mismatch Error

While authenticating a device using RADIUS/TACACS+, you might encounter an authentication failure on ACS for Windows or SE with the failure reason being *key mismatch*. Although the error message is informative enough, it means that shared key does not match between the authentication server and network device. The first step should be to ensure that both keys match. In the case of the Cisco Secure Access Control Server for Windows and Solution Engine, ensure that there is no key configured on the Network Device Group (NDG) level if the device is placed under one. If a key is defined at the

NDG level, that takes precedence over individual AAA client level keys, so ensure that either there is no key at the NDG level if you intend to use different keys for AAA clients, or if you intend to use same key for all AAA client, ensure that the key is correct at the NDG level.

ACS Services Not Starting

ACS services might stop during the course of normal operation due to another database application being installed on the same server as the ACS. The other database application installation interferes with the ACS database installation.

ACS 5.1 Install Failing on VMWare

The VMWare installation fails for ACS 5.1 if minimum requirements are not met as listed in installation guide for ACS 5.1 on VMWare. The most common reason for installation failure is allocation of hard disk space lower than 500GB. To ensure successful installation of ACS 5.1 on VMWare, please follow all the instructions provided in the Installation document:

> http://www.cisco.com/en/US/docs/net_mgmt/cisco_secure_access_control_system/ 5.1/installation/guide/csacs_vmware.html

There are more common problems with installation that you might encounter. The document, Cisco Secure ACS Online Troubleshooting Guide, 4.2, available at Cisco.com covers troubleshooting procedures and tools used for troubleshooting common problems and provides interpretation of error codes on Cisco Secure Access Control Server:

> http://www.cisco.com/en/US/docs/net_mgmt/cisco_secure_access_control_server_ for_windows/4.2/trouble/guide/ACSTrbG42.html

Summary

This chapter provided an overview of two Cisco Secure products; Cisco Secure Access Control Server 4.2 and Cisco Secure Access Control System 5.1, which are used for identity management and access control in a network. More precisely, you have learned:

- Cisco Secure Access Control Server is based on group-based policy model.

- Cisco Secure Access Control System is based on rule-based policy model, which provides more granular control over security policy.

- Cisco Secure Access Control Server is available in two flavors: Cisco Secure Access Control Server for Windows and Cisco Secure Access Control Server Solution Engine (Appliance).

- Cisco Secure Access Control System is available in two flavors as well—one as an appliance and the same can be installed on a VM on VMware.

- Protocol compliance is offered by both products—Cisco Secure Access Control Server and Cisco Secure Access Control System.

- Some of the basic, advanced, and distinctive features offered by both products.

- How to install Cisco Secure Access Control Server 4.2 on Windows server and on Solution Engine.

- How to install Cisco Secure Access Control System 5.1 on Appliance and on VMware.

- How to mitigate a few of the most often encountered issues after installation.

Chapter 3

Getting Familiar with ACS 4.2

In this chapter, you learn the following topics:

- The Seven ACS Services

- A Tour of the ACS GUI

- Administration Control—GUI Control

- Network Configuration—Managing Devices and Servers

- Network Access Profiles

- Interface Configuration

- User Setup—Managing Users

- Group Setup—Managing User Groups

- System Configuration

- Shared Profile Components

- External User Databases

- Reports and Activities—Accounting and Logs

- Working with ACS Log files

One thing you'll notice between ACS 4.2 and ACS 5.1 is that the interface has changed. This might take some getting used to since the ACS interface has basically been the same for years. In this chapter you will discover, or rediscover, the ACS interface of version 4.2. In Chapter 4, you'll have a chance to get familiar with ACS 5.1.

Now you might ask, "Where does it all begin?" The answer is, "With the install." And although that seems to be one of those things that you say, "Uh, yeah" to, it's assumed here that you've already done that. In fact, I personally believe that out of all the Cisco products I've worked with, the ACS is the easiest to install. That is, if you are using a version for Windows; it's even easier if you are using the appliance model.

This chapter begins with a discussion of what is running on your server now that ACS is there.

The Seven Services of ACS

When you install ACS, a number of services begin to run on your machine, each one having a specific purpose. These services include the following:

- CSAdmin

- CSAuth

- CSDBSync

- CSLog

- CSMon

- CSRadius

- CSTacacs

Each of these ACS services runs as a local system service by default. Often you need to modify the ACS services to use a specific domain account to get the access they need. These services can be seen running in Windows Task Manager, as seen in Figure 3-1.

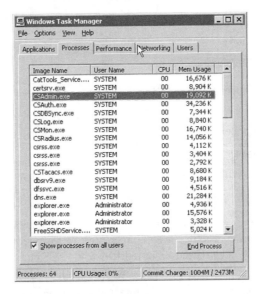

Figure 3-1   *ACS Services*

The sections that follow cover each of these services in greater detail.

CSAdmin

CSAdmin is the service that handles your administrative access to ACS. The CSAdmin service handles the browser interface that you see when working with ACS. You can access the ACS web server by browsing to http://127.0.0.1:2002 on the machine on which it is installed. A link is also placed on the desktop during the install process. You cannot browse to the ACS server remotely until you have configured an administrative user in the ACS interface or using the CLI on an ACS appliance.

Note If you were to restart the ACS services from within the ACS GUI, CSAdmin would be the only service that would not restart. If it did, you would lose connectivity to ACS.

Another important point to mention is that ACS does not stay on port 2002. In fact, as soon as you connect to the web server, it redirects you to a random high number port. This causes some issues with access from outside of firewalls. To get around this issue, you can administratively change the scope of high number ports that you are redirected to in the Administration Control section of the web interface. This will be shown later in this chapter in the section "Administration Control."

CSAuth

When a device initiates a request, it is received by a protocol-specific service on ACS (CSTacacs and CSRadius). These services hand over the authentication and authorization request to the CSAuth service. CSAuth's job is to locate the user, in ACS database or external databases, and determine whether a permit or deny action should be taken.

If a permit action has to be taken, CSAuth also determines the privilege of the user. After that, it hands over the result to the service from which the request was received.

CSAuth is also responsible for all communication between ACS and external databases.

Note Why and how ACS checks external databases is covered in Chapter 5, "Configuring External Databases with ACS." For now, it is important to remember that ACS can use external databases and CSAuth takes care of all communication between the external database and ACS.

CSDBSync

There are times when you might want to add many users and network devices in ACS. Adding them one at a time is a long process. To overcome this, ACS provides the option to load user and device information from an external database, such as a CSV file, or any other relational database, such as SQL. This feature is called *RDBMS synchronization*.

CSDBSync is the service that communicates between the ACS database and the external database for synchronization.

Note   RDBMS synchronization is covered in detailed in Chapter 14, "ACS 4.2 Advanced Configuration."

CSLog

As the name suggests, CSLog is responsible for logging. After CSAuth completes processing an authentication or authorization request, it sends the information to CSLog. CSLog, in turn, captures the event information and stores it in comma separated value (CSV) files.

In addition to these event logs, CSLog also receives accounting packets from CSRadius and CSTacacs and stores the information contained in the packets in CSV files.

All the CSV files maintained by CSLog can be access under the Reports and Activity Section. These files are discussed in detailed later in the chapter.

ACS also enables you to log events and accounting information on a remote server. CSLog handles all communication between the remote logging server and ACS.

CSMon

There are four separate activities that the CSMon service performs:

- It monitors other ACS services.

- It records and reports errors found with other services.

- It notifies the administrator of potential issues with ACS services.

- It uses an application-specific utility to resolve these issues automatically.

CSRadius

CSRadius monitors the RADIUS ports and receives RADIUS packets from AAA clients. CSRadius parses the packets and sends authentication and authorization requests to CSAuth for processing. When it receives a response from CSAuth, CSRadius builds a RADIUS packet using the information from CSAuth and the original packet received from the AAA client. This packet is then sent to the AAA client in response to the request.

In addition to this, CSRadius parses RADIUS accounting packets received and sends them to CSLog for processing.

CSTacacs

Similarly to what CSRadius does, CSTacacs monitors TACACS+ ports and receives TACACS+ packets from AAA clients. It then parses the packets and sends authentication and authorization request to CSAuth for processing. When a response is received, CSTacacs creates a TACACS+ packet and sends to the AAA client in response to the request.

In addition, CSTacacs parses all TACACS+ accounting packets and sends them to CSLog for processing.

The Grand Tour of the ACS Interface

If this is your first time using ACS, it is important to take the time to learn how to navigate the interface.

The main web interface of ACS is divided into frames. You access different menu items on the left side of the page, perform configuration in the middle, and have access to some help on the right side.

Because you use the menu a great deal in your configurations, the next sections look at each menu item and what types of configuration can be performed at each level. This section is not covered in a top-down process, rather in an order that makes sense to setting up your server for functionality. The discussion begins with a look at Administration Control.

Administration Control

The Administration Control section is where you configure all aspects of ACS for administrative access as shown in Figure 3-2. Here you have the ability to add administrators and configure access policy. You can configure information such as IP addresses that are allowed to access ACS, IP addresses that are not allowed to access ACS, and HTTP port allocation here.

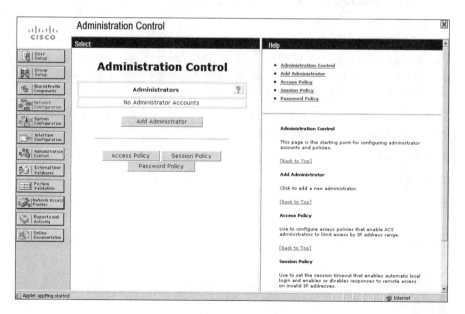

Figure 3-2 *Administration Control*

Session policy enables you to alter the timeout, allow automatic local logins, and respond to invalid IP addresses. You can also choose to lock administrator access after a certain number of failed authentication attempts.

Recall that ACS uses port 2002 as the listening port, but after a connection to that port is made, you are redirected to a random port number. When ACS is positioned behind a firewall, this random port assignment becomes an issue with gaining connectivity. You could simply allow all ports inbound to the ACS server, but that wouldn't be very security-minded. As a better alternative, you have the ability to specify a range of ports used so that you can configure access restrictions within your firewall to match, as seen in Figure 3-3.

Figure 3-3   *HTTP Port Allocation*

Securing Access to ACS

You can take steps to secure ACS by applying administrator passwords and controlling access to the ACS device. The steps that follow demonstrate how to add an administrator and secure access to the ACS administrative interface.

You begin by assigning an administrator password to the ACS device. Follow these steps to complete this task, referring to Figure 3-4:

Step 1.   Select **Administration Control** from the left menu bar.

Step 2.   Select **Add Administrator**.

Step 3.   Enter the required information into the input fields, such as admin name and password.

Step 4.   If this is the first entry for an administrator, select the **Grant All** option.

Note   The **Grant All** option allows your administrator to have full administrative access. Later, as you add more administrators, you can specify what groups they can modify.

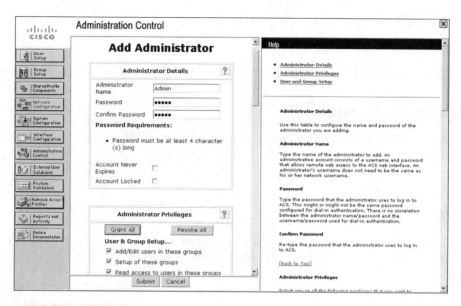

Figure 3-4 *Adding an Administrator to ACS*

Step 5. Select **Submit**.

You now see that your administrator has been added to the ACS device. If you access the ACS device from the server on which it is installed, you will, by default, not need to authenticate. This is against some security policies, so change that. Following the remaining steps will force ACS to authenticate administrators even when they access ACS from the server itself.

Step 6. Select **Session Policy**.

Step 7. Deselect **Allow automatic local login**.

Step 8. Select **Submit**.

Step 9. To test your work, click the X in the top right corner of the screen. Then, you can log back in to the ACS device. If you see Username and Password fields, you were successful.

As discussed earlier, ACS redirects to a random port for GUI access after login. This can be a problem when accessing the GUI from outside a firewall. To restrict the ports used by ACS, go back to the Administration Control section and control the ports that are redirected when ACS is accessed.

Step 10. Select **Access Policy**.

Step 11. Scroll to the HTTP Configuration section.

Step 12. Select the radio button that indicates you want to **Restrict Administration Sessions to the following port range**.

Step 13.   Add a port range, such as 65501 to 65535.

Step 14.   Select **Submit**.

This now restricts the port ranges that ACS redirects your browser to your defined range.

Network Configuration

Network Configuration is where you will add AAA clients to the ACS server. AAA clients can be anything from a firewall to a router. What defines a device as being an AAA client is that it can communicate with the AAA server using the TACACS+ or RADIUS protocol.

Another aspect of Network Configuration is that you can add additional ACS servers here in a distributed configuration or for a database synchronization scenario. In Figure 3-5, you can see the screen that is used for adding an AAA client. Depending on whether you use RADIUS or TACACS+, the interface might look slightly different.

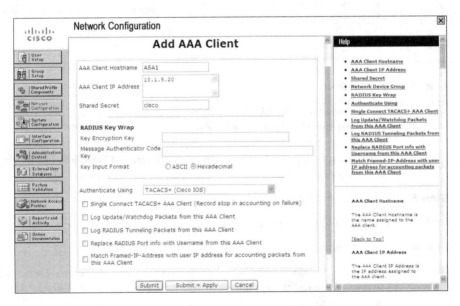

Figure 3-5   *Network Configuration*

The various options that can be configured for TACACS+ clients include the following:

■   **Single Connect TACACS+ AAA Client (Record stop in accounting on failure):**
    Single Connect TACACS+ AAA Client allows a single TCP connection between this
    AAA client and ACS. The normal operation is to establish a separate TCP connection
    for each request. For example, if you are using TACACS+ and you have a user that
    connects to the AAA client, a TCP connection is established when authentication
    occurs. When another user connects, another session is established, and so on. This
    option eliminates those multiple TCP sessions. However, this is not recommended

unless the connection between the TACACS+ AAA client and ACS is extremely reliable. If you decide to use this option and the connection between the ACS and TACACS+ AAA client goes down, ACS never receives accounting stop packets for all users accessing the network through that AAA client. This causes them to remain in the logged in users list until it's purged.

■ **Log Update/Watchdog Packets from this AAA Client:** The Log Update/Watchdog Packets from this AAA Client allows accounting packets sent by the AAA client to be logged by ACS—specifically the logging of update or watchdog packets. It does not control overall logging of accounting packets. Watchdog packets are a means of creating better session length granularity to safeguard against the possibility of a device going down and thus never sending accounting stop packets for the users accessing the network via that device. Customers who have high priority on maintaining session length data might find this more useful than others. An example of an update packet is a RADIUS interim-accounting packet. These packets can be used to account for customer activity and then be used in billing.

■ **Log RADIUS Tunneling Packets from this AAA Client:** The Log RADIUS Tunneling Packets from this AAA Client option allows RADIUS tunneling packets from the AAA client to be logged by ACS.

■ **Replace RADIUS Port Info with Username from this AAA Client:** This enables the use of a username rather than port numbers for session state tracking. This option is useful when the AAA client cannot provide unique port values. For example, if you use the Cisco Secure ACS IP Pools server and the AAA client does not provide a unique port for each user, Cisco Secure ACS assumes that a reused port number indicates that the previous user session has ended, and Cisco Secure ACS can reassign the IP address previously assigned to the session with the non-unique port number. By default, this check box is not selected.

When you make changes to an AAA client, you must submit and restart the ACS services, similar to group changes. If you want to delete an AAA client, you are also required to submit and restart the service for changes to take effect.

Network Access Profiles

The way ACS 4.2 works is by applying a combination of user and group policy to a request. On top of that, a user can belong to a single group only. This leaves no scope for defining policies that can change automatically depending on some factors. For example, you might want to enforce lesser restriction if a user connects via the local network compared to when the same user connects remotely.

To overcome this, ACS provides a feature called Network Access Profiles (NAP). These profiles classify a network access request and apply a policy based on the classification.

Chapter 14 covers NAP in detail along with configuration examples.

Interface Configuration

Moving on to the Interface Configuration menu item, as seen in Figure 3-6, you find a selection from the following subconfiguration links, depending on whether you have selected TACACS+ or a form of RADIUS when you entered your AAA client:

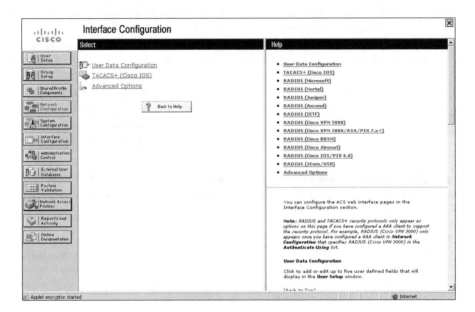

Figure 3-6 *Interface Configuration*

- User Data Configuration

- TACACS+ (Cisco IOS)

- RADIUS (Microsoft)

- RADIUS (Ascend)

- RADIUS (IETF)

- RADIUS (IOS/PIX)

- Advanced Options

Note If you do not see RADIUS options here, you need to add an AAA client that uses the RADIUS protocol. Interface Configuration is directly affected by Network Configuration.

The User Data Configuration link enables you to customize the fields that appear in the user setup and configuration. Here you can add fields such as phone number, work location, supervisor name, or any other pertinent information.

The TACACS+ (Cisco IOS) link enables the administrator to configure TACACS+ settings as well as add new TACACS+ services. You can also configure advanced options that affect what you see in your interface. It is important you understand how this works. Depending on the current configuration of your server, if you go to the TACACS+ link, you might or might not see two columns. If you do see two columns, this means that per-use level attributes have been enabled. Figure 3-7 displays what you see before enabling per-user TACACS+/RADIUS attributes.

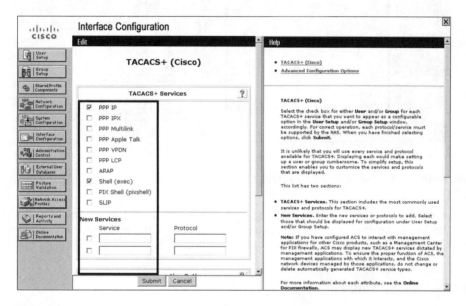

Figure 3-7   *TACACS+ (Cisco IOS) Before User Attributes*

In Figure 3-8, you can see the change to the TACACS+ (Cisco IOS) settings page after going through the following steps:

Step 1.   Select the **Interface Configuration** button on the left side menu.

Step 2.   Select **Advanced Options**.

Step 3.   Select **Per-user TACACS+/RADIUS Attributes**.

Step 4.   Select **Submit**.

Step 5.   Select **TACACS+ (Cisco IOS)**.

You should now have two columns available: User and Group. By selecting these options at the user level or group level, you enable these configuration options within each menu.

Here is where the user-to-group relationship comes into play. If an option is selected to appear in both the user and group configurations, and the user-level configuration is different than the group level, the user-level configuration takes precedence. Most of the features are available in both user and group configurations with a few exceptions. At the

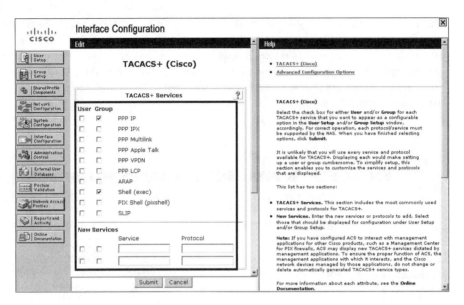

Figure 3-8   *TACACS+ (Cisco IOS) After User Attributes*

user level, you can configure passwords, expiration, and static IP addresses. At the group level, you can configure password aging as well as time-of-day restrictions for different categories.

TACACS+ Settings

To ease your configuration and help make things a little easier while you are learning, you need to disable some of the advanced TACACS+ features. You disable any advanced configurations at this point, and as you increase the functionality of ACS by adding more for it to do, you bring these configuration parameters back. Follow these steps to turn off the advanced TACACS+ settings:

Step 1.   Begin with accessing the Interface Configuration section by clicking the left menu button titled **Interface Configuration**.

Step 2.   In the beginning of this chapter, Interface Configuration was discussed as well as how selecting an option makes certain options visible in the HTML interface. Here, simply select the link **TACACS+ (Cisco IOS)**. This refreshes your screen to the edit page.

Step 3.   Deselect **Advanced TACACS+ Features**.

Step 4.   Select the **Display Time-of-Day** access grid for every TACACS+ service so that you can override the default Time-of-Day settings as shown in Figure 3-9.

Step 5.   Ensure that **Display a window for each service selected in which you can enter customized TACACS+ attributes** is deselected.

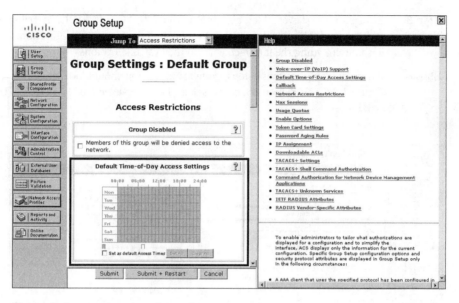

Figure 3-9 *Configuring Time-of-Day Settings*

Step 6.   Ensure that **Display enable default (Undefined) service configuration** is des-elected.

Step 7.   Select **Submit**.

The preceding steps are going to enable you to see a Time-of-Day grid where you have the control to configure Time-of-Day parameters. This might not be the first thing you always want to do; however, it is very noticeable when made visible, and that is the goal here.

To check your work, follow these steps:

Step 1.   Click **Group Setup**.

Step 2.   Select **Edit Settings**.

Step 3.   You should be able to see the Time-of-Day grids.

Advanced Options

Another way to clear out some of the clutter when you are learning is to disable the Advanced Configuration options. You might want to configure these settings, but for now, turn all of them off except for the Per-user TACACS/RADIUS Attributes. To do so, follow these simple steps:

Step 1.   Select **Interface Configuration**.

Step 2.   Select Advanced Options.

Step 3.   Ensure sure that everything except **Per-user TACACS+/RADIUS Attributes** is deselected. This enables you to do some individual user configurations without crowding the interface with all the available options.

Step 4.   After you complete these steps, your configuration should look similar to Figure 3-10. This demonstrates the selection of **Per-user TACACS+/RADIUS Attributes**.

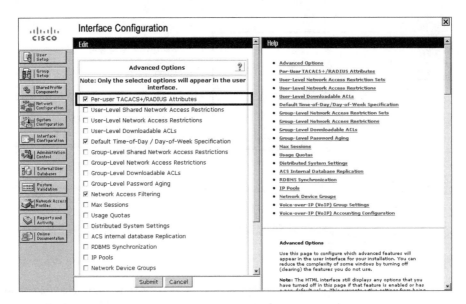

Figure 3-10   *Per-User TACACS+/RADIUS Attributes*

User Setup: Managing Users

When you select the User Setup menu item, your middle frame changes to the Select screen as shown in Figure 3-11. Here you can do a few things, such as add a new user, search for an existing user, find users alphabetically or numerically, or simply list all users at one time.

To begin your configuration, add a username. To do so, follow these steps:

Step 1.   Enter a username; for this example, use **aaauser** and select the **Add/Edit** button.

Step 2.   Now, you can edit user attributes. Moving from top to bottom, you can disable a user account, enter supplementary information, and configure the user's passwords. Figure 3-12 displays the option for authenticating against a Windows database (if you selected Windows Database during installation) or the Cisco Secure database.

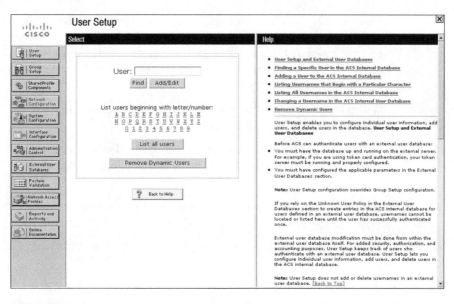

Figure 3-11 *User Setup*

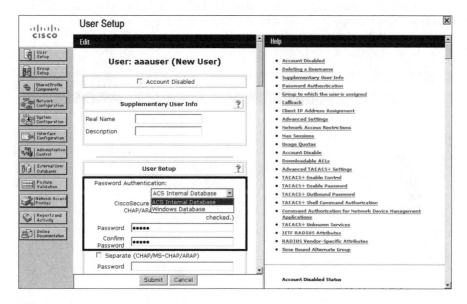

Figure 3-12 *Authentication Location Options*

Step 3.   Enter the password **cisco** for this user. Optionally, you could select the option to use the Windows database. The default is to check the Cisco Secure database.

Here, you can also distinguish which group the user is a member of. By not specifying a group, the user is placed in the default group (group 0). You can have the same attributes to configure in the group setup as you have in the individual user setup; however, user configurations override that of the group of which they are a member.

Within User Setup, you can also configure callback settings, IP address assignment, and account disable properties.

Step 4.   Click **Submit** to create your first AAA user in ACS. Because you have not selected a group, this user is placed in the default (group 0) group.

Note   By selecting the List All Users button after creating your user, you should see a single user entry on the right side of the ACS interface. This ensures that the entry has been successfully created.

Customizing User Attributes

After a user has been added, you might decide that you want to customize the interface a little more. The information displayed under User Setup is good, but you could add more information that might help you in keeping track of users. Notice that in the ACS user configuration, you have the ability, by default, to include supplementary user info. This information includes real name and description, as shown in Figure 3-13.

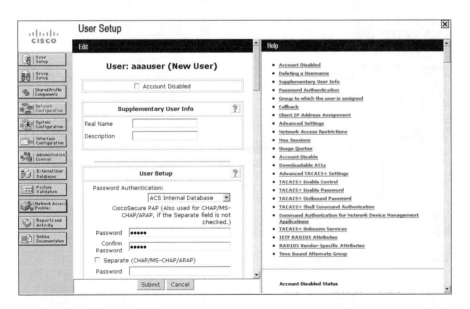

Figure 3-13   *Supplementary User Info*

To add additional fields for more information to be added, follow these steps:

Step 1.   Access the **Interface Configuration** menu.

Step 2.   Select **User Data Configuration**. Place a check mark in the box titled **Display** for number 3 and 4 to indicate that you want these fields to be displayed.

Step 3.   Edit or input the relevant headings for each field you plan to use in addition to the two defaults. The example in Figure 3-14 uses **Extension** and **Cubicle**.

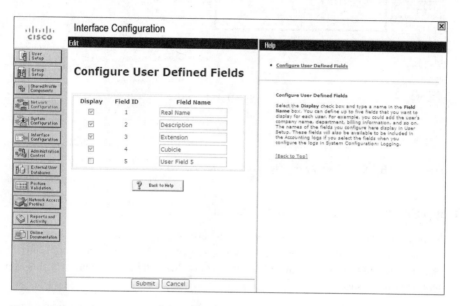

Figure 3-14   *User Data Configuration*

Step 4.   Select **Submit**.

You can check your work by following these steps:

Step 1.   Select **User Setup**.

Step 2.   Enter **aaauser** in the field provided.

Step 3.   Select **Add/Edit**.

Step 4.   You should now see the two new Supplementary User Info fields that you created as shown in Figure 3-15.

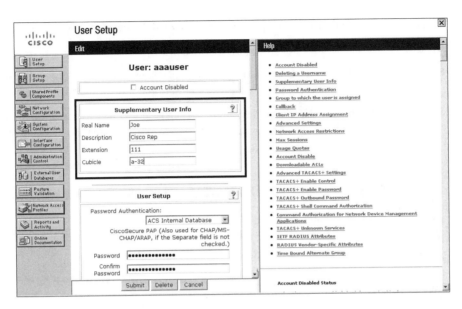

Figure 3-15   *Supplementary User Info (After Edits)*

Group Setup: Managing User Groups

To begin your configuration, recap what you have configured thus far. You have a user called **aaauser** who has a password of **cisco** and is placed in the default group. This user is authenticated to the Cisco Secure database only. To examine the group that this user is in, follow these steps:

Step 1.   Select the Group Setup menu item. As Figure 3-16 illustrates, you have three options from which to choose: Users in Group, Edit Settings, and Rename Group. Users in Group lists all the users assigned to the group that is visible in the drop-down menu. A total of 500 groups numbered 0 through 499 exist.

Step 2.   To view the group settings that your first AAA user is a member of (by default), simply select the **0:Default Group** and then select **Edit Settings**. This selection changes the main window, and you are now in the Group Configuration section, as shown in Figure 3-17.

You can note a few highlights while you are here. First, look at the *Jump To* option at the top of the screen. This feature is a real time-saver. Try it out a few times by jumping to the IP address assignment section and then back to access restrictions. Notice that in the group configuration you have the ability to configure time-of-day access restrictions. This is not available at the user level. You can also configure callback, IP assignment, and TACACS+ settings. Under TACACS+ Settings, you can configure shell command authorizations, apply privilege levels, set auto-commands, and so on.

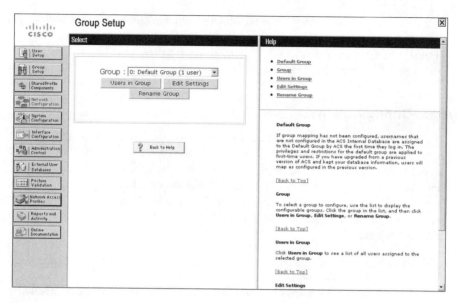

Figure 3-16   *Group Setup*

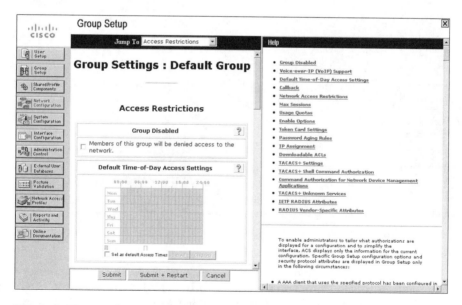

Figure 3-17   *Configuring the Default Group*

Note   Some of the fields might not be visible in either the Group Setup or User Setup screen. As you become more familiar with ACS, you will be able to enable or disable certain fields at either the group level or the user level screens.

When you make group changes, you are required to submit and restart the ACS services. Your changes do not take place until you have done so. If you are making multiple changes to a group, it is best to submit without restart after each change until you have completed all changes, and then restart the ACS services.

System Configuration

Under System Configuration, you find many subconfiguration links beginning with Service Control as shown in Figure 3-18. This is where you can stop and start the ACS services. You can also do so in the Service Control of Windows 2003 or using the CLI **net start** and **net stop** commands (for example, **net stop csadmin**). By stopping the ACS service inside of ACS, you do not stop the ACS web server. If you want to stop the ACS web server, you need to do so in the Service Control of Windows. This web service is called CSAdmin.

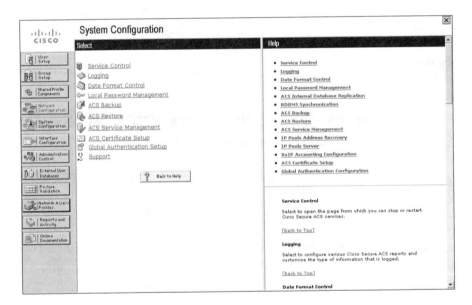

Figure 3-18 *System Configuration*

The next System Configuration feature that you can manipulate is Logging, where you can configure the local logging configuration, such as failed attempts and TACACS+ and RADIUS accounting. You also configure Open DataBase Connectivity (ODBC) and remote logging here.

Date Format Control is straightforward. This is where you can change the format of the date displayed on reports. After you change the format, you must log out of the server to actually see the changes take place.

Note   You can log out of ACS, short of closing the browser, in a few ways. One way is by clicking the Cisco Systems logo in the top left corner of the web browser screen and then selecting the Log Off button. Another method is by clicking on the X in the top right portion of the window.

The next option is Local Password Management. From here, you can set password length as well as password options. You can also configure options for remote password change and logging of password changes.

As for ACS Backup, you can schedule backups to be done manually or at specific times. You can specify a location for the backup files to be stored as well as manage the files. When ACS is backed up, it creates a file with the extension of .dmp. This file is now present when you enter the ACS Restore link. Here you have the ability to select from numerous backup files, as well as determine whether you want to restore the users and groups, system configuration, or both.

ACS Service Management enables the administrator to determine how often to test the availability of ACS authentication services. This is the CSMon service configuration. This allows ACS to test itself and take action when its test is unsuccessful. The available actions, should no authentications be recorded, are as follows:

- Restart all

- Restart RADIUS/TACACS

- Reboot

- Take no action

If the reboot option is selected, this causes the server that is running ACS to reboot. You also have the ability to add custom actions to this list via a script that controls the action to take.

You can also decide that you want to log attempts to log in to disabled accounts. Do this by selecting the check box labeled **Generate event when an attempt is made to log in to a disabled account**.

This is also where you can configure email notifications and Windows Event Log setup.

The ACS Certificate Setup is where you configure the ACS device with digital certificates. You use this when you configure the ACS to use HTTPS for administrative sessions or EAP authentication.

Global Authentication Setup is where you can allow protocols such as PEAP, EAP-TLS, EAP-MD5, and MS-CHAP.

Shared Profile Components

Shared Profile Components enables you to specify shell command authorization sets and PIX shell command authorization sets. By creating these command authorization sets, you can control the commands a user can execute on a device by applying the command authorization set to the user profile in the TACACS+ settings or at the group level. Figure 3-19 displays the Shared Profiles Components configuration menu. By default, you can select Shell Command Authorization Sets and PIX Shell Command Authorization Sets. Optionally, you can configure Downloadable ACLs or Management Center Authorization Sets. For these options to be visible, you must select them in the Interface Configuration page.

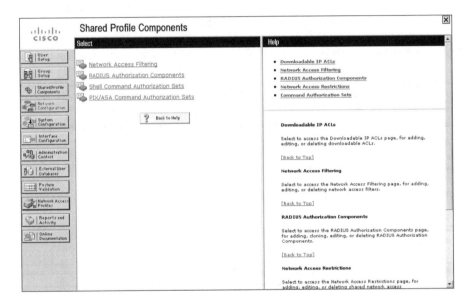

Figure 3-19   *Shared Profile Components*

Other benefits to the Shared Profile Components configuration page is the ability to configure shared network access restrictions and the ability to create a policy once and then use it in more than one group rather that defining the same policy multiple times under multiple groups.

By selecting one of these links, for example, Shell Command Authorization Sets, you are taken to the configuration page for this shared profile component as shown in Figure 3-20. As you can tell, at this point, none are defined.

External User Databases

In this section of the ACS interface, you have the ability to configure an unknown user policy. You also configure database group mappings to external user databases as well as perform the actual database configuration. You can also see the compatible databases here.

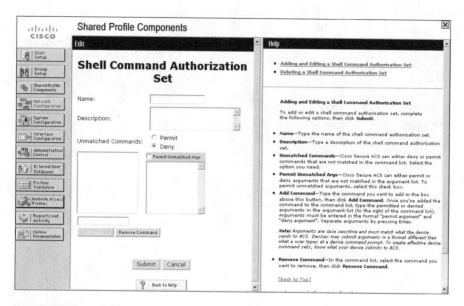

Figure 3-20 *Shell Command Authorization Sets*

The servers available for use as an external database are as follows:

- Windows Database

- Generic LDAP

- External ODBC Database

- LEAP Proxy RADIUS Server

- RADIUS Token Server

- RSA SecurID Token Server

- RSA SecurID Token and LDAP Group Mapping

Each version of ACS includes more and more support for external databases while greatly improving the functionality of the ACS database.

Reports and Activity

The Reports and Activity section provides a wealth of tools in not only troubleshooting, but also in monitoring your network. If you are going to log it, you better look at it. So many times I have been in networks running intrusion prevention systems, SYSLOG, and other types of monitoring, yet nobody takes the time to look through the logs. Figure 3-21 shows the Reports and Activity page.

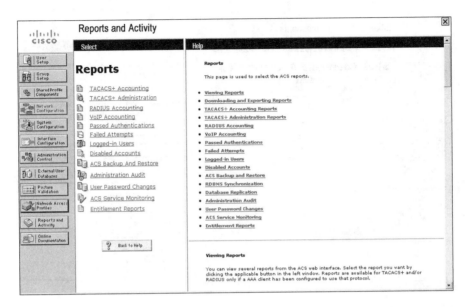

Figure 3-21   *Reports and Activity*

Within ACS, you have the ability as an administrator to monitor your network security on a number of levels. The available logs that ACS keeps for you are as follows:

■ **TACACS+ Accounting:** Accounting information from TACACS+ clients is parsed and stored in these files. All the TACACS+ Accounting reports include information such as time/date, username, type of connection, amount of time logged in, and bytes transferred. The information included in these reports is configurable by the administrator in the System Configuration section under Logging. These reports can be found at Program Files\CiscoSecure ACS v4.x\Logs\TACACS+Accounting.

■ **TACACS+ Administration:** The TACACS+ Administration reports include all the command requests from AAA clients such as routers or firewalls where command authorization is configured. These reports can be found on the hard disk of ACS at Program Files\CiscoSecure ACS v4.x\Logs\TACACS+Administration.

■ **RADIUS Accounting:** Accounting information from the RADIUS clients is parsed and stored in these files. It functions similar to the TACACS+ Accounting logs,; these reports can be found in Program Files\CiscoSecure ACS v4.x\Logs\RADIUSAccounting.

■ **VoIP Accounting:** Clients can send VoIP accounting information to ACS for logging. This report includes information such as VoIP session start and stop times, CLID information, and other attributes. The information included in these reports is configurable by the administrator in the System Configuration section under Logging. These reports can be found in Program Files\CiscoSecure ACS v4.x\Logs\VoIP Accounting.

■ **Passed Authentications:** Passed Authentication reports store information regarding every successful authentication and authorization request. These logs are generated by CSAuth events and do not depend on accounting information from AAA clients. These reports are very important to assess your security policies because they show which users are using various services that are authenticated. A thorough look at these reports will help determine whether some users have more access than they are supposed to have. These reports can be found in Program Files\CiscoSecure ACS v4.x\Logs\Passed Authentications. You should note that this report is not enabled by default and can be enabled from **System Configuration > Logging.**

■ **Failed Attempts:** Failed attempts reports store information regarding every failure authentication and authorization request. These logs are also generated by CSAuth events. This is the first place you should look at if authentication or authorization is failing. These reports provide username, device IP address, and failure reason, among other information, and are usually very precise in pointing out the reason for failure. These reports can be found in Program Files\CiscoSecure ACS v4.x\Logs\Failed Attempts. Figure 3-22 shows the Failed attempts log. You can see that the logs show an authentication failure with the reason **Unknown NAS.** You can make out from the reason that there is a problem with the AAA Client entry in ACS. Similarly, the failure reasons help easily identify the cause of failures in most cases.

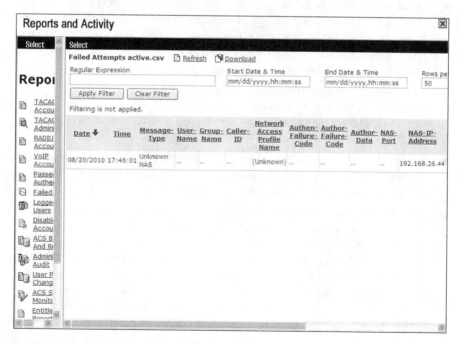

Figure 3-22 *Failed Attempts Report*

■ **Logged-in Users:** Logged-in Users is another report that assists with user administration as well as in troubleshooting users that are failing authentication; when an Accounting Start packet is received from an AAA client, the user is added into this report. The user gets removed from the report when a corresponding Accounting Stop packet is received. This log is not maintained in a CSV format. The idea behind this report is to provide a way in which you can tell how many users are logged in via different devices at a given time. This will help you identify login trends and abnormalities.

- **Disabled Accounts:** This report enables you to view accounts that have been disabled.

- **ACS Backup and Restore:** The ACS Backup and Restore report is available only if the option in Interface Configuration is enabled. This log maintains a history of the dates and times that ACS was backed up and/or restored. This report also shows whether there were any problems during the backup or restore. These reports can be found in Program Files\CiscoSecure ACS v4.x\Logs\Backup and Restore.

- **Remote Database Management Source (RDBMS) Synchronization:** The RDBMS Synchronization report is also available only when the option is configured in Interface Configuration Advanced Options. You don't enable the report; you enable RDBMS Synchronization. This allows ACS to keep report information on RDBMS synchronization. This log also shows whether there were any problems during the RDBMS sync. This logs the time and reason for RDBMS synchronization. These reports can be found in Program Files\CiscoSecure ACS v4.x\Logs\DbSync.

- **Database Replication:** Database Replication is yet another report that must be enabled in Interface Configuration. This report logs the time that the ACS database was replicated to the backup server. This log additionally shows if there were any issues with replication. These reports can be found in Program Files\CiscoSecure ACS v4.x\Logs\DBReplicate.

- **Administration Audit:** Administration Audit logs all the activity in ACS that is performed by administrators. This keeps track of who logged in, what users and groups they made changes to, and what time they logged out. These reports can be found in Program Files\CiscoSecure ACS v4.x\Logs\AdminAudit.

- **User Password Changes:** This report tracks changes to users' passwords performed through the User Changeable Password Module. These reports can be found in Program Files\CiscoSecure ACS v4.x\CSAuth\PasswordLogs.

- **ACS Service Monitoring:** The last report is the ACS Service Monitoring report. This report keeps track of all the events that ACS has had within the services it monitors. An example of a service that might be monitored is CSAdmin or CSTacacs. CSMon can be enabled during the install process. This is, however, configurable. To configure this, you must go to System Configuration and then ACS Service Management. Here, you can choose to monitor the login process, generate events when someone tries to log in to disabled accounts, and so on. These reports can be found in Program Files\CiscoSecure ACSv4.x\Logs\ServiceMonitoring.

As far as viewing these reports goes, you can view them in the ACS interface or from the hard drive of the ACS server if you are using ACS for Windows. The logs are stored as CSV files. Applications such as ACS View can also parse these logs and generate various reports based on these logs.

Note   For more information on ACS View, see
http://www.cisco.com/en/US/partner/products/ps9302/index.html.

Summary

At this point, you should be familiar with the interface of ACS and be prepared to add a user to the database. Remember that the look and feel of your interface depends on what features you have made available in the Interface Configuration section. As you progress with your configuration of ACS, you will add more features and make more configuration options visible in the interface. This is merely a starting point and an overview of ACS 4.2; however, it's important to note that although ACS 4.2 has the largest install base, the latest version of ACS, 5.2, is the next generation of ACS with which you should begin to get acquainted.

Chapter 4

Getting Familiar with ACS 5.1

This chapter covers the following subjects:

- Navigating the ACS 5.1 Graphical User Interface

- Adding Network Groups and Devices

- Adding Users to Internal Repositories

- Policy Elements and Access Services

- Monitoring and Reports

- Using the ACS Command-Line Interface

ACS 5.1 has a completely different user interface from ACS 4.2. Throughout the course of this chapter you will become familiar with the GUI and know where different functions are located. If this is your first time using ACS 5.1, it is important to take the time to learn how to navigate the interface.

The GUI is broken into two frames. You access different menu items on the left side frame (Navigation Pane) and perform configuration in the right side frame (Content Area). The Monitoring and Reports section is the only exception to this. After you launch the Monitoring and Reports Viewer, a new browser window opens. This new window has a layout similar to the original window but contains menu items related to monitoring and reporting. The left side menu is divided further into drop-down menus or drawers. Click on a drawer to expand it and see a list of options. The available drawers are as follows:

- My Workspace

- Network Resources

- Users and Identity Stores

- Policy Elements

- Access Policies

■   Monitoring and Reports

■   System Administration

My Workspace

The My Workspace drawer contains:

■   Welcome Page

■   Task Guide

■   My Account

Welcome Page

The Welcome Page appears when you log in to ACS and provides links to information and shortcuts to some common tasks. Figure 4-1 shows the Welcome Page.

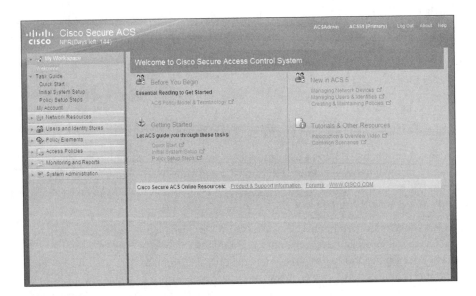

Figure 4-1   *Welcome Page*

Clicking on the links below the Getting Started section on the Welcome Page creates a new frame in the Content Area. This new frame provides help on how to get started with ACS and contains shortcuts to the initial tasks.

Clicking on any other link in the Welcome Page will open a new window containing the help section. ACS 5.1 has a comprehensive help section and can be accessed using the **Help** link in the top-right corner of the ACS GUI.

Task Guide

The Task Guide has three menu items:

- Quick Start
- Initial System Setup
- Policy Setup Steps

These items are shortcuts for the links under the Getting Started section on the Welcome Page.

My Account

My Account provides general information regarding the ACS GUI account and assigned roles, and enables you to change the password of your ACS administrator account. No other changes to the account can be made from this section. See Chapter 15, "ACS 5.1 Advanced Configuration," for information on editing and adding GUI administrator accounts. Figure 4-2 shows the My Account pane.

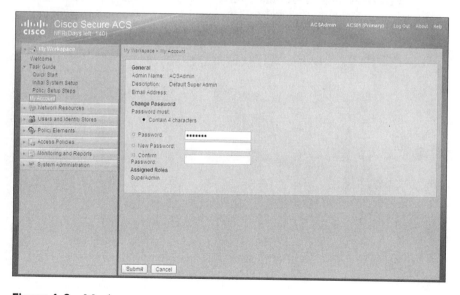

Figure 4-2   *My Account*

Network Resources

AAA clients and external RADIUS servers are defined within this drawer. When ACS receives an AAA request from a network device, it searches the network device repository to find an entry with a matching IP address. If a match is not found, the request will be rejected.

This drawer has four menu items:

■ Network Device Groups

■ Network Devices and AAA Clients

■ Default Network Device

■ External RADIUS Servers

Network Device Groups

AAA clients in the ACS repository can be assigned to Network Device Groups (NDGs). NDGs are logical grouping of devices—for example, by Location or Type—which can be used in policy conditions. For example, all routers in the San Jose location can be assigned a single policy. NDGs simplify creating policies and managing device repository.

NDGs are defined under a hierarchical structure called a Device Group Hierarchy. Each device group hierarchy has a root node under which NDGs are defined. For example, Location and Device Type groups are predefined. The root node of the Location group is All Locations. New NDGs can be created under All Locations. These NDGs can further have other NDGs as child nodes. Figure 4-3 shows a sample hierarchy created under the Locations group. Notice how the NDGs are created countrywise, statewise, or citywise.

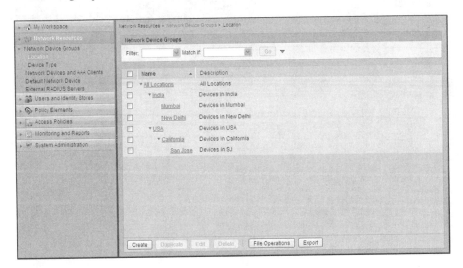

Figure 4-3 *Hierarchical Structure of NDGs*

A maximum of 12 hierarchical groups can be created and each group can have a maximum of six nodes including the root node.

Note The two hierarchical groups provided—Location and Device Types—cannot be deleted or modified. This leaves 10 groups that can be added.

Clicking on the Network Device Groups menu item will display the existing groups in the Content Area as shown in Figure 4-4. The groups also appear as individual submenu items in the Navigation Pane under Network Device Groups. Click on a group name in the Content Area to edit it. New groups can be created by clicking on the **Create** button or the **Duplicate** button.

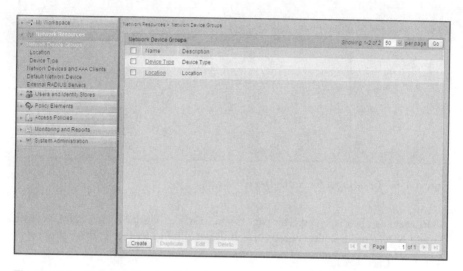

Figure 4-4 *Network Device Groups*

To create a group, follow these steps:

Step 1.   Select **Network Resources > Network Device Groups**.

The Network Device Groups page appears as shown in Figure 4-4.

Step 2.   Click **Create**.

The Hierarchy - General Page appears in the Content Area. Figure 4-5 shows this page.

Step 3.   Enter a name; for this example, use **Routers**.

Step 4.   (Optional) Enter a description.

Step 5.   Enter a root node name. For this example, use **All Routers**.

Remember that this is any name that refers to all the NDGs and devices in this group.

Step 6.   Click **Submit** to create the group.

The group **Routers** now appears in the Navigation Pane as a submenu item under the Network Device Group menu item.

Clicking on the group name, **Routers**, in the Navigation Page will open the Network Device Groups page in the Content Area. Because the group is new, only the root node

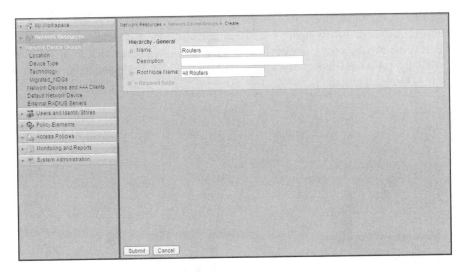

Figure 4-5   *Creating a Network Device Group*

All Routers will be displayed. This page is similar to the one shown in Figure 4-3. You can add NDGs to the **Routers** group from this page. To do so, follow these steps:

Step 1.   Click **Create**.

Step 2.   Enter a name for the group; for our example, use **Core Routers**.

Step 3.   (Optional) Enter a description.

Step 4.   The root node, All Routers, is already selected in the Parent field. If other NDGs existed in the Routers group, you could have clicked on **Select** to see them and select a different parent node.

Step 5.   Click Submit to create the NDG.

Core Routers is now visible under the root node in the Network Device Groups page.

Network Devices and AAA Clients

It is important to remember that a device should be in the ACS repository before AAA requests from that device will be accepted. The Network Devices and AAA Clients menu item shows the repository and enables you to manage the devices. Along with the name and address, the page displays the NDG that the device belongs to. You can use the filter option to search for devices. This page is shown is Figure 4-6. To add an AAA client to the ACS database and enable communications using the TACACS+ or RADIUS protocols, you use the following steps:

Step 1.   Select **Network Resources > Network Devices and AAA Clients**.

Step 2.   Click **Create**.

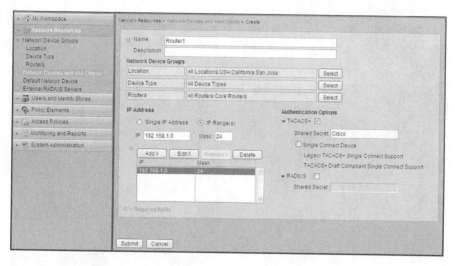

Figure 4-6   *Adding a New AAA Device*

Figure 4-6 shows the Create Network Device page.

Step 3.   Enter the hostname of the AAA client, or if this is going to be a group of devices, enter a name that makes it easily recognizable. For this example, use **Router1**.

Step 4.   (Optional) Enter a description.

Step 5.   All device groups configured in ACS are shown and their root nodes are selected. Click **Select** next to the group you want to change to display the Network Device Groups selection box. Click the radio button next to the desired Network Device Group and click **OK**. For this example, select the **San Jose** and **Core Routers** from the Location and Routers groups.

Step 6.   A device definition can represent a single or multiple devices. Select Single IP Address or IP Range as required. Selecting IP Range will display options for configuring a mask with the IP address. You can add multiple entries for the range. For this example, use a 192.168.1.0 address with a mask of 24.

Step 7.   Select **TACACS+** and/or **RADIUS** and enter the shared secret. You have the option of selecting both protocols for a device. For this example, select **TACACS+** and enter **Cisco** as the shared secret.

Step 8.   Click **Submit**

The device is now listed in the Network Devices and AAA Clients page as shown in Figure 4-7.

Note   The number of devices that you can add in ACS depends on the license type. The number of devices is determined by the number of unique IP addresses that you configure.

This includes the subnet masks that you configure. For example, a subnet mask of 255.255.255.0 implies 256 unique IP addresses and hence the number of devices is 256.

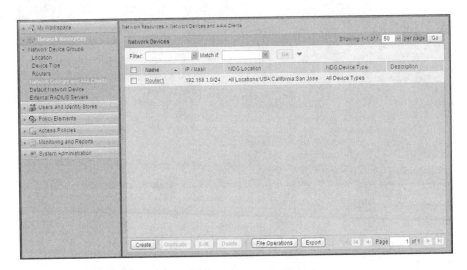

Figure 4-7   *Network Devices and AAA Clients*

Default Network Device

As mentioned previously, a device needs to be in the ACS repository before AAA requests will be accepted from it. There is an exception to this rule. You can configure a default network device. If a request comes from a device that does not specifically exist in the repository, ACS will use the default device profile. In the default network device definition, you provide a shared secret key, network device group, and the protocol(s) to be used. To configure the default network device, follow these steps:

Step 1.   Select **Network Resources > Default Network Device**.

The Default Network Device page appears. Figure 4-8 shows this page.

Step 2.   Select **Enabled** from the drop-down list next to Default Network Device Status.

Step 3.   Click **Select** next to the device groups that you want to modify. For our example, select **San Jose** NDG from the Locations Group.

Step 4.   Select **TACACS+** or **RADIUS** and enter the shared secret for the protocols. You can select one or both the protocols. For this example, select both the protocols and use **Cisco** as the shared secret.

Step 5.   Click **Submit**.

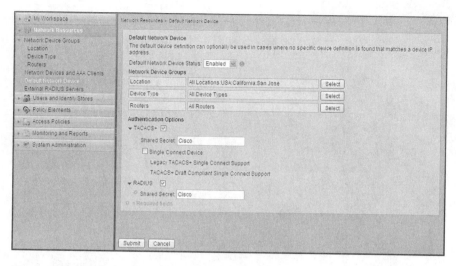

Figure 4-8 *Default Network Device*

External RADIUS Servers

ACS 5.1 can function both as a RADIUS server and a RADIUS proxy server. When it acts as a proxy server, ACS receives authentication and accounting requests from the AAA client and forwards them to the external RADIUS server. ACS accepts the results of the requests and returns them to the client. You must configure the external RADIUS servers in ACS to enable ACS to forward requests to them. You can configure multiple external RADIUS servers. To add a server, follow these steps:

Step 1.   Select **Network Resources > External RADIUS Servers.**

The External RADIUS Servers page appears with a list of configured servers.

Step 2.   Click **Create.**

The Create Server page appears as shown in Figure 4-9.

Step 3.   Enter a name for the server. For this example, use External1.

Step 4.   (Optional) Enter a description.

Step 5.   Enter the server IP address. For this example, use 192.168.1.40.

Step 6.   Enter the shared secret. This secret is used to encrypt the RADIUS request between ACS and the external server. For this example, use **Cisco.**

Step 7.   Click **Advanced Options.**

Step 8.   Verify the authentication and accounting ports.

By default, ports 1812 and 1813 are used. If the external server uses other ports, enter them in the respective fields. This example leaves the ports set to the default values.

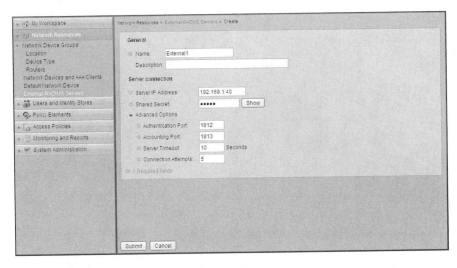

Figure 4-9 *Adding an External RADIUS Server*

Step 9.   Verify the server timeout value.

By default, five seconds timeout period is used. If the server fails to respond in that period, the server will resend the request as many times as specified in the Connection Attempts field. You can specify a timeout value of 1 to 120 seconds. For this example, specify 10 seconds.

Step 10.   Verify the connection attempts value.

By default, ACS will attempt to connect to the external server three times. You can configure ACS to attempt up to 10 times to connect to the external server. For this example, specify five attempts.

Step 11.   Click **Submit**.

Users and Identity Stores

To authenticate and authorize a user or host, ACS uses the user definitions stored in identity stores. There are two types of identity stores:

■   **Internal Identity Stores:** Identity stores that ACS maintains locally are called *internal identity stores*. ACS maintains two different internal identity stores for user and host records. These stores are accessible from the **Internal Identity Stores** menu item in the **Users and Identity Stores** drawer.

■   **External Identity Stores:** Identity stores that reside outside of ACS are called *external identity stores* (or *external user databases* in earlier versions of ACS). Each external identity store requires certain configuration before ACS can obtain information from it. The **External Identity Stores** menu item under the **Users and Identity Stores** drawer can be used to configure these stores.

In this chapter, you add a user and a host to the internal identity stores. External identity stores are discussed in Chapter 5, "Configuring External Databases with ACS."

Before adding a user or host, you should know about identity groups and how to add them.

Identity Groups

Identity groups, as the name suggests, are groups of users or hosts. As in ACS 4.2, users and hosts can be put in a group to apply a uniform policy on them.

> **Note**   A key point to remember is that ACS 4.2 is a group-based server, whereas ACS 5.1 is a policy-based server. This means that users and groups in ACS 5.1 do not have reply attributes configured in their profile. Reply attributes are derived from policy evaluation.

Identity groups are defined in a hierarchical structure like the NDGs. *All Groups* is the root of this hierarchy.

To create an identity group, follow these steps:

Step 1.   Select **Users and Identity Stores > Identity Groups**.

The Identity Groups page appears.

Step 2.   Click **Create**.

The Create Identity Group page appears as shown in Figure 4-10.

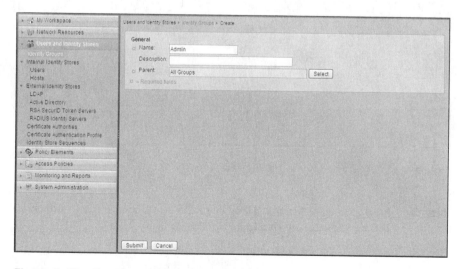

Figure 4-10   *Creating an Identity Group*

Step 3.   Enter a unique name for the group. For our example, use **Admin**.

Step 4.   (Optional) Enter a description.

Step 5.   Click **Select** to select a parent group for this group. For this example, use the Root group.

Step 6.   Click **Submit**.

The Identity Group page appears with the Admin group listed under the root.

Adding a User in the Internal Identity Store

Adding a user to the internal identity store is very simple in ACS 5.1. To add a user, follow these steps:

Step 1.   Select **Users and Identity Stores > Internal Identity Stores > Users**.

The Internal Users page appears.

Step 2.   Click **Create**.

The User Properties page appears as shown in Figure 4-11.

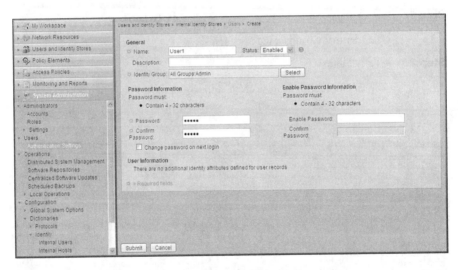

Figure 4-11   *Adding a User to the Internal Identity Store*

Step 3.   Enter a name for the user. This name will be used by the user to authenticate. For our example, use User1.

Step 4.   (Optional) Enter a description.

Step 5.   Click **Select** and select an identity group for the user. For this example, select the Admin group created in the previous section.

Step 6.   Enter the password and confirm the password. The password must match the restriction shown in the Password Information section on the page. By default, the password must be 4 to 32 characters long. For this example, use **Cisco** as the password.

Step 7.   (Optional) An enable password can be entered for users to log in to the privilege mode of devices. This option is enabled by default and can be disabled from the User Authentication settings section. For this example, leave this field blank.

> **Note**   Identity attributes can be used in a policy. For more information on dictionaries and identity attributes see Chapter 15, "ACS 5.1 Advanced Configuration."

Step 8.   Click **Submit**.

The user configuration will be saved and the Internal Users page will appear with the new user listed.

Adding a Host in the Internal Identity Store

Adding a host in the ACS internal data or identity store is not a new concept. In versions of ACS prior to ACS 5.1, the MAC address of a host could be added as a user for MAC address-based authentication. ACS 5.1 provides separate user and host identity stores! Steps for adding a host in the internal identity stores are similar to that of adding a user. To add a host, follow these steps:

Step 1.   Select **Users and Identity Stores > Internal Identity Stores > Hosts**.

The Internal Hosts page appears.

Step 2.   Click **Create**.

The host properties page appears as shown in Figure 4-12.

Step 3.   Enter the MAC address of the host. You can enter the MAC address in any of the following formats:

— xx-xx-xx-xx-xx-xx

— xx:xx:xx:xx:xx:xx

— xxxx.xxxx.xxxx

— xxxxxxxxxxxx

Although you can enter the MAC address in any of the formats in the preceding list, ACS will convert and store the MAC address in the first format. For this example, use **00-19-01-02-AA-EE**.

Step 4.   (Optional) Enter a description.

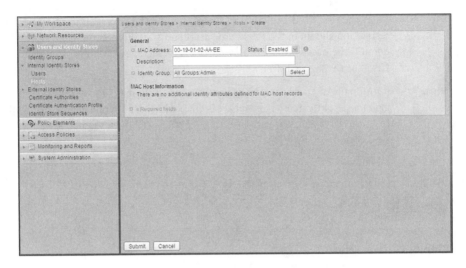

Figure 4-12   *Adding a Host to the Internal Identity Store*

Step 5.   Click **Select** and select an identity group. For our example, use the **Admin** group created in the previous sections.

Step 6.   Click **Submit**.

The host configuration will be saved and the Internal Hosts page will appear with the new host listed.

Note   The Users and Identity Stores drawer contains Certificate Authority and Certificate Authentication Profiles menu items. These are used to configure ACS for Certificate based authentication. These sections are discussed in Chapter 8, "IOS Switches."

The Identity Store Sequences menu item is used to define sequences of databases to be used in a policy. This section is covered in Chapter 5, "Configuring External Databases with ACS."

Policy Elements

You know from Chapter 2 that ACS 5.x is based on a rule-based policy model. You also know that the rules are called *policies* and they consist of conditions and results, which are called *policy elements*. In this section and the next, you will learn more about policy elements and how to create them, the different types of policies, and the flow of a request through different processes in ACS.

Before creating policies, you must create policy elements, which are the building blocks of policies. Policy elements are divided into two types: *session conditions* and *authorization and permissions*.

Session conditions are conditions used to apply policies to requests. Some conditions are available by default, whereas others can be created by you. The following conditions are available by default:

- **Request/Protocol Attributes:** These attributes are derived from the authentication request itself.

- **Identity Attributes:** Identity attributes are derived from the user definition in the internal identity store or external repositories such as LDAP and Active Directory. The attributes need to be mapped in the external database configuration before they become available in the policies. See Chapter 5 for more on external databases and attribute mapping.

- **Identity Groups:** You can map every user and host to an identity group. This group association can be used in policies as a condition.

- **Network Device Groups(NDGs):** Each device is associated with an NDG. This association can be used as a condition in the policies.

The following conditions can be created by you:

- **Date and Time Conditions:** You can create conditions that define specific time intervals across days of the week. These conditions take into account the current date and time and return a true or false result indicating whether the condition is met.

- **Custom Conditions:** You can create conditions based on attributes of various identity and protocol dictionaries which are available in ACS. These conditions allow you to apply policies based on the authentication and authorization requests received from AAA clients.

- **Network Conditions:** You can create conditions based on the following to restrict access:

  - **End Station Filters:** These are based on end stations that initiate and terminate the connection. End stations may be identified by IP Address, MAC Address, or Caller Line Identification (CLI) and Dialed Number Identification Service (DNIS) fields obtained from the request.

  - **Network Device Filters:** Based on the AAA client that processes the request. A network device can be identified by IP address, the name of the device that is defined in the network device repository or the network device group (NDG).

  - **Device Port Filters:** Network device definition might be supplemented by the device port that the end station is connected to.

    These filters or conditions can be included in policy conditions. This set of definitions is matched against those presented in the request. The operator that you use in the condition can either be *match* (in which case the value presented must match at least one entry within the network condition) or *no matches* (in which case it should not match any entry in the set of objects present in the filter).

Authorization and permissions are the results applied to a request that matches a condition in a policy. You can define the following types of results:

- **Authorization Profiles:** You can define a set of attributes and values that is returned to the device in Access-Accept responses for network access requests. These profiles can contain common data such as VLAN information, reauthentication timer, or any RADIUS attribute.

- **Shell Profiles:** You can define a set of permissions that is applied to a user requesting administrative access of a device. Some of these permissions include privilege level, auto command, and custom TACACS+ attributes.

- **Command Sets:** You can define a list of commands that a user can execute on a device during an administrative session.

- **Downloadable ACLs:** You can define downloadable ACLs that can be sent to a device with an Access-Accept message.

If you have worked on previous ACS versions (4.x or 3.x), you must have noticed that many of the policy elements were available earlier in the Group Setup. The difference in ACS 5.x is that these conditions and results are now defined globally and can be used in multiple rules. Group-based configuration required configuring the conditions and results in each group even if they were similar.

Figure 4-13 shows a typical simplified flow of a request through ACS. Note the different places where policy elements are used. At this stage, do not worry about the different policies shown in the figure because they will be covered later in the chapter.

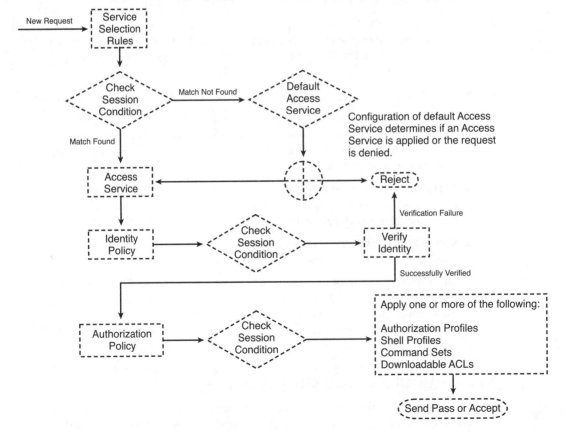

Figure 4-13 *Flow of a Request Through ACS 5.x*

The following sections look at creating the different policy elements.

Session Conditions: Date and Time

To create a Date and Time session condition, follow these steps:

Step 1.   Select **Policy Elements > Session Conditions > Date and Time.**

Step 2.   Click **Create.**

The Date and Time Properties page appears as shown in Figure 4-14.

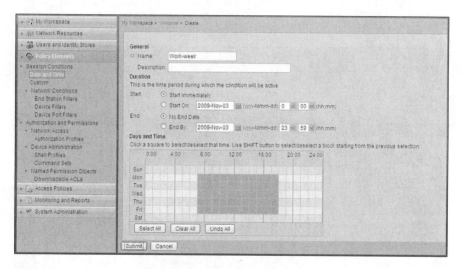

Figure 4-14   *Creating Date and Time Condition*

Step 3.   Enter a name. For this example, use **Work-week.**

Step 4.   (optional) Enter a description.

Step 5.   Define start and end times for this element. During the period defined, the element can be used by policies. You can select *Start Immediately* and *No End Date* for the element to be active always or select a specific date and time during which this element will be active. This is useful when you want to provide some access or privilege for only a certain duration. For our example, select the **Start Immediately** and **No End Date** options.

Step 6.   Select the days and time during which this element will return a positive reply for access request. Each square in the grid is equal to one hour. Select a grid square to make the corresponding time active. For this example, select **7:00 to 18:00 hours, Monday to Friday** as shown in Figure 4-14.

Step 7.   Click **Submit.**

The policy element you created will restrict access to 7:00–18:00 hours on Monday through Friday, when applied to a policy.

Session Conditions: Custom

To create a custom session condition, follow these steps:

Step 1.   Select **Policy Elements > Session Conditions > Custom**.

Step 2.   Click **Create**.

The Custom Condition Properties page appears. This page is shown in Figure 4-15.

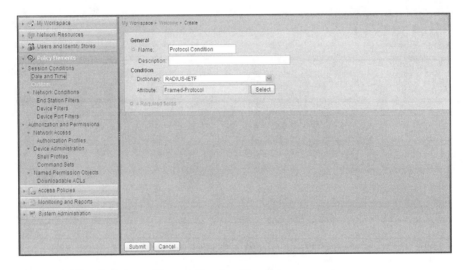

Figure 4-15   *Creating a Custom Session Condition*

Step 3.   Enter a name. For our example, use **Protocol**.

Step 4.   (optional) Enter a description.

Step 5.   Select **Dictionary** from the drop-down list. Different Protocol and Identity dictionaries are available in the drop-down list. For our example, select **RADIUS-IETF**.

Step 6.   Click **Select** next to the Attribute text box and select an attribute. For our example, select **Framed-Protocol**.

Step 7.   Click **Submit**.

The custom condition that you just created will match the Framed-Protocol attribute in a RADIUS request when applied to a policy.

Session Conditions: End Station Filters

To create an end station filter, follow these steps:

Step 1.   Select **Policy Elements > Session Conditions > Network Conditions > End Station Filters**.

Step 2.   Click **Create**.

The End Station Filter Properties page appears as shown in Figure 4-16.

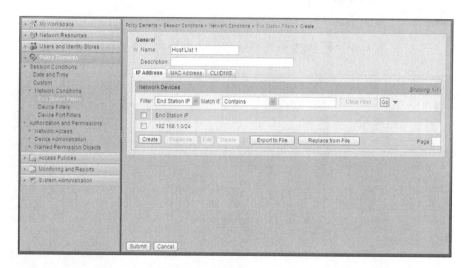

Figure 4-16   *Creating an End Station Filter*

Step 3.   Enter a Name. For this example, use **Host List 1**.

Step 4.   (optional) Enter a description.

Step 5.   End stations can be filtered by IP address, MAC address, or Calling Line ID (CLI)/Dialed Number Identification Service (DNIS). The filter values are added under the respective tabs. For this example, select the **IP Address** tab.

Step 6.   Click **Create**.

A dialog box opens where you can enter an IP address or a range of addresses. For this example, select **IP Range(s)** and enter **192.168.1.0** in the IP text box and **24** in the Mask text box. Click **Ok**.

192.168.1.0/24 is now listed in the *Network Devices* table.

Note that the options in the dialog box will change depending on the tab selected.

Step 7.   Click **Submit**.

The filter you created will match any host in the 192.168.1.0/24 when applied to a policy.

Session Conditions: Device Filters

To create a device filter, follow these steps:

Step 1.   Select **Policy Elements > Session Conditions > Network Conditions > Device Filters**.

Step 2.   Click **Create**.

The Device Filter Properties page appears as shown in Figure 4-17.

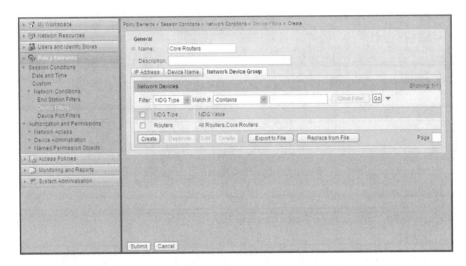

Figure 4-17   *Creating Device Filters*

Step 3.   Enter a name. For this example, use **Core Routers**.

Step 4.   You can enter the IP addresses of devices, the names of devices already in the ACS repository, or a network device group under the respective tabs. For this example, select the **Network Device Group** tab.

Step 5.   Click **Create**.

A dialog box appears where the NDG can be selected. Click **Select** next to the NDG Type text box and select the **Routers** group that you created earlier. Then click on **Select** next to the NDG Value text box and select the **Core Routers** group that you created earlier. Click **Ok**.

The **Core Routers** NDG is now listed in the Network Devices table.

Note that the options in the dialog box will change depending on the tab selected.

Step 6.   Click **Submit**.

The device filter you created will match any device in the Core Routers NDG when applied to a policy.

Session Conditions: Device Port Filters

The steps to create a device port filter are similar to the one you followed to create device filters. The only difference is the addition of a Port text box in the dialog box where you select or enter device information. Figure 4-18 shows the Device Port Filter properties page where the Core Routers NDG is added with port 23.

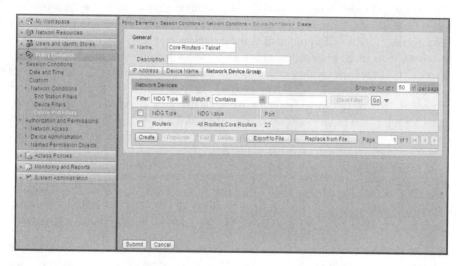

Figure 4-18   *Creating Device Port Filters*

Note   Authorization and permissions policy elements are covered in later chapters.

■   Authorization profiles are covered in Chapter 8, "IOS Switches."

■   Shell profiles and command sets are covered in Chapter 6, "Administrative AAA on IOS."

Downloadable ACLs are covered in Chapter 10, "Cut-Through Proxy AAA on PIX/ASA."

Access Policies

Before you start creating policies, it is important to understand how ACS applies a particular policy to a request and how many policies are available. ACS uses service selection rules and access services to decide on a policy to apply to a request.

Service Selection Rules

Service selection rules decide which access service to send an authentication or authorization request to. You can configure ACS to use a single access service to process all requests or use rules based on session conditions to send requests to different access services. In the case of a rule-based selection, ACS uses the first rule from the top that matches a request.

> **Note**   When rules are used for service selection, ACS provides an option to configure a default rule. If a request does not match any rules in the table, the default rule is applied.

To further understand how this works, take a department store for example. A department store is divided into sections using product category (clothing, sporting goods, jewelry, and so on). An ACS configured to use a single access service is like the department store. All requests go to a single access service, which has different policies. The access service checks session conditions and applies the appropriate policy. Consider a grocery store for another example. A grocery store sells only groceries, but might have sections based on different categories (produce, meat, canned goods, and so on). An ACS configured for rule based service selection is similar to such a store. It will send different kinds of requests to different access services. Each access service equates to a specialized store. These access services will have different policies.

To further understand service selection rules and access services, consider another example. XYZ Inc. has five offices. Each office has routers terminating VPN connections. These routers are going to authenticate and authorize VPN sessions and administrative sessions to a single ACS. There are two ways to configure ACS for the organization:

- **Method 1:** Configure ACS to send all requests to a single access service and configure two policies in the access service. One policy to process all administrative session requests via the TACACS+ protocol and the other to process all VPN session requests via the RADIUS protocol.

- **Method 2:** Configure ACS to send all TACACS+ (administrative sessions) requests to one access service and to send all RADIUS (VPN sessions) request to another access service. Each access service can have one or more policies to process the requests.

Method 1 is easier to configure and maintain; however, it can get very complicated if different authentication or authorization methods need to be applied. For example, one site might need more stringent authorization for VPN sessions than other sites or administrators might need restricted access to remote devices. Further consider an organization with 100 sites and thousands of network devices. In such scenarios, policies will increase in the access service and soon become unmanageable. On the other hand, different access services will have a smaller number of policies and will be easier to manage.

Access Services

Access services are the most basic parts of ACS. They are sets of policies which process all authentication and authorization requests. Every authentication and authorization request has to match a policy in an access service before it is processed. As you already know, a request is sent to an access service by the service selection rules. When an access service receives a request, it checks policies in a top-down manner and applies the first policy that matches the session conditions.

Access services consist of the following types of policies:

■ **Identity Policy:** Specifies how the user should be authenticated and includes the allowed authentication protocols and the user repository to use for password validation. Identity policies can be simple or rule based. Simple policies apply a single policy to all requests. Rule-based policies use session conditions to choose rules for requests.

■ **Group Mapping Policy:** Specifies whether the user's ACS identity group should be dynamically established based on user attributes or group membership in external identity stores. The user's identity group can be used as part of its authorization. Chapter 5 covers group mapping in more detail.

■ **Authorization Policy:** Specifies the authorization rules for the user. Authorization policies can only be rule based.

Note   If a policy is rule based, ACS checks rules in a top-down manner and uses the first rule that matches. ACS also provides an option to configure a default rule. If a request does not match any rules in the table, the default rule is applied.

ACS has two access services by default:

■ **Default Device Admin:** Service selection rules are configured to send all TACACS+ requests to this default access service.

■ **Default Network Access:** Service selection rules are configured to send all RADIUS requests to this default access service.

Creating an Access Service

Access services and their policies bring together different elements from ACS. Hence, before creating an access service, you should determine the network configuration and the degree of refinement that you want individual policies to have. Depending on that, you should add devices and users or user databases. You should also create different policy elements such as session conditions and authorization and permission elements. Ensuring that you have all the required components will save you from moving back and forth between different drawers in the menu.

To create an access service, follow these steps:

Step 1.   Select **Access Policies > Access Services**.

The Access Services page appears.

Step 2.   Click **Create**.

The Access Service General Properties page appears as shown in Figure 4-19.

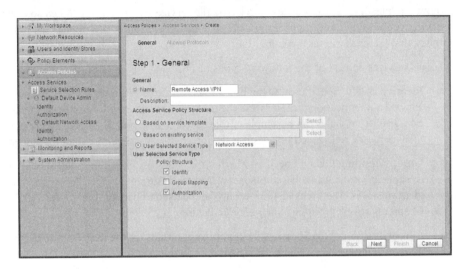

Figure 4-19   *General Properties of a New Access Service*

Step 3.   Enter a name. For this example, use **Remote Access VPN**.

Step 4.   (optional) Enter a description.

Step 5.   Select one of the following options for Access Service Policy Structure:

- **Based on service template:** Creates an access service based on a predefined template. These templates are customized to use a specific condition type. To use this option, select the radio button next to it, and then click **Select** and select a template.

- **Based on existing service:** Creates an access service containing policies based on an existing access service. The new access service does not include the existing service's policy rules. To use this option, select the radio button next to it, and click **Select** and select an existing access service.

- **User Selected Service Type:** Provides you the option to select the access service type. The available options are Network Access, Device Administration, and RADIUS Proxy. The list of policies you can configure depends on your choice of access service type. To use this option, select the radio button next to it and select an access service type from the drop down box. Selecting this option will also display the option to enable or disable different policy types.

For this example, select **User Selected Service Type** and select **Network Access** from the drop-down box. Select **Identity** and **Authorization** in the policy structure.

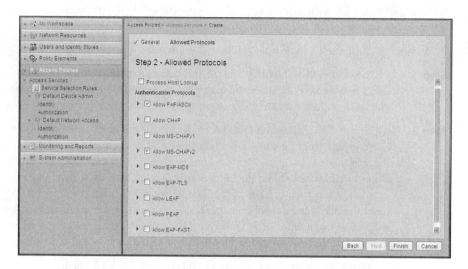

Figure 4-20 *Configuring Allowed Protocols in an Access Service*

Step 6. Click **Next**.

The Allowed Protocols properties page appears as shown in Figure 4-20.

Step 7. This page enables you to select which authentication protocols will be allowed with this access service. PAP, CHAP, MS-CHAPv1, MS-CHAPv2 and various EAP protocols are available as options. You can also enable host lookup (required for machine authentication) from this page. For this example, deselect **Process Host Lookup** and select **Allow PAP/ASCII** and **Allow MS-CHAPv2**.

Step 8. Click **Finish**.

The access service will be saved and will appear as a menu item in the Access Services drawer. Below the menu item, selected policy types will be shown as submenu items. At this point, a prompt will give you an option to activate this service in the Service Selection Rules. For now, click **No**. The Access Services page will appear with the new access service listed in the table.

You are now ready to configure the identity rules and authorization rules for the new access service.

Configuring Identity Policy

As you already know, identity policies can be simple or rule-based. By default, identity policies are simple. When you select Identity under a new Access Service (Remote Access VPN for this example) in the Access Policies drawer, you will find that the Single result selection option is selected and Identity Source is DenyAccess.

If you want to configure a simple policy, follow these steps:

Step 1.   Click **Select** next to **Identity Source** and select an identity store. You can select between certificate-based authentications or different password-based internal or external identity stores.

Step 2.   (Optional) Click **Advanced Options** to display the fail-open options. Fail-open opens enable you to configure the behavior of ACS when authentication fails, the user is not found in an identity store, or there is a process failure. A process failure occurs when ACS is not able to verify the credentials, usually due to external factors such as a network failure between ACS and an external database. To understand the fail-open process, you have to remember that a device will fail over to a different AAA server if the primary server does not respond to a request. Each of the three fail-open options has three possible actions:

- **Reject:** Sends an Access-Reject or Fail reply to the AAA client.

- **Drop:** ACS drops the request, causing the AAA client to retry another fail over to another AAA server.

- **Continue:** Causes ACS to try the next service or rule.

By default ACS will reject a request if authentication fails or a user is not found, and will drop a request if the process fails. Figure 4-21 shows this page with the default Advanced options.

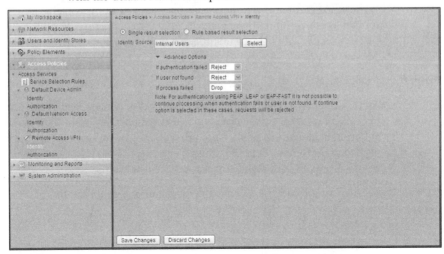

Figure 4-21   *Configuring a Simple Identity Policy*

Step 3.   Click **Save Changes.**

If you want to configure a rule-based identity policy, follow these steps:

Step 1.   Select **Rule based result selection** from the Identity Properties page.

This will change the properties page to a rule-based table format shown in Figure 4-22.

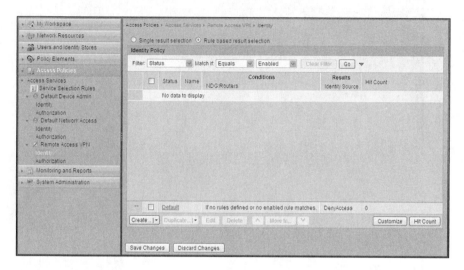

Figure 4-22   *The Identity Policy Page for a Rule-Based Configuration*

Step 2.   The rules of an Identity policy use session conditions to determine which identity store to use for a request. The session conditions available in the Rules Properties page need to be enabled from the Identity Properties page. Click **Customize** to open the Customize Conditions dialog box. Select the conditions that you want to use. For this example, deselect default conditions and select **NDG:Routers** (you created this NDG earlier in this chapter).

Step 3.   Click **Create**.

The Identity Rule properties page appears as shown in Figure 4-23.

Step 4.   Enter a name. For this example, use **Core Routers**.

Step 5.   Select a session condition. In this example, only **NDG:Routers** is available, so select it.

Step 6.   Select an operator from the drop-down box next to the selected condition. The available operators change depending on the condition selected. These are logical operators that allow matching or not matching the user-provided argument with the selected condition. For this example, select **in** from the drop-down box.

Step 7.   For some conditions, such as NDGs, you will see a Select button next to the condition. You can click this button to select the required element. For some conditions, you will get a drop-down box or a text box. For this example, click **Select** and select **Core Routers** NDG.

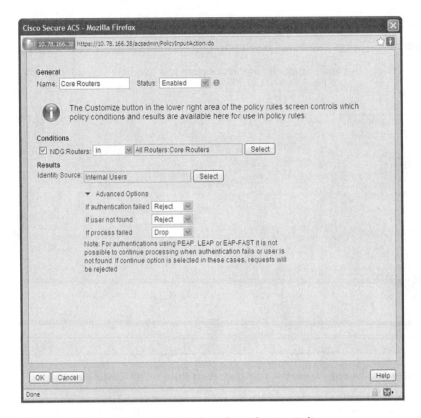

Figure 4-23   *Configuring the Rules of an Identity Policy*

Step 8.   In the Results section, you can select the identity source to be used for this rule. Click **Select** next to Identity Source and select an identity store. You can select between certificate-based authentications or different password-based internal or external identity stores. For this example, use **Internal Users**.

Step 9.   (Optional) Click **Advanced Options** to display the fail-open options. Remember that by default, ACS will reject a request if authentication fails or a user is not found, and will drop a request if the process fails. For this example, leave them set to the default values.

Step 10.   Click OK.

The rule will be saved and the Identity Policy page will appear with the rule listed in the table.

The rule you created will use the Internal Users identity store to authenticate requests that originate from any device in the Core Routers NDG. You can add more rules to use different identity stores for different session conditions.

Now that the identity policy is configured, you can configure the authorization policy to complete the access service.

Configuring Authorization Policy

As mentioned earlier, authorization policies are rule based only. You cannot configure a simple authorization policy, but you can configure a single rule that will match all requests coming to the access service.

ACS also provides a default authorization rule. The default rule is applied if no rules are defined in an authorization policy or if a request does not match any defined rules.

Note   I strongly suggest that you do not use the default rule to avoid security lapses. Using the default rule in most circumstances is like having a gate but leaving it open. You should have explicit rules for all variations of requests you get.

To configure a rule, follow these steps:

Step 1.   Select **Access Policies** > *Access Service you want to change* > **Authorization**. For this example, select **Authorization** under **Remote Access VPN**.

The Authorization Policy page appears.

Step 2.   Rules of an authorization policy use session conditions to determine which authorization and permissions to use for a request. The session conditions available in the Rules Properties page need to be enabled from the Authorization Policy page. Click **Customize** to open the Customize Conditions dialog box. Select the conditions that you want to use. For this example, deselect default conditions and select **Identity Group**.

Step 3.   If the authorization policy for a TACACS+-based access service is being configured, then along with available session conditions, you will need to select available results in the Customize dialog box. Results can be shell profiles or command sets. For this example, you will not have an option to select results because the access service is RADIUS-based. **Authorization Profile** is the only result available with such access services.

Step 4.   Click **Create**.

The Authorization Rule properties page appears as shown in Figure 4-24.

Step 5.   Enter a name. For this example, use **Admins**.

Step 6.   Select a session condition. For this example, select **Identity Group**.

Step 7.   Select an operator from the drop-down box next to the selected condition. The available operators change depending on the condition selected. These

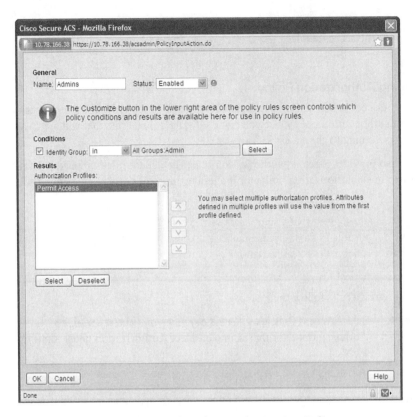

Figure 4-24   *Creating the Rules of an Authorization Policy*

are logical operators that allow matching or not matching a user-provided argument with the selected condition. For our example, select **in** from the drop-down box.

Step 8. For some conditions, such as **Identity Group**, you will see a **Select** button next to the condition. You can click this button to select the required element. For some conditions your will get a drop-down box or a text box. For this example, click **Select** and select the **Admin** group you created earlier.

Step 9. Authorization profiles require you to select a result. Results can be authorization profiles, shell profiles, or command sets depending on the access service. Click **Select** next to the result that you want to configure and select a policy element. For this example, select the **Permit Access** authorization profile, which is available by default.

Step 10. Click **OK.**

The rule will be saved and the Authorization Policy page will appear with the new rule listed in the table.

You have created your first authorization rule, which permits access if the user belongs to the Admin Identity group.

Now that the access service configuration is complete, you will need to create a service selection rule so that this service is used.

Creating Service Selection Rules

As you know, service selection rules decide which access service to apply to a request. By default ACS is configured for rule-based service selection. Two rules are present by default. The first rule, named *Rule-1*, sends all RADIUS requests to the Default Network Access service and the second rule, named *Rule-2*, sends all TACACS+ requests to the Default Device Admin service. To configure ACS to use the Remote Access VPN service that you created, you need to add a new rule for service selection. You have the following choices in this situation:

- Edit Rule-1 to send all requests to the Remote Access VPN service

- Delete Rule-1 and create a new rule

- Create a new rule above Rule-1 that is specific to the Remote Access VPN service

For this example, create a new rule above Rule-1. To do so, follow these steps:

Step 1. Select **Access Policies > Access Services > Service Selection Rules**.

The Service Selection Policy page appears.

Step 2. The session conditions available in a service selection rule properties page can be customized from this page. Click **Customize** and select the required conditions. For this example, select **NDG:Location** and **Protocol**.

Step 3. Select **Rule-1** and click the down arrow on the **Create** button.

Step 4. Select **Create Above**.

The Service Selection Rules properties page appears as shown in Figure 4-25.

Step 5. Enter a name. For this example, use **San Jose VPN**.

Step 6. Select the conditions that define the rule. For this example, select **Protocol** and **NDG:Location**.

Step 7. Select an operator from the drop-down box next to the selected condition. The available operators change depending on the condition selected. These are logical operators that allow matching or not matching a user-provided argument with the selected condition. For this example, select **match** for Protocol and **in** for NDG:Location.

Step 8. For some conditions, such as NDG:Location, you will see a **Select** button next to the condition. You can click this button to select the required element. For some conditions, you will get a drop-down box or a text box. For this example, click **Select** and select **San Jose** for NDG:Location and **RADIUS** for

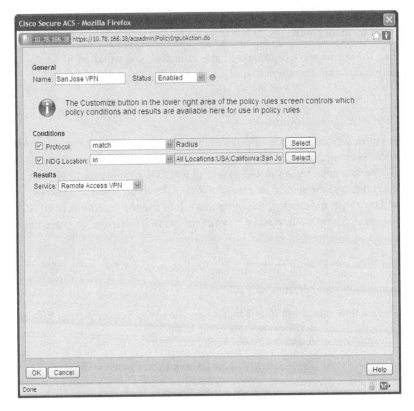

Figure 4-25 *Creating a Service Selection Rule*

Protocol. If you have not created the San Jose group, select the **All Locations** option for NDG:Location.

Step 9. The result of a service selection rule is an access service or DenyAccess. You can use the drop-down box to select the result for the rule. For this example, select **Remote Access VPN** from the drop-down box.

Step 10. Click **Ok**.

The rule will be saved and the Service Selection Policy page will appear with the new rule listed above Rule-1 in the table.

The rule you created will send RADIUS requests originating from devices in the **San Jose** NDG or **All Locations** NDG to the **Remote Access VPN** access service which you created earlier. The access service and policies that you created in the previous sections will authenticate RADIUS requests originating from a device in the **Core Routers** NDG using the **Internal User** identity store. If authentication is successful and the user belongs to the **Admin** identity group, the access will be permitted. Further chapters will help you create more complex access services and policies. The examples in this chapter are used to explain the basic process of creating policies and rules.

Monitoring and Reports

The Monitoring and Reports drawer replaces the Reports and Activity section of previous versions of ACS. You can now view reports based on different criteria such as Access Service, End Point, and Failure Reason, among others. ACS 5.x also introduces a configurable dashboard for reports and alarms.

Note   ACS 5.x has added monitoring, reporting, and troubleshooting capabilities that are similar to those available is ACSView 4.0. ACSView is an independent reporting and monitoring platform available for ACS 4.x.

Covering the entire Monitoring and Reports section in depth is beyond the scope of this book. This section of the text will focus on the reports that are most important and touch on the rest briefly.

The Monitoring and Reports drawer contains the Launch Monitoring and Report Viewer option. Click this option to open the Monitoring and Reports Viewer in another browser window or tab. The layout of the new window is similar to the main window but contains only the following two drawers:

- Monitoring and Reports

- Monitoring Configuration

The Monitoring and Reports drawer contains the following options:

- **DashBoard:** ACS 5.1 provides a new customizable dashboard that contains tabs and portlets where your favorite queries, recent alarms and reports, and health status of ACS reside. Each of these tabs can have multiple portlets, with each portlet containing an application of your choice. You can select an application from the available list. Some of the important applications available in the dashboard by default are as follows:

  - **Recent Five Alarms:** This application is available in the General tab and shows the latest five alarms.

  - **Favorite Reports:** This application contains links to favorite reports. The favorite list is configuration from the Reports option discussed later.

  - **Live Authentications:** This application is available in the Troubleshooting tab and shows authentication requests received in real time. This is a very useful application for troubleshooting. By default, it refreshes every 10 seconds and is configured to monitor RADIUS requests.

  - **NAD Show Command:** A neat little application that can connect to a network device using SSH or Telnet and run a **show** command. You have to provide the login details and the **show** command to run. ACS will display the output in a new window. This is also a very useful application. It saves you from jumping between ACS GUI and Telnet or SSH clients.

  - **ACS Health Status:** Shows the health of the ACS server.

- **Alarms:** ACS 5.x introduces alarms. The monitoring component retrieves data from ACS and generates alarms to notify you of critical system conditions. These alarms can be viewed in the Inbox option in this drawer or can be received through Syslog and email. There are two types of alarms in ACS: Threshold and System. Threshold alarms are defined on logs collected from ACS. You can configure a threshold alarm to notify you of different events such as authentication activity, system health, and process status, among others. System alarms notify you of critical conditions encountered during the execution of the ACS Monitoring and Reporting viewer. System alarms also provide the informational status of system activities, such as data purge events or the failure of the log collector to populate the View database. You cannot configure system alarms. This drawer contains the following options:

    - **Inbox:** Generated alarms can be viewed in the Inbox. After you view an alarm, you can edit the status of the alarm, assign the alarm to an administrator, and add notes to track the event.

    - **Thresholds:** You can configure thresholds from this page. A maximum of 100 thresholds can be configured in an ACS server. Four thresholds exist by default, out of which only the System Errors threshold is enabled.

    - **Schedules:** Each threshold has a schedule associated with it. The schedule defines when a threshold is run. You need to configure schedules on this page before you can use them in thresholds. By default, ACS has a nonstop schedule that monitors events 24 hours a day, seven days a week.

- **Reports:** The Reports section contains different predefined reports that you can use to monitor and troubleshoot ACS. These reports include authentication and authorization reports (similar to passed and failed reports from ACS 4.x), access service reports, ACS configuration and operation audits, and network device summary, among others. You can add any of the reports to your Favorites and those will be displayed in the General tab of the dashboard. The following report categories are available in the catalog:

    - **AAA Protocol:** Contains RADIUS and TACACS+ authentication, authorization (TACACS+ only) and accounting reports, AAA diagnostics, and authentication trend. Passed and failed logs from previous ACS version have been divided into protocol-specific authentication and authorization reports. Figure 4-26 shows the TACACS+ authentication report.

    - **Access Service:** Contains a graphical summary report and a top count report for authentication in respect to access services.

    - **ACS Instance:** Contains different system-related reports such as configuration and operations audit reports, health summary, administrator logins and entitlement reports, and ACS system diagnostics.

    - **Endpoint:** Contains MAC address-based authentication summary reports, MAC address-based top authentications reports, and machine-based top authentication reports.

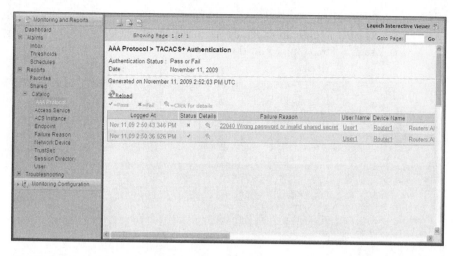

Figure 4-26   *TACACS+ Authentication Report*

- **Failure Reason:** Contains summary and top authentication failure reports. This is one of the most important reporting sections. A close look at this section can tell you about any access attacks being carried out against your network.

- **Network Device:** Contains summary and top authentication reports in respect to network devices. These reports are useful in tracking which devices are generating the maximum number of requests.

- **Session Directory:** Contains active session, terminated sessions, and session history reports for RADIUS and TACACS+. Accounting packets received from devices are used to maintain session information.

- **User:** Contains summary and top authentication reports in respect to users.

- **Troubleshooting:** ACS 5.x contains some nice troubleshooting options. The following options are available in the Troubleshooting section:

- **Connectivity Tests:** You can run a ping, traceroute, and nslookup for a hostname or IP address to see whether the device is reachable from ACS. This is important to see whether the requests from a device and replies from ACS to the device are not getting dropped in the network.

- **ACS Support Bundle:** The support bundle is a zip archive of diagnostic information, including system log files. You can also choose to include ACS configuration, ACS debug log files, ACS localstore log files, and core files. This support bundle will be needed by the Cisco Technical Assistance Center (TAC) for troubleshooting.

- **Expert Troubleshooter:** This section contains some nice tools to check the configuration of a device and ACS. Using RADIUS Authentication troubleshooting tool, you can select a failed or passed log from RADIUS authentication report and have it check the ACS and device configuration to see why the authentication failed or passed. Figure 4-27 shows the report generated by this tool when changing the RADIUS shared key on the device. This section also contains the NAD **show** command application from the dashboard and the Evaluate Configuration Validator, which checks the configuration of a device to see whether it is configured properly for a task such as 802.1x authentication.

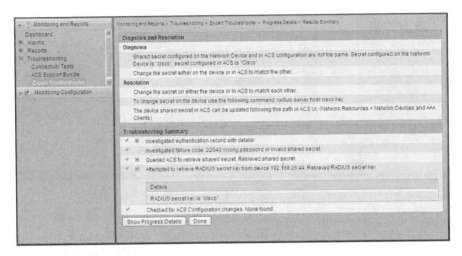

Figure 4-27   *RADIUS Authentication Troubleshooting Tool at Work*

The Monitoring Configuration drawer contains various configuration options for the Monitoring and Report Viewer. Configuration of ACS View (the Monitoring and Reporting part of ACS 5.x) is out of the scope of this book.

Note   The System Administration drawer contains various advanced configuration options for ACS. These options are covered in Chapter 15.

ACS 5.1 Command-Line Interface (CLI)

ACS 5.x, unlike previous versions, provides a CLI for configuration and monitoring along with a GUI. You can access the ACS CLI through a secure shell (SSH) client or the console port.

Two different types of accounts are available for accessing the CLI:

■   **Admin:** Admin accounts have full configuration and monitoring access.

■   **Operator:** Operator accounts have monitoring access only.

This section assumes use of an Admin account to access the CLI.

The ACS CLI is similar to IOS CLI in look, feel, modes, and command structure. You can use the question mark (?) to see the help and the Tab key to complete a command. Logging in to the ACS server places you in the Operator (user) mode or the Admin (EXEC) mode. Typically, logging in requires a username and password.

You can always tell when you are in the Operator (user) mode or Admin (EXEC) mode by looking at the prompt. A right angle bracket (>) appears at the end of the Operator (user) mode prompt; a pound sign (#) appears at the end of the Admin mode prompt, regardless of the submode.

Three command modes are available on the CLI:

■ **EXEC:** EXEC commands primarily include system-level commands such as **show** and **reload** (for example, application installation, application start and stop, copy files and installations, restore backups, and display information). In addition, certain EXEC-mode commands have ACS-specific abilities (for example, start an ACS instance, display and export ACS logs, and reset an ACS configuration to factory default settings).

■ **ACS Configuration:** Commands in this mode can be used to set the debug log level for the ACS management and runtime components, show system settings, reset server certificates and IP address access lists, and manage import and export processes. To access the ACS configuration mode, run the **acs-config** command in EXEC mode as demonstrated in Example 4-1.

Example 4-1   *ACS CLI—Changing to ACS Configuration Mode*

```
ACS51/admin# acs-config
Escape character is CNTL/D.


Username: ACSAdmin
Password:


ACS51/ACSAdmin(config-acs)#
```

■ **Configuration:** Commands in this mode can be used to configure various system options such as interface, repository, SNMP server, and NTP, among others. To access the Configuration mode, run the **configure** command in EXEC mode as demonstrated in Example 4-2.

Example 4-2   *ACS CLI—Changing to Configuration Mode*

```
ACS51/admin# configure
Enter configuration commands, one per line.  End with CNTL/Z.
ACS51/admin(config)#
```

It is not possible to cover all the commands available in the CLI. The list that follows highlights a few important tasks and their related commands:

■ **Starting and Stopping ACS Services:** ACS services can be started or stopped from the EXEC mode using the **acs {start | stop}** command.

- **Reset ACS Configuration:** To reset ACS configuration to the factory default, use the **acs reset-config** command at the EXEC mode.

- **Reset ACSAdmin Password:** To reset the password of the default GUI admin, use the **acs reset-password** command from the EXEC mode.

- **Verify Configuration:** To see the current configuration, use the **show running-config** command from the EXEC mode.

- **Verify Version Information:** To see the current version, use the **show version** command from the EXEC mode.

- **Verify Status of ACS Processes:** To verify the status of the ACS processes, use the **show application status acs** EXEC command.

- **Troubleshoot Connectivity:** To troubleshoot network connectivity, use the **ping** *ip address or hostname*, **traceroute** *ip address or hostname*, and **nslookup** *ip address or hostname* commands from the EXEC mode.

- **Change IP Address:** To change the IP address of the interface, use the **ip address** *ip address subnet mask* command in the Interface mode. To go to the Interface mode, use the **interface GigabitEthernet 0** command in the Configuration mode.

- **Add a Route:** To add a route to the routing table of ACS, use the **ip route** *network-address netmask* **gateway** *gateway-address* command in the Configuration mode.

- **Disable ICMP Echo Response:** To stop the device from sending ICMP echo responses to echo requests received, use the **icmp echo off** command. Use **icmp echo on** command to enable the device to send echo responses.

- **Change Hostname:** To change the hostname of the server, use the **hostname** *name* command in the Configuration mode.

For more details on ACS CLI commands, see the "CLI Reference Guide for the Cisco Secure Access Control System 5.1."

Summary

At this point, you should be familiar with the interface of ACS 5.1 and the process of adding and creating different elements. Remember the flow of adding network devices and users, creating policy elements and access services. You are now prepared to add external user repositories and create complex access services for different AAA scenarios.

Chapter 5

Configuring External Databases (Identity Stores) with ACS

This chapter covers the following subjects:

- External Database or Identity Stores Available in Cisco Secure Access Control Server 4.2 and Cisco Secure Access Control System 5.1

- Configuration of External Databases Available; Active Directory, LDAP, RSA; with Cisco Secure Access Control Server 4.2 and Cisco Secure Access Control System 5.1

Chapter 4, "Getting Familiar with ACS 5.1," explored internal identity stores and detailed how they can be integrated with available policies and rules. At this point, you might be wondering what to do if you already have a database in place? Are you supposed to do some kind of export and import of available databases into Cisco Secure ACS Server? The logical and feasible answer would be to extend Cisco Secure ACS Server to these already present databases, which can be referred as *external databases* or *external identity stores* with reference to Cisco Secure ACS. This approach does not introduce any overhead on the part of Cisco Secure ACS or external identity stores to maintain or sync it with each other. Both entities are maintained separately.

External Databases/Identity Stores

The choices available for external databases or external identity stores are decent enough on Cisco Secure Access Control Server 4.2 and Cisco Secure Access Control System 5.1. This section looks at the different external databases options available on ACS 4.2 and ACS 5.1. You will also learn how these external users or identities are processed in both versions.

External Databases/Identity Stores in Cisco Secure Access Control Server 4.2

On ACS 4.2, users are categorized into three categories:

- **Known Users:** Users who are explicitly added to the ACS internal database. This addition can take place manually by the ACS administrator through the GUI or automatically using Relational Database Management System (RDBMS) synchronization or by using the *CSUtil.exe* database utility.

- **Unknown Users:** Users whose accounts do not exist in the ACS internal database.

- **Discovered Users:** Users whose accounts are created in the ACS internal database after successful authentication by using the Unknown User Policy (through an external database in the policy) on the ACS server. All discovered users are previously unknown users on the ACS server. After they are discovered; the user accounts created on the ACS internal database contain only username and password authentication list settings reflecting the database from where the user was discovered, and a group to which this user is assigned on ACS server as defined by group mapping for the particular external database.

Note   ACS does not import credentials (such as passwords or certificates) for a discovered user.

After ACS 4.2 is integrated with an external database or external identity store, if a user is not explicitly added to the ACS internal database with password authentication list pointing toward the external database, the very first time when a user authenticates, he or she is marked as an unknown user. ACS then checks the configuration of the Unknown User Policy. Depending on the action defined for an unknown user, one of the following actions occurs:

The user is rejected (due to "Fail the attempt" option selection).

An attempt is made to discover the unknown user (due to "Check the following external user databases" option selection) in the selected external user databases.

The **Unknown User Policy** option is available on ACS 4.2 under the **External User Databases > Unknown User Policy** option, as shown in Figure 5-1.

Multiple databases can be selected for unknown user discovery. If a user is not found in one database, the next sequential database is searched. The search order can also be configured in this section for the unknown user. When selecting multiple databases for unknown user discovery, you can place the database at the top of the list that does the following:

- Processes maximum authentication/authorization requests

- Processes requests that are associated with time-sensitive AAA clients or authentication protocols

- Requires the most restrictive mandatory credential types

Note   If a user is not found, a Windows database declares it as an unknown user or bad password, which is the same response when a user's password does not match. Due to this nature of Windows databases, the next sequential database is not attempted when a user is

continues

not found. To overcome this, there is an option available under Windows Database Configuration section. This is covered later in the "Configuring Active Directory" section in this chapter.

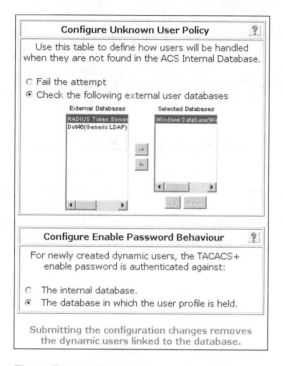

Figure 5-1 *ACS 4.2 Unknown User Policy*

For explanation purposes, assume that Network Access Profile (NAP) is configured on ACS 4.2, and the request matches the criteria defined in one of the NAP policies. In this case, the user is not discovered (if unknown) as defined in the Unknown User Policy section. The unknown user is discovered depending on the database definition available on the particular NAP policy.

Note The unique identifiers for a user are the **username** and **profile name**. Discovered users that are dynamically created through the use of different profiles have distinguished records in the database.

Users can be authenticated on Cisco Secure Access Control Server 4.2 when using the following external databases:

■ Windows User Database

■ Generic LDAP

- Open Database Connectivity (ODBC)–compliant relational databases (ACS for Windows)
- LEAP Proxy Remote Authentication Dial-In User Service (RADIUS) servers
- RADIUS Token server
- RSA SecurID Token Server
- RSA Authentication with LDAP Group Mapping

Note   As discussed in Chapter 2, "Cisco Secure ACS," selection of external database and protocols for authentication depends on the compatibility matrix provided in Table 2-1.

External Databases/Identity Stores in Cisco Secure Access Control System 5.1

In Cisco Secure Access Control System 5.1, there is no concept of known, unknown, and discovered users as there is with Cisco Secure Access Control Server 4.2. In ACS 5.1, an external database or identity store is selected for user authentication and attribute retrieval based on policies and rules. After an external identity store is configured, it can be used in Access Service's **Identity** section, where an identity store of choice can be selected.

ACS 4.2 has an option for selecting multiple external databases so that a user can be searched until it is not found. ACS 5.1 has a similar feature, which is known as *identity store sequences*.

The identity sequence is made up of two components:

- One for authentication
- Other for retrieving attributes

There are two methods of authentication available:

- Certificate based
- Password based

An identity store sequence can be created from the following option: **Users and Identity Stores > External Identity Stores > Identity Store Sequences**.

If you choose to perform certificate-based authentication, a single certificate authentication profile is used, as shown in Figure 5-2.

If you choose to perform password-based authentication (see Figure 5-3), you can define a list of identity databases to be accessed in sequence until the authentication succeeds. If the authentication succeeds, the attributes within the database are retrieved.

In addition, you can configure an optional list of databases from which additional attributes can be retrieved. These additional databases can be configured irrespective of

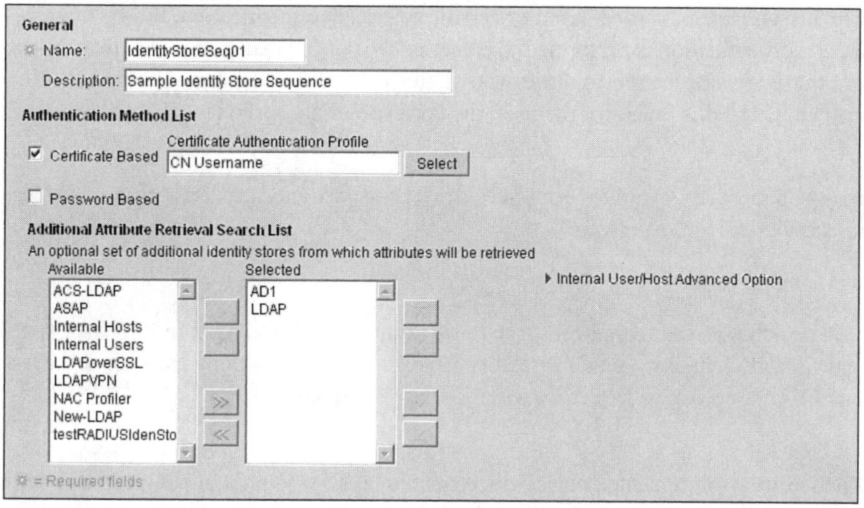

General

* Name: IdentityStoreSeq01

Description: Sample Identity Store Sequence

Authentication Method List

☑ Certificate Based   Certificate Authentication Profile
CN Username   [Select]

☐ Password Based

Additional Attribute Retrieval Search List

An optional set of additional identity stores from which attributes will be retrieved

Available   Selected   ▶ Internal User/Host Advanced Option

ACS-LDAP   AD1
ASAP   LDAP
Internal Hosts
Internal Users
LDAPoverSSL
LDAPVPN
NAC Profiler
New-LDAP
testRADIUSIdenSto

✿ = Required fields

Figure 5-2   *Identity Store Sequence Object Certificate Based Authentication*

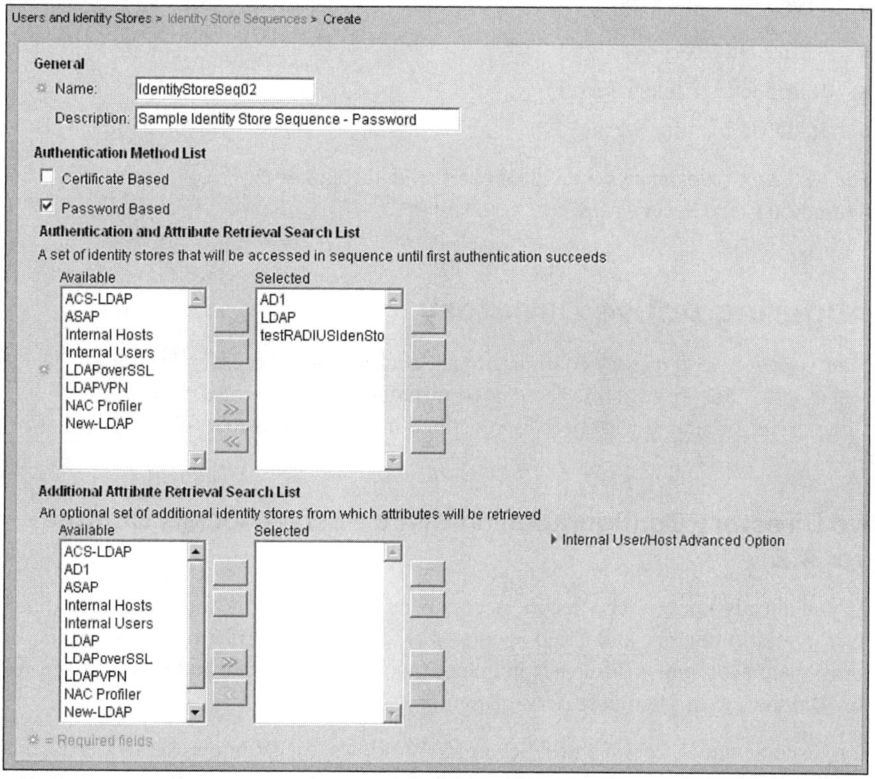

Users and Identity Stores > Identity Store Sequences > Create

General

* Name: IdentityStoreSeq02

Description: Sample Identity Store Sequence - Password

Authentication Method List

☐ Certificate Based

☑ Password Based

Authentication and Attribute Retrieval Search List

A set of identity stores that will be accessed in sequence until first authentication succeeds

Available   Selected

ACS-LDAP   AD1
ASAP   LDAP
Internal Hosts   testRADIUSIdenSto
Internal Users
✿ LDAPoverSSL
LDAPVPN
NAC Profiler
New-LDAP

Additional Attribute Retrieval Search List

An optional set of additional identity stores from which attributes will be retrieved

Available   Selected   ▶ Internal User/Host Advanced Option

ACS-LDAP
AD1
ASAP
Internal Hosts
Internal Users
LDAP
LDAPoverSSL
LDAPVPN
NAC Profiler
New-LDAP

✿ = Required fields

Figure 5-3   *Identity Store Sequence Object Password-Based Authentication*

whether you use password-based or certificate-based authentication. If a certificate-based authentication is performed, the username is populated from a certificate attribute and this username is used to retrieve attributes from all the databases in the list. When a matching record is found for the user, the corresponding attributes are retrieved.

Note   ACS retrieves attributes even for users whose accounts are disabled or whose passwords are marked for change.

Tip   A possible practical application of this feature is when you have an RSA database integrated with Windows Active Directory. The RSA database will be used for authentication and Windows Active Directory will be used to pull user groups.

An identity store sequence object, once created, as shown in Figure 5-3, can be used to process a complex request where multiple identity stores and profiles are involved.

On ACS 5.1, the following external identity stores options are available:

■ LDAP

■ Active Directory

■ RSA SecurID Token Server

■ RADIUS Identity Server

The next section examines individual external databases or external identity stores configured on Cisco Secure ACS.

Configuring Active Directory

Microsoft Active Directory configuration is available on both Cisco Secure ACS 4.2 as well as Cisco Secure ACS 5.1. There lies a difference in the way Microsoft Active Directory is integrated with both as described in the sections that follow.

Active Directory Configuration on Cisco Secure Access Control Server 4.2

As you already know, Cisco Secure Access Control Server 4.2 is available in two platforms: Solution Engine and Cisco Secure ACS for Windows. Due to differences in platform, there lies a minor difference in integrating Solution Engine and Cisco Secure ACS for Windows with Microsoft Active Directory.

For Cisco Secure Access Control Server for Windows, the Windows server needs to be a member server or a domain controller to be able to communicate with the Microsoft Active Directory.

To configure the Windows database on Cisco Secure ACS for Windows, you need to navigate to **External User Databases > Database Configuration > Windows Database > Configure**.

For Solution Engine, there is a minor difference in integration. To ensure solution engine communication with Microsoft Active Directory, you need to install Cisco Secure Remote Agent. This remote agent software needs to be installed on a member server or a domain controller. When installation completes, you need to add a remote agent entry under the Network Configuration section on Solution Engine to make it available for use.

To configure the Windows database on Cisco Secure ACS Solution Engine, navigate to **External Users Databases > Database Configuration > Windows Database > Configure > Windows Authentication Configuration**.

Under this section, you have the following options available for configuration with the Windows database as shown in Figures 5-4, 5-5, 5-6, and 5-7:

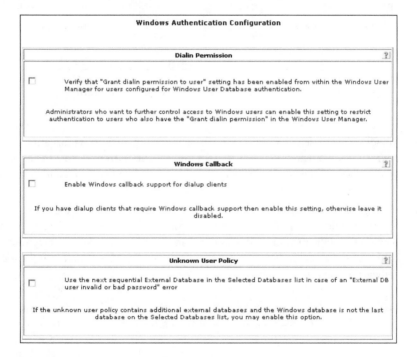

Figure 5-4 *ACS 4.2 Windows Authentication Configuration Section*

- **Dialin Permission:** By enabling this option, network access to users can be restricted based on Windows dial-in permission.

- **Unknown User Policy:** If a user does not exist in the Windows database, or has typed an incorrect password, the error 1326L (bad username or password) is returned. With an unknown user policy, if you have multiple databases and the

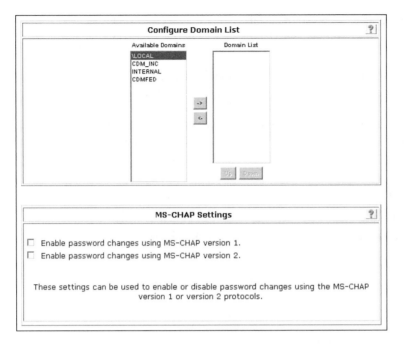

Figure 5-5 *ACS 4.2 Windows Authentication Configuration Section (Continued)*

Windows database is not the last database in the list, ACS treats this error (1326L) as a wrong password and does not attempt authentication from the next external database in the list. This option should be enabled to search external databases in the list after Windows database if the 1326L error is returned.

■ **Configure Domain List:** In a scenario where the same username exists in more than one trusted domain, and it is not practical for users to explicitly specify the domain name while authenticating, a domain list can be configured. ACS will try to authenticate the user normally. If the user authentication fails, ACS will retry authentication for each domain specified in the domain list.

Caution It is advisable to use this option with caution. While this option is configured, a bad password can lock a user out after an unsuccessful authentication attempt is made to each database in list.

■ **MS-CHAP Settings:** These options are required if you want ACS to support MS-CHAP–based password changes for Windows user accounts.

■ **Windows EAP Settings:** The following options are available under this section:

Password change during EAP authentication

Machine Authentication feature on ACS for PEAP and EAP-TLS

Machine Access Restriction

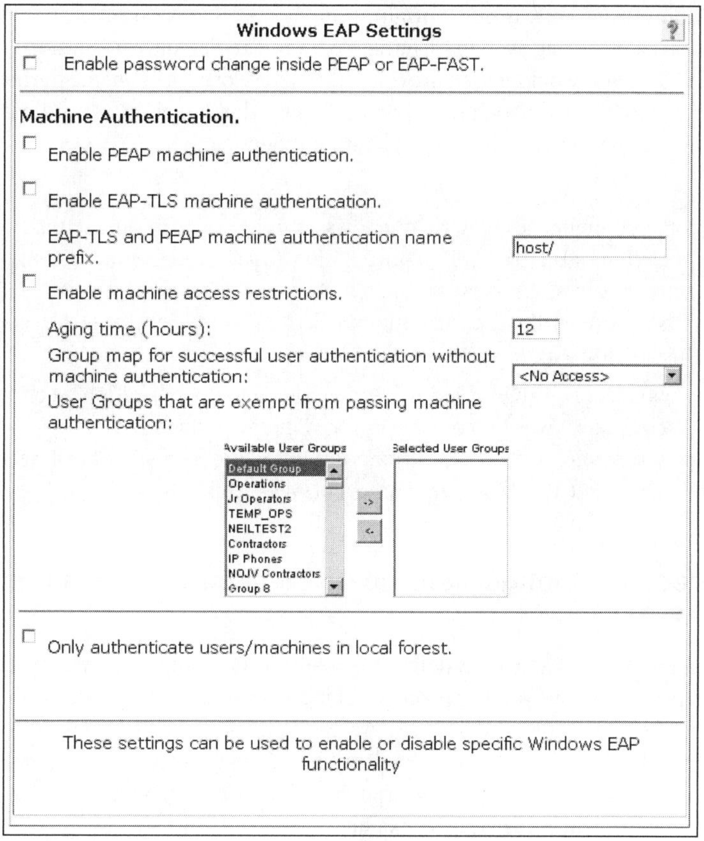

Figure 5-6   *ACS 4.2 Windows Authentication Configuration Section (Continued)*

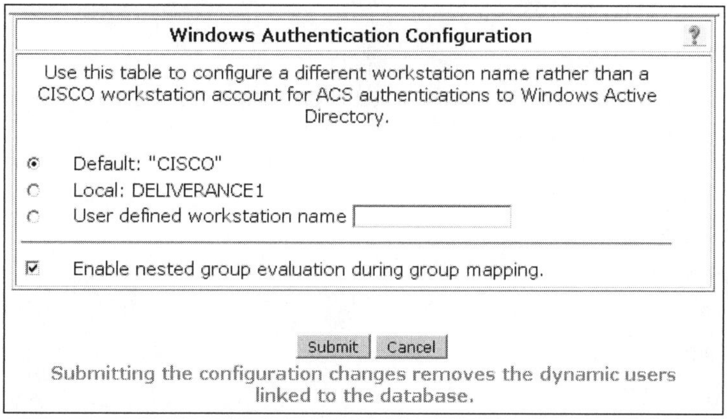

Figure 5-7   *ACS 4.2 Windows Authentication Configuration Section (Continued)*

■ **Windows Authentication Configuration:** For ACS, it is essential to provide a work-station name during Windows authentication. The default workstation name is **CISCO.** If you would like to provide a different workstation name during authentication, it can be specified in this section. This section has another option available that allows evaluation of nested groups during group mapping.

> **Tip** For proper communication with Windows Active Directory, ensure that you follow complete instructions available in "Post-Installation Tasks" available in "Installation guide for Cisco Secure Access Control Server 4.2":
> http://www.cisco.com/en/US/docs/net_mgmt/cisco_secure_access_control_server_for_win dows/4.2.1/Installation_Guide/windows/postin.html.
>
> For remote agents, consult the "Windows Authentication Configuration" section in the "Installing Cisco Secure ACS Remote Agent for Windows" guide:
> http://www.cisco.com/en/US/docs/net_mgmt/cisco_secure_access_control_server_for_sol ution_engine/4.2/installation/guide/remote_agent/rawi.html.

Active Directory Configuration on Cisco Secure Access Control System 5.1

Cisco Secure Access Control System 5.1 is available as an appliance and VMWare. Both available platforms have no difference when it comes to configure Microsoft Active Directory. Previously, the Cisco Secure Access Control Server 4.2 appliance was dependent on an additional piece of software (Remote Agent) to integrate ACS and Windows AD. In ACS 5.1, no such software is required. ACS 5.1 is joined with Microsoft AD with few simple steps, which this section examines.

ACS supports the following Microsoft AD domains:

■ Windows Server 2000

■ Windows Server 2003

■ Windows Server 2008

With an external identity store such as Microsoft AD, ACS 5.1 supports the following authentication protocols:

■ PAP

■ MSCHAPv1

■ MSCHAPv2

■ EAP-GTC

■ PEAP

■ EAP-FAST

■ EAP-TLS

To authenticate user and machine from Microsoft AD, ACS needs to be joined to the AD. Joining ACS with AD is fairly simple as compared to Cisco Secure ACS 4.2 because you do not need to perform post-installation tasks or install remote agent software.

To join ACS with AD, perform the following:

Step 1.   Go to **Users and Identity Stores > External Identity Stores > Active Directory.**

Step 2.   Under **Connection Details**, specify an Active Directory domain name; for example, cisco.com.

Step 3.   Specify a username and password for the account that will be used to join the ACS sever to the AD. Ensure that the account being used has sufficient privileges to search the domain and create a computer account on AD to join ACS into AD.

Step 4.   Press **Test Connection** to ensure that you are able to communicate with AD. A message appears informing you whether the AD server is routable within the network and authenticating the given AD username and password.

Step 5.   If the connection was successful, click **Save Changes.**

If ACS was joined successfully with AD, you should see information under the **Connectivity Status** section including the name of the domain for **Joined to Domain:** and **Connectivity Status:** as **CONNECTED** as shown in Figure 5-8.

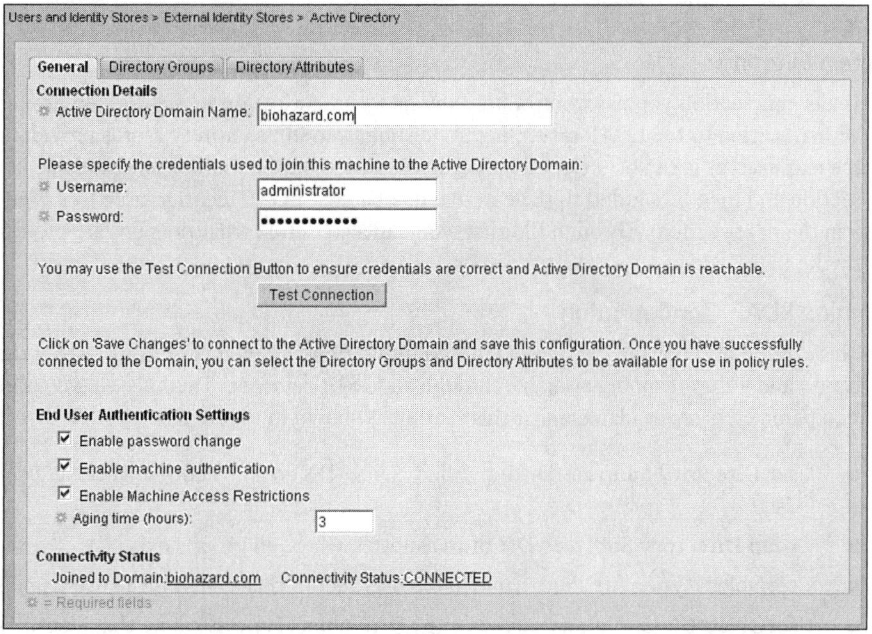

Figure 5-8   *ACS 5.1 Active Directory Identity Store*

> **Tip**   If ACS is not able to join AD, check the following three items for troubleshooting:
> - DNS configuration
> - Time zone configuration
> - Permission of account used on ACS to join AD

Configuring LDAP

Lightweight Directory Access Protocol (LDAP), defined in RFC 2251, is an application protocol for querying and modifying directory services running over TCP/IP. ACS 4.2 and 5.1 integrates with an LDAP external database by using the LDAP protocol.

LDAP Configuration on Cisco Secure Access Control Server 4.2

To configure LDAP on ACS 4.2, you need to navigate to **External User Database > Database Configuration > Generic LDAP**.

Under this section, you have four sections available for configuration:

- Domain Filtering
- Common LDAP Configuration
- Primary LDAP Server
- Secondary LDAP Server

Domain Filtering

Under this section you can control how any user authentication request is submitted for authentication to the LDAP server. It can be submitted in its entirety as it is provided by the end user, or it can be stripped based on the configuration parameters available in this section and then forwarded to the external database or LDAP identity store (see Figure 5-9 in the next section). Through filtering, you can also define what domains are processed by the LDAP server.

Common LDAP Configuration

This section outlines the common LDAP configuration parameters used for user authentication and group mapping available through an LDAP database. The following configuration parameters are available under this section as shown in Figure 5-9.

- **User Directory Subtree:** Distinguished Name (DN) of the subtree where all users exist.
- **Group Directory Subtree:** DN of the subtree where all groups exist.
- **UserObjectType:** Attribute name in the user record that contains the username.
- **UserObjectClass:** Unique value of the LDAP **objectType** attribute that identifies the record as a user.
- **GroupObjectType:** Attribute name in the group record that contains the group name.

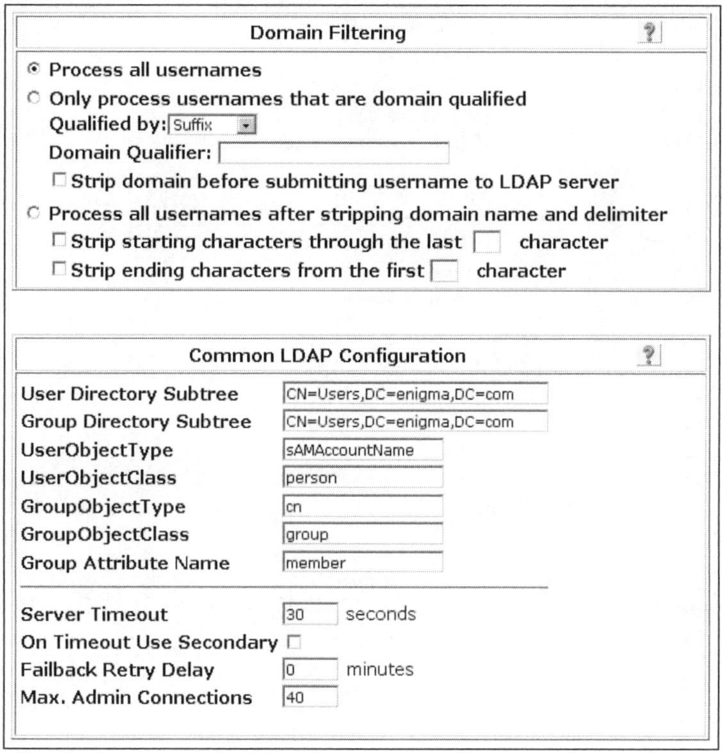

Figure 5-9 *ACS 4.2 LDAP External Database Configuration*

■ **GroupObjectClass:** Unique value of the LDAP **objectType** attribute that identifies the record as a group.

■ **Group Attribute Name:** Attribute name in the group record that contains the list of user records that are a member of that group.

Apart from attribute definition in the preceding list, the following options are also available under this section:

■ Server Timeout

■ On Timeout Use Secondary

■ Failback Retry Delay

■ Max. Admin Connections

Primary and Secondary LDAP Server

In this section, you define the connectivity details for the Primary LDAP server (required) and for the Secondary LDAP server (optional) as shown in Figure 5-10.

By default, the LDAP server listens on TCP/IP port 389. If you want to use secure authentication, port 636 is usually used. If you do not secure communication between ACS and

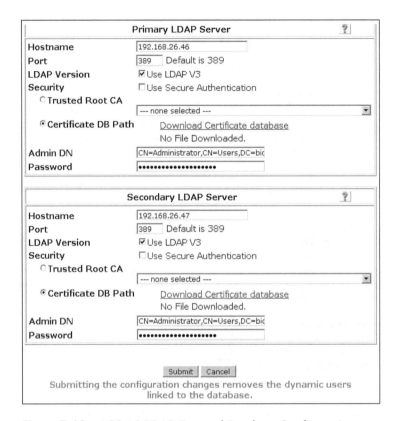

Figure 5-10   *ACS 4.2 LDAP External Database Configuration*

the LDAP server, user credentials are passed to the LDAP server in clear text. ACS uses SSL to encrypt communication between ACS and the LDAP server. If you decide to select the **Use Secure Authentication** option, you must select between **Trusted Root CA** and **Certificate Database Path.** Please note that ACS supports only server-side authentication for SSL communication with the LDAP server. The preferred way to configure secure authentication is by selecting **Trusted Root CA.** To use the **Trusted Root CA** option, you need to obtain a CA certificate from the LDAP server and install it in the ACS server as a trusted root CA (as described in Chapter 8, "IOS Switches," in the section, "Certificate Installation on ACS."

LDAP Configuration on Cisco Secure Access Control System 5.1

To configure LDAP on ACS 5.1, you need to navigate to **Users and Identity Stores > External Identity Stores > LDAP.**

Configuring LDAP on ACS 5.1 is a three-step process:

Step 1. **General.** In this step, you provide a name for the LDAP database or identity store instance, along with a description about this connection in the field provided as illustrated in Figure 5-11.

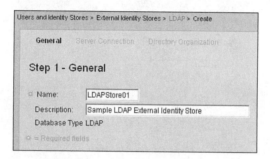

Figure 5-11 *ACS 5.1 LDAP Identity Store Configuration; Step 1*

Step 2. **Server Connection.** In this next step, you need to specify the connection details about the LDAP server as shown in Figure 5-12 so that ACS 5.1 can communicate with the LDAP server.

This section has two subsections.

- **Server Connection:** In this section you can configure to enable or activate your secondary server, as well as how the primary and secondary LDAP server should be contacted in the event that the primary server is not reachable.

- **Primary Server & Secondary Server:** In this section, you provide the IP address or hostname, port, authentication access details, root CA (if you are using secure LDAP), server timeout, and maximum admin connections.

Before proceeding toward the next step, there is a **Test Bind To Server** button provided at the bottom of the page to ensure that connection to primary and secondary (if any) LDAP server is successful based on the information provided in this section. Use the **Test Bind To Server** button to ensure that, based on the information provided, you are able to connect to the LDAP server.

If you are able to connect successfully, you should see the message **Connection test bind Succeeded.** In case there is some issue in establishing a successful connection, a pop-up box will appear with the possible cause.

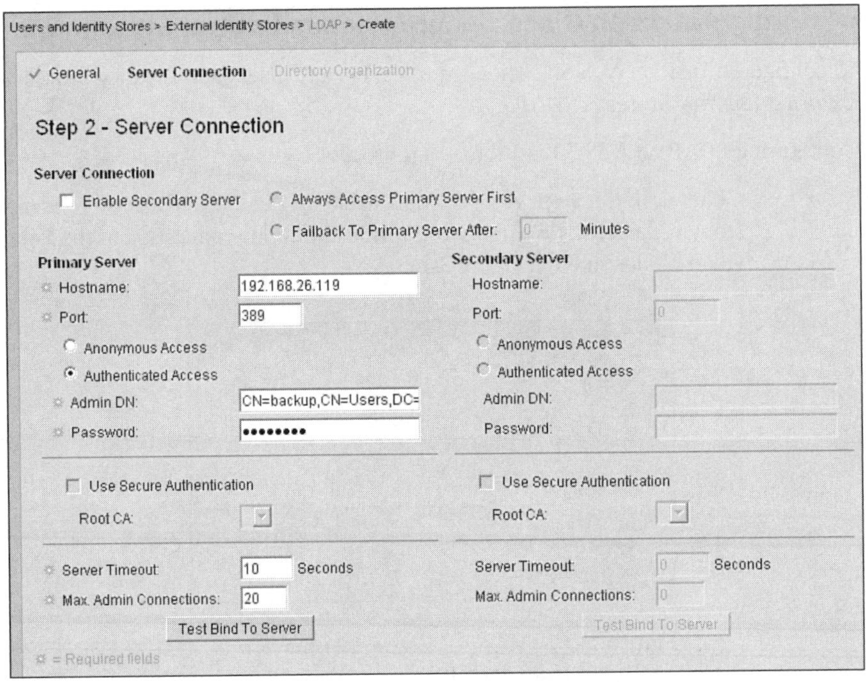

Figure 5-12 *ACS 5.1 LDAP Identity Store configuration; Step 2*

Step 3.   Directory Organization. This section is divided into four subsections as shown in Figure 5-13:

■ **Schema:** In this section you specify the schema of the LDAP server from which you are trying to connect and retrieve information. In this section, you define *Objectclass* and *Attribute name* for *Subject* and *Group*. In this section you also specify whether **Subject** objects contain reference to groups or **Group** objects contain reference to subjects, along with how subjects in a group are stored in a member attribute. All this information needs to be collected beforehand from the LDAP administrator to ensure successful information verification or retrieval from the identity store.

■ **Directory Structure:** In this section you define from where search should begin to search a **Subject** as specified by **Subject Search Base**, and for **Group** as specified by **Group Search Base**.

■ **Username Prefix\Suffix Stripping:** If it is required to send subject or username information to the identity store, that can be configured on this section according to need.

■ **MAC Address Format:** If you have built a MAC address database on the LDAP server, in order to authenticate the MAC addresses you need to specify the format in which MAC address need to be searched in the LDAP identity store.

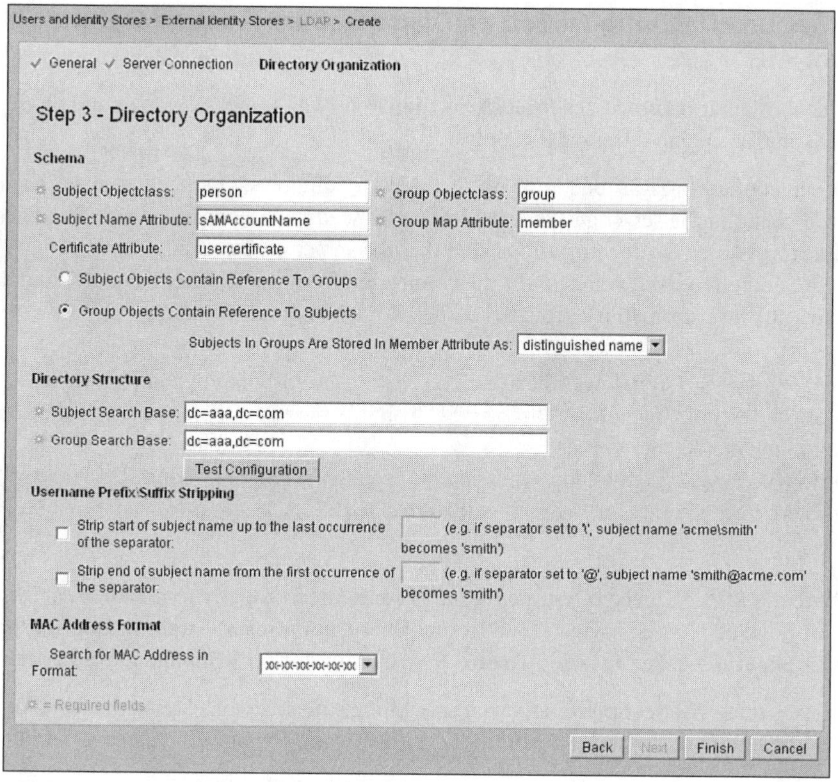

Figure 5-13   *ACS 5.1 LDAP Identity Store Configuration; Step 3*

Before finishing and submitting this step, ensure that you are able to retrieve the information successfully using the **Test Configuration** button provided for testing under the **Directory Structure** subsection.

If information is retrieved successfully, you should see the number of subjects and groups in the information provided in the pop-up box.

Configuring RSA SecureID

RSA SecureID provides two-factor authentication, which is one of the more secure means of authentication available today. In this two-factor authentication, the user provides a personal identification number (PIN) along with a single-use token generated from a time code algorithm. Because the token is a single-use token, it can be used only once; also, different tokens are generated at fixed intervals. Therefore, for authentication, a correct token along with a PIN need to be provided. A correct combination of both provides a higher degree of certainty that the user being authenticated is a valid user.

RSA SecureID Configuration on Cisco Secure Access Control Server 4.2

The configuration processes for RSA SecureID on ACS 4.2 for Windows and on the ACS 4.2 solution engine differ only slightly.

When configuring RSA SecureID on ACS 4.2 for Windows, you need to install the RSA ACE client on the server and the *sdconf.rec* file needs to be copied to the \Windows directory\system32 directory. To ensure that the server is able to communicate with the RSA SecureID server, you can test the connection from the Control Panel by running the Test Authentication utility provided in the ACE client application.

Tip Do not restart Windows when the RSA ACE client installation completes. Please refer to the section "Using RSA Token-Card Client Software" in the end user guide for ACS 4.2 for complete details:
http://www.cisco.com/en/US/docs/net_mgmt/cisco_secure_access_control_server_for_win dows/4.2.1/User_Guide/UsrDb.html#wp461844.

After the RSA ACE client is installed and is configured properly to communicate with RSA SecureID server, navigate to **External User Databases > Database Configuration > RSA SecureID Token Server > Create New Configuration > Submit > Configure**.

If everything was set up properly, you should see a message displaying the name of the RSA SecureID server and the path to the authenticator dynamic link library (DLL).

For the ACS 4.2 Solution Engine, the process of integrating RSA SecureID is even simpler. You only need to obtain the *sdconf.rec* file from the RSA administrator and upload it to the ACS 4.2 solution engine through a FTP server.

Navigate to **External User Databases > Database Configuration > RSA SecureID Token Server**, fill in the FTP server details, and select *Upload sdconf.rec*.

Note It takes one successful authentication for ACS to get the node secret from RSA SecurID Token Server.

RSA SecureID Configuration on Cisco Secure Access Control System 5.1

Configuring RSA SecureID as an external identity store is very similar to the process that you followed for ACS 4.2 Solution Engine.

On ACS 5.1, navigate to **Users and Identity Stores > External Identity Stores > RSA SecurID Token Servers** and click on **Create** to create a new instance for RSA SecureID on ACS 5.1.

Provide a name to this RSA instance under the General section, and upload the *sdconf.rec* file provided by the RSA administrator for ACS 5.1 Server and ACS 5.1 will begin communicating with RSA SecureID for two-factor authentication.

Note   It takes one successful authentication for ACS to get the node secret from RSA SecurID Token Server.

Group Mapping

The group mapping feature in external user databases or identity stores is used to associate users to an ACS group. This can be done to create logical association to the ACS groups, but is primarily done for the purpose of assigning authorization profiles based on group membership in external databases or identity stores.

Group Mapping on Cisco Secure Access Control Server 4.2

For ACS 4.2, in the case of the TACACS+ protocol, all the authorization attributes or profiles are configured at group level or user level. If you want to assign authorization to a specific group of users based on group membership they share on an external database, you need to map that external group to an ACS group and assign authorization to that ACS group.

In the case of the RADIUS protocol, you have the option to use a Network Access Profile (NAP) where it is not necessary to configure authorization attributes for an ACS group. Authorization attributes can be assigned depending on certain conditions, however, and among those conditions, group membership can be one of the deciding factors.

With ACS 4.2, every user needs to be a part of some group, so group mapping is very essential for any user, be it ACS local, internal user, or unknown user discovered from an external database.

To configure group mapping on ACS 4.2, navigate to **External User Databases > Database Group Mappings**.

For a database to appear under the section Database Group Mappings, it must first be configured under the **External User Databases > Database Configuration** section.

An unknown user on ACS 4.2, after being discovered, is assigned a group on ACS. The process of electing a group (group mapping) is described in this section.

Before delving into the group mapping options available for different external databases, you first need to understand group mapping order. On ACS 4.2, any user known or discovered can be a part of only a single ACS group. Even if the discovered user is a member of multiple groups on external database, on ACS, the user can be associated to only a single ACS group.

Say, for instance, you have a user on Microsoft Active Directory that is a member of three groups; namely, Group01, Group02, and Group3. On ACS, you create two mappings:

- If a user is a member of Group01 and Group02, map to ACS group ACSGroup01.
- If a user is a member of Group01 and Group03, map to ACS group ACSGroup02.

The user in question satisfies both conditions. Should this user be associated with group ACSGroup01 or ACSGroup02? The user cannot be a part of both groups in ACS 4.2.

This condition is controlled and resolved by group mapping order. ACS starts at the top of the list of group mapping for the external database. It sequentially checks user group membership in the external database against each group mapping in the list. As soon as the first group set mapping match is found, ACS assigns the user to the ACS group and the group mapping process stops.

Moving back to the original user in question, if you have the ACSGroup01 mapping above ACSGroup02 mapping, the user will be mapped to ACSGroup01 and vice versa.

Figure 5-14 shows an example of External User Database (LDAP) group mapping.

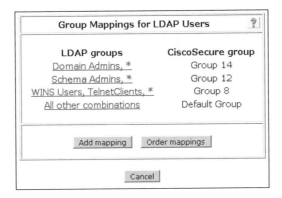

Figure 5-14   *ACS 4.2 Group Mapping and Group Mapping Order*

Tip   The order of group mappings is important. When defining mappings for users who belong to multiple groups, ensure that they are in the correct order so that users are mapped to the correct ACS group.

Group Mapping on Cisco Secure Access Control System 5.1

ACS 5.1 provides more advanced features and flexibility when it comes to group mapping.

The external identity store option available on ACS 5.1 has LDAP, Active Directory, RSA SecurID Token Servers, and RADIUS Identity Servers.

Out of all the external identity store options available on ACS 5.1, you can achieve group mapping with three external identity stores:

- LDAP
- Active Directory
- RADIUS Identity Servers

After you have created an instance for LDAP and Active Directory on ACS 5.1, two tabs or options automatically appear in that instance configuration:

- Directory Groups
- Directory Attributes

In the case of RADIUS Identity Stores, you get Directory Attributes only.

On ACS 5.1, the group mapping option feature available is dependent on the attribute retrieval from the external identity store.

Group Mapping with LDAP Identity Stores

When you create an LDAP identity store, ACS also creates a new dictionary for that store with two attributes: **ExternalGroups** and **IdentityDn**.

A custom condition for group mapping from the **ExternalGroups** attribute is created; the condition name has the format **LDAP** *ID_store_name*:**ExternalGroups** for LDAP identity stores.

If you create policy conditions from attributes of user or subject records to be referenced in policy rules from the Directory Attributes section in the identity stores, these conditions have the format **LDAP** *ID_store_name : attribute* for LDAP identity stores.

To view or edit the customer conditions created, navigate to **Policy Elements > Session Conditions > Custom**.

For LDAP, to make groups available as options in the rule table for group mapping conditions, the groups need to be selected under the Directory Group section: **Users and Identity Stores > External Identity Stores > LDAP > Directory Groups**.

Select the groups under **Selected Directory Groups** column using the **Add** or **Select** option as shown in Figure 5-15. The list populated in this section will be used as option when creating the policy condition.

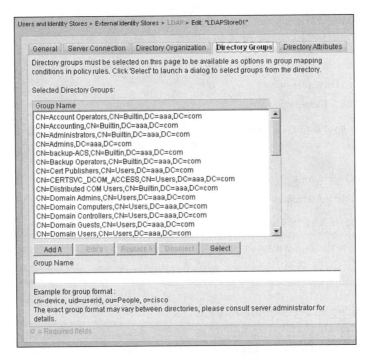

Figure 5-15   *Directory Groups for LDAP Identity Store*

Group Mapping with AD Identity Stores

When you configure an AD identity store, ACS also creates a new dictionary for that store with two attributes: **ExternalGroups** and **IdentityAccessRestricted**.

A custom condition for group mapping from the **ExternalGroups** attribute is created; the condition name has the following format:

AD1:ExternalGroups

If you create policy conditions from attributes of user or subject records to be referenced in policy rules from the Directory Attributes section in the identity stores, these conditions have the following format:

AD1 : *attribute*

To view or edit the customer conditions created, navigate to **Policy Elements > Session Conditions > Custom**.

For Active Directory, to make groups available as options in the rule table for group mapping conditions, the groups need to be selected under Directory Group section: **Users and Identity Stores > External Identity Stores > Active Directory > Directory Groups** as shown in Figure 5-16.

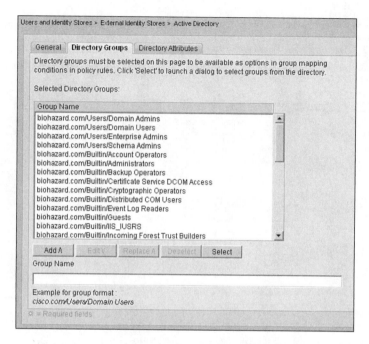

Figure 5-16   *Directory Groups for Active Directory*

Select the groups under **Selected Directory Groups** column using the **Add** or **Select** option. The list items populated in this section will be used as options when creating policy condition.

Group Mapping with RADIUS Identity Stores

In ACS 5.1, to the provide per-user group mapping feature for RADIUS Identity Servers identity stores, you use the attribute retrieval and authorization mechanism for users that are authenticated with a RADIUS identity store. For this, you must configure the RADIUS identity store to return authentication responses that contain the **[009\001]** *cisco-av-pair* attribute with the following value:

    ACS:CiscoSecure-Group-Id=N,

This is configured from **Users and Identity Stores > External Identity Stores > RADIUS Identity Servers > Edit the RADIUS Identity server instance > Directory Attributes**, as shown in Figure 5-17.

N can be any ACS group number from 0 through 499 that ACS assigns to the user. Then this attribute is available in the policy configuration pages of the ACS web interface while creating authorization and group mapping rules.

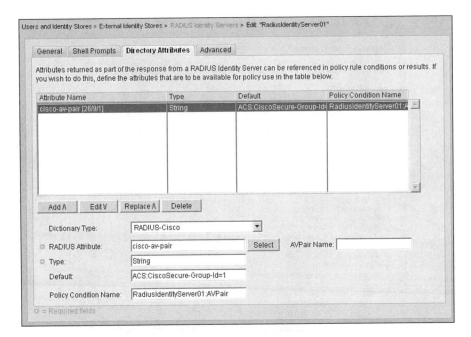

Figure 5-17   *Directory Attributes Section for RADIUS Identity Server*

Note   On ACS 4.2, the same feature is available for group mapping for LEAP proxy
RADIUS server and RADIUS token server. For complete details, please refer to "RADIUS-
Based Group Specification" under the "User Group Mapping and Specification" section of
"User Guide for Cisco Secure Access Control Server 4.2," which you find here:

http://www.cisco.com/en/US/docs/net_mgmt/cisco_secure_access_control_server_for_win
dows/4.2.1/User_Guide/GrpMap.html#wp961623.

Group Mapping Conditions for LDAP, AD, and RADIUS Identity Databases

After attributes have been defined and groups have been selected, you can proceed
toward the final step of using these group mapping conditions. For that you need to navigate to section **Access Policies > Access Services.**

You can create a new Access Service or edit an existing one. To make use of the group
mapping feature, you can either enable **Group Mapping** under **Policy Structure**, or you
can use it under **Authorization**, as shown in Figures 5-18 and 5-19.

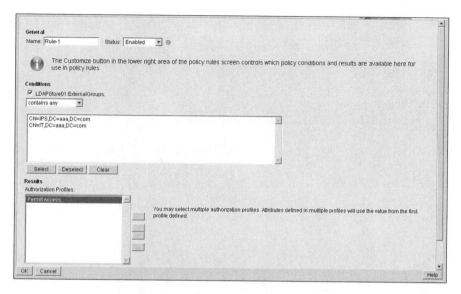

Figure 5-18   *Authorization Rule Using ExternalGroups as Condition*

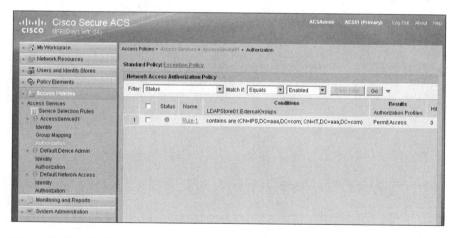

Figure 5-19   *Authorization Policy*

If you have enabled **Group Mapping** under **Policy Structure,** using this policy you can associate a user in an external identity store to an ACS group based on the group membership a user has with an external identity store, as shown in Figures 5-20 and 5-21.

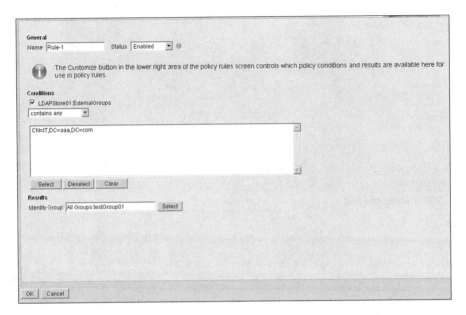

Figure 5-20 *Group Mapping Rule Using ExternalGroups as Condition*

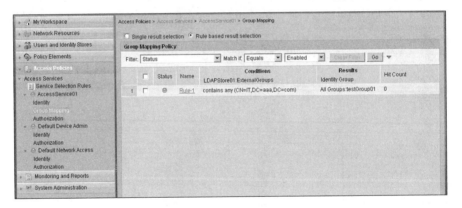

Figure 5-21 *Group Mapping Policy*

Make sure that you have selected **Rule based result selection** under Group Mapping
Policy for an Access Service. When done, you will have the option to **Create** a rule; in
this section, you can create a rule according to the specified requirements and associate a
user to a particular group on ACS. Another way to utilize the group mapping feature is
under the Authorization policy. Under Authorization, you can use the **ExternalGroups**
attribute as one of the conditions and, depending on the result, authorization can be
applied.

Summary

This chapter discussed what external databases or external identity stores are and how they can be integrated with ACS 4.2 and ACS 5.1. Apart from that, you also learned the following:

- On ACS 4.2, users fall under three categories: known, unknown, and discovered users.

- On ACS 4.2, the Unknown User Policy decides how an unknown user is discovered.

- On ACS 4.2, various external database options are available: Windows User Database, Generic LDAP, ODBC, LEAP Proxy RADIUS servers, RADIUS Token Servers, and RSA SecureID.

- On ACS 5.1, you have the following external identity store options available: LDAP, Active Directory, RSA SecurID Token Server, and RADIUS Identity Store.

- On ACS 5.1, you have two methods of authentication available: certificate-based and password-based.

- You learned the individual configuration settings for Active Directory, LDAP and SecurID server on ACS 4.2 and ACS 5.1.

- Using external group membership associations, users from external databases or identity stores can be assigned different authorization attributes.

- On ACS 4.2, Group Mapping Order is important. It starts from top to bottom and terminates as soon as the first group set mapping is found.

- On ACS 5.1, external groups are identified using the **ExternalGroups** attribute. This attribute can be used in Access Service for the Group Mapping policy or Authorization policy as a condition.

Chapter 6

Administrative AAA on IOS

This chapter covers the following subjects:

- Introduction to Administrative Sessions, Authentication, and Privilege Levels

- Enabling AAA on IOS

- Method Lists

- Authentication of Administrative Sessions

- Troubleshooting Authentication

- Authorization of Administrative Sessions

- Command Authorization

- Troubleshooting Authorization

- Accounting of Administrative Sessions and Commands

Previous chapters provided you with the opportunity to become familiar with ACS 4.2 and 5.1, depending on what you are using in your workplace. This chapter begins discussing how to use AAA to accomplish various administrative tasks on Cisco IOS devices. This chapter explores the way a router is accessible for management and how those points of management are handled by default. You will then look at local users and how to authenticate them, followed by a lab scenario of creating and using a privilege level. After the local lab scenario, this chapter moves into a discussion of external AAA and various configurations of authentications to the AAA Server, as well as Authorization and Accounting. You will also learn valuable troubleshooting techniques in this chapter.

Local Database

Cisco IOS provides four methods for administrative access—**console, vty, auxiliary,** and **HTTP.** Administrative access is granted based on Username and/or Password. By default, the console port is usually unprotected to allow initial configuration. Access to **vty** port is not allowed until a password, called the *line password*, is manually configured using the following commands:

```
Router(config)#line vty 0 4
Router(config-line)#password password
```

You can create a database of users in the router, called the *local database*, and use it to authenticate administrative sessions instead of using just a password. To add a user to the local database, use the following command in the global configuration mode:

```
username user password password
```

After creating the database, you will need to configure the router to use the local database for authentication instead of the line password. To do this, use the following commands:

```
line {console | vty | aux} line_number [line_number_end]
login authentication local
```

Note   As soon as this command is entered, the authentication prompt on login will change from Password to Username. If a local database does not exist, you will not be able to log in to the device.

Similar to the console, vty, and auxiliary lines, the built-in HTTP server can be configured to use the local database for authentication using the following command:

```
ip http authentication local
```

Privilege Levels

All the users in the local database that you just created have an equal level of access. It is usually desired to have different levels of access for users depending on their job role, experience, and so on. Such authorization can also be configured on the device without an AAA server.

For this, IOS provides 16 levels of access, called *privilege levels*. The number of commands available to a user depends on the privilege level. Higher privilege levels provide more commands.

By default, the following three levels are defined on the device:

- **privilege level 0:** Includes the **disable, enable, exit, help,** and **logout** commands. You cannot really access this level because after login, the first level accessible is level 1. Hence, the commands defined in this level are available to all users and do not affect the configuration of the device.

- **privilege level 1:** Normal level on Telnet; includes all user-level commands at the *router>* prompt. This level is also known as *User-EXEC mode.* Commands at this level do not affect the configuration of the device.

- **privilege level 15:** Includes all enable-level commands at the *router#* prompt. At this level, all commands are available and any configuration can be viewed or changed. This level is also known as *Privileged-EXEC mode.*

When you log in to a device using Telnet or Console, you arrive at level 1 after authentication. To get to level 15, you have to use the **enable** command and enter the configured enable secret. The enable secret is configured using the following command in the global configuration mode:

`enable secret` *password*

As you already know, all commands that can change configuration of the device are available at level 15. Access to this level is not something that you will want to give to everyone. To provide differential access, you will need to reduce the privilege level of a command from 15 to one of the custom levels (2 to 14). For example, if you want **user1** to be able to use the **clock** command, you will need to reduce the privilege level of the command. After that, **user1** can access the custom level and use the **clock** command. The user will not have access to any other level 15 commands.

To enter the custom privilege level, the users will need an enable secret for that level. Enable secret for a custom level can be configured using the following command:

`enable secret level` *level password*

To enter the custom privilege level, users have to use the following command at level 1:

`enable` *level*

To reduce the privilege level of a command and make it available at a lower privilege level, use the following global configuration command:

`privilege` *mode* `[all] level` *level command*

Table 6-1 explains the command syntax.

Example 6-1 shows the configuration required to create a custom level 2 where the users have access to level 15 commands **show running-config, configure, hostname,** and **clock.**

Example 6-1 *Custom Level Configuration*

```
Router(config)#username user1 password 7 13061E010803
Router(config)#enable secret level 2 test
Router(config)#privilege exec level 2 configure terminal
Router(config)#privilege exec level 2 show running-config
Router(config)#privilege configure all level 2 clock
Router(config)#privilege configure level 2 hostname
```

Note   When the privilege level of **show running-config** command is reduced, users at the custom level will not be able to see the entire configuration. Users will see only the configuration related to the commands they can execute.

Table 6-1 *Syntax Description: Privilege Command*

Command Option	Description
mode	Configuration mode for the command whose privilege you are reducing. Command example of modes are as follows: **exec:** Privileged EXEC mode **configure:** Global configuration mode **interface:** Interface configuration mode **router:** Routing configuration mode
all	(Optional) Changes the privilege level for all the suboptions to the same level. For example, the **all** keyword with the **show** command will allow the users of the custom level to execute all show commands.
level *level*	Specifies the privilege level you are configuring for the specified command or commands. The *level* argument must be a number from 0 to 15.
command-string	Command whose privilege level you want to reduce.

Lab Scenario #1: Local Authentication and Privilege Levels

XYZ Inc. is installing a new router in a small network. It has basic access restriction in place using vty and console line passwords. The company wants to use a local database now. It also wants to configure level 5 on IOS, such that users at this level can shut down interfaces and change interface duplex and speed. Your task is to configure the router to support that requirement. In addition, **user1** and **user2** with a password of abcd should exist in the local database. The enable secret for level 5 should be **limited**.

Lab Setup

This lab scenario requires any device running Cisco IOS. IP connectivity is not necessary because verification can be done using the console port.

Lab Solution

Step 1.   Add users in the local database:

```
Router(config)#username user1 password abcd
Router(config)#username user2 password abcd
```

Step 2.   Create an enable secret for level 5:

```
Router(config)#enable secret level 5 limited
```

Step 3.   Change privilege level for the required commands:

```
Router(config)#privilege exec level 5 configure terminal
Router(config)#privilege configure level 5 interface
Router(config)#privilege interface level 5 shutdown
Router(config)#privilege interface all level 5 duplex
Router(config)#privilege interface all level 5 speed
```

Lab Verification

To verify the solution, login to the device and enter level 5. You should have **default, duplex, exit, help, no, shutdown, and speed** commands available in the interface configuration mode. You can verify this using the **?** command at the mode.

Using AAA

In the previous sections you learned how to use the local database and privilege levels on IOS to secure access to the device. When you have a large number of network devices, it is difficult to manage access information. Imagine adding a new user on 100 devices! For such situations, you can make use of the AAA framework on IOS and authenticate and authorize users using TACACS+ or RADIUS.

Note   IOS supports both TACACS+ and RADIUS for administrative AAA but using TACACS+ is highly recommended due to support of command authorization.

By default, the AAA model is disabled on IOS. To enable AAA, enter the following command in global configuration mode of a Cisco router:

```
Router(config)#aaa new-model
```

Note   As soon as AAA model is enabled, it will overwrite every other authentication method configured on the lines and default to authentication using local database. We cannot stress enough the importance of having a local user configured before enabling AAA. Failure to do so can lead to unwanted password recovery procedure in certain situations.

You can disable AAA functionality with a single command. To disable AAA, use the following command in global configuration mode:

```
Router(config)#no aaa new-model
```

> **Note**   When the AAA model is disabled, all AAA configurations remain in the memory and are applied back when the AAA model is re-enabled. This can cause problems if the device is off network or AAA servers are unreachable. We recommend removing all AAA configurations before disabling the AAA model.

Before you can configure authentication using AAA, you need to add the IP address, shared secret key, and optionally the port of the AAA server to be used. To add the server details, use the following command:

```
radius-server host {hostname | ip-address} [key secret-key] [auth-port number]
[acct-port number]
```

or

```
tacacs-server host {hostname | ip-address} [key secret-key] [port number]
```

> **Note**   If you use a hostname, ensure that the device is able to resolve it. Port configuration is optional and you should configure it only if your AAA server is not listening on default ports.

You can add multiple RADIUS or TACACS+ servers. Each new server is added below the previous one. The device will query each server starting from the top until it gets a response.

All the servers added in this fashion form a group called *group RADIUS* or *group TACACS+* depending on the protocol. In effect, *group RADIUS* contains all the RADIUS servers added in the device and *group TACACS+* contains all TACACS+ servers added in the device. Under normal circumstances, these default groups are used for all AAA purposes. In situations where you want to use some servers for a particular type of AAA and some for other types, you will need to create custom server groups and assign the servers to them. To create a custom server group and assign the servers, use the following commands:

```
Router(config)#aaa group server {radius | tacacs+} group-name
Router(config-sg-radius)#server {hostname | ip-address}
```

> **Note**   You can assign servers to custom groups only after adding them in the device to the default groups. After the servers have been assigned to the custom server group, they will belong to the custom as well as the default group. They can be used by calling the custom or the default group. An exception to this rule can be made using the **server-private** command inside the group; however, this will not be discussed here to avoid complication.

From this point, you use a method list to configure what method in which to use AAA. A *method list* is a list that defines the point of authentication, authorization, or accounting and the method to be used. The section that follows discusses *method lists* in detail.

Configuring Authentication on IOS Using AAA

After enabling AAA and adding AAA servers, it is finally time to configure authentication. As mentioned earlier, method lists are used to define the method to be used for a point of authentication (also called service). There are many points of authentication, authorization and accounting or services in an IOS device such as login, PPP, enable, and dot1x. Different services are discussed throughout this book.

The syntax for a method list created on a Cisco router is shown here in a generic form:

```
aaa authentication service {default | list-name} method1 [method2] [method3] ...
[methodn]
```

As you already know, *service* is the point of authentication, authorization, or accounting that this method applies to. This section looks at authentication of administrative sessions on the console, vty, and aux lines. For this, use the **login** service.

The second option (*list-name*) to determine is the name of the list. If **default** is used, this list applies to all variations of the *service*. For this case, the default list will apply to the console, vty, aux lines, and HTTP sessions. If **default** is not used, the list will need to be applied to each variation of service manually. For example, two method lists are created for the **login** service. One is the **default** list and another is named **MYAUTH**. The **default** list gets applied to console, vty, and aux lines as soon as it is created. The **MYAUTH** list does nothing unless it is manually applied to one of the lines. At this stage, if **MYAUTH** list is applied to the console, it will override the **default** list for the console only. The remaining lines will continue to use the default list.

Finally, you must select the method of authentication. The method can be one of the AAA server groups (group RADIUS, group TACACS+, or a custom server group) or any of the local options available for the particular service. If multiple methods are configured, the first option will act as the primary option and the subsequent methods will act as failover options in the order they are specified. Table 6-2 shows the different methods available for the **login** service.

Example 6-2 shows some method lists for the **login** service.

Example 6-2 *Authentication Method Lists for Login Service*

```
Router(config)#aaa authentication login default group tacacs+ local
Router(config)#aaa authentication login MYAUTH local
Router(config)#aaa authentication login TEST group tacacs+ group radius enable
Router(config)#aaa authentication login TEST2 group tacacs+ line
Router(config)#aaa authentication login TEST3 group MYGROUP local
```

Table 6-2   *Methods Available for Authentication of Login Service*

Method	Description
group *group-name*	Specifies an AAA server group to be used for authentication. *group-name* can be RADIUS, TACACS+ or any custom server group. The device will try to contact each server in the group, starting from the top, until it gets a response. If all the servers are unreachable, the device fails over to the next method configured in the list.
local	Specifies that the local database should be used for authentication. It is highly recommended to have the local database as a failover method when using RADIUS or TACACS+ as the first method.
line	Specifies that the line password configured under individual lines should be used for authentication.
enable	Specifies that the enable secret or enable password should be used for login authentication also.
none	Specifies that authentication should be disabled. If you use this method, users will be given access without authentication.

Note   The device will use failover methods only when it fails to get a response from the current method. If an authentication failure is received, the device will not failover. The only exception to this rule occurs when the local database is the first option. In such cases, if the username does not exist in the local database, the next configured method is used.

You can apply a named method list to console, vty, or aux line using the following command:

```
Router(config-line)#login authentication list-name
```

A named method list can be applied to HTTP sessions using the following command:

```
Router(config)#ip http authentication aaa login-authentication list-name
```

Before moving to the next section, take some time to understand the complete configuration given in Example 6-3. This example shows the configuration required to authenticate Telnet and aux lines using TACACS+ with that local database as failover while authentication is disabled on the console.

Example 6-3   *Authentication Configuration*

```
Router(config)#aaa new-model
Router(config)#aaa authentication login default group tacacs+ local
Router(config)#aaa authentication login noauth none
Router(config)#tacacs-server host 192.168.1.10 key mykey
```

```
Router(config)#tacacs-server host 192.168.1.11 key mykey2
Router(config)#line con 0
Router(config-line)#login authentication noauth
```

Configuring ACS 4.2 and 5.1 for Authentication

Now that you have configured the device for authentication using TACACS+ or RADIUS, it is time to configure ACS to accept the requests from the device and authenticate users. Configuring ACS for authentication of login services requires the following steps:

Step 1.   Add the device as an AAA client in ACS.

Step 2.   Create a user.

Step 3.   (ACS 5.1 only) Create an access service for the authentication request.

You already know how to add an AAA client, create a user, and access services from the coverage in Chapter 3, "Getting Familiar with ACS 4.2," and Chapter 4, "Getting Familiar with ACS 5.1," depending on your ACS version. In case you have forgotten, or have skipped the previous chapters, refer to these chapters.

Verifying and Troubleshooting Authentication

During the initial configuration of AAA, the most common reason for failure is a communication problem between the device and the AAA server. A quick way to verify authentication is to use the following command on the device:

```
test aaa group group-name username password {legacy | new-code}
```

Note   The **legacy** and **new-code** options refer to the TACACS+ code path to use. Newer IOS versions do not have the **legacy** option. I personally prefer the **legacy** option because it provides better debugs then the **new-code** options.

If the user is successfully authenticated, the communication between the device and the AAA server is working properly. If not, check the following:

- The hostname or IP address of the AAA server is correctly added in the device. If you are using hostname, make sure it can be resolved by the device.

- Verify IP communication between the device and the AAA server using ping.

- Ensure that the device can reach the AAA server on TACACS+ or RADIUS ports. A firewall or access list might be blocking these ports.

- Ensure that the shared secret key is same on the device and the server. With TACACS+, the secret key mismatch will be obvious in the AAA server logs; however, with RADIUS, the AAA server will report an authentication failure due to a user password mismatch.

- For ACS 5.1, ensure that an access service is properly configured to authenticate the request.

When troubleshooting authentication, the following debugs are most useful:

debug aaa authentication

debug {tacacs | radius}

The debugs will help pinpoint the problem area. Example 6-4 shows the debug seen when authentication fails due to key mismatch and Example 6-5 shows the debugs seen when the AAA server is unreachable.

Example 6-4   debug aaa authentication *and* debug tacacs+: *Key Mismatch*

```
Router#debug aaa authentication
Router#debug tacacs
AAA: parse name=<no string> idb type=-1 tty=-1
AAA/MEMORY: create_user (0x66396144) user='vivek' ruser='NULL' ds0=0 port=''
rem_addr='NULL' authen_type=ASCII service=LOGIN priv=1 initial_task_id='0', vrf=
(id=0)
TAC+: send AUTHEN/START packet ver=192 id=-1181286511
TAC+: Using default tacacs server-group "tacacs+" list.
TAC+: Opening TCP/IP to 192.168.26.22/49 timeout=5
TAC+: Opened TCP/IP handle 0x6639719C to 192.168.26.22/49
TAC+: 192.168.26.22 (3113680785) AUTHEN/START/LOGIN/ASCII queued
TAC+: (3113680785) AUTHEN/START/LOGIN/ASCII processed
TAC+: received bad AUTHEN packet: length = 6, expected 82417
TAC+: Invalid AUTHEN/START/LOGIN/ASCII packet (check keys).

TAC+: Closing TCP/IP 0x6639719C connection to 192.168.26.22/49
TAC+: Using default tacacs server-group "tacacs+" list.
AAA/MEMORY: free_user (0x66396144) user='vivek' ruser='NULL' port=''
rem_addr='NULL' authen_type=ASCII service=LOGIN priv=1 vrf= (id=0)
```

Example 6-5   debug aaa authentication *and* debug tacacs+: *Server Unreachable*

```
Router#debug aaa authentication
Router#debug tacacs
AAA: parse name=<no string> idb type=-1 tty=-1
AAA/MEMORY: create_user (0x66395E08) user='vivek' ruser='NULL' ds0=0 port=''
rem_addr='NULL' authen_type=ASCII service=LOGIN priv=1 initial_task_id='0', vrf=
(id=0)
TAC+: send AUTHEN/START packet ver=192 id=729631450
TAC+: Using default tacacs server-group "tacacs+" list.
TAC+: Opening TCP/IP to 10.10.10.10/49 timeout=5
TAC+: TCP/IP open to 10.10.10.10/49 failed — Connection timed out; remote host
not responding
```

If the device is able to reach the AAA server, the logs on the server will be more useful than debugs to troubleshoot the problem. Chapter 3 and 4 cover the ACS logs in more detail.

Authorization of Administrative Sessions

The previous section taught you how to authenticate administrative sessions using TACACS+ and RADIUS. With such configuration, all users have equal access to the device. As discussed earlier, the level of access should be regulated depending on job role, experience, and so on. For this, you can configure the device to authorize administrative sessions. Authorization will not only determine whether a user has administrative access to the device, it will also determine the level of access a user has. Using Attribute-Value pairs, you can customize the level of access every user has.

Configuring authorization on IOS also involves creating method lists. The authorization method lists are similar to authentication method lists and the generic syntax for them is as follows:

```
aaa authorization service {default | list-name} method1 [method2] [method3] ...
[methodn]
```

To authorize administrative sessions, you have to use the **exec** service. A **default** method list will apply to all administrative services whereas a named method list would need to be applied to console, vty, aux, or HTTP sessions manually.

Note   Authorization does not get applied to console unless the **aaa authorization console** command is present in the configuration. By default, the command is not present in the configuration.

Table 6-3 shows the different methods available for **exec** authorization.

Example 6-6 shows some method lists for EXEC authorization.

Table 6-3   *Methods Available for EXEC Authorization*

Method	Description
group *group-name*	Specifies an AAA server group to be used for authorization. *group-name* can be RADIUS, TACACS+ or any custom server group.
local	Specifies that the local database should be used for authorization. It is highly recommended to have the local database as a failover method when using RADIUS or TACACS+ as the first method.
if-authenticated	Allows the user to access the requested function if the user is authenticated. The **if-authenticated** method is a terminating method. Therefore, if it is listed as a method, any methods listed after it will never be evaluated. Using **if-authenticated** as the first method is equivalent to not having an authorization if authentication has succeeded.
none	Specifies that authentication should be disabled. If you use this method, users will be given access without authentication.

Example 6-6 *Method Lists for EXEC Authorization*

```
Router(config)#aaa authorization exec default group tacacs+ local
Router(config)#aaa authorization exec MYlist group tacacs+ if-authenticated
Router(config)#aaa authorization exec testlist local
Router(config)#aaa authorization exec fortelnet group tacacs+ none
```

You can apply a named method list to a console, vty, or aux line using the following command:

```
Router(config-line)#authorization exec list-name
```

A named method list can be applied to HTTP sessions using the following command:

```
Router(config)#ip http authentication aaa exec-authorization list-name
```

Before moving to the next section, consider the configuration given in Example 6-7. This example builds on Example 6-3 and adds EXEC authorization for all administrative sessions except those on the console.

Example 6-7 *EXEC Authorization Configuration*

```
Router(config)#aaa new-model
Router(config)#aaa authentication login default group tacacs+ local
Router(config)#aaa authentication login noauth none
Router(config)#aaa authorization exec default group tacacs+ local
Router(config)#tacacs-server host 192.168.1.10 key mykey
Router(config)#tacacs-server host 192.168.1.11 key mykey2
Router(config)#line con 0
Router(config-line)#login authentication noauth
```

Note   If you are wondering why there is no named method list applied on the console for EXEC authorization, recall that authorization does not get applied to the console until the **aaa authorization console** command is present in the configuration.

Configuring ACS 4.2 and 5.1 for EXEC Authorization

After configuring the device to authorize administrative sessions, you now need to configure ACS to accept these requests, authorize the service, and optionally send additional attributes to customize the access levels.

As mentioned earlier, you can use TACACS+ and RADIUS for authentication, authorization, and accounting of administrative sessions; however, using TACACS+ is highly recommended due to better support for these sessions—especially the ability for command authorization. Hence we will cover only TACACS+ configuration in this section.

When EXEC authorization has been enabled, the device will send a TACACS+ authorization request to the AAA server immediately after authentication to check whether the user is allowed to start an administrative session. So, the user or group profile in ACS 4.2 and the access service in ACS 5.1 should have the Shell (EXEC) service enabled.

To enable the service in ACS 4.2, follow these steps:

Step 1.   If you want to enable the service at the user level, ensure that **Per-user TACACS+/RADIUS Attributes** is enabled in **Interface Configuration > Advanced Options.**

Step 2.   Select **Interface Configuration > TACACS+ (Cisco IOS)** and enable **Shell (exec)** for User and/or Group, as shown in Figure 6-1.

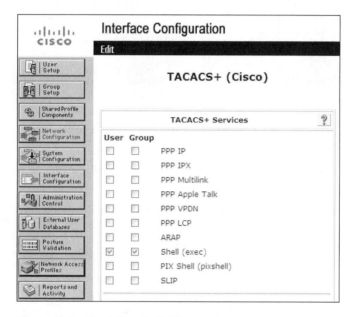

Figure 6-1   *Enabling Shell (EXEC) Service in ACS 4.2*

Step 3.   If you want to enable the service for the group, select the group in the **Group Setup** page and click **Edit Settings.** If you want to enable the service for the user, type the username in **User Setup** page and click **Add/Edit.**

Step 4.   Scroll down to **TACACS+ Settings.**

Step 5.   Select **Shell (Exec)**, as shown in Figure 6-2.

Step 6.   Select **Submit** from **User Setup** page or **Submit + Restart** from **Group Setup** page.

ACS 5.1 has a default access service called **Default Device Admin** that allows local users to authenticate. It also has a default authorization policy that allows EXEC authorization for all users. Recommend practice dictates changing the default policy and applying the **Deny Access** shell profile, which you can perform from the **Access Policies > Default**

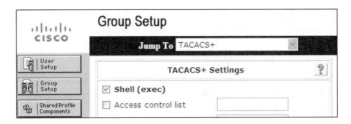

Figure 6-2   *Permitting Shell (EXEC) in an ACS 4.2 Group*

Device Admin > Authorization page. After changing the default authorization policy, create a new policy as per the following steps:

Step 1.   Select **Access Policies > Default Device Admin > Authorization** and click **Create.**

This will bring up the policy creation page.

Step 2.   Enter a name.

Step 3.   Select **Identity Group** of the users. You also can select any condition that identifies the request.

Step 4.   In the *Results* section, click **Select** next to **Shell Profiles** and select **Permit Access** shell profile from the list.

Figure 6-3 shows the policy creation page after completing the preceding steps.

Step 5.   Click **OK.**

This will bring you back to the Authorization Policy page.

Step 6.   Click **Save Changes.**

> **Note**   If you do not want to use the **Default Device Admin** access service, you can create a new **Access Service** and configure the **Service Selection Rules** accordingly. The preceding steps can be repeated for creating an authorization policy inside the new **Access Service.** For steps to create a new **Access Service** and changing the **Service Selection Rule,** see Chapter 4.

Now you know how to configure ACS so that the EXEC authorization is successful. You can also configure ACS to push additional attributes to the device. The following list discusses some of the attributes that you can use to customize the administrative session on a per user or group level:

■   **Default Privilege Level:** Defines the default privilege level of the user. Upon successful authentication and authorization, the user will land in this privilege level instead of level 1. This is a very useful attribute to ensure that users get the correct privilege level on login and do not have to use the **enable** command. Certain

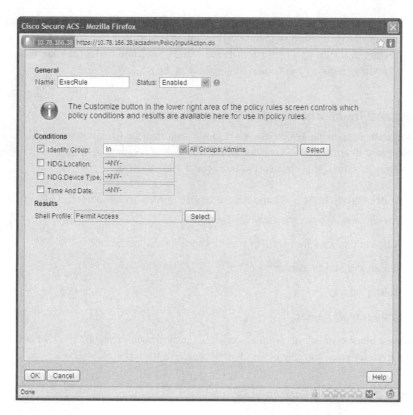

Figure 6-3   *Creating an Authorization Policy for EXEC Authorization*

administrative HTTP sessions to the device require this attribute to be set to 15. To configure this attribute, select the **Privilege Level** option under **TACACS+ Settings** in the group or user profile in ACS 4.2. In ACS 5.1, the **Default Privilege Level** attribute is available under the **Common Tasks** tab when creating or editing a shell profile.

- **Auto Command:** You can use the Auto Command attribute to send a command from the ACS to the device, which will be executed as soon as authorization is complete. The user will see the output of the command and the session will be closed. In effect, the user does not get an interactive shell. This is a useful feature if you want the user to see a menu or just certain information such as running configuration, version, interface status, and so on. Ensure that you are assigning a default privilege level of 15 if you want to execute a level 15 command such as **show running-config**. This option is also available under **TACACS+ Setting** in the group or user profile page in ACS 4.2 and under the **Common Tasks** tab when creating or editing a shell profile in ACS 5.1.

- **Timeout:** You can use this attribute to define the absolute timeout of the administrative session for a user in minutes. This option is also available under **TACACS+ Setting** in the group or user profile page in ACS 4.2 and under the **Common Tasks** tab when creating or editing a shell profile in ACS 5.1.

■   **Idle Timeout:** You can use this attribute to define the idle timeout value for an administrative session in minutes. This option is also available under **TACACS+ Setting** in the group or user profile page in ACS 4.2 and under the **Common Tasks** tab when creating or editing a shell profile in ACS 5.1.

Verifying and Troubleshooting EXEC Authorization

If authentication using TACACS+ is working, authorization usually works well also. Most problems with authorization are due to the absence of required attributes or incorrect attributes or values. If authorization fails, check the following:

■   User or group in ACS 4.2 and access service in ACS 5.1 has Shell (EXEC) privilege.

■   Attribute values are correctly configured.

The following debugs are useful in troubleshooting authorization:

■   **debug aaa authorization**

■   **debug tacacs**

■   **debug tacacs packet**

Example 6-8 shows debugs from a successful authorization session. You can see the privilege level, timeout, and idle timeout attributes sent from the ACS server.

Example 6-8   *EXEC Authorization Debugs*

```
Router#debug aaa authorization
Router#debug tacacs
TPLUS(00006349)/0/6639796C: Processing the reply packet
TPLUS: Processed AV idletime=1
TPLUS: Processed AV priv-lvl=15
TPLUS: Processed AV timeout=10
TPLUS: received authorization response for 25417: PASS
AAA/AUTHOR/EXEC(00006349): processing AV cmd=
AAA/AUTHOR/EXEC(00006349): processing AV idletime=60
AAA/AUTHOR/EXEC(00006349): processing AV priv-lvl=15
AAA/AUTHOR/EXEC(00006349): processing AV timeout=600
AAA/AUTHOR/EXEC(00006349): Authorization successful
```

Command Authorization

Earlier in the chapter you learned about using privilege levels in IOS to limit the commands available to a user during an administrative session. Configuring and maintaining privilege levels on hundreds of IOS devices is not an easy task. To make this easier to manage, IOS allows using TACACS+ to control which commands a user can execute on the device. After command authorization is enabled, the device will send each command to the TACACS+ server for authorization. If authorization is successful, the command will be executed. If the authorization fails, the user will see a failure message and the command will not be executed.

To do this, you will need to configure command authorization on the IOS device and apply shell command authorization sets on the user or group profile in ACS.

Before configuring command authorization, you should have authentication working on the device with TACACS+.

Configuring command authorization also requires creating method lists, the generic syntax for which is as follows:

```
aaa authentication commands level {default | list-name} method1 [method2]
[method3] ... [methodn]
```

The command authorization method list is similar to the EXEC authorization method list with the exception of the *level* option. The *level* option indicates the privilege level on which command authorization has to be applied. You can apply command authorization on any level from 0 to 15 using a separate method list for each level.

Note The *level* option in the method list indicates the level of the commands on which authorization has to be enabled. It does not indicate the level of the user. What it means is that if a user at privilege level 15 executes a privilege level 1 command, command authorization will be applied only if it has been enabled for level 1 commands.

Command authorization on level 15 does not affect the global configuration mode and its submodes unless the following command is present in the configuration:

```
aaa authorization config-commands
```

If a named method list is used, you will need to apply the list individually to console, vty, aux, or HTTP sessions. Recall that authorization does not apply to console unless the **aaa authorization console** command is present in the configuration. For a list of methods available for command authorization, refer to Table 6-3.

You can apply a named method list to console, vty, or aux line using the following command:

```
Router(config-line)#authorization commands level list-name
```

You can apply a named method list to HTTP sessions using the following command:

```
Router(config)#ip http authentication aaa command-authorization level list-name
```

Before moving to the next section, consider the configuration given in Example 6-9. This example builds on Example 6-7 and adds command authorization for level 0, 1, and 15 on all administrative sessions except those on the console.

Example 6-9   *Command Authorization Configuration*

```
Router(config)#aaa new-model
Router(config)#aaa authentication login default group tacacs+ local
Router(config)#aaa authentication login noauth none
Router(config)#aaa authorization exec default group tacacs+ local
Router(config)#aaa authorization commands 0 default group tacacs+ local
Router(config)#aaa authorization commands 1 default group tacacs+ local
Router(config)#aaa authorization commands 15 default group tacacs+ local
Router(config)#tacacs-server host 192.168.1.10 key mykey
Router(config)#tacacs-server host 192.168.1.11 key mykey2
Router(config)#line con 0
Router(config-line)#login authentication noauth
```

Configuring ACS 4.2 and 5.1 for Command Authorization

As you already know, when command authorization is enabled, the device sends each command and its arguments to the TACACS+ server for authorization. The user or group profile in ACS 4.2 and the authorization policy in 5.1 should have a command authorization set applied to it. A command authorization set is a list of commands and their arguments that are permitted or denied for the user or group it is applied to.

To create a command authorization set in ACS 4.2, perform the following steps:

Step 1.   Select **Shared Profile Components.**

Step 2.   Select **Shell Command Authorization Sets.**

Step 3.   Select the **Add** button.

Step 4.   Enter a name for your shell command authorization set.

Step 5.   Enter a description for your shell command authorization set.

Step 6.   You have two options in the form of radio buttons for unmatched commands.

The option to select a permit action versus a deny action here is determined based on the amount of commands you want to allow a user to have access to. For example, if you want a user with this command level to have access to all except a few commands, it makes sense to select Permit and create a list of denied commands. On the other hand, if you want to permit only a few commands, it makes sense to select Deny and create a list of commands permitted.

For this example, select **Deny.**

Step 7.   The large box on the left is populated as you enter commands in the small text box below it. In the small text box, enter the word **show** for this example.

Step 8.   Select the **Add Command** button.

After performing step 8, you can see the **show** command placed in the large box on the left side of the configuration page.

Step 9. Select the command with your mouse. This highlights the command in blue.

Step 10. If you place a check mark next to the words **Permit Unmatched Arguments**, any argument not listed in the box below the check mark will be permitted. If the box below the check mark is empty, all arguments are permitted. For our example, do not place a check mark there.

Step 11. To create a list of arguments that are permitted or denied with the selected command (**show** in our case), use the following format:

`{permit | deny}` *argument*

You can add entries for as many arguments as you want. Remember that the arguments are case sensitive.

For this example, enter **permit running-config**.

At this point, your command authorization set reads like this: Any command that does NOT match "**show running-config**" will be denied. Users to whom this set is applied will not be able to execute any commands apart from **show running-config**. To include any other commands, simply follow steps 7 through 11.

Figure 6-4 shows a command set created to allow some commands and deny the rest.

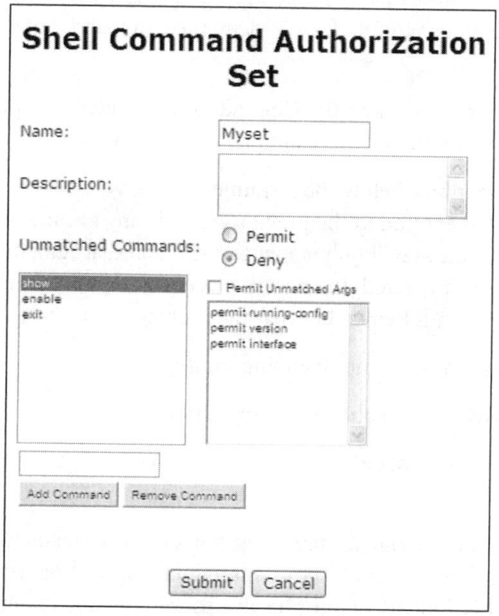

Figure 6-4 *Command Authorization Set in ACS 4.2*

Step 12. Click **Submit.**

To create a **Command Authorization Set** in ACS 5.1, follow these steps:

Step 1. Select **Policy Elements > Authorization and Permissions > Device Administration > Command Sets.**

Step 2. Click **Create.**

Step 3. Enter a name for your shell command authorization set.

Step 4. Enter a description for your shell command authorization set.

Step 5. You have an option to select the check box next to **Permit any command that is not in the table below.**

The option between allowing versus not allowing commands not listed in the table is determined based on the number of commands you want to allow a user to have access to. For example, if you want a user with this command level to have access to all except a few commands, it makes sense to place a check mark here and create a list of denied commands. On the other hand, if you want to permit only a few commands, it makes sense to not place a check mark here and create a list of commands permitted.

For this example, do not place a checkmark here.

Step 6. Below the table, you have three fields: **Grant, Command** and **Arguments.** Select **Permit** or **Deny** in the drop-box below the **Grant** field depending on whether you want to allow or deny the command. For this example, select **Permit.**

Step 7. In the text box under the **Command** field, enter the command you want to permit or deny. For this example, enter **show.**

Step 8. In the text box below the **Argument** field, you can enter an argument of the command entered in the previous step. If any argument is entered, the permit or deny action will only apply to the entered argument of the command. If no argument is entered, the permit or deny action will apply to all arguments of the command. Remember that the arguments are case sensitive.

For this example, enter **running-config.**

Step 9. Click **Add** button above the **Grant** field.

The **show** command and its argument that you entered are now listed in the table.

At this point, your command authorization set reads like this: Any command that does NOT match **show running-config** will be denied. Users to whom this set is applied will not be able to execute any commands apart from **show running-config.** To include any other commands or arguments of previously entered commands, simply follow steps 6 through 9. Figure 6-5 shows a command set created to allow some commands and deny the rest.

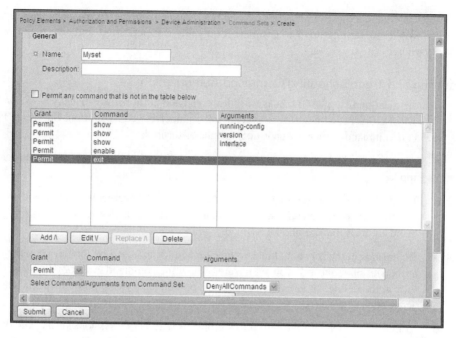

Figure 6-5 *Command Set in ACS 5.1*

Step 10. Click **Submit**.

You can apply the command authorization sets created in the preceding list using the following methods:

■ (ACS 4.2 only) In user or group edit page, select **Assign a Shell Command Authorization Set for any network device** and select your command set from the drop-down list. Click **Submit** from the User edit page or **Submit + Restart** from the group edit page.

■ (ACS 5.1 only) Ensure that **Command Sets** is selected as a result in the Authorization Policy page of your access service and select your command set in the correct authorization policy. In case you are not sure about results and authorization policies, refer to Chapter 4.

Before moving on to the next section, you should know that ACS applies pattern matching to the arguments. That is, the argument **permit and** matches any argument that contains the string **any**. Thus, for example, permit **any** would allow not only the argument **any** but also the arguments **company** and **anywhere**. To limit the extent of pattern matching, you can add the following expressions:

■ **Dollar Sign ($):** Expresses that the argument must end with what has gone before. Thus permit **any$** would match **any** or **company**, but not **anywhere**.

■ **Caret (^):** Expresses that the argument must begin with what follows. Thus permit **^any** would match **any** or **anywhere**, but not **company**.

You can combine these expressions to specify absolute matching. In the example given, you would use permit ^any$ to ensure that only **any** was permitted, and not **company** or **anywhere**.

Verifying and Troubleshooting Command Authorization

If authentication using TACACS+ is working, command authorization usually works well also. Most problems with authorization are due to incorrect configuration. Check the following if command authorization is not working as desired:

- User or group in ACS 4.2 and access service in ACS 5.1 has the correct command set applied.

- The device is configured to authorize commands of the correct levels. Remember that the level of the command is important for deciding the levels for which command authorization should be enabled.

- Commands in the set should match the case and format used by the device in the authorization request. If you are unsure of how the command is sent by the device, look at the debugs or failure logs on ACS. Sometimes devices will omit special characters such as slash (/).

- Command authorization often causes problems with HTTP sessions such as the ones opened by SDM. This is because SDM issues a series of commands when it starts up and they are not present in the command set. Look at ACS failure logs to see the commands that need to be permitted for SDM to work properly.

The following debugs are useful in troubleshooting authorization:

- **debug aaa authorization**
- **debug tacacs**
- **debug tacacs packet**

Example 6-10 shows debugs from a successful command authorization request. You can see that the authorization request from the device contains the command and argument entered by the user.

Example 6-10 *Debug Output for Command Authorization*

```
Router#debug aaa authorization
Router#debug tacacs
Router#debug tacacs packet
AAA/AUTHOR/TAC+: (2000424917): user=vivek
AAA/AUTHOR/TAC+: (2000424917): send AV service=shell
AAA/AUTHOR/TAC+: (2000424917): send AV cmd=show
AAA/AUTHOR/TAC+: (2000424917): send AV cmd-arg=running-config
AAA/AUTHOR/TAC+: (2000424917): send AV cmd-arg=<cr>
TAC+: Using default tacacs server-group "tacacs+" list.
TAC+: Opening TCP/IP to 192.168.40.7/49 timeout=5
TAC+: Opened TCP/IP handle 0x66925BD8 to 192.168.40.7/49
```

```
TAC+: 192.168.40.7 (2000424917) AUTHOR/START queued
TAC+: (2000424917) AUTHOR/START processed
TAC+: (2000424917): received author response status = PASS_ADD
```

Accounting of Administrative Sessions

Restricting access to a network device alone is not enough for complete security of the device. Restrictions should be followed by regular monitoring. IOS provides the accounting feature to help monitor administrative sessions and commands entered in the session.

Similar to authentication and authorization, accounting also requires creating method lists. The syntax for accounting of EXEC sessions is as follows:

aaa accounting exec {default | *list-name*} {stop-only | start-stop} group { tacacs+ | radius} [group {tacacs+ | radius}] ...

The syntax for command accounting is as follows:

aaa accounting commands *level* {default | *list-name*} {stop-only | start-stop} group { tacacs+ | radius} [group {tacacs+ | radius}] ...

In the preceding commands, a default list will apply to all administrative sessions whereas a named list will need to be applied to individual lines manually. Another important consideration when enabling accounting is whether you need accounting records only when the session stops only or also when the session starts. This is denoted by the **stop-only** and **start-stop** keywords in the syntax.

Accounting can use only a server group as a method. You can use multiple server groups as failover.

Example 6-11 builds on Example 6-9 and adds EXEC and command accounting.

Example 6-11 *Accounting Configuration*

```
Router(config)#aaa new-model
Router(config)#aaa authentication login default group tacacs+ local
Router(config)#aaa authentication login noauth none
Router(config)#aaa authorization exec default group tacacs+ local
Router(config)#aaa authorization commands 0 default group tacacs+ local
Router(config)#aaa authorization commands 1 default group tacacs+ local
Router(config)#aaa authorization commands 15 default group tacacs+ local
Router(config)#aaa accounting exec default start-stop group tacacs+
Router(config)#aaa accounting commands 0 default stop-only group tacacs+
Router(config)#aaa accounting commands 1 default stop-only group tacacs+
Router(config)#aaa accounting commands 15 default stop-only group tacacs+
Router(config)#tacacs-server host 192.168.1.10 key mykey
Router(config)#tacacs-server host 192.168.1.11 key mykey2
Router(config)#line con 0
Router(config-line)#login authentication noauth
```

You can apply named lists for EXEC and command accounting to the lines using the following commands:

```
Router(config-line)#accounting exec list-name
Router(config-line)#accounting commands level list-name
```

Configuring ACS for Accounting

There is no configuration required on ACS to accept accounting if the device is added as an AAA client.

You can see the EXEC accounting logs in ACS 4.2 under **Reports and Activity > TACACS+ Accounting** and command accounting logs under **Reports and Activity > TACACS+ Administration**.

In ACS 5.1, you can see both the EXEC and command accountings logs under **AAA Protocol > TACACS+ Accounting**.

Note   If authentication is working, accounting will work. The only exception to this is when you are using RADIUS and the device cannot reach ACS at the configured accounting port. In such situations, ensure that the accounting port is properly configured and is not blocked by a firewall or ACL. You can use **debug accounting** and **debug radius** to troubleshoot accounting.

Lab Scenario #2: Authentication, Authorization, and Accounting of Administrative Sessions Using TACACS+

XYZ Inc. has purchased Cisco ACS and it wants to use TACACS+ to authenticate connecting to its router using Telnet. In addition to that, the company wants to ensure that users belonging to the Admins group land in privilege level 15 directly after login and are able to execute all commands except **shutdown**. It also wants all sessions and commands to be logged in ACS using TACACS+.

You task is to configure the device and ACS to meet all these requirements and ensure that console and aux lines are not affected.

The IP address of the router is 192.168.1.1 and the IP address of ACS is 192.168.1.10.

Lab Setup

You require a simple setup connecting an IOS device to your ACS. The router should have IP connectivity to ACS.

Before starting the lab, add the device in ACS as an AAA client. If you are using ACS 4.2, rename a group to **Admins**. If you are using ACS 5.1, create an identity group named **Admins**. You can use the **Default Device Admin** access service for this lab. You also need to create an authorization policy in the access service that matches the **Admins** identity group.

Lab Solution

Step 1.   Configure the device for authentication, authorization, and accounting:

```
Router(config)#aaa new-model
Router(config)#tacacs-server host 192.168.1.10 key mykey
Router(config)#aaa authentication login default line
Router(config)#aaa authentication telnet group tacacs+ line
Router(config)#aaa authorization exec telnet group tacacs+ none
Router(config)#aaa authorization commands 0 telnet group tacacs+ none
Router(config)#aaa authorization commands 1 telnet group tacacs+ none
Router(config)#aaa authorization commands 15 telnet group tacacs+ none
Router(config)#aaa accounting exec telnet start-stop group tacacs+
Router(config)#aaa accounting commands 0 telnet stop-only group
tacacs+
Router(config)#aaa accounting commands 1 telnet stop-only group
tacacs+
Router(config)#aaa accounting commands 15 telnet stop-only group
tacacs+
Router(config)#aaa authorization config-commands
Router(config)#line vty 0 4
Router(config-line)#login authentication telnet
Router(config-line)#authorization exec telnet
Router(config-line)#authorization commands 0 telnet
Router(config-line)#authorization commands 1 telnet
Router(config-line)#authorization commands 15 telnet
Router(config-line)#accounting exec telnet
Router(config-line)#accounting commands 0 telnet
Router(config-line)#accounting commands 1 telnet
Router(config-line)#accounting commands 15 telnet
```

Step 2.   Create a command set in ACS that denies the command **shutdown** with all arguments and permits all other commands.

Step 3.   (ACS 4.2 only) Apply the command set to ACS 4.2 group called **Admins** and select **Shell (exec)** and **Privilege Level** under **TACACS+ Settings** and enter **15** in the text box next to it. Click **Submit + Restart**

Step 4.   (ACS 5.1 only) Create a shell profile and set **Default Privilege Level** to **15**. Apply this shell profile and the command set to the authorization policy created at the start of the lab.

Lab Verification

To verify the solution, create a user in the **Admins** group and initiate a Telnet session to the device. Authenticate using the user from the **Admins** group. You will notice that the session starts in level 15 and the user is able to execute any command except the **shutdown** command in the interface configuration mode.

Lab Scenario #3: Authentication and Authorization of HTTP Sessions

XYZ Inc. wants to manage its routers using Cisco Security Device Manager (SDM). The company wants SDM sessions to be authenticated from ACS using TACACS+. Users in the **Admin** group should be able to access SDM without any problems.

Your task is to configure the device and ACS to fulfill the preceding requirement.

The IP address of the router is 192.168.1.1 and the IP address of ACS is 192.168.1.10. Ensure that console, vty, and aux are still authenticated using line passwords.

Lab Setup

You require a simple setup connecting an IOS device to your ACS. The router should have IP connectivity to ACS. SDM is not really required for this lab.

Before starting the lab, add the device in ACS as an AAA client. If you are using ACS 4.2, rename a group to **Admins**. If you are using ACS 5.1, create an identity group named **Admins**. You can use the **Default Device Admin** access service for this lab. You also need to create an authorization policy in the access service that matches the **Admins** identity group.

Lab Solution

Step 1.   Configure the device for authentication and authorization:

```
Router(config)#aaa new-model
Router(config)#tacacs-server host 192.168.1.10 key mykey
Router(config)#aaa authentication login default line
Router(config)#aaa authentication login sdm group tacacs+
Router(config)#aaa authorization exec sdm group tacacs+
Router(config)#ip http server
Router(config)#ip http authentication aaa login-authentication sdm
Router(config)#ip http authentication aaa exec-authorization sdm
```

Step 2.   (ACS 4.2 only) Edit the **Admins** group and select **Shell (exec)** under **TACACS+ Settings**. Also select **Privilege Level** and enter **15** in the text box next to it. Click **Submit + Restart**.

Step 3.   (ACS 5.1 only) Create a shell profile and set **Default Privilege Level** to **15**. Apply this shell profile in the authorization policy created at the start of the lab.

Lab Verification

To verify the solution, launch a web browser and connect to the router at 192.168.1.1. HTTP authentication and authorization should be successful and you should see SDM loading. If you do not have SDM, you will see the default web interface of the device.

Summary

This chapter is the most crucial one in understanding AAA implementation on Cisco devices. The following will be used throughout this book and it is important that you understand them well and are comfortable with all variations:

Method lists

- ACS 4.1 configuration including group/user setup and command sets

- ACS 5.2 configuration including access services, shell profiles, and command sets

This chapter also covered troubleshooting steps for AAA on IOS, which will be used throughout the book.

Chapter 7

Administrative AAA on ASA/PIX

This chapter covers the following subjects:

- Introduction to Administrative sessions, Authentication, and Privilege levels on Cisco Security appliances

- Authentication of administrative sessions on Cisco Security Appliances

- Troubleshooting authentication on Cisco Security Appliances

- Authorization of administrative sessions on Cisco Security Appliances

- Command authorization on Cisco Security Appliances

- Troubleshooting authorization on Cisco Security Appliances

- Accounting of Administrative sessions and commands on Cisco Security Appliances

Cisco security appliances, including the Cisco PIX Firewall and Cisco Adaptive Security Appliance (ASA) have become staples of network security found in enterprise networks today. Their very design is security focused and the use of them within an authenticated infrastructure is a given. In this chapter, you will learn two aspects of the Cisco security appliance:

- How to perform authentication and authorization using local database.

- How to perform authentication, authorization, and accounting (AAA) using AAA servers.

You'll also learn some valuable tips for troubleshooting AAA issues should they arise.

Note The term "ASA" is used in this chapter to represent both the PIX Firewall as well as the ASA running OS version 7.0 and later. Where a feature is relevant only to ASA or PIX, it will be specifically mentioned.

Local Database

ASA provides three methods for administrative access to the device:

- Console (also called serial)

- Telnet/SSH

- HTTP

Administrative access is granted based on username and/or password. By default, the console port is usually unprotected to allow initial configuration.

Access to the device through Telnet and SSH is protected using a default password of **cisco**. This can be changed using the **password** *password* command.

Note   Before the security appliance can authenticate a Telnet, SSH, or HTTP user, you must first configure access to the security appliance using the **telnet, ssh**, and **http** commands. These commands identify the IP addresses that are allowed to communicate with the security appliance. More information regarding allowing Telnet, SSH, and HTTP access to ASA can be found at the following URL:

http://www.cisco.com/en/US/docs/security/asa/asa80/configuration/guide/mgaccess.html

In the ASA, you can create a database of users called the *local database*, and use it to authenticate administrative sessions instead of using just a password. To add a user to the local database, use the following command in the global configuration mode:

```
username user password password
```

After creating the database, you will need to configure the ASA to use the local database for authentication instead of just the password. To do this, use the following command:

```
aaa authentication {telnet | ssh | http | serial} console LOCAL
```

Note   As soon as this command is entered, the authentication prompt on login will change from password to username. If a local database does not exist, you will not be able to login to the device.

Privilege Levels

All users in the local database that you just created have an equal level of access. It is usually desired to have differing levels of access for users depending on their job role, experience, and so on. Such authorization can also be configured on the device without an AAA server.

Similar to Cisco IOS, ASA also provides 16 levels of access called *privilege levels*. By default, the following three levels are defined on the device:

- **privilege level 0:** Includes the **show checksum, show curpriv, enable, help, show history, login, logout, page, show pager, clear pager, quit,** and **show version** commands. You cannot really access this level because after login the first level accessible is level 1. Hence, the commands defined in this level are available to all users and do not affect the configuration of the device.

- **privilege level 1:**   Normal level on Telnet; includes all user-level commands at the *ASA>* prompt. This level is also known as *User-EXEC mode*. Commands at this level do not affect the configuration of the device.

- **privilege level 15:** Includes all enable-level commands at the *ASA#* prompt. At this level, all commands are available and any configuration can be viewed or changed. This level is also known as *Privileged-EXEC mode*.

When you login to the device, you arrive at privilege level 1. To get to level 15, you have to use the **enable** command and enter the configured enable password. The enable password is configured using the following command in global configuration mode:

```
enable password password
```

As you already know, all commands that can change configuration of the device are available at level 15. Access to this level is not something which you will want to give to everyone. To provide differential access, you will need to reduce the privilege level of a command from 15 to one of the custom levels (2 to 14). For example, if you want **user1** to be able to use the **clock** command, then you will need to reduce the privilege level of the command. After this, **user1** can access the custom level and use the **clock** command. The user will not have access to any other level 15 command.

To enter the custom privilege level, the users will need an enable password for that level. The enable password for a custom level can be configured using the following command:

```
enable password password level privilege-level
```

To enter the custom privilege level, users have to use the following command at level 1:

```
enable level
```

To reduce the privilege level of a command and make it available at a lower privilege level, use the following global configuration command:

```
privilege [show | clear | cmd] level level [mode mode] command command
```

Table 7-1 explains the command syntax for this command. Repeat this command for each command you want to reassign.

Starting with OS version 8.0(2), by default, ASA does not match the privilege level of the command with the privilege level of the user. To enforce this match, use the following command:

```
aaa authorization command LOCAL
```

Table 7-1 *Syntax Description:* **privilege** *Command*

Command Option	Description
show | clear | cmd	These optional keywords let you set the privilege only for the **show, clear,** or configure form of the command. The configure form of the command is typically the form that causes a configuration change. If you do not use one of these keywords, all forms of the command are affected. Example: If you want a user at level 2 to only view the access lists configured on the device, then you will change the privilege level for the **show** form of the **access-list** command. If you want the user to add or delete access lists, then you will change the privilege level for the configure form of the command.
mode *mode*	Configuration mode for the command whose privilege you are reducing. Command example of modes are: **exec:** Privileged EXEC mode **configure:** Global configuration mode **interface:** Interface configuration mode **router:** Routing configuration mode
level *level*	Specifies the privilege level you are configuring for the specified command or commands. The level argument must be a number from 0 to 15.
command	Command whose privilege level you want to reduce.

Previous versions of the OS match the privilege level of the command and the user without additional configuration.

Example 7-1 shows the configuration required to create a custom level where the users have access to the configuration mode and can use any form of the **hostname** and **clock** commands.

Example 7-1 *Custom Level Configuration*

```
ASA(config)#username user1 password tJsDL6po9m1UFs.h encrypted
ASA(config)#enable password y.tvDXf6yFbMTAdD encrypted
ASA(config)#aaa authorization command LOCAL
ASA(config)#privilege level 2 mode exec command configure
ASA(config)#privilege level 2 mode configure command clock
ASA(config)#privilege level 2 mode configure command hostname
```

Lab Scenario #4: Local Authentication and Privilege Levels on ASA

XYZ Inc. is installing a new ASA in a small network. They have basic access restriction in place using login and enable passwords. They want to use a local database now for Telnet and SSH authentication. They also want to configure level 5 on the device, such that users at this level can shutdown interfaces and change interface duplex and speed. Your task is to configure the ASA to support their requirement. In addition to that, **user1** and **user2** with a password of abcd should exist in the local database. The enable password for level 5 should be **limited**.

Lab Setup

This Lab Scenario requires an ASA or PIX running OS 7.x or later. IP connectivity is necessary to test Telnet/SSH.

Lab Solution

Step 1. Add users in the local database:

```
ASA(config)#username user1 password abcd
ASA(config)#username user2 password abcd
```

Step 2. Create an enable password for level 5:

```
ASA(config)#enable password limited level 5
```

Step 3. Change privilege level for the required commands:

```
ASA(config)#privilege level 5 mode exec command configure
ASA(config)#privilege level 5 mode configure command interface
ASA(config)#privilege level 5 mode interface command speed
ASA(config)#privilege level 5 mode interface command duplex
ASA(config)#privilege level 5 mode interface command shutdown
```

Step 4. Enable authentication using local database:

```
ASA(config)#aaa authentication telnet console LOCAL
ASA(config)#aaa authentication ssh console LOCAL
```

Step 5. (For ASA 8.0(2) and later only) Enable command authorization:

```
ASA(config)#aaa authorization command LOCAL
```

Lab Verification

To verify the solution, login to the device and enter level 5 using the **enable 5** command. You should be able to enter the interface configuration mode and execute the **shutdown**, **speed**, and **duplex** commands. You should not be able to execute any other command.

Using AAA

In the previous sections you learned how to use the local database and privilege levels on ASA to secure access to the device. ASA also supports the AAA framework for administrative access. You already know that AAA provides an easy and centralized method of identity management and access control. In this section you will learn to configure ASA to use TACACS+ for authentication, authorization, and accounting of administrative sessions.

Note ASA supports both TACACS+ and RADIUS for administrative AAA but using TACACS+ is highly recommended due to support of command authorization.

Before you can configure authentication using AAA, you need to add the IP address, shared secret key, and optionally the port of the AAA server to be used. On ASA, the AAA servers are added to server groups. These protocol-specific server groups contain one or more servers and are referenced to in the authentication, authorization, and accounting commands.

You can define up to 100 server groups in single mode or four server groups per context in multiple mode on the ASA. Each group can have up to 16 servers in single mode or four servers in multiple mode.

When the ASA needs to contact an AAA server, it tries to contact the first server defined in the group. It will keep moving down the server list until it gets a response. If no response is received from any of the servers in the group, ASA will use the fallback method, if defined. If you do not have a fallback method, then the AAA transaction is deemed failed.

Note As you already know, the fallback method defines what method to use for AAA if the primary method, AAA server group in this case, is not available. The types of fallback methods available depend on the service for which AAA is being configured. Sections relevant to different services discuss available fallback methods throughout the book.

The server group needs to be created before adding a server to it. To create the server group, use the following command:

```
aaa-server group-tag protocol {tacacs+ | radius}
  exit
```

Now you can add servers to this group using the following commands:

```
aaa-server group-tag host [(ifname)] {ip-address | hostname}
  key shared-secret-key
  exit
```

In the preceding command, pay special attention to the *ifname* parameter. This parameter denotes the interface through which the AAA server can be reached. This parameter defaults to the **inside** interface and in some OS versions, ASA will not reference the routing table before sending the AAA request. It will send the request out the interface mentioned in the **aaa-server host** command. You should enter the correct interface name in the **aaa-server host** command to ensure that the ASA can reach the AAA server.

Note   If you use a hostname to define the server, ensure that the device is able to resolve it.

Example 7-2 shows an AAA server added in ASA. Subsequent sections will build on this example.

Example 7-2   *AAA Server Group in ASA*

```
ASA(config)#aaa-server myserver protocol tacacs+
ASA(config-aaa-server-group)#exit
ASA(config)#aaa-server myserver (inside) host 192.168.10.1
ASA(config-aaa-server-host)#key secretkey
```

Now that you have added a server group, you have to consider what happens when the servers in the group are not available. When all the servers in a group fail to respond, the group is considered inactive. If a fallback method is configured in the authentication, authorization, or accounting command, the group will be marked inactive for a default period of 10 minutes. During this period, all requests will use the fallback method.

The method and period used by ASA to mark a server as active again might not be suitable in all environments. To overcome this, ASA allows you to choose between the following two methods of reactivation of servers:

- **Depletion Mode:** This is the default mode used by ASA. In this mode, when a server is unresponsive, it is marked as inactive. It remains inactive until all servers in the group are marked inactive. When this happens, a configurable timer, 10 minutes by default, is started. During this time, the fallback method is used by all requests. At the end of the configured time, all servers in the group are marked active and ASA tries to contact the servers for new requests. If the servers are still unresponsive, the cycle is repeated.

- **Timed Mode:** In this mode, unresponsive servers are marked inactive for a period of 30 seconds. After this period, they are marked active and new requests can be sent to the servers. If the server is still unresponsive, then the 30 second cycle is repeated.

> **Note**   If a fallback method is not configured, ASA continues to retry the servers in the group.

You can configure the reactivation method using the following commands:

```
aaa-server group-tag protocol {tacacs+ | radius}
  reactivation-mode {depletion [deadtime minutes] | timed}
```

The **depletion** and **timed** keywords define the reactivation mode and the optional **deadtime** parameter defines the time to be used for the depletion mode.

Configuring Authentication on ASA Using AAA

After adding AAA servers, you can begin to configure AAA on ASA. In this section you will learn how to configure authentication of all administrative sessions including console, Telnet, SSH, and HTTP.

To enable authentication using AAA, use the following command in global configuration mode:

```
aaa authentication {ssh | telnet | serial | http} console group-tag [LOCAL]
```

The *group-tag* parameter is case sensitive. If you specify the **LOCAL** keyword, ASA will fallback to the local database if the AAA servers in the specified group do not respond.

Before moving to the next section, take some time to understand the complete configuration given in Example 7-3. This example builds up on Example 7-2 to enable authentication of Telnet and SSH using AAA with local database as failover.

Example 7-3   *Authentication Configuration on ASA Using TACACS+*

```
ASA(config)#aaa-server myserver protocol tacacs+
ASA(config-aaa-server-group)#exit
ASA(config)#aaa-server myserver (inside) host 192.168.10.1
ASA(config-aaa-server-host)#key *****
ASA(config-aaa-server-host)#exit
ASA(config)#aaa authentication telnet console myserver LOCAL
ASA(config)#aaa authentication ssh console myserver LOCAL
```

Configuring ACS 4.2 and 5.1 for Authentication

Now that you have configured the device for authentication using TACACS+ or RADIUS, it is time to configure ACS to accept the requests from the device and authenticate users. Configuring ACS for authentication of login services requires the following steps:

Step 1.   Add the device as an AAA client in ACS.

Step 2.   Create a user.

Step 3.   (ACS 5.1 only) Create an access service for the authentication request.

You already know how to add an AAA client, create a user, and access services from Chapter 3 and 4 depending on your ACS version. In case you have forgotten or have skipped the previous chapters, please refer back to them.

Verifying and Troubleshooting Authentication

During initial configuration of AAA, the most common reason of failure is a communication problem between the device and the AAA server. A quick way to verify authentication is to use the following command on the device:

test aaa-server authentication *group-tag* **username** *username* **password** *password*

If the user is successfully authenticated then the communication between the device and the AAA server is working properly. If not, check the following:

- The hostname or IP address of the AAA server is correctly added in the device. If you are using hostname then make sure it can be resolved by the device.

- Verify IP communication between the device and the AAA server using ping.

- Ensure that the device can reach the AAA server on TACACS+ or RADIUS ports. A firewall or access list might be blocking these ports.

- Ensure that shared secret key is the same on both the device and the server. In case of TACACS+, a mismatch of the secret key will be obvious in the AAA server logs; however, in the case of RADIUS, the AAA server will report an authentication failure due to a user password mismatch.

- In the case of ACS 5.1, ensure that an access service is properly configured to authenticate the request.

When troubleshooting authentication, the following debugs are most useful:

- **debug aaa authentication**
- **debug {tacacs | radius all}**

The debugs will help pinpoint the problem area. Example 7-4 shows the debug seen when authentication fails due to key mismatch and Example 7-5 shows the debugs seen when the AAA server is unreachable.

Example 7-4   debug aaa authentication *and* debug tacacs: *Key Mismatch*

```
ASA#debug tacacs
ASA#debug aaa authentication
mk_pkt - type: 0x1, session_id: 413
 user: test
 Tacacs packet sent
```

```
Sending TACACS Start message. Session id: 413, seq no:1
Received TACACS packet. Session id:1160274910   seq no:2
tacp_procpkt_authen: ERROR
TACACS Session finished. Session id: 413, seq no: 1
```

Example 7-5   debug aaa authentication *and* debug tacacs: *Server Unreachable*

```
ASA#debug tacacs
ASA#debug aaa authentication
mk_pkt - type: 0x1, session_id: 419
 user: test
 Tacacs packet sent
Sending TACACS Start message. Session id: 419, seq no:1
TACACS Request Timed out. Session id: 419, seq no:1
TACACS Session finished. Session id: 419, seq no: 1
```

If the device is able to reach the AAA server, then the logs on the server will be more useful than debugs to troubleshoot the problem. ACS logs are covered in detail in Chapter 3 and 4.

Authorization of Administrative Sessions

In the previous section, you learned how to authenticate administrative sessions using TACACS+. Such configuration does not check whether a valid user should have access to the shell. For optimum security, you should have explicit control over who can access the shell of the device. Authorization of administrative sessions, or EXEC authorization as it is commonly called, forces the device to check for explicit shell access permission in a user profile.

To enable EXEC authorization, use the following command in the global configuration mode:

```
aaa authorization exec authentication-server
```

Configuring ACS 4.2 and 5.1 for EXEC Authorization

The steps to configure ACS 4.2 and 5.1 for EXEC authorization of sessions on ASA and IOS are same. These steps are covered in Chapter 6 under the section "Configuring ACS 4.2 and 5.1 for EXEC Authorization."

One exception for ASA is that it does not support any attributes except the *default privilege level* attribute. Even the support for the default privilege level attribute is different on ASA. This attribute affects only the privilege level of the user on Adaptive Security Device Manager (ASDM). The ASA will put the user in level 1 in the CLI irrespective of the value of this attribute.

Verifying and Troubleshooting EXEC Authorization

If authentication using TACACS+ is working then authorization usually works well also. Most problems with authorization are due to absence of required attributes or incorrect attributes or values. If authorization fails, check the following:

- User or group in ACS 4.2 and access service in ACS 5.1 has Shell (EXEC) privilege
- Attribute values are correctly configured

The following debugs are useful is troubleshooting authorization:

- **debug aaa authorization**
- **debug tacacs**

Example 7-6 shows debugs from a successful authorization request.

Example 7-6 *EXEC Authorization debugs on ASA*

```
ASA#debug tacacs
ASA#debug aaa authorization
mk_pkt - type: 0x2, session_id: 641
mkpkt - authorize user: vivek
 Tacacs packet sent
Sending TACACS Authorization message. Session id: 641, seq no:1
Received TACACS packet. Session id:1834132148  seq no:2
tacp_procpkt_author: PASS_ADD

tacp_procpkt_author: PASS_REPL

Attributes = priv-lvl

TACACS Session finished. Session id: 641, seq no: 1
```

Command Authorization

Like Cisco IOS, ASA also supports authorization of commands entered by the user. Once command authorization is enabled, the device will send each command to the TACACS+ server for authorization. If authorization is successful, the command will be executed. If the authorization fails, the user will see a failure message and the command will not be executed.

To do this, you will need to configure command authorization on ASA and apply shell command authorization sets on the user or group profile in ACS.

Before configuring command authorization, you should have session authentication working on the device with TACACS+. In addition to that, you have to configure ASA to authenticate the enable password using TACACS+ instead of the local enable password. To do this, use the following command in global configuration mode:

```
aaa authentication enable console group-tag [LOCAL]
```

Note   When ASA is configured to authenticate the enable password from the TACACS+ server, the enable password for every user will be different. The enable password of the user is configured in the User Profile in ACS and it can be configured to be the same as the login password of the user. In addition to configuring the enable password on the user profile, on ACS 4.2 you need to set the Maximum Enable Privilege for the user to 15 for enable authentication to work. The Maximum Enable Privilege option can be found in the User Setup Page under Advanced TACACS+ Settings section.

To enable command authorization, use the following command in the global configuration mode:

```
aaa authorization command group-tag [LOCAL]
```

Note   When enable authentication and command authorization are enabled, they affect the console session also. Ensure that console sessions are authenticated using TACACS+ also; otherwise, the console user will not be able to login to the privilege mode or execute any command. You should also use the LOCAL database as a fall back method for command authorization to prevent a lock out situation if the TACACS+ server is not reachable.

Example 7-7 builds up on Example 7-3 to add enable authentication and command authorization.

Example 7-7   *Command Authorization Configuration on ASA*

```
ASA(config)#aaa-server myserver protocol tacacs+
ASA(config-aaa-server-group)#exit
ASA(config)#aaa-server myserver (inside) host 192.168.10.1
ASA(config-aaa-server-host)#key *****
ASA(config)#aaa authentication telnet console myserver LOCAL
ASA(config)#aaa authentication ssh console myserver LOCAL
ASA(config)#aaa authentication enable console myserver LOCAL
ASA(config)#aaa authorization command myserver LOCAL
```

Configuring ACS 4.2 and 5.1 for Command Authorization

The steps to configure ACS 4.2 and 5.1 for command authorization of sessions on ASA and IOS are identical and you can find coverage of this process in Chapter 6 under the section "Configuring ACS 4.2 and 5.1 for Command Authorization."

Verifying and Troubleshooting Command Authorization

If authentication using TACACS+ is working, then command authorization usually works well also. Most problems with authorization are due to incorrect configuration. Check the following if command authorization is not working as desired:

- User or group in ACS 4.2 and access service in ACS 5.1 have the correct command set applied.

- Commands in the set should match the case and format used by the device in the authorization request. If you are unsure of how the command is sent by the device, take a look at the debugs or failure logs on ACS. Sometimes devices will omit special characters such as slash (/).

- Command authorization often causes problem with ASDM sessions. This is because ASDM issues a series of commands when it starts up and they are not present in the command set. Take a look at ACS failure logs to see the commands that need to be permitted for ASDM to work properly.

The following debugs are useful is troubleshooting authorization:

- **debug aaa authorization**

- **debug tacacs**

Example 7-8 shows the debugs from a successful command authorization request.

Example 7-8 debug aaa authorization *and* debug tacacs: *Command Authorization*

```
ASA#debug aaa authorization
ASA#debug tacacs
mk_pkt - type: 0x2, session_id: 683
mkpkt - authorize user: vivek
cmd=configure
cmd-arg=terminal  Tacacs packet sent
 Sending TACACS Authorization message. Session id: 683, seq no:1
 Received TACACS packet. Session id:281835371  seq no:2
tacp_procpkt_author: PASS_ADD
tacp_procpkt_author: PASS_REPL
 TACACS Session finished. Session id: 683, seq no: 1
```

Accounting of Administrative Sessions and Commands

ASA provides accounting feature to help monitor administrative sessions and commands entered in a session.

To enable accounting for administrative sessions, use the following command in the global configuration mode:

```
aaa accounting {telnet | ssh | serial} console group-tag
```

To enable accounting for commands entered in a sessions, use the following command in the global configuration mode:

aaa accounting command [**privilege** *level*] *group-tag*

You can use the optional **privilege** *level* parameter to specify the level for which you want to enable command accounting. The command can be repeated to configure accounting for multiple levels.

Example 7-9 builds on Example 7-7 to enable accounting for Telnet and SSH sessions and all commands entered in an administrative session.

Example 7-9   *Accounting Configuration on ASA*

```
ASA(config)#aaa-server myserver protocol tacacs+
ASA(config-aaa-server-group)#exit
ASA(config)#aaa-server myserver (inside) host 192.168.10.1
ASA(config-aaa-server-host)#key *****
ASA(config-aaa-server-host)#exit
ASA(config)#aaa authentication telnet console myserver LOCAL
ASA(config)#aaa authentication ssh console myserver LOCAL
ASA(config)#aaa authentication enable console myserver LOCAL
ASA(config)#aaa authorization command myserver LOCAL
ASA(config)#aaa accounting telnet console myserver
ASA(config)#aaa accounting ssh console myserver
ASA(config)#aaa accounting command myserver
```

There is no configuration required on ACS to accept accounting, if the device is added as an AAA client.

You can see the EXEC accounting logs in ACS 4.2 under **Reports and Activity > TACACS+ Accounting** and command accounting logs under **Reports and Activity > TACACS+ Administration.**

In ACS 5.1 you can see both the EXEC and command accountings logs under **AAA Protocol > TACACS+ Accounting.**

Lab Scenario #5: Authentication, Authorization and Accounting of Administrative Sessions on ASA using TACACS+

XYZ Inc. has purchased Cisco ACS and they want to use TACACS+ to authenticate all administrative session on their ASA. In addition to that, they want to ensure that users belonging to the **Admins** can execute all commands except **shutdown.** They also want that all sessions and commands should be logged in ACS using TACACS+.

Your task is to configure the ASA and ACS to meet all of these requirements. XYZ Inc. does not use ASDM so you can ignore HTTP sessions for this task.

The IP address of the ASA is 192.168.1.1 and the IP address of ACS is 192.168.1.10.

Lab Setup

You require a simple setup connecting an ASA to your ACS. The ASA should have IP connectivity to ACS.

Before starting the lab, add the ASA in ACS as an AAA client. If you are using ACS 4.2, then rename a group to **Admins**. If you are using ACS 5.1, then create an Identity Group named **Admins**. You can use the **Default Device Admin** access service for this lab. You also need to create an Authorization Policy in the access service which matches the **Admins** Identity Group.

You should also have the following configuration on the ASA before starting the lab:

```
telnet 0 0 inside
ssh 0 0 inside
```

Lab Solution

Step 1. Configure the device for authentication, authorization and accounting:

```
ASA(config)#aaa-server ACS protocol tacacs+

ASA(config)#aaa-server ACS (inside) host 192.168.1.10

ASA(config-aaa-server-host)#key mykey

ASA(config-aaa-server-host)#exit

ASA(config)#aaa authentication telnet console ACS LOCAL

ASA(config)#aaa authentication ssh console ACS LOCAL

ASA(config)#aaa authentication serial console ACS LOCAL

ASA(config)#aaa authentication enable console ACS LOCAL

ASA(config)#aaa authorization command ACS LOCAL

ASA(config)#aaa accounting telnet console ACS

ASA(config)#aaa accounting ssh console ACS

ASA(config)#aaa accounting serial console ACS

ASA(config)#aaa accounting command ACS
```

Step 2. Create a command set in ACS which denies the command **shutdown** with all arguments and permits all other commands.

Step 3.   (ACS 4.2 only) Apply the command set to ACS 4.2 group called **Admins** and select **Shell (exec)** under TACACS+ Settings. Click **Submit + Restart**

Step 4.   (ACS 5.1 only) Apply the default **Permit** shell profile and the command set to the authorization policy created at the start of the lab.

Lab Verification

To verify the solution, create a user in the **Admins** group and initiate a Telnet or SSH to the ASA. Authenticate using the user from the **Admins** group. You will notice that the user is able to execute any command except the **shutdown** command in the interface configuration mode.

Summary

In this chapter you learned the basics of AAA configuration on ASA and PIX running OS version 7.0 and later. Understanding these basic steps is crucial to implementing advanced AAA discussed later in this book. Along with the configuration, this chapter also discussed troubleshooting steps for AAA on ASA/PIX. Most of these troubleshooting techniques will be used later in the book as well.

Chapter 8

IOS Switches

This chapter covers the following subjects:

- 802.1X, Extensible Authentication Protocol (EAP) and EAP over LANs (EAPOL)

- Different Types of EAP Available

- Configuration Examples Based on Some EAP Types Available for ACS 4.2 and ACS 5.1

This chapter examines the 802.1X standard and the components involved in it that can be used to secure the LAN or wireless LAN (WLAN) infrastructure. The chapter essentially examines Layer 2 security and how Access Control Server (ACS) will help secure the LAN and WLAN infrastructure. This chapter focuses on LAN infrastructure, as Chapter 9, "Access Points," focuses on the WLAN infrastructure.

Introduction to 802.1X, EAP, and EAPOL

802.1X is an IEEE standard for media-level access control, offering the capability to permit or deny network connectivity, control VLAN access, and apply traffic policy, based on user or machine identity. The basic idea behind the standard is to authenticate and authorize before a user can connect to the physical or logical port of a Layer 2 device in order to gain access to VLAN or WLAN infrastructure.

The IEEE 802.1X restricts unauthorized clients from connecting to the LAN or WLAN infrastructure by using a client and server-based access control and authentication protocol.

The 802.1X standard defines three main entities that take part in the access control method set up in this standard:

- **Client or Supplicant:** The device that needs access or requests access to the LAN/WLAN infrastructure or Layer 2 device services. The device must be running 802.1X-compliant client software so that it can respond to requests from a Layer 2 device.

- **Authenticator:** The device responsible for relaying information between the authentication server and the supplicant. The authenticator is a Layer 2 device that acts as an intermediary or proxy between the client and the authentication server, by requesting identity information from the client, verifying that information with the authentication server, and replaying the response returned by the authentication server to the client or supplicant.

■ **Authentication Server:** The device responsible for performing actual authentication and authorization on behalf of the authenticator. The authentication server validates the identity of the client or supplicant and notifies the Layer 2 device acting as authenticator, which relays information to the client. For the purposes of this chapter, the authentication server would be Cisco Secure ACS and the protocol would be RADIUS.

Figure 8-1 provides an overview based on the different roles.

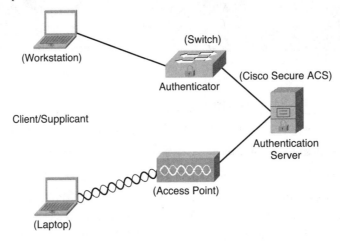

Figure 8-1   *802.1X Device Roles*

Figure 8-2 provides a more generic overview of the 802.1X architecture.

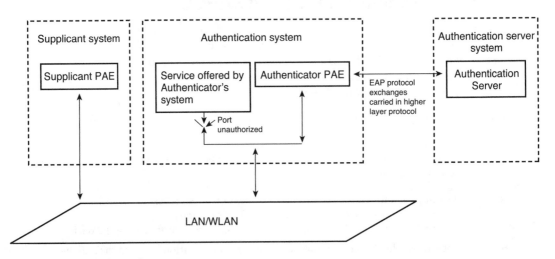

Figure 8-2   *802.1X Architecture*

The port access entity (PAE) specified in Figure 8-2 refers to the entity on a given device that performs the 802.1X algorithm and protocol operation.

Now that you have a general overview of 802.1X, the text that follows delves into this standard a little deeper and examines and how it works.

Extensible Authentication Protocol (EAP) is the key protocol used to pass the authentication information between the supplicant and the authentication server.

IEEE 802.1X defines encapsulation of EAP over IEEE 802 and is known as EAP over LANs (EAPOL). EAPOL was originally designed for Ethernet but was extended to suit other technologies such as wireless and Fiber Distribution Data Interface (FDDI).

EAP is an authentication framework, not a specific authentication mechanism. It provides some common functions and negotiation of authentication methods called *EAP methods*. EAP methods support different authentication types, such as token cards, one-time passwords, certificates, and public key authentication.

The sections that follow look at EAP and EAPOL so that you understand them better before proceeding any further.

EAP

EAP is an authentication framework that supports multiple authentication methods. Basically, EAP allows two entities to exchange information that is specific to the authentication method these entities want to use. The content of these authentication specific methods is not defined in EAP.

This is one of the advantages offered by the EAP architecture—its flexibility. The authenticator need not be updated to support different or new authentication methods—only the client/supplicant and the authentication server can implement some of or all the authentication methods.

Today, there are many authentication methods or EAP authentication methods available, some of which are defined in the IETF RFCs (EAP-MD5, EAP-OTP, EAP-GTC, EAP-TLS, and more) and some of which are vendor-specific methods (PEAP, LEAP, EAP-TTLS).

EAP specifies that four types of messages can be sent:

- **Request(0x01):** Used to send messages from the authenticator to the supplicant
- **Response(0x02):** Used to send messages from the supplicant to the authenticator
- **Success(0x03):** Sent by the authenticator to indicate access is granted
- **Failure(0x04):** Sent by the authenticator to indicate access is refused

Figure 8-3 illustrates the EAP message format and the list that follows describes each of the fields.

- **Code:** The one-byte Code field indicates the type of message (Request, Response, Success or Failure).

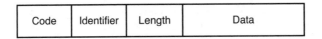

Figure 8-3 *EAP Message Format*

- **Identifier:** The one-byte Identifier field contains an unsigned integer used to match requests with responses. Each new request uses a new identifier number.

- **Length:** The two-byte Length field indicates the total number of bytes in the entire packet.

- **Data:** The value of the variable-length (including zero byte) Data field defines the way the Data field is to be interpreted.

The EAP message format shown in Figure 8-3 is used to send

- EAP Request
- EAP Response
- EAP Success
- EAP Failure

For the EAP Request and EAP Response, one more field is introduced: the *Type* field, as illustrated in Figure 8-4. The one-byte Type field defines the type of request or response. Only one Type is used in each packet and the response Type matches the request.

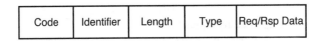

Figure 8-4 *EAP Request/Response Message*

For EAP Success and EAP Failure, the Data field is of zero bytes in length. The rest of the structure remains the same as shown previously in Figure 8-3.

As previously stated, the EAP Request and EAP Response messages are subdivided using the EAP Type field. Some common EAP types are as follows:

- Identity (1)
- Notification (2)
- NAK (3)
- MD5-Challenge (4)
- One-Time Password (OTP) (5)
- Generic Token Card (6)
- EAP-TLS (13)

- LEAP (17)
- EAP-TTLS (21)
- PEAP (25)
- EAP-FAST (43)

The most important predefined *Type* is *Identity* (Type = 1) because this is used as a part of the EAP introduction phase:

- **EAP-Request/Identity (Code = 1, Type = 1):** Sent by authenticator to a new supplicant.
- **EAP-Response/Identity (Code = 2, Type = 1):**   In response to EAP-Request/Identity, supplicant replies with this message containing its username or some other identifier that will be understood by the authentication server.

For details on other EAP types, please refer to the EAP RFC (RFC 2284). For other EAP types or methods, you need to refer to individual RFCs or drafts.

The section that follows looks at EAPOL to continue the discussion on 802.1X.

EAPOL

The EAP RFC does not specify how messages should be communicated. So, to communicate EAP messages, you need to find a way to *encapsulate* them. To solve this puzzle, IEEE 802.1X defined a protocol called EAP over LAN (EAPOL) to get EAP messages to be communicated between the supplicant and the authenticator. EAPOL was originally designed for Ethernet but was extended to suit other technologies.

Figure 8-5 illustrates the frame format for EAPOL frames.

Ethernet MAC Header	Protocol Version	Packet Type	Packet Body Length	Packet Body

Figure 8-5   *EAPOL Frame Format*

The five types of EAPOL messages are as follows:

- **EAPOL-Packet (0):** Contains an encapsulated EAP frame. This is what the majority of EAPOL frames are.
- **EAPOL-Start (1):** A supplicant can send an EAPOL-Start frame instead of waiting for a challenge from the authenticator (EAPOL-Packet [EAP-Identity/Request]).
- **EAPOL-Logoff (2):** Used to return the state of the port to unauthorized when the supplicant has finished using the network.
- **EAPOL-Key (3):** Used to exchange cryptographic keying information.

■   **EAPOL-Encapsulated-ASF-Alert (4):** Provided as a method of allowing Alerting Standards Forum (ASF) alerts to be forwarded through a port that is in the unauthorized state.

Message Exchange in 802.1X

Now you know what EAP and EAPOL are, it's time to return to the general discussion of 802.1X. As discussed previously, there are three entities in 802.1X: supplicant, authenticator, and authentication server. Messages are exchanged among these three entities. 802.1X uses EAP, or more specifically EAPOL, to pass these messages between supplicant and authenticator and between authenticator and authentication server using RADIUS by encapsulating EAP in RADIUS, sometimes referred to as *EAP over RADIUS*.

Figure 8-6 illustrates a typical EAPOL/802.1X exchange.

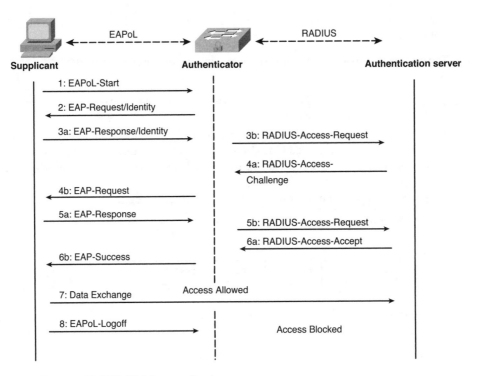

Figure 8-6   *EAPOL/802.1X Message Exchange*

The operation process in 802.1X is as follows:

Step 1.   Generally, the authenticator sends the first EAP-Request message of the identity type to the supplicant to ask for the supplicant's identity. The supplicant can also start this process if it so desires by sending EAPOL-Start.

Step 2.   If the supplicant sends EAPOL-Start, the authenticator requests the supplicant's identity by sending EAP-Request/Identity.

Step 3. In response, the client sends its information in EAP-Response/Identity frame. The supplicant decapsulates the information from the EAPOL frame and passes over the EAP information in it to the authentication server using the RADIUS protocol as RADIUS-Access-Request.

Step 4. The RADIUS server negotiates with the supplicant by sending RADIUS-Access-Challenge to the authenticator, which encapsulates the EAP information in an EAPOL frame and passes it over to the supplicant as EAP-Request.

Step 5. In response to EAP-Request, the supplicant sends back EAP-Response over to the authenticator, that again decapsulates the EAP information and sends it to the authentication server using RADIUS-Access-Request.

Step 6. There are several exchanges of EAP-Response/RADIUS-Access-Request and RADIUS-Access-Challenge/EAP-Request before finally the RADIUS server sends RADIUS-Access-Accept, which signifies that user was authenticated. When this response is received by the authenticator, the authenticator decapsulates the EAP information and sends it to the supplicant as EAP-Success. At this point, the port is authorized and the supplicant is allowed to communicate.

Step 7. At this stage, the supplicant can proceed with data exchange.

Step 8. After data exchange has finished and the supplicant leaves the access port, it sends EAPOL-Logoff to the authenticator to let it know that it has left the port and it can now be brought back to the blocked or unauthorized state.

EAP Types

The previous section explained that the EAP-Request/Response identity frame has a field called Type. This field has various values that also help in deciding what EAP authentication method to use after it is negotiated between the supplicant and the authentication server.

A few of the different EAP authentication types available are as follows:

- **EAP-MD5:** EAP-MD5 (Message Digest) Challenge is an EAP authentication type defined in RFC 3748. It offers minimal security. It is typically not recommended because it might allow the user's password to be compromised because the MD5 hash function is vulnerable to dictionary attacks. In this EAP authentication type, there is only one-way authentication; there is no mutual authentication between EAP peer and EAP server. Because it provides authentication only of the EAP peer to the EAP server and does not provide EAP server authentication, this EAP authentication method is also vulnerable to man-in-the-middle attacks.

- **LEAP:** Lightweight Extensible Authentication Protocol (LEAP) is a proprietary EAP authentication type developed by Cisco Systems. This is primarily used in Cisco WLANs. This protocol was distributed through the Cisco Certified Extensions (CCX) as part of getting 802.1X and dynamic Wired Equivalent Privacy (WEP) adoption, in the absence of a security standard in industry. LEAP encrypts data transmissions using dynamically generated WEP keys. It also supports mutual authentication. Although LEAP supports mutual authentication, user credentials can still be easily compromised. Recommended practice dictates that if you must use LEAP, this should be done only with sufficiently complex passwords.

■ **PEAP:** Protected Extensible Authentication Protocol (PEAP) is jointly developed by Cisco Systems, Microsoft, and RSA Security. This EAP authentication method allows for secure transport of authentication data, thus providing very good security. This is accomplished by creating a tunnel between PEAP clients and an authentication server. In PEAP, only a server-side public key infrastructure (PKI) certificate is required to create a secure Transport Layer Security (TLS) tunnel to protect user authentication. The requirement to have only a server-side certificate simplifies the implementation and administration of secure LAN/WLAN.

There are two certified PEAP subtypes available:

■ PEAPv0/EAP-MSCHAPv2

■ PEAPv1/EAP-GTC

Note   The terms PEAPv0 and PEAPv1 refer to the outer authentication method—the mechanism that creates the secure TLS tunnel to protect subsequent authentication transactions. EAP-MSCHAPv2 and EAP-GTC refer to the inner authentication method, which facilitates user or device authentication.

■ **EAP-TLS:** EAP-TLS (Transport Layer Security) is defined in RFC 5216. The security offered by the TLS protocol is strong because it provides certificate-based and mutual authentication. It uses PKI to secure communication to an authentication server. As opposed to PEAP, EAP-TLS has more administrative overhead because it requires client-side certificates along with a server-side certificate to perform authentication. The reason EAP-TLS is considered one of the most secure EAP authentication types is that even if a password is compromised, it is not enough to break into EAP-TLS–enabled systems because the hacker still needs to have the client-side private key. Security provided by EAP-TLS can be made more secure if you introduce smart cards because in smart cards the client-side keys are housed on the card itself. In the event of the theft of a smart card, it is much more likely to be noticed than password theft, which makes recognizing the potential for a security break much easier to mitigate by simply revoking the smart card.

■ **EAP-FAST:** EAP-FAST (Flexible Authentication via Secure Tunneling) is defined in RFC 4851 and was developed by Cisco Systems. The protocol was designed to address the weaknesses of LEAP while preserving the lightweight implementation. Instead of using a certificate, mutual authentication is achieved by means of a Protected Access Credential (PAC). A PAC file is issued on a per-user basis, which can be managed dynamically by the authentication server. EAP-FAST uses PAC to establish a TLS tunnel in which client credentials are verified. The PAC can be provisioned to the client either manually or automatically. Manual provisioning is delivered to the client via disk or a secured network distribution method. Automatic provisioning is an in-band distribution.

EAP-FAST has three phases:

- **Phase 0:** An optional phase in which the PAC can be provisioned manually or dynamically.

- **Phase 1:** In this phase, the client and the authentication server uses the PAC to establish TLS tunnel.

- **Phase 2:** In this phase, the client credentials are exchanged inside the encrypted tunnel.

EAP-FAST can also be used without PAC files using certificate-based mutual authentication as in TLS.

Tip When automatic PAC provisioning is enabled, EAP-FAST has a slight vulnerability in that an attacker can intercept the PAC and subsequently use it to compromise user credentials. This vulnerability is mitigated by manual PAC provisioning or by using server certificates for the PAC provisioning phase (Phase 0).

PEAPv0/EAP-MSCHAPv2

PEAPv0/EAP-MSCHAPv2 is commonly known as "PEAP." After EAP-TLS, PEAPv0/EAP-MSCHAPv2 is the second most widely supported EAP standard in the world. PEAPv0/EAP-MSCHAPv2 is natively supported in many operating systems. This version of PEAP was defined in Internet draft "draft-kamath-pppext-peapv0."

The support for inner EAP methods in PEAPv0 varies from vendor to vendor. Other known forms of PEAPv0 are PEAPv0/EAP-SIM and PEAPv0/EAP-TLS (PEAP-EAP-TLS).

PEAP-EAP-TLS require a client-side digital certificate located on the client's hard drive or a smart card. PEAP-EAP-TLS is very similar in operation to EAP-TLS, but provides slightly more protection due to the fact that portions of the client certificate that are unencrypted in EAP-TLS are encrypted in PEAP-EAP-TLS.

PEAPv1/EAP-GTC

PEAPv1/EAP-GTC was created by Cisco as an alternative to PEAPv0/EAP-MSCHAPv2. It allows the use of an inner authentication protocol other than Microsoft's MSCHAPv2.

EAP-GTC (Generic Token Card) is defined in RFC 3748. It carries a text challenge from the authentication server, and a reply that is assumed to be generated by a security token.

This version of PEAP is defined in the IETF internet draft "draft-josefsson-pppext-eap-tls-eap-10."

Note To use PEAPv0/EAP-MSCHAPv2 or PEAPv0/EAP-GTC, you must ensure that both client and server support it.

Table 8-1 *Comparison of EAP Authentication Types*

	Message Digest 5 (MD5)	Lightweight Extensible Authentication Protocol (LEAP)	Protected Extensible Authentication Protocol (PEAP)	Flexible Authentication via Secure Tunneling (FAST)	Transport Level Security (TLS)
Authentication Attributes	One way	Mutual	Mutual	Mutual	Mutual
Client side certificate required	No	No	No	No (PAC)	Yes
Server side certificate required	No	No	Yes	No (PAC)	Yes
Deployment difficulty	Easy	Moderate	Moderate	Moderate	Difficult (Client certificate deployment required)
Security	Poor	High (Only with strong passwords)	High	High	Very High

EAP Authentication Type Summary

Table 8-1 summarizes the key features of the various EAP authentication types described up to this point in the chapter.

What you have learned so far is very generic, vendor-neutral 802.1X learning. The rest of the chapter focuses on Cisco switch-based 802.1X configuration.

802.1X Configuration on a Cisco Switch

To enable 802.1X port-based authentication, you need to perform following tasks:

Note Earlier 802.1X commands on Cisco IOS are being replaced by authentication manager commands, but they provide the same functionality as earlier 802.1X commands. The authentication manager commands were introduced in Cisco IOS Software Release 12.2(50)SE & 12.2(50)SG as you will find here:

http://www.cisco.com/en/US/docs/switches/lan/catalyst3750/software/release/12.2_50_se/configuration/guide/sw8021x.html#wp1430322.

Step 1. Enable AAA on the switch:

```
Device(config)# aaa new-model
```

Step 2.   Configure the switch for RADIUS server communication:

```
Device(config)# radius-server host {hostname| ip_address}
Device(config)# radius-server key string
```

Step 3.   Create an 802.1X port-based authentication and authorization method list:

```
Device(config)# aaa authentication dot1x default method1 [method2...]
Device(config)# aaa authorization network default method1 [method2...
```

Step 4.   Globally enable 802.1X port-based authentication:

```
Device(config)# dot1x system-auth-control
```

Step 5.   Enter the interface configuration mode for the specific interface:

```
Device(config)# interface type slot/port
```

Step 6.   Set the port to access mode:

```
Device(config-if)# switchport mode access
```

Step 7.   Enable port-based authentications on the interface:

New commands:

```
Device(config-if)# authentication port-control auto
Device(config-if)# dot1x pae authenticator
```

Old command:

```
Device(config-if)# dot1x port-control auto
```

Example 8-1 shows the full basic 802.1X configuration on a Cisco IOS switch.

Example 8-1   *Basic 802.1X Configuration on a Cisco IOS Switch*

```
Router(config)# aaa new-model
!
Router(config)# radius-server host 172.120.39.46
Router(config)# radius-server key cisco
!
Router(config)# aaa authentication dot1x default group radius
Router(config)# aaa authorization network default group radius
!
Router(config)# dot1x system-auth-control
!
Router(config)# interface fastethernet 5/1
Router(config-if)# authentication port-control auto
Router(config-if)# dot1x pae authenticator
Router(config-if)# end
```

Note   The 802.1X protocol is supported on Layer 2 static-access ports, voice VLAN ports, and Layer 3 routed ports, but it is not supported on trunk port, dynamic ports, dynamic access ports, EtherChannel ports, Switch Port Analyzer (SPAN) or Remote SPAN (RSPAN) destination ports.

Note   When 802.1X is enabled on a switchport, until a supplicant is authenticated, the switchport remains in the unauthorized state. In this unauthorized state, only EAPOL traffic is allowed to pass and all other traffic is dropped. On Cisco switches along with EAPOL, CDP/LDP is also allowed.

802.1X Host Modes

Host mode on an 802.1X-enabled port decides whether to allow only one client to authenticate (which is there by default) or to allow multiple clients or some other special condition.

There are four host modes available and one mode that are applied with all other four modes.

The four host modes are as follows:

■   Single-host mode

■   Multiple-host mode

■   Multidomain authentication mode

■   Multiauthentication mode

Pre-authentication open access is the mode that is applied with the other four modes. The sections that follow describe these modes in more detail and how to configure them.

Single-Host Mode

In this mode, only one client can be connected to an 802.1X-enabled port. The commands to configure this mode are as follows.

Note   Earlier 802.1X commands on Cisco IOS are being replaced by authentication manager commands, but they provide the same functionality as earlier 802.1X commands. The authentication manager commands were introduced in Cisco IOS Software Release 12.2(50)SE & 12.2(50)SG, the information for which you can find here:

http://www.cisco.com/en/US/docs/switches/lan/catalyst3750/software/release/12.2_50_se/configuration/guide/sw8021x.html#wp1430322.

For Cisco IOS switches, the new command to configure this mode is as follows:

```
Router(config-if)# authentication host-mode single-host
```

For Cisco IOS switches, the old command to configure this mode is as follows:

```
Router(config-if)# dot1x host-mode single-host
```

Multiple-Host Mode

In this mode you can attach multiple clients to the 802.1X-enabled port. The feature of this mode is that only one client must be authorized for all clients to grant network access. The commands to configure this mode are as follows.

For Cisco IOS switches, the new command to configure this mode is as follows:

```
Router(config-if)# authentication host-mode multi-host
```

For Cisco IOS switches, the old command to configure this mode is as follows:

```
Router(config-if)# dot1x host-mode multi-host
```

Multidomain Authentication Mode

In this mode, also known as Multidomain Authentication (MDA) mode, an IP Phone and a single host behind the IP Phone are authenticated independently, even though both the IP Phone and host machine are connected to a single switch port on the switch. *Multidomain* in this mode refers to two domains:

- Data domain
- Voice domain

Only two MAC addresses are allowed on a port where MDA is enabled. The switch can place the client machine in a data VLAN and the IP Phone in a voice VLAN, even though they appear on the same switch port. The commands to configure this mode are as follows.

For Cisco IOS switches, the command to configure this mode is as follows:

```
Router(config-if)# authentication host-mode multi-domain
```

Note   To authorize a voice device, the AAA server must be configured to send a Cisco Attribute-Value (AV) pair attribute with a value of device-traffic-class=voice. Without this value, the switch treats the voice device as a data device.

Multiauthentication Mode

Also known as *multiauth mode*, this mode allows for one 802.1X client on a voice VLAN and multiple authenticated 802.1X clients on a data VLAN. In multiauth mode, each client connected needs to be authenticated individually; this is the main difference between multiple-host mode and multiauth mode.

For Cisco IOS switches, the command to configure this mode is as follows:

```
Router(config-if)# authentication host-mode multi-auth
```

Note   When a switchport is in multiauth mode, VLAN assignment through a RADIUS server, guest VLAN and authentication fail, and VLAN features do not activate.

Pre-Authentication Open Access

The pre-authentication open access mode, which can be used with the four host modes, allows a device to gain network access before authentication. This is useful to test 802.1X functionality; it is like a pilot feature that is turned off after the administrator is comfortable with the 802.1X deployment. Whenever this is applied on a switchport, it is always recommended that you should use static ACLs to restrict Layer 3 traffic. Pre-authentication open access can be configured additionally with any of the four host modes.

To configure pre-authentication open access on Cisco IOS switches, use the following command:

```
Router(config-if)# authentication open
```

Note   Please refer to prerequisites and expected behavior for a platform/Cisco IOS version for 802.1X host modes. The operation might differ by platform/version.

802.1X Authentication Features

The authentication features available on Cisco IOS with 802.1X are as follows:

- Guest VLAN

- Restricted VLAN

- Inaccessible Authentication Bypass

- VLAN Assignment
- MAC Authentication Bypass

- ACL Assignment and Redirect URLs

And many more. To get detail on which feature does what, and how already existing feature co-exists with 802.1X, please refer to the 802.1X section in the configuration guide of the respective switch platform and IOS/Catalyst OS.

We will look at few features in this section. Namely, Guest VLAN, Restricted VLAN, MAC Authentication Bypass, and VLAN Assignment.

Guest VLAN

To provide limited services to non-802.1X-compliant clients, you can make use of the guest VLAN feature. When you enable guest VLAN on an 802.1X port, the switch assigns clients to a guest VLAN when the switch does not receive a response to its EAP request/identity frame or when EAPOL packets are not sent by the client and no fallback authentication methods are enabled.

By default, the switch maintains the EAPOL packet history. If an EAPOL packet is detected on the interface during the lifetime of the link, the switch determines that the device connected to that interface is an 802.1X-capable supplicant, and the interface will not change to the guest VLAN state. The EAPOL packet history is cleared if the interface link status goes down.

If you want the interface to change to the guest VLAN state for a non-802.1X-capable client, regardless of the EAPOL packet history, use the following global configuration command:

```
Switch(config)# dot1x guest-vlan supplicant
```

To configure a guest VLAN, the new command on a Cisco IOS switch is as follows:

```
Router(config-if)# authentication event no-response action authorize vlan vlan-id
```

To configure a guest VLAN, the old command on a Cisco IOS switch is as follows:

```
Router(config-if)# dot1x guest-vlan vlan-id
```

Restricted/Authentication Failed VLAN

If you want to provide limited service to clients who fail authentication, you can configure a restricted VLAN or an authentication failed VLAN. One thing that you need to note is that these clients are 802.1X compliant, so they cannot be assigned to the guest VLAN.

You can configure a port to be in a restricted VLAN after a specified number of failed authentication attempts. The switch counts the failed authentication attempts, with the failed attempt count incrementing when the RADIUS server replies with an Access-Reject EAP failure or an empty response without an EAP packet. When this count exceeds the configured maximum number of authentication attempts, the port is assigned to the restricted VLAN. After a port is moved to the restricted VLAN, the failed attempt counter for the port is reset and EAPOL-Start messages from the client are ignored.

Note   You can configure a VLAN to be both the guest VLAN and the restricted VLAN if you want to provide the same services to both types of users.

To configure a restricted VLAN, the new command on a Cisco IOS switch is as follows:

```
Router(config-if)# authentication event fail [retry retries] action authorize
vlan vlan-id
```

The default *retries* value is 2 and is configurable from 1 to 5.

To configure a restricted VLAN, the old commands on a Cisco IOS switch are as follows:

```
Router(config-if)# dot1x auth-fail vlan vlan-id
Router(config-if)# dot1x auth-fail max-attempts max-attempts
```

The default *max-attempts* value is 3 and is configurable from 1 to 3.

After three failed authentication attempts, the supplicant is moved to a restricted or authentication fail VLAN.

Note   For configuration guidelines and restrictions, please refer to the device documentation section for 802.1X configuration because guidelines and restrictions can differ for IOS version and/or device platform:
http://www.cisco.com/en/US/docs/switches/lan/catalyst3750/software/release/12.2_50_se/configuration/guide/sw8021x.html#wp1177420.

MAC Authentication Bypass

You can now even configure a switch to allow clients based on their MAC addresses by using the MAC Authentication Bypass (MAB) feature. This can be useful in scenarios where 802.1X authentication times out while waiting for an EAPOL response from the client connected to the port, in which case the switch will try to authorize the client by using MAB. Devices such as printers, fax machines, and so on fall under this category.

When this feature is enabled, the switch uses the MAC address as the client identity. For this to be successful, the authentication server must have a database of allowed client MAC addresses.

After a client is detected on the port, the switch waits for an Ethernet frame from the client. The switch then sends the authentication server a RADIUS-access/request as illustrated in Figure 8-7.

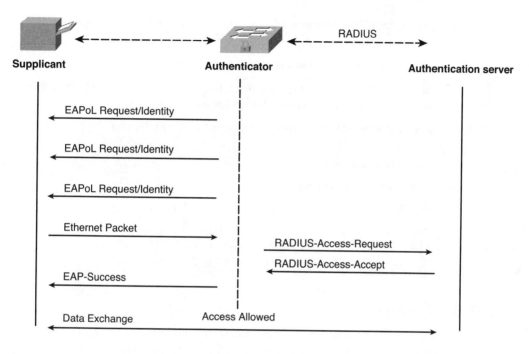

Figure 8-7   *MAC Authentication Bypass (MAB)*

To configure MAB on a Cisco IOS switch, the new command is as follows:

```
Router(config-if)# mab [eap]
```

To configure MAB on a Cisco IOS switch, the old command is as follows:

```
Router(config-if)# dot1x mac-auth-bypass [eap]
```

Note   The **eap** keyword tells MAB to use the EAP protocol (inside of RADIUS) for the authentication, instead of just sending the MAC address as the username/password.

VLAN Assignment

If you want to specify a VLAN to which a user should be assigned after successful 802.1X authentication, you can do this with VLAN assignment feature. The RADIUS server database can be configured to maintain username-to-VLAN mapping. During authentication, the RADIUS server can send VLAN assignment information to the switch so that a user can be assigned to a RADIUS server–defined VLAN.

The VLAN assignment feature is automatically enabled when you configure 802.1X authentication on an access port. For VLAN assignment to work, you must ensure that network authorization is configured on the switch to allow interface configuration from the RADIUS server.

To configure the VLAN assignment feature on a Cisco IOS switch, enter the following command:

```
Switch(config)# aaa authorization network default method1 [method2...]
```

To configure the VLAN assignment feature on a Catalyst OS switch, no equivalent command exists, and none is required to turn this feature on.

The following RADIUS IETF attributes are configured in RADIUS server:

- [64] Tunnel-Type = VLAN
- [65] Tunnel-Medium-Type = 802
- [81] Tunnel-Private-Group-ID = *VLAN name* or *VLAN ID*

Note   The *VLAN name* or *VLAN ID* being specified in attribute 81 must exist on the switch configuration; otherwise, authorization will not work for VLAN assignment.

802.1X Timers

Configuring 802.1X configuration on a switch might not be sufficient enough to get it to work. You might be required to tweak a few 802.1X times to get it to work in an acceptable manner. There are different 802.1X timers available that can be tweaked to get the desired result. The sections that follow take a look at a few of these timers, including the following:

- Quiet period
- Switch-to-client retransmission time
- Switch-to-client retransmission time for EAP-Request frames
- Switch-to-authentication-server retransmission time for Layer 4 packets
- Switch-to-client frame retransmission number

Quiet Period

When the switch cannot authenticate the client for some reason (for example, failed authentication), the switch remains idle for a set period of time and then tries again. The idle time is determined by the quiet-period value. The default is 60 seconds. This timer can be tweaked to provide a faster response.

To configure this timer on a Cisco IOS switch, enter the following command:

```
Router(config-if)# dot1x timeout quiet-period seconds
```

The value range for the *seconds* parameter is 0 to 65535 seconds.

Switch-to-Client Retransmission Time (tx-period)

The client responds to the EAP-request/identity frame from the switch with an EAP-response/identity frame. If the switch does not receive this response, it waits a set period of time, which is known as the *retransmission time*, and then retransmits the frame. You can tweak the amount of time that the switch waits for notification from 1 to 65535 seconds. The default is 30 seconds.

To configure this timer on a Cisco IOS switch, enter the following command:

```
Router(config)# dot1x timeout tx-period seconds
```

Switch-to-Client Retransmission Time for EAP-Request Frames (supp-timeout)

The client notifies the switch that it received the EAP-request frame. If the switch does not receive this notification, the switch waits a set period of time and then retransmits the frame. This timer can be tweaked to set the amount of time that the switch waits for notification from 1 to 65535 seconds. The default is 30 seconds.

To configure this timer on a Cisco IOS switch, enter the following command:

```
Router(config-if)# dot1x timeout supp-timeout seconds
```

Switch-to-Authentication-Server Retransmission Time for Layer 4 Packets (server-timeout)

The authentication server notifies the switch each time it receives a transport layer packet (Layer 4). When the switch does not receive a notification after sending a packet, it waits a set period of time and then retransmits the packet. This can be tweaked to set the amount of time that the switch waits for notification from 1 to 65535 seconds. The default is 30 seconds.

To configure this timer on a Cisco IOS switch, enter the following command:

```
Router(config-if)# dot1x timeout server-timeout seconds
```

Switch-to-Client Frame Retransmission Number (max-reauth-req)

The client notifies the switch that it received the EAP-request frame. If the switch does not receive this notification, the switch waits a set period of time, and then retransmits the frame. Apart from tweaking supp-timeout, we can tweak the number of times that the switch sends an EAP-request/identity frame to the client before restarting the authentication process from 1 to 10. The default is 2.

To configure this timer on a Cisco IOS switch, enter the following command:

```
Router(config-if)# dot1x max-reauth-req count
```

Configuring Accounting

Accounting is an essential part of the AAA architecture. An 802.1X accounting packet can indicate the following information to the RADIUS server:

■   When a user successfully authenticates

■   When a user logs off

■   When the link goes down on an 802.1X port

■   When a reauthentication succeeds

■   When a reauthentication fails

There are three types of RADIUS accounting packets sent by a switch:

■   **START:** Sent when a new user session starts.

■   **INTERIM:** Sent during an existing session for updates.

■   **STOP:** Sent when a session terminates.

To configure 802.1X accounting on a Cisco IOS switch, enter the following command:

```
Router(config)# aaa accounting dot1x default start-stop group radius
```

Certificate Installation on ACS

A certificate installed on an ACS server can be used for various purposes. A certificate can be used to secure an administrative session by enabling HTTPS (enabled by default in ACS 5.x) or to configure PEAP- or EAP-TLS-related authentications. The certificate installed on an ACS server is an identity certificate for a server. This section covers the steps required to install a certificate on an ACS server when you have an in-house Windows 2003 certificate authority.

On both ACS 4.2 & ACS 5.1, you have two options from which to install a certificate:

■   **Self-Signed Certificate:** Certificate is issued to ACS server as an ACS server certificate. ACS cannot be used to issue certificate to any entity other than itself.

■   **External Certificate Authority:** This includes any in-house or third-party certificate authority.

The self-signed certificate cannot be used for EAP-TLS authentication. The sections that follow show how to install a certificate using the external certificate authority.

The following checklist outlines the prerequisite items to install a certificate from an external certificate authority:

ACS Server certificate, which is issued by an external certificate authority

Certificate authority certificate

Intermediate certificate(s) authority certificate (only if certificate is issued to the ACS server from an intermediate certificate authority)

A note is provided to extract the private key file that is used to load the server certificate (identity certificate) for the ACS server. This is needed in situations where customers get a certificate with an embedded private key (.pfx file) from a third-party CA.

Certificate Installation on ACS 4.2

To install a certificate on ACS 4.2, perform the following steps:

Step 1.   Go to **System Configuration > ACS Certificate Setup > Generate Certificate Signing Request.**

Step 2.   Fill in the information for certificate signing request, that is: certificate subject, private key file, private key password, retype private key password, key length, digest to sign with.

For example:

```
Certificate subject: cn=SJACSCert,ou=TAC,o=Cisco,s=SJ,c=US
Private key file: ACSPrivateKey.pvk
Private key password: *****
Retype private key password: *****
Key length: 1024 bits
Digest to sign with: SHA1
```

Step 3.   After filling the information, click **Submit.**

After clicking **Submit,** you will get the screen shown in Figure 8-8.

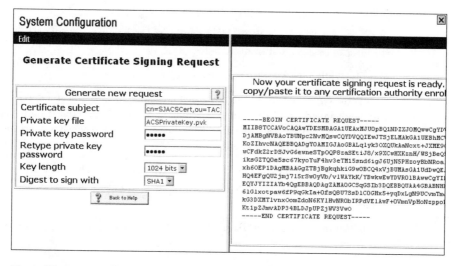

Figure 8-8 *Certificate Signing Request on ACS 4.2*

Copy the generated CSR (Certificate Signing Request) and save it in a notepad.

In certificate subject, CN (commonName) is the only mandatory field, the others can be skipped.

In ACS 4.2, you can specify the exact location of the private key file. For example:

```
Private key file: C:\ACS\ACSPrivateKey.pvk
```

Tip   When using the ACS Solution Engine, only specify the filename in the Private key file field without specifying the file location.

Note   When obtaining a certificate from a third-party CA, it might provide you with a certificate that contains the identity certificate and the private key file. You need to convert the provided certificate into a format understandable by the ACS server. This can be done using OpenSSL toolkit:

openssl.exe pkcs12 –in *.pfx file name>* **-out** *<output filename.pem>*

Password: *Private key password*

PEM Password: *new password*

confirm PEM Password: *new password*

This will generate a file that should be used on ACS for both the ACS certificate and the private key. The private key password will be the PEM password during file generation.

Step 4.   Go to the certificate authority. In this example, you will access CA (Certificate Authority) using HTTP(S).

In the case of Windows 2003 CA, if configured to be accessible via HTTP, the CA can be accessed from

```
http(s)://<IP of Windows 2003 CA server>/certsrv
```

Access the CA server using the preceding URL and go to **Request a certificate > advanced certificate request > Submit a certificate request by using a base-64-encoded CMC or PKCS #10 file**, or submit a renewal request by using a base-64-encoded PKCS #7 file.

Paste the CSR obtained in step 3 under Saved Request and choose **Web Server** as the certificate template, and then click **Submit** as illustrated in Figure 8-9.

Download the certificate as Base 64–encoded. This will give us the ACS server certificate.

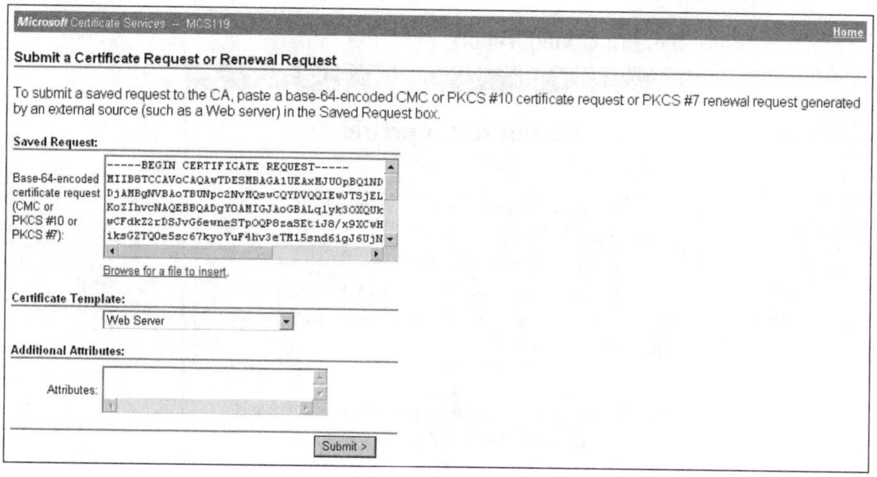

Figure 8-9   *Certificate Generation Using CSR*

Now you also need a CA certificate, which you can download from the CA home page option Download a CA certificate, certificate chain, or CRL.

Download CA certificate as Base 64–encoded too.

Now you have two certificates.

Step 5.   First install the CA certificate on ACS server from **System Configuration > ACS Certificate Setup > ACS Certification Authority Setup.**

Specify the location of the CA certificate and press **Submit.**

After the CA certificate is loaded, check it as a trusted certificate under **System Configuration > ACS Certificate Setup > Edit Certificate Trust List.**

Finally, install the ACS server certificate on the ACS server from **System Configuration > ACS Certificate Setup > Install ACS Certificate.**

Specify the location of the ACS server certificate and type the private key password.

Now the ACS Server certificate will be installed as specified in Figure 8-10.

As mentioned in the message, to commit the changes on ACS, you need to go to **System Configuration > Service Control** and click **Restart.** After services are restarted, you will get the installed certificate as shown in Figure 8-11.

Tip   With the ACS Solution Engine, if you plan to install the certificate by generating CSR from ACS SE, when specifying the location of ACS server certificate on FTP server, do not click on the link to specify the private key file location—only type the private key password after the ACS server certificate location has been specified on the FTP server.

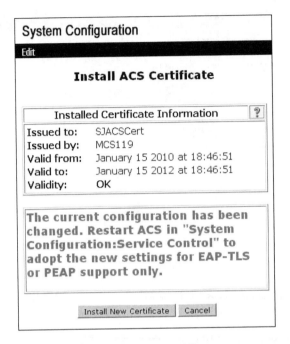

Figure 8-10   *ACS Server Certificate*

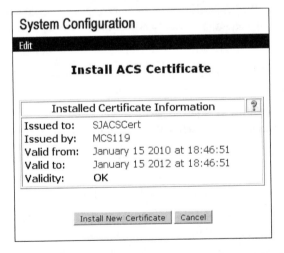

Figure 8-11   *ACS Certificate Installed on ACS 4.2*

Certificate Installation on ACS 5.1

As you already know, there are various ways of installing certificate on ACS, but this section focuses on installing a certificate using a CSR from an in-house Microsoft CA. To install certificate on ACS 5.1, you need to follow these steps:

Step 1.   Go to **System Administration > Configuration > Local Server Certificates > Local Certificates > Add**

The wizard will provide four options from which to select to install a server certificate on ACS:

```
Import Server Certificate
Generate Self Signed Certificate
Generate Certificate Signing Request
Bind CA Singed Certificate
```

Each option has some descriptive text to explain what the option means. For demonstration purposes, the **Generate Certificate Signing Request** option is selected as illustrated in Figure 8-12. After selecting the option, click **Next**.

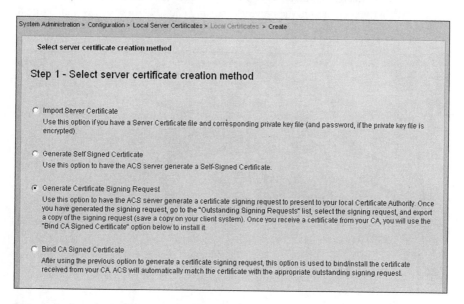

Figure 8-12   *Select Server Certificate Creation Method*

Step 2.   In this section, you provide details for **Certificate Subject** and **Key Length** and click **Finish**. For demonstration purposes, the following information is filled in as illustrated in Figure 8-13:

```
Certificate Subject: cn=SJACSCert,ou=TAC,o=Cisco,s=SJ,c=US
Key Length: 1024
```

Figure 8-13 *CSR Details*

After clicking **Finish,** you get a message from the ACS server:

A server certificate signing request has been generated and can be viewed in the "Outstanding Signing Requests" list.

Step 3. Go to the section **System Administration > Configuration > Local Server Certificates > Outstanding Signing Requests.** In this section check the CSR that you created in the previous step and click **Export** as shown in Figure 8-14.

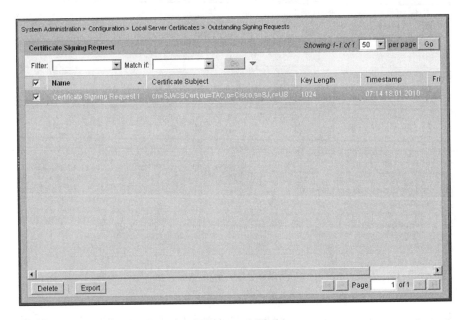

Figure 8-14 *Downloading the CSR from ACS 5.1*

This will prompt you to save the CSR in *pem* format.

Step 4. Open the downloaded *pem* file in WordPad or a similar text editor, and the CSR will appear similar to what you saw in the case of ACS 4.2 in Figure 8-8.

Copy this request and follow step 4 from the previous section, "Certificate Installation on ACS 4.2." This will provide us with a ACS server certificate for ACS 5.1.

Step 5.   To install a CA certificate on ACS 5.1, you need to go to **Users and Identity Stores > Certificate Authorities** and click on **Add**.

In the resulting page, shown in Figure 8-15, specify the CA certificate location and specify whether you want to use it for EAP-TLS authentication to trust/not trust clients and click **Submit**. This results in the page shown in Figure 8-16.

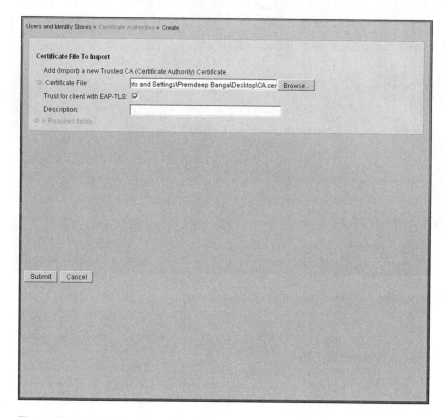

Figure 8-15   *CA Certificate Install on ACS 5.1*

Step 6.   Finally, install the server certificate on ACS 5.1 by going to **System Administration > Configuration > Local Server Certificates > Local Certificates > Add**.

This time, as illustrated in Figure 8-17, you need to select the **Bind CA Signed Certificate** option and press **Next**. This enables the ACS server to bind the CSR generated previously with the server certificate obtained from the CA.

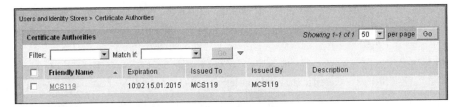

Figure 8-16   *CA Certificate Installed on ACS 5.1*

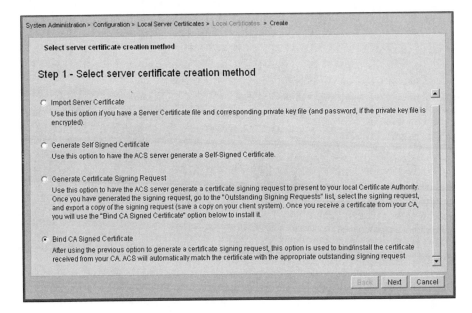

Figure 8-17   *Bind CA Signed Certificate Option*

On the next page, shown in Figure 8-18, you need to specify the ACS server certificate location. In addition, you also need to specify the purpose of the certificate, that is, for EAP protocol or for Management Interface purposes. After the information has been provided, click **Finish** to load the server certificate on ACS. Figure 8-19 shows the final screen.

Configuring EAP-MD5 on ACS

This section provides configuration details for EAP-MD5 on ACS 4.2 and ACS 5.1.

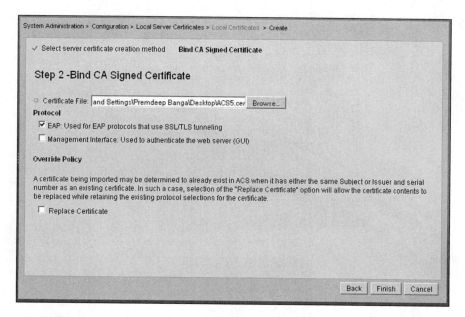

Figure 8-18   *Server Certificate Installation on ACS 5.1*

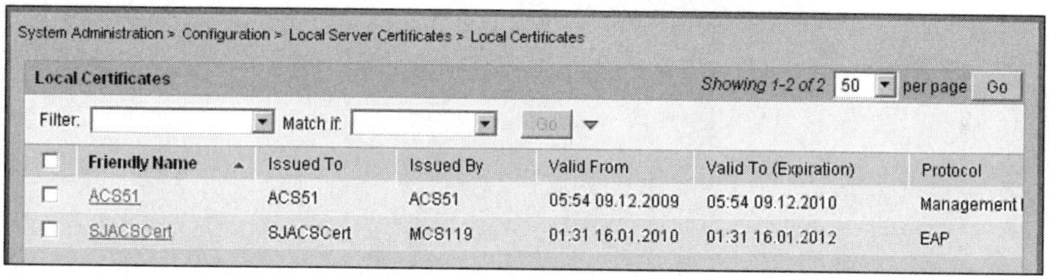

Figure 8-19   *Server Certificate(SJACSCert) Installed on ACS 5.1*

EAP-MD5 Configuration on ACS 4.2

To configure/enable EAP-MD5 on ACS 4.2, go to **System Configuration** > **Global Authentication Setup** and under **EAP-MD5**, check **Allow EAP-MD5** and click **Submit + Restart** as shown in Figure 8-20.

EAP-MD5 Configuration on ACS 5.1

In ACS 5.1, for EAP-MD5 to be allowed under the access policy, go to **Access Policies** > **Access Services**.

You can create a new access service or edit an already configured access service.

Go to the **Allowed Protocols** section in the access policy, as shown in Figure 8-21, and check **Allow EAP-MD5** in the access policy to allow it and click **Submit**.

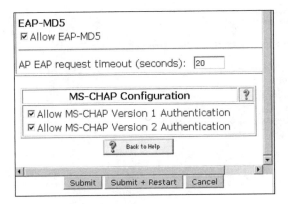

Figure 8-20   *EAP-MD5 on ACS 4.2*

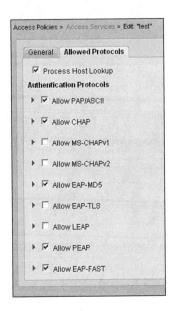

Figure 8-21   *EAP-MD5 on ACS 5.1*

Configuring PEAP on ACS

Before configuring ACS for PEAP authentication, ensure that you have an ACS server certificate already installed on ACS 4.2 and ACS 5.1. The ACS server certificate can be self-signed or obtained from an external CA.

PEAP Configuration on ACS 4.2

On ACS 4.2, go to **System Configuration** > **Global Authentication Setup**.

Under **PEAP**, check the PEAP version that you want to allow:

- Allow EAP-MSCHAPv2

- Allow EAP-GTC

- Allow Posture Validation

- Allow EAP-TLS

After selecting the PEAP version, click on **Submit + Restart**.

Figure 8-22 shows an example where EAP-MSCHAPv2 has been enabled.

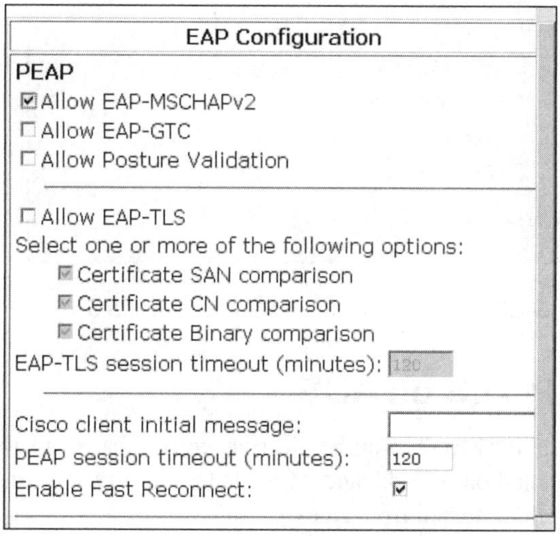

Figure 8-22   *PEAP/EAP-MSCHAPv2 on ACS 4.2*

PEAP Configuration on ACS 5.1

In ACS 5.1, PEAP needs to be allowed under the access policy. Go to **Access Policies** > **Access Services**.

You can create a new access service or edit an already configured access service.

Go to the **Allowed Protocols** section in the access policy, as shown in Figure 8-23, and check **Allow PEAP** in the access policy to allow it. Expand the **Allow PEAP** option to select any of the PEAP versions that you want to allow.

Figure 8-23 shows an example where EAP-MSCHAPv2 has been enabled.

You can configure other related PEAP settings from: **System Administration** > **Configuration** > **Global System Options** > **PEAP Settings**.

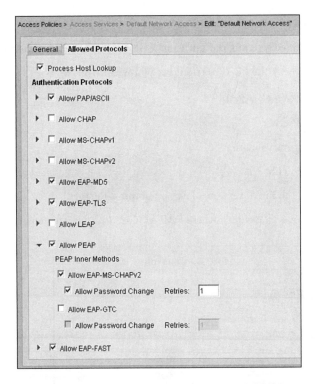

Figure 8-23   *PEAP/EAP-MSCHAPv2 on ACS 5.1*

Configuring EAP-TLS on ACS

Before configuring ACS for EAP-TLS authentication, ensure that you have an ACS server certificate already installed on ACS 4.2 and ACS 5.1. The ACS server certificate can *not* be self signed, it must be obtained from an external CA.

EAP-TLS Configuration on ACS 4.2

On ACS 4.2, go to **System Configuration > Global Authentication Setup**. Under **EAP-TLS** check **Allow EAP-TLS**, as shown in Figure 8-24, and click **Submit + Restart** to commit the changes made on ACS configuration.

EAP-TLS Configuration on ACS 5.1

In ACS 5.1, EAP-TLS needs to be allowed under the access policy. Go to **Access Policies > Access Services.** You can create a new access service or edit an already configured access service.

Go to the **Allowed Protocols** section in the access policy, and check **Allow EAP-TLS** in the access policy to allow it, as shown in Figure 8-25, and then click **Submit**.

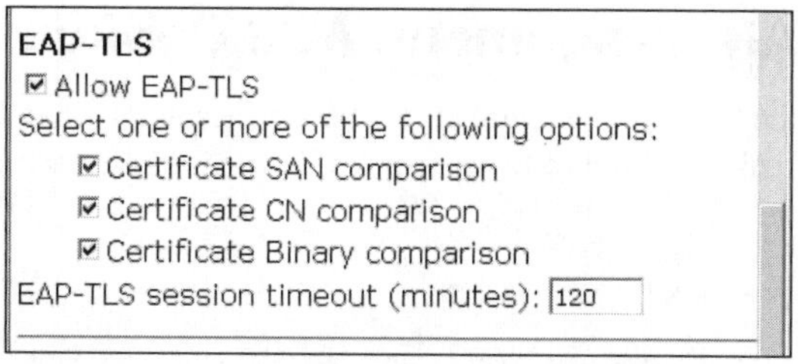

```
EAP-TLS
☑ Allow EAP-TLS
Select one or more of the following options:
    ☑ Certificate SAN comparison
    ☑ Certificate CN comparison
    ☑ Certificate Binary comparison
EAP-TLS session timeout (minutes): [120  ]
```

Figure 8-24   *EAP-TLS on ACS 4.2*

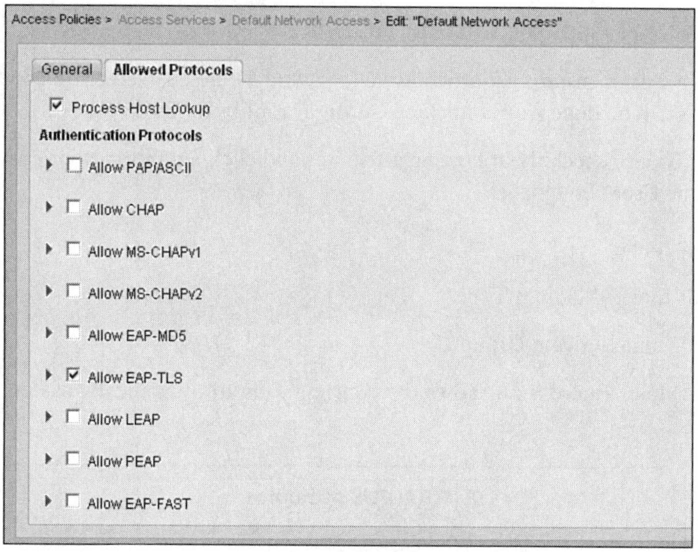

Access Policies > Access Services > Default Network Access > Edit: "Default Network Access"

| General | **Allowed Protocols** |

☑ Process Host Lookup

Authentication Protocols

▶ ☐ Allow PAP/ASCII

▶ ☐ Allow CHAP

▶ ☐ Allow MS-CHAPv1

▶ ☐ Allow MS-CHAPv2

▶ ☐ Allow EAP-MD5

▶ ☑ Allow EAP-TLS

▶ ☐ Allow LEAP

▶ ☐ Allow PEAP

▶ ☐ Allow EAP-FAST

Figure 8-25   *EAP-TLS on ACS 5.1*

You can configure other related EAP-TLS settings from **System Administration > Configuration > Global System Options > EAP-TLS settings.**

For EAP-TLS authentication on ACS 5.1, you must also configure the certificate authentication profile according to your requirements. By default, there exists a predefined certificate authentication profile called CN Username. Certificate authentication profiles define how X509 certificate information is to be used for a certificate-based request. In these profiles, you can select from a list of available attributes to be used as the username. The selected attribute is used to populate the username field and is used to query the LDAP or AD identity store. You can configure the certificate authentication profile on ACS 5.1 from **Users and Identity Stores > Certificate Authentication Profile.**

Dynamic VLAN Assignment: ACS Configuration

As discussed in the "VLAN Assignment" section earlier in the chapter, following vendor-specific tunnel attributes need to be configured in the RADIUS server for dynamic VLAN assignment:

- [64] Tunnel-Type = VLAN

- [65] Tunnel-Medium-Type = 802

- [81] Tunnel-Private-Group-ID = VLAN name or VLAN ID

Dynamic VLAN Assignment for ACS 4.2

On ACS 4.2, first ensure that attributes 64, 65, and 81 are enabled to be configured on ACS. This can be done from **Interface Configuration > RADIUS (IETF)**.

For User/Group, check the following attributes and click **Submit** to configure the attributes on the User/Group level:

- [064] Tunnel-Type

- [065] Tunnel-Medium-Type

- [081] Tunnel-Private-Group-ID

As an example, Figure 8-26 shows the configuration to dynamically assign VLAN 10 to a user.

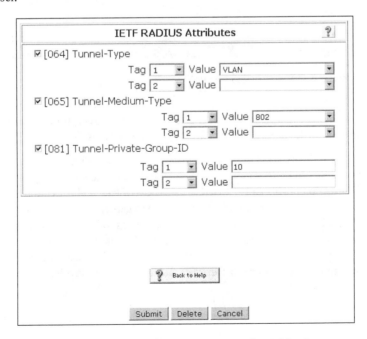

Figure 8-26   *Dynamic VLAN Assignment for ACS 4.2*

Dynamic VLAN Assignment for ACS 5.1

For ACS 5.1, you first need to create an authorization profile that will have the RADIUS IETF attributes for VLAN assignment. Go to **Policy Elements > Authorization and Permissions > Network Access > Authorization Profiles.**

Create or edit an authorization profile and go to the **RADIUS Attributes** tab. In this section, configure the attributes for dynamic VLAN assignment. As an example, create an authorization profile to assign a user in VLAN 10 with the following attribute configuration:

- Dictionary Type: **RADIUS-IETF**
- RADIUS Attribute: **Tunnel-Type**
- Attribute Type: **Tagged Enum**
- Attribute Value: **Static: VLAN**
- Tag: **1**
- Dictionary Type: **RADIUS-IETF**
- RADIUS Attribute: **Tunnel-Medium-Type**
- Attribute Type: **Tagged Enum**
- Attribute Value: **Static: 802**
- Tag: **1**
- Dictionary Type: **RADIUS-IETF**
- RADIUS Attribute: **Tunnel-Private-Group-ID**
- Attribute Type: **Tagged String**
- Attribute Value: **Static: 10**
- Tag: **1**

Figure 8-27 illustrates the preceding configuration.

After the authorization profile is created, you can apply the profile using the access policy's authorization section.

There is another way to accomplish this and an easier one. To configure this, go to **Policy Elements > Authorization and Permissions > Network Access > Authorization Profiles > Create/Edit > Common Tasks > VLAN > VLAN ID/Name.**

Here you can specify VLAN statically by choosing the **Static** option and specifying the VLAN ID/name in the **Value** box provided. You can also choose the **Dynamic** option and specify an external identity store from which the value can be retrieved. If you choose **Dynamic**, you need to specify the external identity store dictionary from which the value will be populated. The external identity store dictionary is configured under **External Identity Stores.**

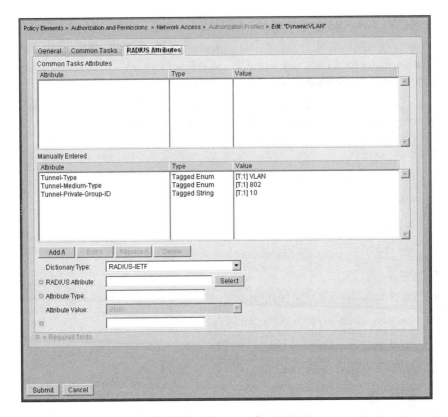

Figure 8-27   *Dynamic VLAN Assignment for ACS 5.1*

Lab Scenario #7: Configuring Switch, ACS, and Windows XP for 802.1X Authentication Using EAP-MD5

ABC Inc. has a requirement to secure all the Windows XP workstations connected to the Layer 2 switch port. The company has three departments: HR, Finance, and Development. All three departments have access to the conference hall. A requirement dictates that whenever any members of the HR team moves to the conference hall, they should be authenticated using ACS and then placed into VLAN 5; similarly, members of the Finance team should be assigned to VLAN 6, and members of the Development team should be assigned to VLAN 7 should they move to the conference hall. You need to configure the switch, client, and ACS for EAP-MD5 authentication.

Lab Setup

This lab setup requires one switch, one ACS server, and one Windows XP client that can be used by any department individual to log in. Figure 8-28 shows the setup required.

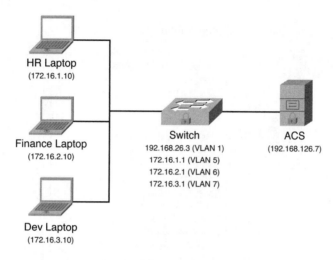

Figure 8-28   *Setup for Lab 7*

Lab Solution

The solution to this scenario assumes certain things that are very basic and are expected to be configured by the candidate using the knowledge obtained from previous sections.

The assumptions are as follows:

A. Switch entry exists in ACS configuration.

- For ACS 5.1: Under **Network Resources > Network Devices and AAA Clients**

- For ACS 4.2: Under **Network Configuration > ... > AAA Clients**

B. Three groups have been created in the ACS configuration: HR, Finance, and Development.

- For ACS 5.1: Under **Users and Identity Stores > Identity Groups**

- For ACS 4.2: Under **Group Setup**

C. Users exist under each group configured in section B:

- ACS 5.1: Under **Users and Identity Stores > Internal Identity Stores > Users**

- ACS 4.2: **User Setup**

ACS 4.2 Configuration Requirement

A. Ensure that RADIUS attributes for dynamic VLAN assignment are enabled for the group. Go to **Interface Configuration > RADIUS (IETF)** and check that the following attributes are configured as illustrated in Figure 8-29:

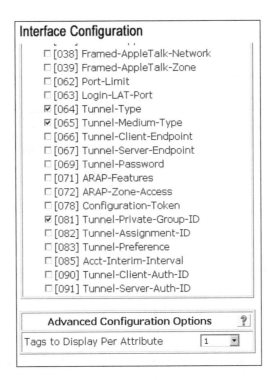

Figure 8-29 *Attributes for Dynamic VLAN Assignment*

- **[064] Tunnel-Type**

- **[065] Tunnel-Medium-Type**

- **[081] Tunnel-Private-Group-ID**

If you are not sending multiple attributes for other RADIUS IETF attributes, change **Tags to Display Per Attribute** to **1**.

B. Under each individual group, configure the attributes as shown in Figure 8-30:

HR group:

- [064] Tunnel-Type, Tag: **1**, Value: **VLAN**

- [065] Tunnel-Medium-Type, Tag: **1**, Value: **802**

- [081] Tunnel-Private-Group-ID, Value: **5**

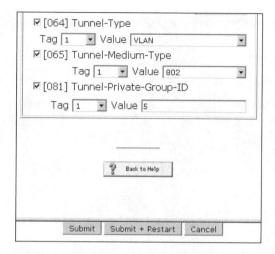

Figure 8-30   *Attributes Configured for the HR Group on ACS 4.2*

Finance group:

■ [064] Tunnel-Type, Tag: **1**, Value: **VLAN**

■ [065] Tunnel-Medium-Type, Tag: **1**, Value: **802**

■ [081] Tunnel-Private-Group-ID, Value: **6**

Development group:

■ [064] Tunnel-Type, Tag: **1**, Value: **VLAN**

■ [065] Tunnel-Medium-Type, Tag: **1**, Value: **802**

■ [081] Tunnel-Private-Group-ID, Value: **7**

C. Although by default EAP-MD5 is enabled on ACS, you can verify that it is enabled from **System Configuration > Global Authentication Setup.**

After configuring for attributes for individual group and ensuring the EAP-MD5 is enabled, click **Submit + Restart** to ensure that settings take effect.

ACS 5.1 Configuration Requirement

A. Create a device filter named **Dot1xSwitch** for the switch configured under the **Network Resources > Network Devices and AAA Clients** section.

The device filter can be created from **Policy Elements > Session Conditions > Network Conditions > Device Filters** as shown in Figure 8-31.

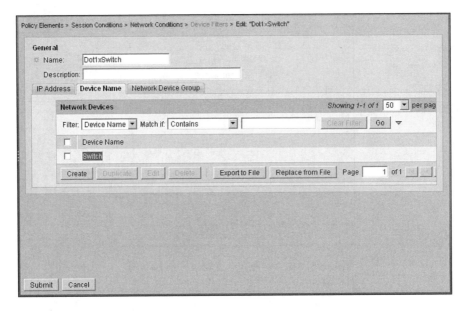

Figure 8-31   *Device filter on ACS 5.1*

B. Create three authorization profiles under **Policy Elements > Authorization and Permissions > Network Access > Authorization Profiles:**

- HR VLAN Profile

- Finance VLAN Profile

- Development VLAN Profile

Under the RADIUS Attributes tab, configure following two attributes for each profile:

- Dictionary Type: **RADIUS-IETF**

- RADIUS Attribute: **Tunnel-Type**

- Attribute Type: **Tagged Enum**

- Attribute Value: Static: **VLAN**

- Tag: **1**

- Dictionary Type: **RADIUS-IETF**

- RADIUS Attribute: **Tunnel-Medium-Type**

- Attribute Type: **Tagged Enum**

- Attribute Value: **Static: 802**

- Tag: **1**

For the last attribute required for dynamic VLAN assignment, you must use the values 5, 6, and 7 for the Attribute Value for each respective profile:

■ Dictionary Type: **RADIUS-IETF**

■ RADIUS Attribute: **Tunnel-Private-Group-ID**

■ Attribute Type: **Tagged String**

■ Attribute Value: **Static: 5**

■ Tag: **1**

■ Dictionary Type: **RADIUS-IETF**

■ RADIUS Attribute: **Tunnel-Private-Group-ID**

■ Attribute Type: **Tagged String**

■ Attribute Value: Static: **6**

■ Tag: **1**

■ Dictionary Type: **RADIUS-IETF**

■ RADIUS Attribute: **Tunnel-Private-Group-ID**

■ Attribute Type: Tagged **String**

■ Attribute Value: **Static: 7**

■ Tag: **1**

As an example, Figure 8-32 shows what the HR VLAN profile will look like.

Note   VLAN assignment on ACS 5.1 can also be configured using a common task as described in the section "Dynamic VLAN Assignment for ACS 5.1."

C. Create an access service named **Dot1xPolicy** under **Access Policies > Access Services** as shown in Figure 8-33. For **Policy Structure** for access services, check only **Identity** and **Authorization**. Under **Allowed Protocols**, use only **Allow EAP-MD5** as shown in Figure 8-34.

D. Create a rule to match and to apply the access service configured in the previous step from **Access Policies > Access Services > Service Selection Rules** as shown in Figure 8-35. Under **Conditions**, select

■ Protocol: **match: Radius**

■ Device Filter: **match: Dot1xSwitch**

For Results, select **Dot1xPolicy** as the service.

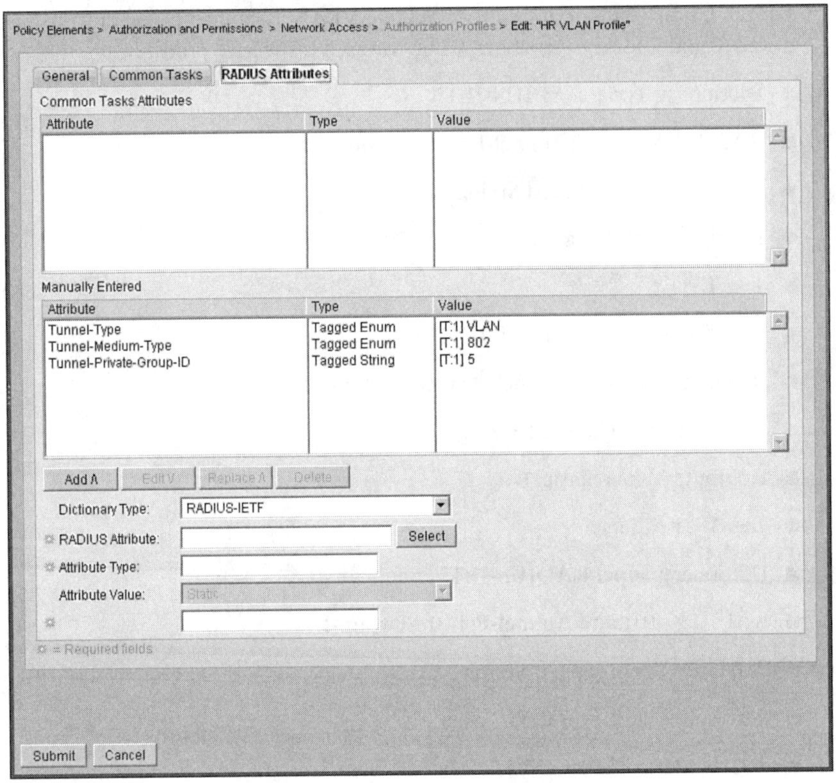

Figure 8-32 *Authorization Profile HR VLAN Profile on ACS 5.1*

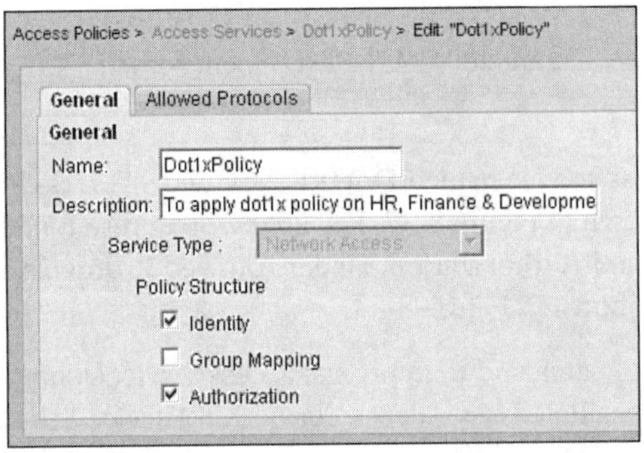

Figure 8-33 *Access Service* Dot1xPolicy
for Dynamic VLAN Assignment

Note Choose the **Customize** button to create the required conditions.

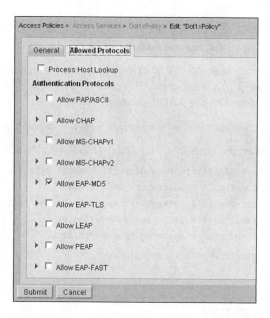

Figure 8-34   *EAP-MD5 as the Only Allowed Protocol Under Access Service*

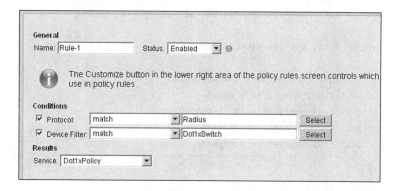

Figure 8-35   *Rules to Apply Dot1xPolicy*

Switch Configuration Requirements

Step 1.   Enable the AAA model on the switch:

```
Switch(config)# aaa new-model
```

Step 2.   Configure the RADIUS server configuration on the switch:

```
Switch(config)# radius-server host 192.168.26.7 key cisco
```

Step 3.   Enable 802.1X globally on the switch:

```
Switch(config)# dot1x system-auth-control
```

Step 4.   Configure the switch for 802.1X authentication:

```
Switch(config)# aaa authentication dot1x default group radius
```

Step 5.   Configure the switch for 802.1X authorization, which is mandatory for dynamic VLAN assignment. This command tells the switch to process attributes returned by the RADIUS server:

```
Switch(config)# aaa authorization network default group radius
```

Step 6.   Configure the interface for single host mode 802.1X authentication:

```
Switch(config)# interface GigabitEthernet1/0/24
Switch(config-if)# switchport mode access
Switch(config-if)# authentication port-control auto
Switch(config-if)# dot1x pae authenticator
Switch(config-if)# spanning-tree portfast
```

Example 8-1 shows the full switch configuration.

Example 8-1   *802.1X Configuration on Switch*

```
Switch(config)# aaa new-model
Switch(config)# radius-server host 192.168.26.7 key cisco
!
Switch(config)# aaa authentication dot1x default group radius
Switch(config)# aaa authorization network default group radius
!
Switch(config)# dot1x system-auth-control
!
Switch(config)# interface GigabitEthernet1/0/24
Switch(config-if)# switchport mode access
Switch(config-if)# authentication port-control auto
Switch(config-if)# dot1x pae authenticator
Switch(config-if)# spanning-tree portfast
```

Client Configuration Requirements

You need to configure the Windows XP client for MD5 authentication, which can be done from **Control Panel > Network Connections > Select the LAN connection > Right-click > Properties > Authentication.**

From the screen in Figure 8-36, ensure that **Enable IEEE 802.1X authentication** is checked.

Select **MD5-Challenge** under **Choose a network authentication method.**

Tip   If the Authentication tab is not available, start the Wireless Zero Configuration service on Windows XP Service Pack 2 and Wired AutoConfig on Windows XP Service Pack 3.

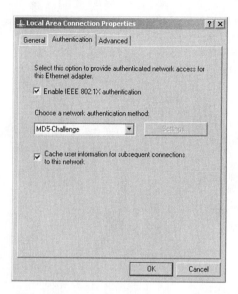

Figure 8-36 *MD5 Configuration on Client*

When the client is plugged in the switch port configured for 802.1X authentication, the client PC will get a balloon on the LAN network connection in the system tray. Click on the balloon and it will pop up with a login window as shown in Figure 8-37.

Figure 8-37 *Login Windows for MD5 Authentication*

Example 8-2 displays the show dot1x **interface gigabitEthernet 1/0/24 details** output after successful authentication. This output can be a starting point while troubleshooting issues related to 802.1X. This provides you with information about the configuration on the switchport and the current state of the switchport.

The **Dot1x Info for** *Interface* section covers the configuration part of the interface and provides information about the following:

■ PAE

■ Port Control

■ Control Direction

■ Host Mode

■ Quiet Period

■ Server Timeout

■ Supplicant Timeout

■ ReAuth Max

■ Max Request

■ Tx Period

The current state of the switchport is under the **Dot1x Authenticator Client List** section. This section provides you with following information.

■ **Supplicant:** MAC address of the supplicant

■ **Session ID:** Session ID used for authentication, authorization and accounting

■ **Auth SM State:** Shows current authentication state

■ **Port Status:** Current port status

Based on the information available from this output, further action plans can be drawn to troubleshoot the issue.

Example 8-2   show dot1x interface gigabitEthernet 1/0/24 details *Command Output*

```
Switch#sh dot1x interface gigabitEthernet 1/0/24 details
Dot1x Info for GigabitEthernet1/0/24
— — — — — — — — — — — — — — — — — —·
PAE                      = AUTHENTICATOR
PortControl              = AUTO
ControlDirection         = Both
HostMode                 = SINGLE_HOST
QuietPeriod              = 60
ServerTimeout            = 0
SuppTimeout              = 30
ReAuthMax                = 2
MaxReq                   = 2
TxPeriod                 = 30


Dot1x Authenticator Client List
```

```
_ _ _ _ _ _ _ _ _ _ _ _ _ _ _ _ _ _.
Supplicant                 = 0018.8ba8.34cc
Session ID                 = C0A81A030000001002791E32
   Auth SM State           = AUTHENTICATED
   Auth BEND SM State      = IDLE
Port Status                = AUTHORIZED
```

Example 8-3 displays the **show dot1x interface gigabitEthernet 1/0/24 statistics** output after successful authentication. This command is useful in understanding the type of EAP information received or sent on/from the switchport:

- **RxStart:** Number of valid EAPOL-start frames received

- **RxLogoff:** Number of EAPOL-logoff frames received

- **RxResp:** Number of valid EAP-response frames (other than response/identity) received

- **RxRespID:** Number of EAP-response/identity frames received

- **RxInvalid:** Number of EAPOL frames with unrecognized frame type received

- **RxLenError:** Number of EAPOL frames with invalid body length field received

- **RxTotal:** Number of valid EAPOL frames (any type) received

- **TxReq:** Number of EAP-request frames (other than request/identity) sent

- **TxReqID:** Number of EAP-request/identity frames sent

- **TxTotal:** Number of EAPOL frames (any type) sent.

- **RxVersion:** Number of packets received in IEEE 802.1X version 1 format

- **LastRxSrcMAC:** Source MAC address carried in the most recently received EAPOL frame

Example 8-3   show dot1x interface gigabitEthernet 1/0/24 statistics *Command Output*

```
Switch#sh dot1x interface gigabitEthernet 1/0/24 statistics
Dot1x Authenticator Port Statistics for GigabitEthernet1/0/24
_ _ _ _ _ _ _ _ _ _ _ _ _ _ _ _ _ _ _ _ _ _
RxStart = 12     RxLogoff = 0     RxResp = 2      RxRespID = 10
RxInvalid = 0    RxLenErr = 0     RxTotal = 24


TxReq = 12       TxReqID = 73     TxTotal = 95


RxVersion = 1    LastRxSrcMAC = 0018.8ba8.34cc
```

Example 8-4 displays the **show authentication interface gigabitEthernet 1/0/24** output after successful authentication. This output shows authentication manager events on the switch. This is useful in determining the method (dot1x, mab or webauth) by which a supplicant is authenticated; the current domain (Data or Voice) under which the supplicant is placed; and the current status for the switchport.

The following are the status values that can be found in the **show authentication** output:

- **Idle:** It means session has been initialized and no methods have been run yet.
- **Running:** It means a method is running for this session.
- **No methods:** It means no method has provided a result for this session.
- **Authc Success:** It means a method has resulted in authentication successful for this session.
- **Authc Failed:** It means a method has resulted in authentication fail for this session.
- **Authz Success:** It means all features have been successfully applied for this session.
- **Authz Failed:** It means a feature has failed to be applied for this session.

Example 8-4   show authentication interface gigabitEthernet 1/0/24 *Command Output*

```
Switch#sh authentication interface gigabitEthernet 1/0/24


Client list:
Interface  MAC Address     Method   Domain   Status         Session ID
  Gi1/0/24   0018.8ba8.34cc  dot1x    DATA     Authz Success
C0A81A030000001202885332


Available methods list:
  Handle  Priority  Name
    3        0        dot1x
Runnable methods list:
  Handle  Priority  Name
    3        0        dot1x
```

Example 8-5 displays the **show authentication sessions gigabitEthernet 1/0/24** output after successful authentication. This is another useful command to check the state of a switchport (that is, domain, host mode, username, status, VLAN policy, and so on). In this show output, you will also have State, which can have following values:

- **Not run:** The method has not run for this session.
- **Running:** The method is running for this session.
- **Failed over:** The method has failed and the next method is expected to provide a result.
- **Authc Success:** The method has provided a successful authentication for the session.
- **Authc Failed:** The method has provided a failed authentication for the session.

Example 8-5   show authentication sessions interface gigabitEthernet 1/0/24

```
Switch#sh authentication sessions interface gigabitEthernet 1/0/24
            Interface:  GigabitEthernet1/0/24
          MAC Address:  0018.8ba8.34cc
```

```
          IP Address:   Unknown
         User-Name:     userhr
            Status:     Authz Success
            Domain:     DATA
   Security Policy:     Should Secure
   Security Status:     Unsecure
    Oper host mode:     single-host
   Oper control dir:    both
      Authorized By:    Authentication Server
        Vlan Policy:    5
    Session timeout:    N/A
       Idle timeout:    N/A
  Common Session ID:    C0A81A030000001202885332
    Acct Session ID:    0x00000018
             Handle:    0x9B000012


Runnable methods list:
     Method    State
     dot1x     Authc Success
```

Example 8-6 displays the **show vlan** output before authentication. This command can be used before the authentication process to check current VLAN for the switchport.

Example 8-6   show vlan *Output Before Authentication*

```
Switch#sh vlan

VLAN Name                             Status    Ports
---- -------------------------------- --------- -------------------------------
1    default                          active    Gi1/0/2, Gi1/0/3, Gi1/0/4
                                                Gi1/0/5, Gi1/0/6, Gi1/0/7
                                                Gi1/0/8, Gi1/0/9, Gi1/0/10
                                                Gi1/0/11, Gi1/0/12, Gi1/0/13
                                                Gi1/0/14, Gi1/0/15, Gi1/0/16
                                                Gi1/0/17, Gi1/0/18, Gi1/0/19
                                                Gi1/0/20, Gi1/0/21, Gi1/0/22
                                                Gi1/0/23, Gi1/0/24
2    VLAN0002                         active
3    VLAN0003                         active
5    HR_VLAN                          active
6    FIN_VLAN                         active
7    DEV_VLAN                         active
```

Example 8-7 displays the **show vlan** output after authentication. This command can be used to verify the dynamic VLAN assignment feature to ensure that the switchport has successfully transitioned to required VLAN.

Example 8-7 show vlan *Output After Authentication*

```
Switch#sh vlan

VLAN Name                             Status    Ports
---- -------------------------------- --------- -------------------------------
1    default                          active    Gi1/0/2, Gi1/0/3, Gi1/0/4
                                                Gi1/0/5, Gi1/0/6, Gi1/0/7
                                                Gi1/0/8, Gi1/0/9, Gi1/0/10
                                                Gi1/0/11, Gi1/0/12, Gi1/0/13
                                                Gi1/0/14, Gi1/0/15, Gi1/0/16
                                                Gi1/0/17, Gi1/0/18, Gi1/0/19
                                                Gi1/0/20, Gi1/0/21, Gi1/0/22
                                                Gi1/0/23
2    VLAN0002                         active
3    VLAN0003                         active
5    HR_VLAN                          active    Gi1/0/24
6    FIN_VLAN                         active
7    DEV_VLAN                         active
```

Example 8-8 displays an excerpt of the **debug radius authentication** output. This debug can be used to troubleshoot authentication failures. In this debug, you can verify the information passed between the authentication server and the switch. As shown in the debugs in Example 8-8, you can clearly see information such as User-Name, Tunnel-Type, Tunnel-Medium-Type, and Tunnel-Private-Group being passed over to the RADIUS server.

Example 8-8 debug radius authentication *Output Excerpt*

```
RADIUS: Received from id 1645/14 192.168.26.7:1645, Access-Accept, len 92
RADIUS:  authenticator 87 37 FD CD 11 DB 4C 1F - B7 A9 58 05 C7 29 A2 FD
RADIUS:  User-Name           [1]    8    "userhr"
RADIUS:  Class               [25]   24
RADIUS:   43 41 43 53 3A 41 43 53 35 31 2F 35 33 33 30 34   [CACS:ACS51/53304]
RADIUS:   37 34 37 2F 33 38                  [ 747/38]
RADIUS:  Tunnel-Type         [64]   6    01:VLAN                 [13]
RADIUS:  Tunnel-Medium-Type  [65]   6    01:ALL_802              [6]
RADIUS:  EAP-Message         [79]   6
RADIUS:   03 60 00 04                        [ `]
RADIUS:  Message-Authenticato[80]   18
RADIUS:   1D 23 36 43 D2 E9 F7 53 DA 9A 83 07 D6 BB 85 74         [ #6CSt]
```

```
RADIUS:  Tunnel-Private-Group[81]  4   01:"5"
RADIUS(00000018): Received from id 1645/14
RADIUS/DECODE: EAP-Message fragments, 4, total 4 bytes
```

To view the log for successful authentications and failures on ACS 4.2, you need to go to **Reports and Activity > Passed Authentications** and **Reports and Activity > Failed Attempts**.

For ACS 5.1, you first need to go to **Monitoring and Reports > Launch Monitoring & Report Viewer**.

This will launch a new browser window with Cisco Secure ACS View. In Cisco Secure ACS View, you need to go to the following:

- **Monitoring & Reports > Reports > catalog > AAA Protocol > RADIUS Authentication**

- **Monitoring & Reports > Reports > catalog > AAA Protocol > AAA Diagnostics**

Lab Scenario #8: Configuring Switch, ACS, and Windows XP for 802.1X Authentication Using PEAP

The lab setup will remain the same as Lab Scenario #7; the only requirement that will change is to change the authentication method from EAP-MD5 to PEAP.

Lab Solution

The ACS 4.2 configuration requirement is to install the CA (the CA that issued the ACS server identity certificate) and server certificate (the identity certificate for ACS) and enable PEAP on ACS 4.2 as described earlier in the section "Configuring PEAP on ACS."

The ACS 5.1 configuration requirement is to install the CA (CA that issued ACS server identity certificate) and server certificate (the identity certificate for ACS) and check only the **Allow PEAP** and **PEAP Inner Methods** as **Allow EAP-MS-CHAPv2** in the **Dot1xPolicy** on ACS 5.1 as described previously in the section "Configuring PEAP on ACS."

For the switch configuration requirement, the configuration will remain the same as configured in Lab Scenario #7.

The client configuration requirements for this lab are satisfied as follows:

A. Ensure that the CA certificate that was installed on the ACS server is also installed on the client machine because, in PEAP, the client validates the RADIUS (ACS) server certificate during authentication.

B. Configure the Windows XP client for PEAP authentication from **Control Panel > Network Connections > Select the LAN connection > Right click > Properties > Authentication**. Ensure that **Enable IEEE 802.1X authentication** is checked and select

Protected EAP (PEAP) under Choose a network authentication method as shown in Figure 8-38.

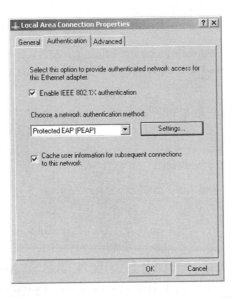

Figure 8-38   *PEAP Configuration on Client Machine*

Example 8-9 displays an excerpt of the **debug dot1x all** output. Before authorizing a port, there are multiple exchanges that take place between the supplicant and the RADIUS server. The debug shown has some portions removed to make it more understandable. In these debugs, you can clearly see the following:

```
EAP-Request/Identity (EAP code: 0x1 and type: 0x1)
```

You can also see that EAP authentication attempted is PEAP as the type shown in the debug is 0x19 (equivalent to decimal 25, PEAP).

At the end you can see authentication passing and an EAP success (EAP code: 0x3).

Example 8-9   debug dot1x all *Output Excerpt*

```
dot1x-packet:dot1x_mgr_send_eapol :EAP code: 0x1  id: 0x2  length: 0x0005 type:
0x1  data:
dot1x-ev:FastEthernet6:Sending EAPOL packet to group PAE address
dot1x-ev:dot1x_mgr_pre_process_eapol_pak: Role determination not required on
FastEthernet6.
dot1x-registry:registry:dot1x_ether_macaddr called
dot1x-ev:dot1x_mgr_send_eapol: Sending out EAPOL packet on FastEthernet6
EAPOL pak dump Tx
EAPOL Version: 0x2  type: 0x0  length: 0x0005
EAP code: 0x1  id: 0x2  length: 0x0005 type: 0x1
```

```
dot1x-packet:dot1x_txReq: EAPOL packet sent out for the default authenticator
dot1x-sm:Fa6:0000.0000.0000:auth_bend_idle_request_action called
<!—Output Removed—>
@@@ dot1x_auth_bend Fa6: auth_bend_response -> auth_bend_request
dot1x-sm:Fa6:0015.c547.81c6:auth_bend_response_exit called
dot1x-sm:Fa6:0015.c547.81c6:auth_bend_request_enter called
dot1x-packet:dot1x_mgr_send_eapol :EAP code: 0x1  id: 0xB  length: 0x002B type:
0x19 data:
dot1x-ev:FastEthernet6:Sending EAPOL packet to group PAE address
dot1x-ev:dot1x_mgr_pre_process_eapol_pak: Role determination not required on
FastEthernet6.
dot1x-registry:registry:dot1x_ether_macaddr called
dot1x-ev:dot1x_mgr_send_eapol: Sending out EAPOL packet on FastEthernet6
EAPOL pak dump Tx
EAPOL Version: 0x2  type: 0x0  length: 0x002B
EAP code: 0x1  id: 0xB  length: 0x002B type: 0x19

dot1x-packet:dot1x_txReq: EAPOL packet sent to client (0015.c547.81c6)
dot1x-sm:Fa6:0015.c547.81c6:auth_bend_response_request_action called
dot1x-ev:dot1x_mgr_pre_process_eapol_pak: Role determination not required on
FastEthernet6.
dot1x-err:No dot1x subblockdot1x-packet:dot1x_mgr_send_eapol :EAP code: 0x1  id:
0x2  length: 0x0005 type: 0x1  data:
dot1x-ev:FastEthernet6:Sending EAPOL packet to group PAE address
dot1x-ev:dot1x_mgr_pre_process_eapol_pak: Role determination not required on
FastEthernet6.
dot1x-registry:registry:dot1x_ether_macaddr called
dot1x-ev:dot1x_mgr_send_eapol: Sending out EAPOL packet on FastEthernet6
EAPOL pak dump Tx
EAPOL Version: 0x2  type: 0x0  length: 0x0005
EAP code: 0x1  id: 0x2  length: 0x0005 type: 0x1
dot1x-packet:dot1x_txReq: EAPOL packet sent out for the default authenticator
dot1x-sm:Fa6:0000.0000.0000:auth_bend_idle_request_action called
<!—Output Removed—>
dot1x-ev:dot1x_mgr_send_eapol: Sending out EAPOL packet on FastEthernet6
EAPOL pak dump Tx
EAPOL Version: 0x2  type: 0x0  length: 0x0004
EAP code: 0x3  id: 0xB  length: 0x0004

dot1x-packet:dot1x_txReq: EAPOL packet sent to client (0015.c547.81c6)
%LINEPROTO-5-UPDOWN: Line protocol on Interface FastEthernet6, changed state to
up
```

Example 8-10 displays an excerpt of the **debug eap all** output. In this debug output, you can see all the exchanges; that is, EAP-Request/identity, EAP-Response/identity, and EAP-Success.

Example 8-10   debug eap all *Output Excerpt*

```
EAP-AUTH-EVENT: Current method = Identity
    eap_authen : idle during state eap_auth_tx_packet
@@@ eap_authen : eap_auth_tx_packet -> eap_auth_idle
EAP-AUTH-EVENT: Sending packet to lower layer for context 0x20000015
EAP-AUTH-TX-PAK: Code:REQUEST  ID:0x2   Length:0x0005  Type:IDENTITY

EAP-EVENT: Started 'Authenticator ReqId Retransmit' timer (30s) for EAP sesion
handle 0x20000015
EAP-EVENT: Started EAP tick timer
EAP-EVENT: Sending lower layer event 'EAP_TX_PACKET' on handle 0x20000015
EAP-EVENT: Received event 'EAP_RX_PACKET' on handle 0x20000015
EAP-AUTH-RX-PAK: Code:RESPONSE  ID:0x2   Length:0x0009  Type:IDENTITY

    Payload:  74657374
    eap_authen : during state eap_auth_idle, got event 1(eapRxPacket)
@@@ eap_authen : eap_auth_idle -> eap_auth_received

EAP-EVENT: Received event 'EAP_RX_PACKET' on handle 0x20000015
EAP-AUTH-RX-PAK: Code:RESPONSE  ID:0x6   Length:0x0070  Type:25
    Payload:  80000000661603010061010000005D030 ...
    eap_authen : during state eap_auth_idle2, got event 1(eapRxPacket)
@@@ eap_authen : eap_auth_idle2 -> eap_auth_received2
EAP-AUTH-EVENT: EAP Response received by context 0x20000015
EAP-AUTH-EVENT: EAP Response type = Method (25)


EAP-EVENT: eap_aaa_reply
EAP-AUTH-AAA-EVENT: Server status: PASS
EAP-AUTH-AAA-EVENT: Response contains MS MPPE Send Key, length:50
EAP-AUTH-AAA-EVENT: Response contains MS MPPE Recv Key, length:50
EAP-EVENT: Sending lower layer event 'EAP_KEY_AVAILABLE' on handle 0x20000015
EAP-AUTH-AAA-EVENT: Authorization not required for this context
EAP-EVENT: Received event 'EAP_AAA_SUCCESS' on handle 0x20000015

    eap_authen : during state eap_auth_aaa_idle, got event 5(eapAAASuccess)
@@@ eap_authen : eap_auth_aaa_idle -> eap_auth_success
EAP-EVENT: Sending lower layer event 'EAP_SUCCESS' on handle 0x20000015
EAP-EVENT: Received free context (0x20000015) from lower layer
EAP-EVENT: Received event 'EAP_DELETE' on handle 0x20000015
EAP-AUTH-EVENT: Freed EAP auth context
EAP-EVENT: Freed EAP context
EAP-EVENT: Stopped EAP tick timer
%LINEPROTO-5-UPDOWN: Line protocol on Interface FastEthernet6, changed state to up
```

Lab Scenario #9: Configuring Switch, ACS, and Windows XP for 802.1X Authentication Using EAP-TLS

The lab setup will remain the same as Lab Scenario #7; the only requirement that will change is the authentication method from EAP-MD5 to EAP-TLS.

Lab Solution

ACS 4.2 configuration requirement:

The ACS 4.2 configuration requirement is to install CA (the CA that issued the ACS server identity certificate and the CA that issued certificates to supplicants) and server certificate (the identity certificate for ACS) and enable EAP-TLS on ACS 4.2 as described in the section "Configuring EAP-TLS on ACS."

The ACS 5.1 configuration requirement is to install the CA and ACS server certificate on ACS 5.1 and check only **Allow EAP-TLS** in **Dot1xPolicy** on ACS 5.1 as described in the section "Configuring EAP-TLS on ACS."

For the switch configuration requirement, the configuration will remain the same as configured in Lab Scenario #7.

The client configuration requirements for this lab are satisfied as follows:

A. Ensure that the CA certificate and a client certificate issued to the client are installed on the client machine.

B. Configure the Windows XP client for EAP-TLS authentication from **Control Panel > Network Connections > Select the LAN connection > Right click > Properties > Authentication**. Ensure that **Enable IEEE 802.1X authentication** is checked and Select **Smart Card or other Certificate** under **Choose a network authentication method** as shown in Figure 8-39. Further, click on **Settings** and select **Use a certificate on this computer** option. Also choose the **Validate server certificate** option and click **Trusted root certificate authority** and select the root certification authority server for the enterprise EAP-TLS clients and ACS server.

Useful show Commands

show commands can provide very useful and meaningful output and can assist in troubleshooting various issues. **show** commands are generally used for confirming the change made in a device configuration or the current state/status of/on the device.

Useful **show** commands in Cisco IOS switches include the following:

show dot1x [**all** | **interface** *type slot/port*]: Displays IEEE 802.1x statistics, administrative status, and operational status for the switch or for the specified port.

- **show authentication registrations:** Displays details of all methods registered with the Auth Manager.

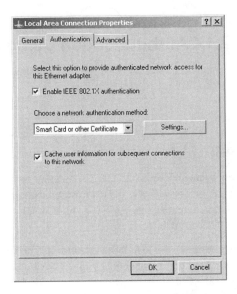

Figure 8-39 *EAP-TLS Configuration on Client*

show authentication interface *interface*: Displays all the Auth Manager details associated with the specified interface.

show authentication method *method*: Displays all clients authorized by a specified authentication method. Valid values are dot1x, mab and webauth.

show authentication sessions [**handle** *handle*] [**interface** *interface*] [**mac** *mac*] [**method** *method*] [**session-id** *session-id*]: Displays details of the current Auth Manager sessions (for example, client devices).

show mab {**all** | **interface** *type slot/port*} [**detail**]: Displays MAC authentication bypass (MAB) information.

Troubleshooting 802.1X

The following commands can be useful while troubleshooting 802.1X issues:

- **debug aaa authentication:** Displays debug messages for authentication only.

- **debug aaa authorization:** Displays debug messages for authorization only.

- **debug aaa accounting:** Displays debug messages for accounting only.

debug dot1x [**all** | **errors** | **events** | **feature** | **packets** | **redundancy** | **registry** | **state-machine**]: Enables debugging of the 802.1x feature.

debug eap [**all** | **method**] [**authenticator** | **peer**] {**all** | **errors** | **events** | **packets** | **sm**}: Enables debugging of the Extensible Authentication Protocol (EAP) activity.

debug radius [**accounting** | **authentication** | **brief** | **elog** | **failover** | **retransmit** | **verbose**]: Displays RADIUS debugging messages for all users and sessions, including decoded RADIUS messages.

Tip   Make sure that you turn off debug after required logs are collected. This can be done by using *no* for of the **debug** command or all the debugs can be turned off in one go by using the command **undebug all.**

Note   It is recommended that debugs/traces on the device must be enabled with caution as they can affect CPU utilization and device performance. It is best to use debug commands during periods of lower network traffic and fewer users. Debugging during these periods decreases the likelihood that increased debug command processing overhead will affect system use.

Summary

This chapter familiarized you with 802.1X concepts as well as explored 802.1X configuration from a Cisco switch perspective. In addition, the key takeaways and concepts covered in this chapter are as follows:

- 802.1X standard has three main entities: client or supplicant, authenticator, and authentication server.

- EAP is the key protocol in 802.1X used to pass the authentication information between the supplicant and authentication server.

- In EAP, four type of messages can be sent: Request, Response, Success, and Failure.

- EAP requests and responses are subdivided using the EAP Type filed.

- EAPOL is used to encapsulate the EAP messages.

- EAPOL has five messages: EAPOL-Packet, EAPOL-Start, EAPOL-Logoff, EAPOL-Key, and EAPOL-Encapsulated-ASF-Alert.

- A few of the more common EAP types are EAP-MD5, LEAP, PEAP, EAP-TLS, and EAP-FAST.

- 802.1X basic configuration on switch.

- 802.1X host modes: single, multiple, multidomain, multiauthentication, and pre-authentication open access.

- Guest and restricted VLAN feature with 802.1X.

- MAC authentication bypass feature for non 802.1X-compliant supplicants.

- Dynamic VLAN assignment for 802.1X-authenticated clients.

- Some of the more commonly used 802.1X timers are quiet period, tx-period, supp-timeout, server-timeout, and max-req.

- 802.1X accounting includes START, INTERIM, and STOP accounting packet types.

- How to configure EAP-MD5, PEAP, and EAP-TLS on ACS 4.2 and ACS 5.1.

Access Points

This chapter covers the following subjects:

- 802.1X and Wireless

- Configuring 802.1X on Access Points and Wireless LAN Controller

- Configuration Example Based on Some EAP Types Available on ACS 4.2 and ACS 5.1

This chapter is an extension of Chapter 8, "IOS Switches." The fundamental concepts that you learned in the previous chapter also apply to wireless infrastructure. The configuration part on ACS will also remain the same while configuring Protected Extensible Authentication Protocol (PEAP) and Extensible Authentication Protocol-Transport Layer Security (EAP-TLS). In the case of wireless infrastructure, you need only configure a wireless device for EAP authentication (authenticator). In today's world, whenever there is wireless (802.11) deployment, it is mostly bundled with 802.1X security to enhance network security.

Using what you learned from the previous chapter, this chapter shows how you can configure the Access Point (AP) and Wireless LAN Controller (WLC) for EAP authentication (authenticator).

Configuring Wireless NAS for 802.1X Authentication on an AP

Configuring an AP can be done from either the web interface or from the command-line interface (CLI). This section looks at configuration from the web interface.

The step-by-step procedure that follows looks at the configuration portion for EAP authentication and RADIUS server configuration on an Access Point; assuming that you already have a Service Set Identifier (SSID) configured with Wi-Fi Protected Access/Temporal Key Integrity Protocol (WPA/TKIP) or Wi-Fi Protected Access version

2/Advanced Encryption Standard (WPA2/AES) configured on it. The configuration steps are as follows:

Step 1.   Log in to the Access Point graphical user interface to generate the resulting screen in Figure 9-1.

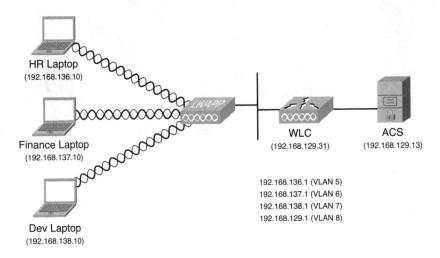

HR Laptop
(192.168.136.10)

Finance Laptop
(192.168.137.10)

Dev Laptop
(192.168.138.10)

WLC
(192.168.129.31)

ACS
(192.168.129.13)

192.168.136.1 (VLAN 5)
192.168.137.1 (VLAN 6)
192.168.138.1 (VLAN 7)
192.168.129.1 (VLAN 8)

Figure 9-1   *Access Point Web Interface*

Step 2.   Go to the **SECURITY > Server Manager** section to configure the RADIUS server in the Access Point configuration. In this section, specify the RADIUS server hostname or IP address and the shared secret key under Corporate Servers as shown in Figure 9-2.

In this section, you will also see the Default Server Priorities. Here you configure the global priority of the RADIUS server for various authentication and accounting tasks. You can configure the same RADIUS server as the primary server for EAP authentication and accounting as shown in Figure 9-3.

Step 3.   Go to **SECURITY > Encryption Manager** to configure TKIP or AES for the VLAN.

As Figure 9-4 shows, you are configuring TKIP (WPA) as the cipher for VLAN 15.

If the requirement is to configure AES so that WPA2 can be enabled, you can configure the cipher as shown in Figure 9-5.

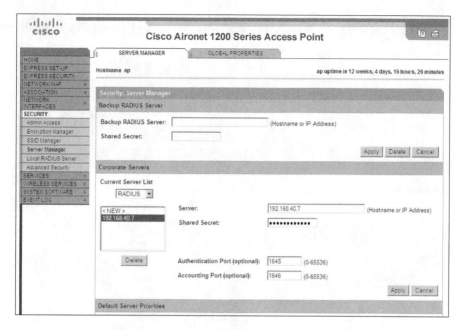

Figure 9-2 *RADIUS Server Configuration*

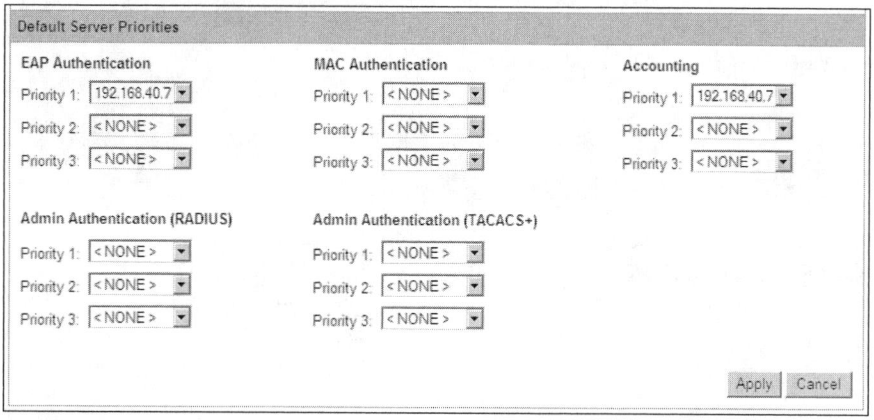

Figure 9-3 *RADIUS Server for EAP Authentication and Accounting*

Step 4.   Now select the SSID associated with the VLAN for which you configured a
cipher in step 3 from **SECURITY > SSID Manager** (see Figure 9-6).

Step 5.   After selecting the SSID that needs to be configured for 802.1X authentication, move to the section Client Authentication Settings.

Select Open Authentication and choose with EAP from the drop-down options.

Select Network EAP and keep the selection as <NO ADDITION>.

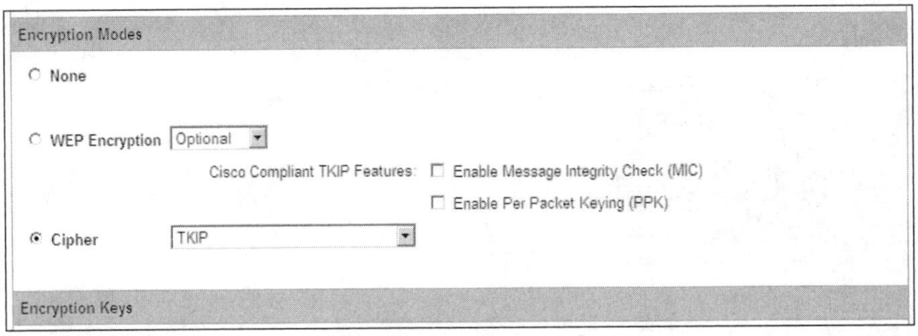

Figure 9-4 *Cipher TKIP on VLAN*

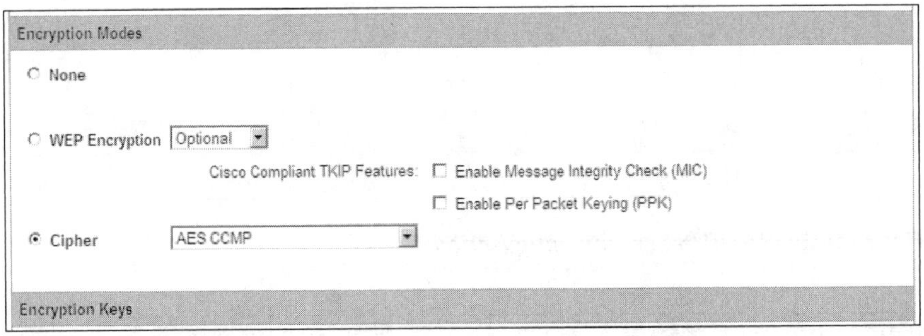

Figure 9-5 *Cipher AES on VLAN*

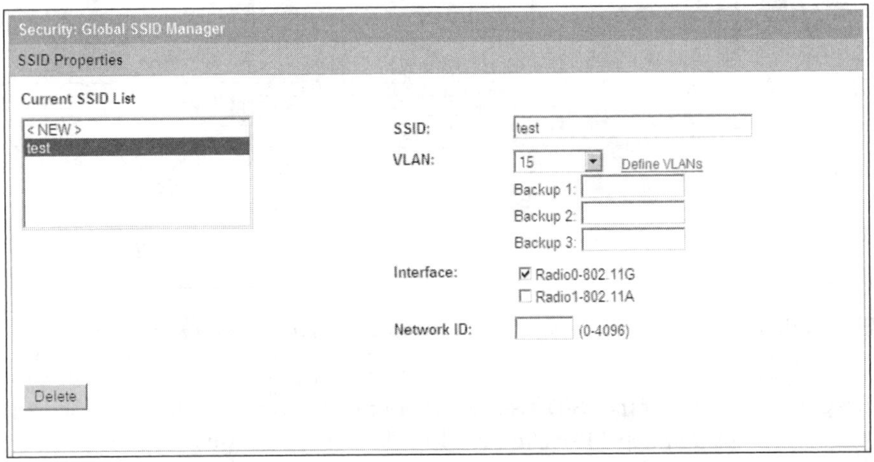

Figure 9-6 *SSID for 802.1X Authentication*

Also under Client Authentication Settings, you can either specify a particular RADIUS server for authentication or you can let it be the default; that is, Use

Defaults. The Use Defaults option refers to RADIUS server priority as defined in step 2.

Figure 9-7 shows the configuration for this step.

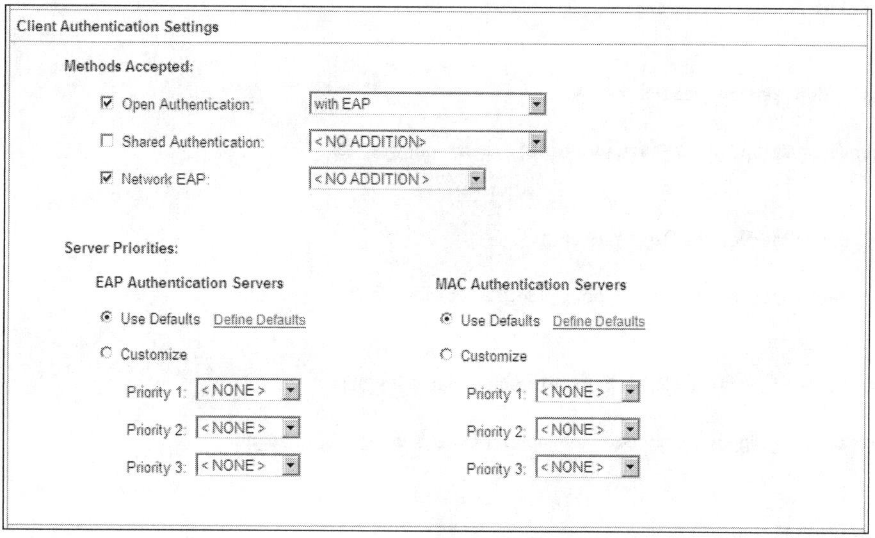

Figure 9-7   *Client Authentication Settings on SSID*

Step 6.   The final step is to specify the key management on the AP. For both WPA and WPA2, you will have the same setting on the AP.

For Key Management, choose Mandatory and check WPA as shown in Figure 9-8.

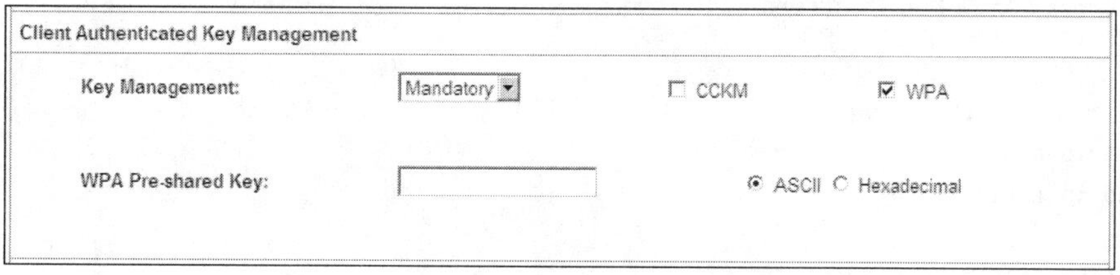

Figure 9-8   *Client Authenticated Key Management*

Note   Configuring RADIUS accounting is similar to specifying the server for the EAP authentication on an Access Point. You can choose to send accounting information to a specific RADIUS server in a specific order, or you can send the accounting information to a RADIUS server as defined under Default Server Priorities by checking Use Defaults for the SSID.

Example 9-1 illustrates CLI-based configuration example for a Cisco Access Point using WPA/TKIP. This CLI configuration is equivalent to one shown through the GUI.

Example 9-1   *802.1X Configuration on an Access Point*

```
aaa new-model
!
aaa group server radius rad_eap
 server 192.168.40.7 auth-port 1812 acct-port 1813
!
aaa group server radius rad_acct
 server 192.168.40.7 auth-port 1812 acct-port 1813
!
aaa authentication login eap_methods group rad_eap
aaa accounting network acct_methods start-stop group rad_acct
!
dot11 ssid test
   vlan 15
   authentication open eap eap_methods
   authentication network-eap eap_methods
   authentication key-management wpa
   accounting acct_methods
!
interface Dot11Radio0
 no ip address
 no ip route-cache
 !
 encryption mode ciphers tkip
 !
 encryption vlan 15 mode ciphers tkip
 !
 ssid test
 !
```

Configuring Wireless NAS for 802.1X Authentication on a WLC

The Cisco Wireless LAN Controller (WLC) is a part of Cisco Unified Wireless Network (CUWN) solution. Along with WLC, the CUWN solution consists of associated Lightweight Access Point Protocol (LWAPP) APs.

The following step-by-step procedure outlines the configuration required for 802.1X authentication on WLC:

Step 1.   Log in to the WLC to get to the screen shown in Figure 9-9.

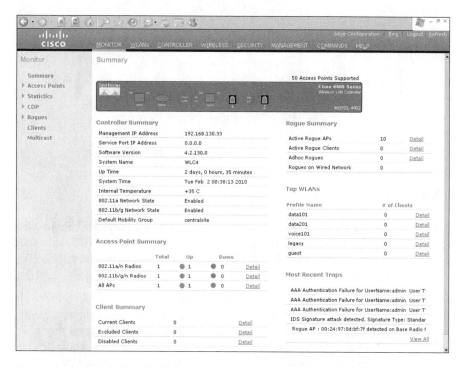

Figure 9-9   *WLC Graphical User Interface*

Step 2.   Configure the RADIUS server for authentication. If accounting is desired, a RADIUS server instance must be added exclusively for accounting, too.

To add a RADIUS server for authentication, go to **SECURITY > AAA > RADIUS > Authentication > New**

In the resulting screen in Figure 9-10, fill in the RADIUS server details. Ensure that the Network User option is enabled for wireless client authentication. You can also specify the global priority of the server entry on WLC (the lower the number, the higher the priority). The shared secret can be specified either in ASCII format or hex format.

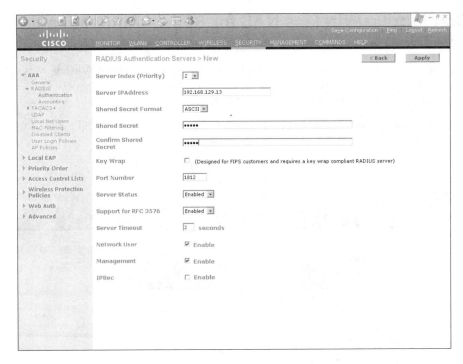

Figure 9-10   *Adding RADIUS Server for Authentication on WLC*

The Key Wrap is designed for Federal Information Processing Standards (FIPS) customers and requires a key-wrap–compliant RADIUS authentication server. Cisco Secure Access Control Server is among compliant RADIUS authentication servers.

To add the RADIUS server for accounting, go to **SECURITY > AAA > RADIUS > Accounting > New** for the resulting screen in Figure 9-11. All the fields are similar to those used while creating an authentication server instance on WLC. The only difference in the configuration would be to specify the correct port number for RADIUS accounting.

Step 3.   Now select and edit the SSID on which you want to configure 802.1X. The assumption here is that the security on the SSID is WPA/WPA2 TKIP/AES.

Go to **WLANs > Edit the SSID > Security** to get to the screen shown in Figure 9-12.

Go to the AAA Servers tab under **Security** for an SSID and choose the authentication server or authentication and accounting server both in this section; as shown in Figure 9-13.

This would be the minimum configuration required on WLC for 802.1X authentication.

If you are passing attributes/VSA from AAA server, for the WLC to acknowledge and apply them, you must allow AAA override. This option enables you to apply VLAN tagging, QoS, and ACLs to individual clients based on the returned RADIUS attributes from the AAA server.

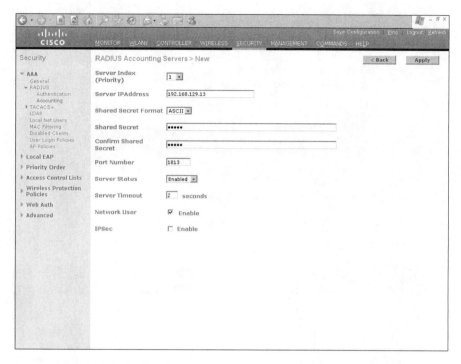

Figure 9-11   *Adding a RADIUS Server for Accounting on WLC*

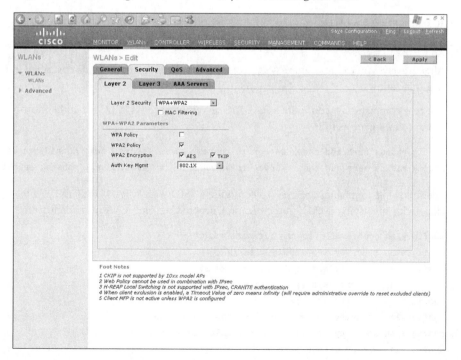

Figure 9-12   *Layer 2 Security on SSID*

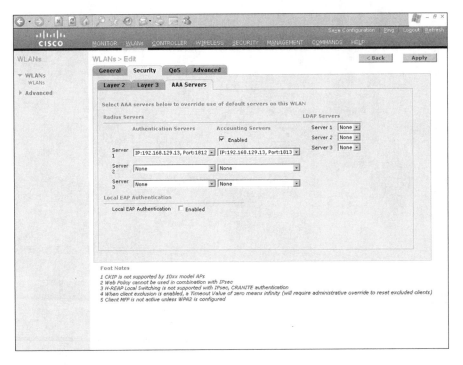

Figure 9-13   *AAA Servers Section Under SSID Configuration*

To configure AAA override; go to **WLANs > Edit SSID > Advanced.**

Check **Allow AAA Override** and apply the settings as shown in Figure 9-14.

Alternatively, you can configure WLC from the CLI using the commands described in the text that follows.

The two commands to configure a RADIUS server instance on WLC for authentication and accounting are as follows:

```
config radius auth add index server-ip-address port# {ascii | hex} shared-secret
config radius acct add index server-ip-address port# {ascii | hex} <shared_secret>
```

The following commands are used to configure a SSID with WPA/WPA2 TKIP/AES, along with specifying 802.1X authentication, accounting, and AAA override feature:

```
config wlan create wlan-id profile-name ssid
config wlan security wpa enable wlan-id
config wlan security wpa wpa1 enable wlan-id
config wlan security wpa wpa2 enable wlan-id
config wlan security wpa wpa1 ciphers tkip enable wlan-id
config wlan security wpa wpa2 ciphers aes enable wlan-id
config wlan security wpa akm 802.1X enable wlan-id
config wlan radius_server auth enable wlan-id
```

```
config wlan radius_server acct enable wlan-id
wlan radius_server auth add wlan-id server-id
wlan radius_server acct add wlan-id server-id
wlan aaa-override enable wlan-id
config wlan enable wlan-id
```

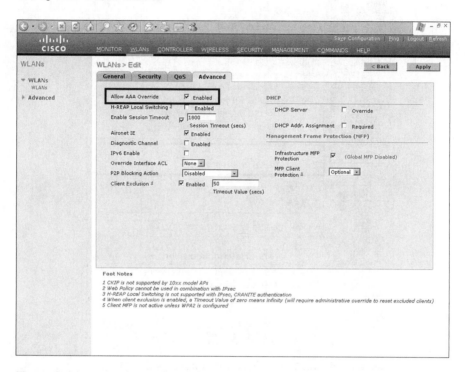

Figure 9-14   *AAA Override on WLC*

Configuring ACS 4.2 for LEAP

On ACS 4.2, you will find LEAP configuration under the Global Authentication Setup section.

To configure LEAP on ACS 4.2, go to **System Configuration > Global Authentication Status**.

Ensure that the Allow LEAP option is checked under the LEAP section as shown in Figure 9-15.

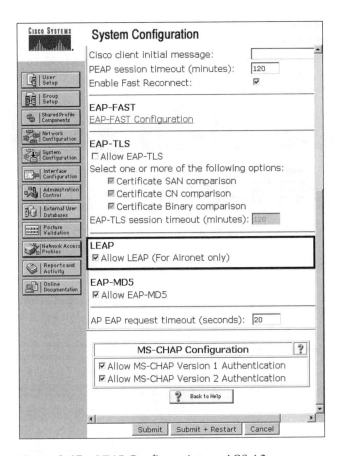

Figure 9-15   *LEAP Configuration on ACS 4.2*

Configuring ACS 5.1 for LEAP

To allow LEAP on ACS 5.1 it needs to be allowed on an access service. To allow LEAP on an already configured access service, go to **Access Policies > Access Services.**

Edit the desired access service and go to the Allowed Protocols tab to enable LEAP as shown in Figure 9-16.

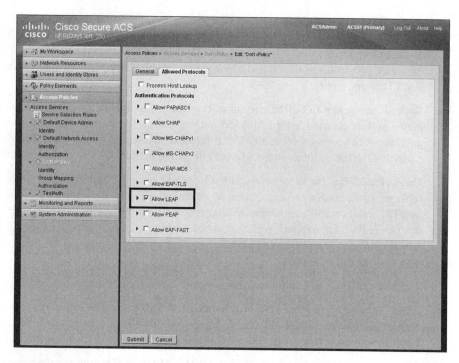

Figure 9-16   *LEAP Configuration on ACS 5.1*

Configuring ACS 4.2 for EAP-FAST

EAP-FAST configuration options are available under the Global Authentication Setup section on ACS 4.2. To configure EAP-FAST, go to **System Configuration > Global Authentication Setup > EAP-FAST Configuration.**

This section contains all configuration parameters related to EAP-FAST. To enable EAP-FAST, check Allow EAP-FAST.

If you are configuring anonymous Protected Access Credential (PAC) provisioning, you must configure the following:

Note   PACs are strong shared secrets that enable ACS and an EAP-FAST end user client to authenticate each other and establish a TLS tunnel for use in EAP-FAST phase two. Before that, PACs need to be supplied to the end user client (that is, provisioned). Automatic PAC provisioning sends a new PAC to an end user client over a secured network connection. Automatic PAC provisioning requires no intervention of the network user or an ACS administrator provided that you configure ACS and the end user client to support automatic provisioning.

- **Active master key TTL:** The amount of time that a master key is used to generate new PACs. A master key expires when it is older than the sum of the master key TTL and the retired master key TTL. When the TTL that is defined for the master key expires, it is considered retired and a new master key is generated. The default master key TTL is one month.

- **Retired master key TTL:** The amount of time the PACs generated by using a retired master key are acceptable for EAP-FAST authentication. When an end-user client gains network access by using a PAC that is based on a retired master key, ACS sends a new PAC to the end-user client. The default retired master key TTL is three months.

- **Tunnel PAC TTL:** The duration that a PAC is used before it expires and must be replaced. If the master key that is used to generate the Tunnel PAC has not expired, new PAC creation and assignment is automatic. If the master key used to generate the Tunnel PAC that expired, you must use automatic or manual provisioning to provide the end-user client with a new PAC.

- **Authority ID Info:** This field is mandatory. It is the textual identity of the ACS server, which an end user can use to determine which ACS server to be authenticated against.

- **Allow anonymous in-band PAC provisioning:** ACS provisions an end-user client with a PAC by using EAP-FAST phase zero. ACS establishes a secured connection with the end-user client for the purpose of providing the client with a new PAC.

- **Allowed inner methods (EAP-GTC & EAP-MSCHAPv2):** This option determines which inner EAP methods can run inside the EAP-FAST TLS tunnel. For anonymous in-band provisioning, you must enable EAP-GTC and EAP-MS-CHAP for backward compatibility. If you selected **Allow anonymous in-band PAC provisioning**, you must select EAP-MS-CHAP (phase zero) and EAP-GTC (phase two).

Figure 9-17 and Figure 9-18 show the configuration of the items in the preceding list.

Configuring ACS 5.1 for EAP-FAST

To allow EAP-FAST on ACS 5.1, it needs to be allowed on the access service. To allow EAP-FAST on an already configured access service, go to **Access Policies > Access Services**.

Edit the desired access service and go to the Allowed Protocols tab to enable EAP-FAST as shown in Figure 9-20.

Also configure the suboptions of EAP-FAST. Allow the inner method that needs to be allowed. For anonymous PAC provisioning, check the option **Allow Anonymous In-Band PAC Provisioning**. With anonymous in-band PAC provisioning, the inner methods used are MS-CHAPv2 and EAP-GTC. In this section, you can define Tunnel PAC TTL, which restricts the lifetime of PAC. The default value is one day.

In this section you also have an option for a proactive PAC update. This option is configured as percentage of the remaining TTL. This ensures that the end-user client has a valid PAC. The default value is 10%.

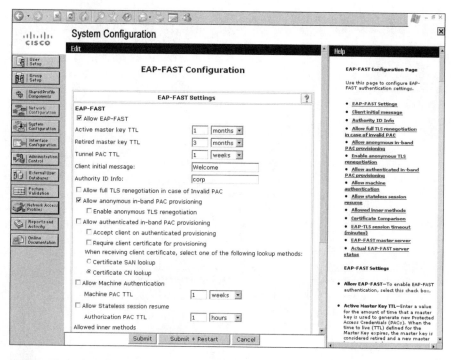

Figure 9-17 *EAP-FAST Configuration on ACS 4.2*

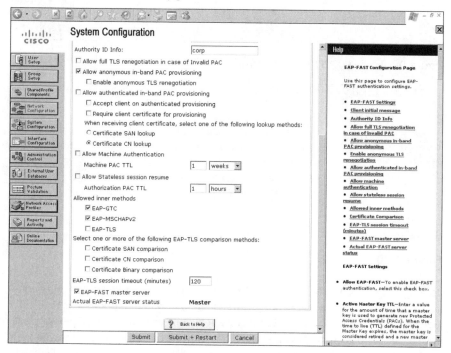

Figure 9-18 *EAP-FAST Configuration on ACS 4.2*

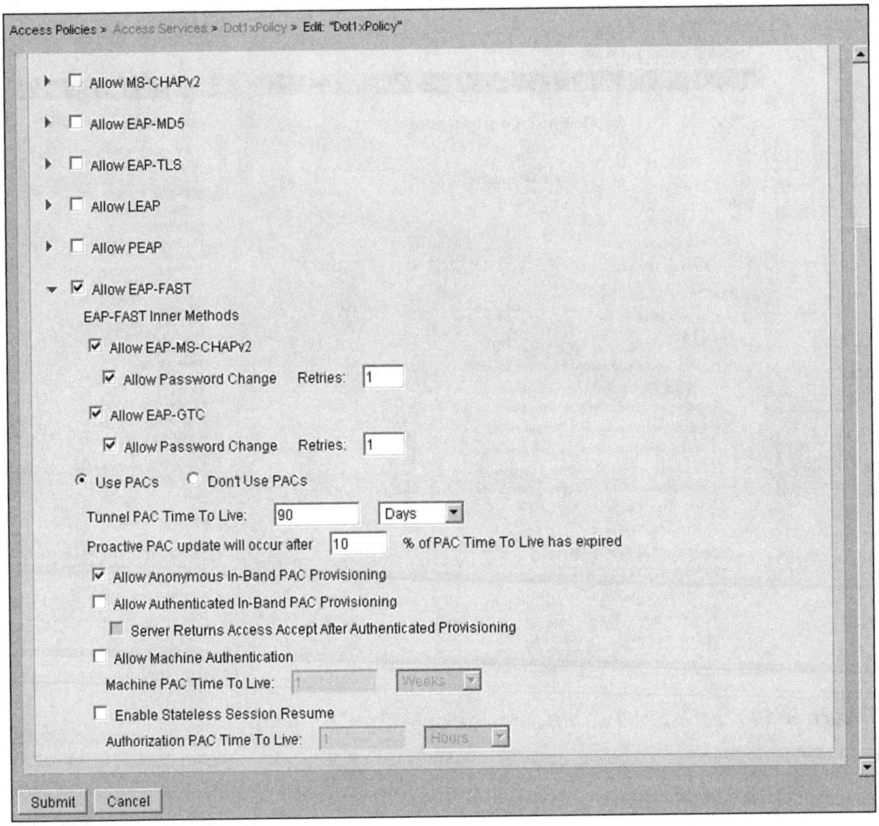

Figure 9-19   *EAP-FAST Configuration on ACS 5.1*

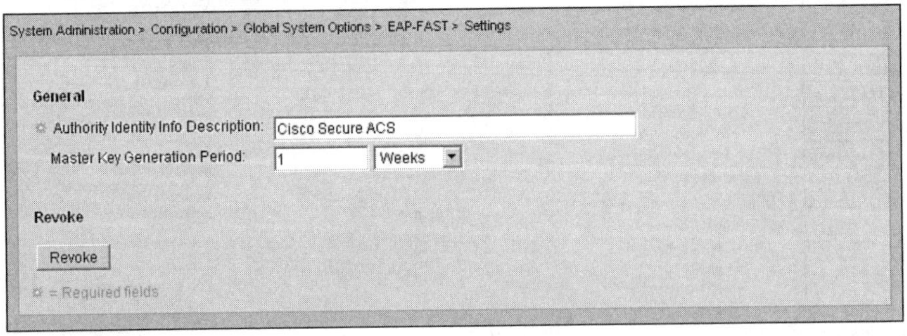

Figure 9-20   *EAP-FAST Settings on ACS 5.1*

If you need to change the authority ID for the server or master key generation period, go to **System Administration > Configuration > Global System Options > EAP-FAST > Settings** as shown in Figure 9-20. In this section, you can also use the **Revoke** option to revoke all previous master keys and PACs. The **Revoke** operation should be used with caution because revoking master keys and PACs will cause all the end-user clients to obtain new PACs from the server.

Lab Scenario #10: Configure WLC, ACS and Cisco Secure Services Client for 802.1X Authentication Using LEAP

ABC Inc. has a requirement to secure all the Windows XP workstations connected through its wireless network. The company has three departments: HR, Finance, and Development, but has only a single SSID—data101_1. All members of each team connecting to the corporate wireless network must be authenticated using ACS and then placed into the following VLANs:

■ **HR team:** VLAN 5

■ **Finance team:** VLAN 6

■ **Development team:** VLAN 7

For this lab scenario, you will need to configure the WLC, client, and ACS for LEAP authentication.

Lab Setup

The lab setup requires one switch, one ACS server, one Lightweight Access Point Protocol (LWAPP) AP, one WLC, and one Windows XP machine with Cisco Secure Services Client installed for wireless communication. Figure 9-21 shows the required setup.

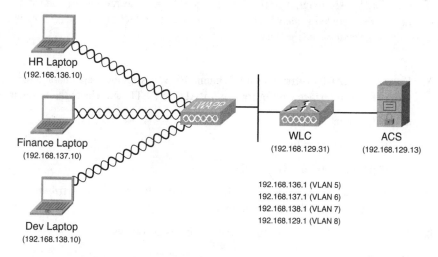

Figure 9-21 *Setup for Lab Scenario #10*

Lab Solution

The solution to this scenario assumes certain things that are very basic and are expected to be configured by the candidate using the knowledge obtained from previous sections. Only 802.1X-related configuration on WLC will be covered in this solution section.

The assumptions are as follows:

A.   A WLC entry exists on ACS configuration:

- ACS 5.1: Under **Network Resources > Network Devices and AAA Clients**

- ACS 4.2: Under **Network Configuration > ... > AAA Clients**

B.   Three groups are created in the ACS configuration: HR, Finance, and Development:

- ACS 5.1: Under **Users and Identity Stores > Identity Groups**

- ACS 4.2: Under **Group Setup**

C.   Users are configured under each of the three groups.

- ACS 5.1: Under **Users and Identity Stores > Internal Identity Stores > Users**

- ACS 4.2: **User Setup**

ACS 4.2 Configuration Requirements

Note   Dynamic VLAN assignment requirements are the same as required in the Chapter 8 Lab Scenarios. For detailed screenshots for the configuration section, please refer back to the Lab Scenario sections in Chapter 8.

A.   Ensure that RADIUS attributes for dynamic VLAN assignment are enabled for the group. Go to **Interface Configuration > RADIUS (IETF)** and check the following:

- **[064] Tunnel-Type**

- **[065] Tunnel-Medium-Type**

- **[081] Tunnel-Private-Group-ID**

If you are not sending multiple attributes for other RADIUS IETF attributes, change the **Tags to Display Per Attribute** to **1**.

B.   Under individual groups configure the attributes as follows:

HR group:

- [064] Tunnel-Type, Tag: **1**, Value: **VLAN**

- [065] Tunnel-Medium-Type, Tag: **1**, Value: **802**

- [081] Tunnel-Private-Group-ID, Value: **5**

Finance group:

- [064] Tunnel-Type, Tag: **1**, Value: **VLAN**

- [065] Tunnel-Medium-Type, Tag: **1**, Value: **802**

- [081] Tunnel-Private-Group-ID, Value: **6**

Development group:

- [064] Tunnel-Type, Tag: **1**, Value: **VLAN**

- [065] Tunnel-Medium-Type, Tag: **1**, Value: **802**

- [081] Tunnel-Private-Group-ID, Value: **7**

C.   From the section **System Configuration > Global Authentication Setup**, check Allow LEAP under the LEAP section.

After configuring attributes for individual group and ensuring the LEAP is enabled, click **Submit + Restart** to ensure that settings take effect.

ACS 5.1 Configuration Requirements

A.   Create a device filter named **Dot1xWLC** for the WLC configured under the **Network Resources > Network Devices and AAA Clients** section.

- The device filter can be created from **Policy Elements > Session Conditions > Network Conditions > Device Filters**.

B.   Create three authorization profiles under **Policy Elements > Authorization and Permissions > Network Access > Authorization Profiles**:

- HR VLAN Profile

- Finance VLAN Profile

- Development VLAN Profile

Under the RADIUS Attributes tab, configure following two attributes for each profile:

Note   VLAN assignment on ACS 5.1 can also be configured using common task as described in the section, "Dynamic VLAN Assignment for ACS 5.1," in Chapter 8.

- Dictionary Type: **RADIUS-IETF**

- RADIUS Attribute: **Tunnel-Type**

- Attribute Type: **Tagged Enum**

- Attribute Value: **Static: VLAN**

Tag: **1**

- Dictionary Type: **RADIUS-IETF**
- RADIUS Attribute: **Tunnel-Medium-Type**
- Attribute Type: **Tagged Enum**
- Attribute Value: **Static: 802**

Tag: **1**

For the last attribute required for dynamic VLAN assignment, you must have the values 5, 6, and 7 for the Attribute Value for each respective profile:

- Dictionary Type: **RADIUS-IETF**
- RADIUS Attribute: **Tunnel-Private-Group-ID**
- Attribute Type: **Tagged String**
- Attribute Value: Static: **5**

Tag: **1**

- Dictionary Type: **RADIUS-IETF**
- RADIUS Attribute: **Tunnel-Private-Group-ID**
- Attribute Type: **Tagged String**
- Attribute Value: **Static: 6**

Tag: **1**

- Dictionary Type: **RADIUS-IETF**
- RADIUS Attribute: **Tunnel-Private-Group-ID**
- Attribute Type: **Tagged String**
- Attribute Value: Static: **7**

Tag: **1**

C. Create an access service named **Dot1xPolicy** under **Access Policies > Access Services.**

- For **Policy Structure** for access services, only check **Identity & Authorization.**

Under **Allowed Protocols,** only allow LEAP.

D. Create a rule to match and to apply the access service configured in the previous step from **Access Policies > Access Services > Service Selection Rules.** Under **Conditions** select the following:

- Protocol: **match: Radius**
- Device Filter: **match: Dot1xWLC**
- For **Result,** select **Dot1xPolicy**

WLC Configuration Requirements

Please refer to the section "Configuring Wireless NAS for 802.1X Authentication on a WLC" in this chapter to configure the SSID for 802.1X. Ensure that you enable AAA override to allow dynamic VLAN assignment.

Client Configuration Requirements

On the client, ensure that Cisco Secure Services Client (CSSC) is already installed. In CSSC, add SSID by clicking the Add SSID option. Add the SSID data101_1 and choose the appropriate security setting corresponding to WLC configuration.

Under the 802.1X Configuration section, select LEAP as the EAP method and password as the credential type as shown in Figure 9-22.

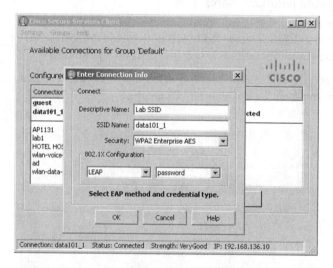

Figure 9-22   *CSSC LEAP Configuration*

Lab Scenario #11: Configure WLC, ACS, and Cisco Secure Services Client for 802.1X Authentication Using EAP-FAST

The lab setup will remain the same as Lab Scenario #10, with the only requirement change being the shift from LEAP to EAP-FAST.

Lab Solution

The lab solution for the changed requirement will require changes in some sections of the solution provided for Lab Scenario #10. The sections that follow cover only the changes that should be made to get this lab setup to work.

ACS 4.2 Configuration Requirements

Refer to step C in the "ACS 4.2 Configuration Requirements" section for the Lab Scenario #10 Solution. Under **System Configuration > Global Authentication Setup**, configure EAP-FAST instead of LEAP in the screens shown previously in Figure 9-17 and Figure 9-18. The rest of the configuration remains the same.

ACS 5.1 Configuration Requirements

Refer to step C in the "ACS 5.1 Configuration Requirements" section for the Lab Scenario #10 solution. Under Allowed Protocols, configure EAP-FAST instead of LEAP in the screen shown previously in Figure 9-19. The rest of the configuration remains the same.

Client Configuration Requirements

On the client, ensure that Cisco Secure Services Client (CSSC) is already installed. On CSSC, add SSID by clicking the **Add SSID** option. Add the SSID **data101_1** and choose the appropriate security setting corresponding to WLC configuration.

Under the 802.1X Configuration section, select EAP-FAST as the EAP method and password as the credential type as shown in Figure 9-23.

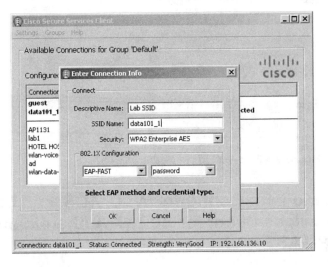

Figure 9-23 *CSSC EAP-FAST Configuration*

Troubleshooting 802.1X

The following commands can be useful while troubleshooting 802.1X issues on WLC:

```
debug aaa [all | events | detail] enable
debug dot1x [packet | events | states] enable
```

Example 9-2 illustrates output from **debug aaa events enable** from the Cisco WLC. In these debugs you can clearly see RADIUS message exchanges. These message exchanges can be used to track the issue during troubleshooting. In addition, the **debug mac address** *mac-address* command can prove very useful when troubleshooting a particular end-user client.

Example 9-2   debug aaa events enable *Output*

```
(Cisco Controller) >debug mac addr 00:22:68:d2:f6:a8
(Cisco Controller) >debug aaa events enable
(Cisco Controller) >
*Aug 11 17:28:20.961: 00:22:68:d2:f6:a8 DHCP    server id: 1.1.1.1  rcvd server
id: 192.168.28.47
*Aug 11 17:33:48.498: apfVapRadiusInfoGet: WLAN(1) dynamic int attributes
srcAddr:0x0, gw:0x0, mask:0x0, vlan:0, dpPort:0, srcPort:0
*Aug 11 17:33:48.498: 00:22:68:d2:f6:a8 Successful transmission of Authentication
Packet (id 27) to 192.168.28.101:1812, proxy state 00:22:68:d2:f6:a8-00:00
*Aug 11 17:33:48.501: ****Enter processIncomingMessages: response code=11


*Aug 11 17:33:48.501: ****Enter processRadiusResponse: response code=11


<!— output truncated—>
*Aug 11 17:33:48.639: 00:22:68:d2:f6:a8 Access-Challenge received from RADIUS
server 192.168.28.101 for mobile 00:22:68:d2:f6:a8 receiveId = 12
*Aug 11 17:33:48.642: apfVapRadiusInfoGet: WLAN(1) dynamic int attributes
srcAddr:0x0, gw:0x0, mask:0x0, vlan:0, dpPort:0, srcPort:0
*Aug 11 17:33:48.642: 00:22:68:d2:f6:a8 Successful transmission of Authentication
Packet (id 31) to 192.168.28.101:1812, proxy state 00:22:68:d2:f6:a8-00:00
*Aug 11 17:33:48.645: ****Enter processIncomingMessages: response code=2


*Aug 11 17:33:48.645: ****Enter processRadiusResponse: response code=2


*Aug 11 17:33:48.645: 00:22:68:d2:f6:a8 Access-Accept received from RADIUS server
192.168.28.101 for mobile 00:22:68:d2:f6:a8 receiveId = 12
*Aug 11 17:33:48.645: 00:22:68:d2:f6:a8 Applying new AAA override for station
00:22:68:d2:f6:a8
*Aug 11 17:33:48.645: 00:22:68:d2:f6:a8 Override values for station
00:22:68:d2:f6:a8        source: 4, valid bits: 0x0
    qosLevel: -1, dscp: 0xffffffff, dot1pTag: 0xffffffff, sessionTimeout: -1
dataAvgC: -1, rTAvgC
*Aug 11 17:33:48.646: 00:22:68:d2:f6:a8 Inserting new RADIUS override into chain
for station 00:22:68:d2:f6:a8
```

```
*Aug 11 17:33:48.646: 00:22:68:d2:f6:a8 Override values for station
00:22:68:d2:f6:a8       source: 4, valid bits: 0x0
   qosLevel: -1, dscp: 0xffffffff, dot1pTag: 0xffffffff, sessionTimeout: -1
dataAvgC: -1, rTAvgC
*Aug 11 17:33:48.656: 00:22:68:d2:f6:a8 Sending Accounting request (0) for station
00:22:68:d2:f6:a8
*Aug 11 17:33:48.657: apfVapRadiusInfoGet: WLAN(1) dynamic int attributes
srcAddr:0x0, gw:0x0, mask:0x0, vlan:0, dpPort:0, srcPort:0
*Aug 11 17:33:48.657: 00:22:68:d2:f6:a8 Successful transmission of Accounting-
Interim (id 6) to 192.168.28.101:1813, proxy state 00:22:68:d2:f6:a8-00:00
*Aug 11 17:33:48.661: ****Enter processIncomingMessages: response code=5

*Aug 11 17:33:48.661: ****Enter processRadiusResponse: response code=5

*Aug 11 17:33:48.661: 00:22:68:d2:f6:a8 Accounting-Response received from RADIUS
server 192.168.28.101 for mobile 00:22:68:d2:f6:a8 receiveId = 0
```

Example 9-3 illustrates output from the **debug aaa detail enable** command. This debug can be used to check the Attribute Value Pair (AVP) being sent and received for troubleshooting purposes on a Cisco WLC.

Example 9-3 debug aaa detail enable *Command Output*

```
(Cisco Controller) >debug aaa detail enable
AuthenticationRequest: 0x18e5ecf4

   Callback.....................................0x109fa804
   protocolType.................................0x00140001
   proxyState...................................00:22:68:D2:F6:A8-0E:00
   Packet contains 12 AVPs (not shown)
   AuthorizationResponse: 0x13e8fd98
   structureSize................................125
   resultCode...................................255
   protocolUsed.................................0x00000001
   proxyState...................................00:22:68:D2:F6:A8-0E:00
   Packet contains 3 AVPs (not shown)
<!— Output truncated —>
   AuthorizationResponse: 0x13e8fd98
   structureSize................................239
   resultCode...................................0
   protocolUsed.................................0x00000001
   proxyState...................................00:22:68:D2:F6:A8-0E:04
   Packet contains 6 AVPs:
       AVP[01] Framed-IP-Address........................0xffffffff (-1) (4 bytes)
       AVP[02] EAP-Message..............................0x030a0004 (50987012) (4
bytes)
       AVP[03] Microsoft / MPPE-Send-Key................DATA (32 bytes)
```

```
     AVP[04] Microsoft / MPPE-Recv-Key...............DATA (32 bytes)
     AVP[05] Class...................................CACS:0/18f0f/c0a81c2f/2 (23
bytes)
     AVP[06] Message-Authenticator..................DATA (16 bytes)
 AccountingMessage Accounting Interim: 0x18e646dc
 Packet contains 18 AVPs:
     AVP[01] User-Name..............................admin (5 bytes)
     AVP[02] Nas-Port...............................0x00000002 (2) (4 bytes)
     AVP[03] Nas-Ip-Address.........................0xc0a81c2f (-1062724561)
 (4 bytes)
     AVP[04] Framed-IP-Address......................0xc0a81c51 (-1062724527)
 (4 bytes)
     AVP[05] Class...................................CACS:0/18f0f/c0a81c2f/2 (23
bytes)
     AVP[06] NAS-Identifier..........................cisco47 (7 bytes)
< !—output truncated — >
     AVP[10] Acct-Status-Type........................0x00000003 (3) (4 bytes)
     AVP[11] Acct-Input-Octets.......................0x0000aadc (43740) (4 bytes)
     AVP[12] Acct-Output-Octets......................0x00001f60 (8032) (4 bytes)
     AVP[13] Acct-Input-Packets......................0x00000327 (807) (4 bytes)
     AVP[14] Acct-Output-Packets.....................0x00000037 (55) (4 bytes)
     AVP[15] Acct-Session-Time.......................0x0000022d (557) (4 bytes)
     AVP[16] Acct-Delay-Time.........................0x00000000 (0) (4 bytes)
     AVP[17] Calling-Station-Id......................192.168.28.81 (13 bytes)
```

Example 9-4 illustrates output from the **debug dot1x events enable** command. This is
another useful debug that can be used for troubleshooting to track the message exchange
that takes place between the end-user client and the RADIUS server through Cisco WLC.

Example 9-4   debug dot1x events enable *Command Output*

```
(Cisco Controller) >debug dot1x events enable
 00:22:68:d2:f6:a8 Processing RSN IE type 48, length 20 for mobile
00:22:68:d2:f6:a8
 00:22:68:d2:f6:a8 Received RSN IE with 0 PMKIDs from mobile 00:22:68:d2:f6:a8
 00:22:68:d2:f6:a8 Disable re-auth, use PMK lifetime.
 00:22:68:d2:f6:a8 Sending EAP-Request/Identity to mobile 00:22:68:d2:f6:a8 (EAP
Id 1)
 00:22:68:d2:f6:a8 Received EAPOL START from mobile 00:22:68:d2:f6:a8
 00:22:68:d2:f6:a8 Sending EAP-Request/Identity to mobile 00:22:68:d2:f6:a8 (EAP
Id 2)
 00:22:68:d2:f6:a8 Received EAPOL EAPPKT from mobile 00:22:68:d2:f6:a8
 00:22:68:d2:f6:a8 Received EAP Response packet with mismatching id (currentid=2,
eapid=1) from mobile 00:22:68:d2:f6:a8
 00:22:68:d2:f6:a8 Received EAPOL EAPPKT from mobile 00:22:68:d2:f6:a8
```

```
00:22:68:d2:f6:a8 Received Identity Response (count=2) from mobile
00:22:68:d2:f6:a8
 00:22:68:d2:f6:a8 Processing Access-Challenge for mobile 00:22:68:d2:f6:a8
 00:22:68:d2:f6:a8 WARNING: updated EAP-Identifer 2 ===> 9 for STA
00:22:68:d2:f6:a8
 00:22:68:d2:f6:a8 Sending EAP Request from AAA to mobile 00:22:68:d2:f6:a8 (EAP
Id 9)
< !— output truncated — >
 00:22:68:d2:f6:a8 Received EAP Response from mobile 00:22:68:d2:f6:a8 (EAP Id 11,
EAP Type 25)
 00:22:68:d2:f6:a8 Processing Access-Challenge for mobile 00:22:68:d2:f6:a8
 00:22:68:d2:f6:a8 Sending EAP Request from AAA to mobile 00:22:68:d2:f6:a8 (EAP
Id 12)
 00:22:68:d2:f6:a8 Received EAPOL EAPPKT from mobile 00:22:68:d2:f6:a8
 00:22:68:d2:f6:a8 Received EAP Response from mobile 00:22:68:d2:f6:a8 (EAP Id 12,
EAP Type 25)
 00:22:68:d2:f6:a8 Processing Access-Accept for mobile 00:22:68:d2:f6:a8
 00:22:68:d2:f6:a8 Setting re-auth timeout to 1800 seconds, got from WLAN config.
 00:22:68:d2:f6:a8 Station 00:22:68:d2:f6:a8 setting dot1x reauth timeout = 1800
 00:22:68:d2:f6:a8 Creating a PKC PMKID Cache entry for station
00:22:68:d2:f6:a8 (RSN 2)
 00:22:68:d2:f6:a8 Adding BSSID 00:17:59:08:6c:d0 to PMKID cache for station
00:22:68:d2:f6:a8
New PMKID: (16)
     [0000] 35 87 7c d1 34 4e a3 eb 0c 18 9c 34 e4 4d aa ce
 00:22:68:d2:f6:a8 Disabling re-auth since PMK lifetime can take care of same.
 00:22:68:d2:f6:a8 PMK sent to mobility group
 00:22:68:d2:f6:a8 Sending EAP-Success to mobile 00:22:68:d2:f6:a8 (EAP Id 12)
```

The following commands can be useful while troubleshooting 802.1X issues on autonomous AP:

```
debug dot11 aaa authenticator state-machine
debug dot11 aaa authenticator process or debug dot11 aaa dot1x process
debug radius authentication
debug aaa authentication
```

Example 9-5 illustrates output from the debug dot11 aaa authenticator process command. This debug can be used during troubleshooting authentication issues with an end-user client through a Cisco Access Point. You can also use the debug condition mac-address *mac-address-of-client* to debug a particular end-user client message exchange.

Example 9-5   debug dot11 aaa authenticator process *Command Output*

```
ap#debug condition mac-address 0022.68d2.f6a8
ap#debug dot11 aaa authenticator process
 dot11_auth_dot1x_start: in the dot11_auth_dot1x_start
```

```
dot11_auth_parse_client_pak: Received EAPOL packet from 0022.68d2.f6a8
dot11_auth_parse_client_pak: Received EAPOL packet from 0022.68d2.f6a8
dot11_auth_parse_client_pak: id is not matching req-id:1resp-id:2, waiting for
response
dot11_auth_parse_client_pak: Received EAPOL packet from 0022.68d2.f6a8
dot11_auth_dot1x_parse_aaa_resp: Received server response: GET_CHALLENGE_RESPONSE
dot11_auth_dot1x_parse_aaa_resp: found eap pak in server response
dot11_auth_dot1x_parse_aaa_resp: found session timeout 20 sec
dot11_auth_parse_client_pak: Received EAPOL packet from 0022.68d2.f6a8
dot11_auth_dot1x_parse_aaa_resp: Received server response: GET_CHALLENGE_RESPONSE
dot11_auth_dot1x_parse_aaa_resp: found eap pak in server response
dot11_auth_parse_client_pak: Received EAPOL packet from 0022.68d2.f6a8
dot11_auth_dot1x_parse_aaa_resp: Received server response: GET_CHALLENGE_RESPONSE
dot11_auth_dot1x_parse_aaa_resp: found eap pak in server response
dot11_auth_dot1x_parse_aaa_resp: found session timeout 20 sec
dot11_auth_parse_client_pak: Received EAPOL packet from 0022.68d2.f6a8
dot11_auth_dot1x_parse_aaa_resp: Received server response: GET_CHALLENGE_RESPONSE
dot11_auth_dot1x_parse_aaa_resp: found eap pak in server response
dot11_auth_dot1x_parse_aaa_resp: found session timeout 20 sec
dot11_auth_parse_client_pak: Received EAPOL packet from 0022.68d2.f6a8
dot11_auth_dot1x_parse_aaa_resp: Received server response: PASS
dot11_auth_dot1x_parse_aaa_resp: found eap pak in server response
dot11_auth_dot1x_parse_aaa_resp: Found AAA_AT_MS_MPPE_SEND_KEY in server response
dot11_auth_dot1x_parse_aaa_resp: AAA_AT_MS_MPPE_SEND_KEY session key length 32
dot11_auth_dot1x_parse_aaa_resp: Found AAA_AT_MS_MPPE_RECV_KEY in server response
dot11_auth_dot1x_parse_aaa_resp: AAA_AT_MS_MPPE_RECV_KEY session key length 32
```

Summary

In Chapter 8, you learned about the basic concepts of 802.1X and its practical approach in a wired environment. In this chapter, you learned how to apply your knowledge of 802.1X in a wireless environment. As 802.1X is more popular among wireless deployments to secure the wireless access, that is easily accessible. The key concepts and skills learned in this chapter are as follows:

- Enabling and configuring LEAP on ACS 4.2 and ACS 5.1

- Enabling and configuring EAP-FAST on ACS 4.2 and ACS 5.1

- Configuring SSID on autonomous access point for 802.1X authentication

- Configuring SSID on WLC for 802.1X authentication

- AAA override on WLC to apply RADIUS attributes returned by AAA server

- Lab exercise illustrating practical application of LEAP and EAP-FAST using Cisco Secure Services Client

Chapter 10

Cut-Through Proxy AAA on PIX/ASA

This chapter covers the following subjects:

- Overview of Cut-Through Proxy AAA

- Configuring PIX/ASA for Cut-Through Proxy AAA

- Downloadable Access Lists

- Configuring ACS 4.2 to Support Cut-Through Proxy Authentication and Authorization

- Configuring ACS 5.1 to Support Cut-Through Proxy Authentication and Authorization

Traditionally, access control lists (ACLs) have been used to restrict access to network resources. Although effective, ACLs are static in nature. ACLs cannot be used in environments where the source and/or destination address of the traffic is not known or is not static. For example, consider a network where an IP address is assigned dynamically using Dynamic Host Configuration Protocol (DHCP) and access to the Internet is not required for everyone. Because the source address of the traffic is not static, ACLs cannot be used to restrict access here.

For such requirements, PIX and ASA provide the cut-through proxy AAA feature. Using this feature, you can make authentication and authorization mandatory for certain types of sessions. Even if the interface ACL allows the session, ASA/PIX will intercept it for authentication. Access is granted based on the user profile.

Note This chapter uses ASA to refer to the security appliance. All concepts and commands discussed here also apply to PIX version 7.0 and later unless mentioned otherwise.

Cut-Through Proxy Authentication

> **Note** Throughout this section it is assumed that authorization and accounting is not con-
> figured unless mentioned otherwise. Authorization and accounting are covered later in this
> chapter.

Figure 10-1 shows the steps involved in cut-through proxy authentication. The ASA
device shown is configured to enforce authentication on all outbound HTTP sessions.
When an unauthenticated user from the inside network initiates an HTTP session to a
web server on the outside network, ASA intercepts the connection and sends a challenge
to the user.

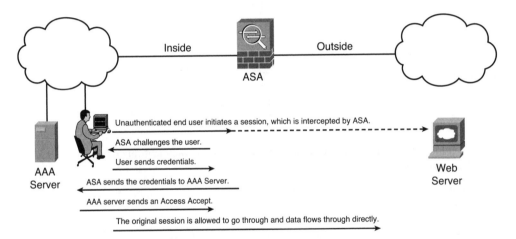

Figure 10-1 *Cut-Through Proxy Authentication*

When the user replies with his/her credentials, ASA sends the credentials to an AAA
server for verification. If the AAA server responds with an Access Accept or PASS message, ASA allows the original session to go through normally. At this point, the session
continues between the end user and the web server directly.

You should remember the following rules before configuring cut-through proxy authentication:

■ You can configure ASA to enforce authentication on multiple types of sessions;
however, the user needs to authenticate only once. This means that the first authentication by the user will be valid for all types of sessions that require authentication.

■ When the user authenticates, ASA starts a timer called User Authentication or a
uauth timer. When this timer expires, the user will need to authenticate again. This
timer is discussed in detail later in the chapter.

- ASA supports direct authentication with FTP (TCP port 21), Telnet (TCP port 23), HTTP (TCP port 80), and HTTPS (TCP port 443). A user must first authenticate with one of these services before the security appliance allows other traffic requiring authentication.

- For Telnet and FTP, the security appliance generates an authentication prompt. For HTTP, the security appliance uses basic HTTP authentication and provides an authentication prompt. For HTTPS, the security appliance generates a custom login screen.

ASA provides means to authenticate users using Virtual Telnet and HTTP sessions in case you do not want to enforce authentication on the supported protocols. This means if you want to authenticate any other type of traffic, say RDP (TCP port 3389), users will need to initiate a Virtual Telnet or HTTP session to the ASA and authenticate first. When authenticated, they can initiate the other type of sessions. Virtual HTTP and Virtual Telnet sessions are discussed in detailed later in the chapter.

You can use RADIUS or TACACS+ for cut-through proxy authentication. There is no difference as far as choice of protocol is concerned for authentication, but there are differences when authorization is required.

You already know the commands for adding an AAA server on ASA from Chapter 7, "Administrative AAA on ASA/PIX ," which are repeated here for your reference:

```
aaa-server server_tag protocol {radius | tacacs+}
aaa-server server_tag [(nameif)] host ip_address
key shared_key
```

There are two ways of configuring cut-through proxy authentication. The legacy command is as follows:

```
aaa authentication include service  interface_name inside_ip inside_mask
[outside_ip outside_mask] {server_tag | LOCAL}
```

Table 10-1 explains the command options.

For example, assuming that the AAA group is radius_servers in Figure 10-1, Example 10-1 shows the command to enforce authentication for an outbound HTTP connection:

Example 10-1 *Enforcing Authentication for an Outbound HTTP Connection*

```
ASA(config)#aaa authentication include http inside 0 0 radius_servers
```

Another command you should know about is the **aaa authentication exclude** command. This command will exclude specified IP addresses from authentication. The syntax for the **exclude** command is as follows:

aaa authentication exclude *service interface_name inside_ip inside_mask [outside_ip outside_mask] {server_tag | LOCAL}*

The options for the **exclude** commands are same as the **include** command and have the same meaning.

Table 10-1   aaa authentication include *Command Options*

Syntax	Description
include	Specifies that the traffic specified by the command should be authenticated before being allowed to go through.
service	Specifies the services that require authentication. You can specify one of the following values: **any** **tcp/0** (To specify all TCP traffic) **ftp** **http** **https** **ssh** **telnet** **tcp**/*port[-port]* **udp**/*port[-port]* **icmp**/*type*
inside_ip	Specifies the IP address of the local/internal host that is the source or destination of the traffic. Whether the IP address is source or destination depends on which interface the command is applied to. When applied to a higher security interface, the inside address is the source. Use 0 to mean all hosts.
inside_mask	Specifies the network mask for the inside IP address. 0 in an octet means anything is allowed. 255 in an octet means an exact match is required in the IP address.
interface_name	Specifies the interface that receives the traffic.
outside_ip	Specifies the remote/outside host which is the source or destination of the traffic. Whether the IP address is source or destination depends on which interface the command is applied to. When applied to a higher security interface the outside address is the destination. Use 0 to mean all hosts.
outside_mask	Specifies the network mask for the outside IP address. 0 in an octet means anything is allowed. 255 in an octet means an exact match is required in the IP address.
server_tag	Specifies the AAA server group to be used for this authentication.
LOCAL	Specifies that the local database is to be used for this authentication

Example 10-2 shows the command required to exclude a host from the authentication configured in Example 10-1.

Example 10-2 *Excluding a Host from Authentication*

```
ASA(config)#aaa authentication exclude http inside 192.168.1.1 255.255.255.255
radius_servers
```

The new and Cisco-recommended command for configuring cut-through proxy authentication is the **aaa authentication match** command. This command uses an access list to define traffic that needs to be included in or excluded from authentication. The syntax of the command is as follows:

```
aaa authentication match acl_name interface_name {server_tag | LOCAL}
```

You will notice that this command is simpler than the aaa authentication **include** command. The *acl_name* parameter defines the ACL to be used for authentication. The *interface_name* parameter defines the interface on which the traffic is being received and the *server_tag* parameter defines the AAA server group to be used for this authentication. The LOCAL parameter tells the ASA to use the local database for authentication.

You must use an extended access list to configure this method of cut-through proxy authentication. Permit statements in the access list define which traffic needs to be authenticated. Deny statements define which traffic needs to be excluded from authentication.

Example 10-3 shows the commands required to combine Example 10-1 and Example 10-2 in the **aaa authentication match** command.

Example 10-3 *Configuring Cut-Through Proxy Authentication with the* aaa authentication match *Command*

```
ASA(config)#access-list httpauth deny tcp host 192.168.1.1 any eq 80
ASA(config)#access-list httpauth permit tcp any any eq 80
ASA(config)#aaa authentication match httpauth inside radius_servers
```

Note You cannot use both the new and the legacy commands together. You must use either **aaa authentication match** (the new and Cisco-recommended method) or **aaa authentication include** (the legacy method) on an ASA/PIX device. In addition, the legacy method is much slower than the new method.

Virtual Telnet, Virtual HTTP, and HTTP Redirection

As mentioned earlier, ASA supports direct authentication with HTTP, HTTPS, FTP, and Telnet protocols only. If authentication is required for any other protocol, the user must authenticate using the supported protocols first. If you do not want to enforce authentication for any of the supported protocols, you can use the Virtual Telnet, Virtual HTTP, or HTTP Redirection features in ASA.

Consider the network shown in Figure 10-2. In the sample network, authentication is required for all outbound Remote Desktop Protocol (RDP) (TCP/3389) traffic, but no other traffic requires authentication. Because RDP traffic cannot be authenticated directly, you will need to use one of the features described in the sections that follow.

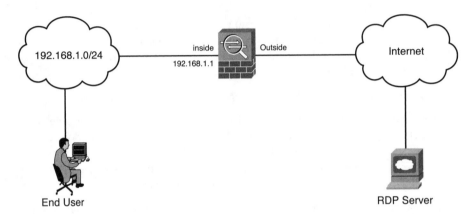

Figure 10-2 *Need for Virtual Telnet, Virtual HTTP, or HTTP Redirection*

Each of the three methods of authenticating unsupported protocols—Virtual Telnet, Virtual HTTP and HTTP Redirection—have their own advantages and disadvantages. Your network, the technical level of the end users, security considerations, and other related considerations determine which method is best for you.

Virtual Telnet

The Virtual Telnet feature enables you to configure an IP address to which users can Telnet to authenticate. When an unauthenticated user Telnets to this IP address, the user is challenged for a username and password, and then authenticated by the AAA server or the local database. When authenticated, the user sees the message "Authentication Successful" and is disconnected. The user can now access other services that require authentication.

The Virtual Telnet IP address should be an unused IP address from the network and routable to the ASA. Ideally it should be in the same subnet as the interface where the traffic in received. ASA will respond to ARP requests for this IP address.

To better understand Virtual Telnet, consider the example of the network shown previously in Figure 10-2. To authenticate RDP sessions, the administrator would need commands similar to the following:

```
access-list rdp permit tcp 192.168.1.0 255.255.255.0 any eq 3389
aaa authentication match rdp inside radgroup
```

When an unauthenticated end user initiates an outbound RDP session, ASA will drop it. Because RDP cannot be authenticated directly, Virtual Telnet can be used to authenticate the user. The IP address to be used in this case would need to be in the 192.168.1.0/24 subnet. For this example, 192.168.1.2 can be used for Virtual Telnet. After Virtual Telnet is configured, the end user will need to Telnet to 192.168.1.2 and provide a username and password. If authentication is successful, the user will see a message to that effect and will be disconnected. The user can now initiate the outbound RDP session.

While configuring Virtual Telnet, you should remember the following:

- The **aaa authentication include** or **aaa authentication match** command should include Telnet traffic to the virtual IP address. In the previous example, **access-list rdp permit tcp 192.168.1.0 255.255.255.0 host 192.168.1.2 eq 23** command would need to be added.

- For inbound users (from lower security to higher security), the ACL applied to the source interface should allow Telnet traffic to the Virtual Telnet address. For outbound users, there is an explicit permit statement for traffic; however, if you apply an access list to an inside interface, be sure to allow access to the Virtual Telnet address.

- For inbound users, you must add a **static** command for the Virtual Telnet IP address, even if NAT is not required (using the **no nat-control** command). An identity NAT command is typically used. The **static** statement is not required for outbound users.

- A user will stay authenticated until the uauth timer expires. The user can reconnect to the Virtual Telnet IP address to log out. uauth is discused later in the chapter.

To configure Virtual Telnet, use the following command in the global configuration mode:

virtual telnet *virtual_telnet_ip_address*

For the example in this section, the command to configure Virtual Telnet is **virtual telnet 192.168.1.2**.

Virtual HTTP

Virtual HTTP is similar to Virtual Telnet. In this case, the end user uses HTTP to authenticate instead of Telnet. The IP address, ACL, and static statement considerations discussed in the Virtual Telnet section also apply to Virtual HTTP.

ASA uses basic HTTP authentication for Virtual HTTP. It redirects all HTTP connections that require AAA authentication to the HTTP server on the security appliance, where the user is prompted for a username and password. After the user is authenticated, ASA redirects the HTTP connection back to the original server, but it does not include the username and password.

To configure Virtual HTTP, use the following command in the global configuration mode:

```
virtual http virtual_http_ip_address
```

In the network shown previously in Figure 10-2, if Virtual HTTP is used for authentication outbound RDP sessions, the commands shown in Example 10-4 will be required:

Example 10-4   *Virtual HTTP Configuration*

```
ASA(config)#access-list rdp permit tcp 192.168.1.0 255.255.255.0 any eq 3389
ASA(config)#access-list rdp permit tcp 192.168.1.0 255.255.255.0 host 192.168.1.2
eq 80
ASA(config)#aaa authentication match rdp inside radgroup
ASA(config)#virtual http 192.168.1.2
```

HTTP Redirection

Redirection is an improvement over the Virtual HTTP method in that it provides an improved user experience when authenticating. The users can connect to the ASA's interface IP address directly using HTTP or HTTPS and will get an authentication page similar to the one shown in Figure 10-3. Optionally, HTTP traffic that requires authentication can also be redirected to this authentication page.

Figure 10-3   *Authentication Page for Redirection*

As you can see from Figure 10-3, this page provides some information—unlike a simple authentication prompt on a browser. In addition to that, you can use the interface address of the ASA instead of having to use a different address.

You can configure HTTP Redirection using the following command in the global configuration mode:

aaa authentication listener http[s] *interface_name* [**port** *portnum*] [**redirect**]

Table 10-2 explains the command options.

Note   Redirection, or listener as it is sometimes called, can sometimes be unavailable to users who are directly authenticating to ASA. It is better to ask the users to connect to http://asa-ip-address/netaccess/constatus.html.

Another benefit of HTTP Redirection is that the users can explicitly log out by connecting to the ASA's IP address. They will see a page similar to the one shown in Figure 10-4.

Table 10-2 *HTTP Redirection Command Options*

Option	Description
http[s]	Specifies the protocol that you want to listen for, either HTTP or HTTPS. Enter this command separately for each protocol.
interface_name	Specifies the interface on which you enable redirection.
port *number*	Specifies the port number that the security appliance listens on for direct or redirected traffic; the defaults are 80 (HTTP) and 443 (HTTPS). You can use any port number and retain the same functionality, but be sure your direct authentication users know the port number; redirected traffic is sent to the correct port number automatically, but direct authenticators must specify the port number manually. You should also consider other web services for which the ASA device is configured. If ASDM or WEBVPN will be used on this ASA, you will need to change the port numbers.
redirect	Redirects HTTP traffic requiring authentication to the authentication page. Without this command option, the traffic will not be allowed through and the user will need to connect to the ASA directly for authentication first.

This page also shows users the login duration. It is useful in cases where the usage is billed to the user or access durations are restricted.

Figure 10-4 *Redirection Logout Page*

Although HTTP Redirection has some benefits over Virtual HTTP, you cannot use HTTP Redirection if the destination web server of the original HTTP traffic also requires authentication. This is because HTTP Redirection sends the username and password that you used to authenticate with the ASA to the HTTP server; you are not prompted separately for the HTTP server username and password. Assuming the username and password are not the same for the AAA and HTTP servers, the HTTP authentication fails.

Virtual HTTP, on the other hand, enables you to authenticate separately to ASA and the destination server.

uauth Timer

When a cut-through proxy authentication is successful, ASA stores the authentication and authorization information in its cache. The cache entry contains IP address, authorization information, and cache timers. The entry is created on the first authentication and is valid for any kind of traffic. This means that if more than one kind of traffic needs authentication, the first authentication will be sufficient for all of them as long as the cache entry exists.

The uauth timer determines how long ASA will maintain the cache entry. When the uauth timer expires, the entry is removed, and the user will need to authenticate again. The uauth timer can be absolute or inactivity based. This means that the uauth timer can be made to expire after a fixed period or if there is no activity for a defined period. Example 10-5 shows a uauth cache with default timers.

Example 10-5   *Uauth Cache*

```
user 'vivek' at 10.78.166.175, authenticated
    absolute    timeout: 0:05:00
    inactivity timeout: 0:00:00
```

By default, the uauth timer expires in 5 minutes, irrespective of activity status. You can change the uauth timer default using the following global configuration command:

timeout uauth *hh*:*mm*:*ss* [**absolute** | **inactivity**]

To configure absolute and inactivity timers together, use the command twice. You must ensure that the uauth duration is shorter than the **xlate** duration. The **xlate** duration defines the idle time after which an address translation slot is freed. ASA will not accept a timer which is longer than the **xlate** timer.

You can disable caching by using a uauth timer of 0. The timer can be set to a maximum of 1193:0:0.

Configuring ACS for Cut-Through Proxy Authentication

Configuring ACS 4.2 and 5.1 for cut-through proxy authentication requires the steps you followed for configuring administrative authentication of ASA. Refer to Chapter 7 to recall the steps you used. A summary of required steps is as follows:

Step 1.   Add ASA as an AAA client with the correct shared key and protocol.

Step 2.   Add a user.

Step 3.   For ease of learning, ensure that you use a new group so that previous configuration does not cause problems.

Verifying and Troubleshooting Cut-Through Proxy Authentication

The most common problems with cut-through proxy authentication relate to the communication between the ASA and AAA server as discussed in Chapter 7. For the most part, when communication between the ASA device and the AAA server is working, cut-through proxy authentication works like a charm. Few problems that arise with cut-through proxy authentication itself are related to the authentication configuration on ASA. You should verify that the following are true:

- The **aaa authentication match** or **aaa authentication include** commands are correct. Check the ACL used for the **match** command. Ensure that the Virtual Telnet or Virtual HTTP session is added in the authentication command.

- Ensure that the Virtual Telnet, Virtual HTTP, or HTTP Redirection address is accessible by users. This includes verifying the routing, NAT configuration, and interface access lists.

- Ensure that the authentication commands are using the correct server group.

The **show uauth** command is very important when verifying and troubleshooting cut-through proxy authentication as demonstrated in Example 10-6. Two important things you should notice in the command are the *Most Seen Authenticated Users* number and the cache entries themselves. If the cache entry is empty or the most seen number is 0, your users are not being prompted for authentication or are not able to get to the virtual addresses.

Example 10-6   show uauth *Command Output*

```
ASA(config)# show uauth
                         Current     Most Seen
Authenticated Users        1            1

Authen In Progress         0            2
user 'vivek' at 10.78.166.175, authenticated
   absolute    timeout: 0:05:00
   inactivity timeout: 0:00:00
```

If authentication is working well and users are complaining about repeatedly needing to authenticate, you might need to adjust the uauth timers.

Note   When the uauth cache is disabled by setting the uauth timeout to 0, HTTPS authentication might not work. If a browser initiates multiple TCP connections to load a web page after HTTPS authentication, the first connection is let through, but the subsequent connections trigger authentication. As a result, users are continuously presented

continues

continued

with an authentication page, even if the correct username and password are entered each time. To work around this, the uauth timeout must be enabled and set to at least 1.

Before moving to authorization of cut-through traffic, complete Lab Scenario #12 so that the authentication concepts are clear. Remember that if cut-through proxy authentication is not working, authorization will not work.

Lab Scenario #12: Authenticating Cut-Through Traffic on ASA

XYZ Inc. is hosting an application server inside its internal network. The employees and partners need to initiate an FTP connection and connect to TCP port 8764 from the Internet to the server. The company wants the users to authenticate to its AAA server before they can access the services on the server. Users connect to the 200.10.30.4 address, which is translated into the inside host address. They have a free IP address, 200.10.30.5, which can be used for Virtual Telnet. Your task is to configure the ASA device to authenticate FTP and Virtual Telnet connections to the AAA server at 10.1.10.2 in the inside network.

Lab Setup

This Lab Scenario requires one ASA device and at least a Layer 2 switch. Figure 10-5 shows the setup required for the scenario. Apart from the solution that follows, you will need to configure an access list on the Outside interface on ASA to permit the required traffic.

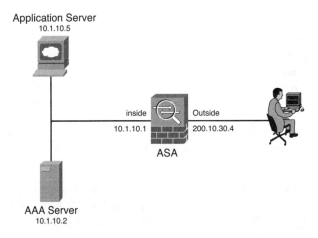

Figure 10-5 *Lab Setup for Scenario #12*

Lab Solution

Note   For ACS configuration required for this lab, see Lab #5.

Step 1.   Create a server group and add the AAA server:

```
ASA(config)#aaa-server myservers protocol tacacs+
ASA(config-aaa-server-group)#exit
ASA(config)#aaa-server myservers host 10.1.10.2
ASA(config-aaa-server-host)#key seckey
ASA(config-aaa-server-host)#exit
```

Step 2.   Create an access list for the traffic that needs to be authenticated:

```
ASA(config)#access-list authlist permit tcp any host 200.10.30.4 eq
ftp
ASA(config)#access-list authlist permit tcp any host 200.10.30.4 eq
8764
ASA(config)#access-list authlist permit tcp any host 200.10.30.5 eq
telnet
```

Step 3.   Configure ASA to authenticate the traffic on the outside interface:

```
ASA(config)#aaa authentication match authlist outside myservers
```

Step 4.   Configure Virtual Telnet:

```
ASA(config)#virtual telnet 200.10.30.5
```

Lab Verification

To verify the solution, you will need to Telnet to 200.10.30.5 from a host in the outside network and enter the AAA credentials. Example 10-7 shows sample output from the Telnet session.

Example 10-7   *Virtual Telnet Session Output for Lab Scenario #12*

```
LOGIN Authentication
Username: vivek
Password:
authentication approved
Authentication Successful
Connection closed by foreign host.
```

After a successful authentication, you can use the **show uauth** command to see the cache entry as shown in Example 10-8.

Example 10-8 show uauth *Output for Lab Scenario #12*

```
ASA# sh uauth
                              Current     Most Seen
Authenticated Users          1           1
Authen In Progress           0           2
user 'vivek' at 200.10.30.10, authenticated
    absolute   timeout: 0:05:00
    inactivity timeout: 0:00:00
```

Cut-Through Proxy Authorization

ASA supports authorization of cut-through traffic using both TACACS+ and RADIUS. Authorizing cut-through traffic enables you to control which group of users can access which service. For example, consider a network where you want all users to authenticate before any traffic is allowed to the Internet. You also want to restrict which group of users can access which service on the Internet. This is where authorization comes into the picture.

Remember that the choice of protocol *does not* matter when *authenticating* cut-through traffic but it *does* matter when *authorizing* the traffic. This is because RADIUS and TACACS+ have different ways of authorizing cut-through traffic. Remember that TACACS+ can initiate multiple authorization requests to the AAA server independent of the authentication request. RADIUS, on the other hand, authorizes along with the authentication process. Hence it cannot initiate multiple authorization requests. So, a RADIUS server must return all authorization information in the Access-Accept packet.

Owing to the way each protocol works, ACS has to be configured as follows:

TACACS+: Every time there is traffic which needs to be authorized, ASA sends a service authorization request to the AAA server. This request is similar to the request sent for command authorization of administrative sessions. On ACS, you need to apply command authorization sets to the user or group or policy as the case may be.

RADIUS: For authorization using RADIUS, you need to configure downloadable ACLs on ACS and apply them to the user or group or policy as necessary. These access lists are downloaded from ACS to the ASA and applied on the interface for the user. By default, the interface access list will override any conflicting access control entry.

Note TACACS+ is more resource intensive because it initiates a request every time there is a traffic that needs to be authorized.

As with authentication, ASA supports a legacy **include** command and the new **match** command for authorization of cut-through traffic using TACACS+. The commands are similar to the authentication commands:

```
aaa authorization include service interface_name inside_ip inside_mask
[outside_ip outside_mask] {server_tag | LOCAL}
```

```
aaa authorization match acl_name interface_name {server_tag | LOCAL}
```

For a definition of the command options of the **include** command, see Table 10-1.

Configuring ACS 4.2 and 5.1 for Cut-Through Proxy Authorization Using TACACS+

As mentioned earlier, the authorization request for cut-through traffic is similar to the authorization request for command authorization. In the case of command authorization, if the ASA device needs to authorize the **configure terminal** command, it sends the following request:

service=shell

cmd=configure terminal

In the case of cut-through traffic, if the ASA device needs to authorize a Telnet session to destination 172.16.26.1, it sends the following request:

service=shell

cmd=telnet 172.16.26.1

Here, **telnet** is the command and the destination IP address is the argument. The command authorization set applied to the user should permit the command and the argument.

Note   When ASA needs to authorize well-known protocols such as Telnet, HTTP, and so on, it sends the name of the protocol. If it has to authorize any other protocol, the request is sent as cmd=*protocol/port destination address.*

Note   Chapter 6, "Administrative AAA on IOS," covers creating and applying command authorization sets in greater detail.

To configure ACS to allow authorization of cut-through traffic, you will need to create a command authorization set and apply it to the user or its group. This time the command sets will contain the protocol name as the command and the destination addresses as arguments. Figure 10-6 shows a command authorization set that permits a Telnet connection to 172.16.26.1 and denies it for 172.16.26.2 in ACS 4.2. Figure 10-7 shows the same command set in ACS 5.1.

Remember that ACS looks for a minimum match in arguments. This means that permit 172.16.26.1 will permit destination addresses that contain 172.16.26.1, such as 172.16.26.10. If you want to restrict the match to only the given address, use the dollar sign ($) at the end.

Figure 10-6   *Command Authorization Set in ACS 4.2 for Cut-Through Traffic*

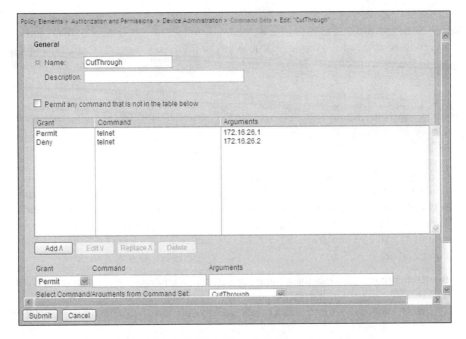

Figure 10-7   *Command Set in ACS 5.1 for Cut-Through Traffic*

You can also allow all destination addresses for a protocol by leaving the Arguments box blank and selecting the Permit Unmatched Args check box in ACS 4.2. You can leave the Arguments box blank in ACS 5.1 to permit all destination addresses.

Apart from the command authorization sets, you will need to give the user **Shell (EXEC)** privilege in ACS 4.2. You might recall that this privilege can be given in User or Group Setup in ACS 4.2. In ACS 5.1, you do not need to be given this privilege.

Configuring ACS 4.2 for Cut-Through Proxy Authorization Using RADIUS

As mentioned earlier, RADIUS requires authorization attributes to be sent along with the Access-Accept packet. Hence, you will need to configure downloadable access lists (DACLs) on ACS and apply them to the user or its group.

DACLs are standard IP access lists configured in ACS. These access lists use the same syntax as the normal IP ACLs on the device. When a user authenticates, these ACLs are sent as attribute-value pairs in the Access-Accept packet.

Note   The process by which DACLs are sent to the device has been simplified here for better understanding. In reality, two RADIUS Access-Request packets are involved in the process.

When the device receives the AV pairs containing the downloaded ACL, it stores the ACL in its memory and associates it with the uauth cache. The traffic from the authenticated user has to be permitted by the downloaded ACL or the interface ACL before it is allowed to go through.

Before creating DACLs, ensure that **User-Level Downloadable ACLs** and/or **Group-Level Downloadable ACLs** options are selected in the **Interface Configuration > Advanced Options** section.

To create a DACL, follow these steps:

Step 1.   Select Shared **Profile Components > Downloadable IP ACLs**.

Step 2.   Click **Add**.

The Downloadable IP ACLs page appears. Each downloadable IP ACL can contain multiple sets of access control entries. All the entries in all the sets configured will be sent to the device.

Step 3.   Enter a name. For this example, use **CutThrough**.

Step 4.   (Optional) Enter a description.

Step 5.   Click **Add.**

The Downloadable IP ACL Content page appears as shown in Figure 10-8. You can create your set of entries in this page.

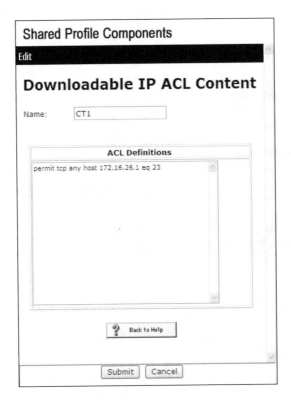

Figure 10-8   *Creating Downloadable ACL in ACS 4.2*

Step 6.   Enter a name for the set. For this example, use **CT1**.

Step 7.   Enter an ACL definition. Remember that you have to use the access list format supported by the device. On ASA, the simplified command to create an ACL is as follows:

```
access-list id {deny | permit} {any | host ip_address | ip_address
subnet_mask}
```

or

```
access-list id {deny | permit} protocol src_ip mask [operator port]
dest_ip mask [operator port]
```

On ACS, each entry in the set starts with the **permit** or **deny** keyword. The rest of the syntax remains the same. For this example, the ACL should permit Telnet traffic to 172.16.26.1. Figure 10-8 shows the configuration required for this example.

Step 8. Click **Submit**.

The set you created is added to the Downloadable ACL. At this stage, you can create more sets, although this option is not pursued for the purposes of this example.

Step 9. Click **Submit**.

The downloadable ACL is saved.

After the downloadable ACL is created, you have to apply it to a user or the group of the user with the following steps:

Step 1. Select **User Setup** or **Group Setup** from the main ACS menu.

Step 2. Enter a username or select a group.

Step 3. Scroll to the Downloadable ACLs section.

Step 4. Select Assign IP ACL.

Step 5. Select the downloadable ACL from the drop-down box. For this example, select **CutThrough**.

Step 6. Click **Submit** in User Setup or **Submit+Apply** in Group Setup.

Configuring ACS 5.1 for Cut-Through Proxy Authorization Using RADIUS

Note If you have skipped the previous section, "Configuring ACS 4.2 for Cut-Through Authorization Using RADIUS," you should read it once to understand how authorization works when RADIUS is used.

As with ACS 4.2, you will need to configure downloadable ACLs in ACS 5.1 for cut-through proxy authorization to work with RADIUS. To create downloadable ACLs in ACS 5.1, follow these steps:

Step 1. Select **Policy Elements > Authorization and Permissions > Named Permission Objects > Downloadable ACLs**.

The Downloadable ACLs page appears with a list of existing ACLs.

Step 2. Click **Create**.

The Create Downloadable ACLs page appears as shown in Figure 10-9.

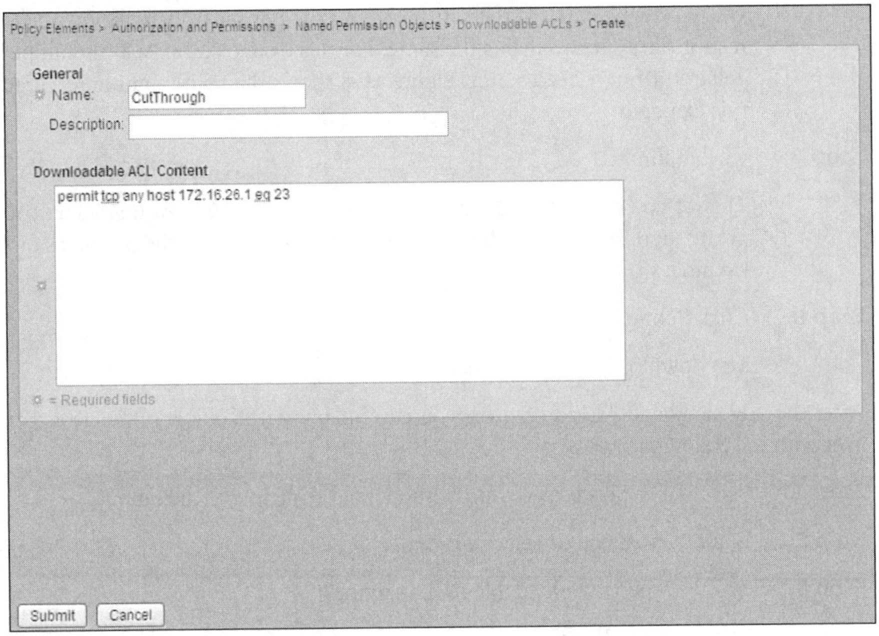

Figure 10-9 *Creating Downloadable ACLs in ACS 5.1*

Step 3.   Enter a name. For this example, use **CutThrough**.

Step 4.   (Optional) Enter a description.

Step 5.   Enter an ACL definition. Remember that you have to use the access list format supported by the device. On ASA, you can use one of the following simplified commands to create an ACL:

```
access-list id {deny | permit} {any | host ip_address | ip_address
subnet_mask}
access-list id {deny | permit} protocol src_ip mask [operator port]
dest_ip mask [operator port]
```

On ACS, each entry in the set starts with the **permit** or **deny** keyword. The rest of the syntax remains the same. For this example, the ACL should permit Telnet traffic to 172.16.26.1. Figure 10-9 shows the configuration required for this example.

Step 6.   Click **Submit**.

The ACLs is saved and is now listed in the Downloadable ACLs page.

Because RADIUS-based authorization policies allow only authorization profiles as results, you will need to create bind the DACL to an authorization profile.

Authorization profiles are discussed in detail in Chapter 4, "Getting Familiar with ACS 5.1." To create an authorization profile and bind the DACLs to it, follow these steps:

Step 1.   Select **Policy Elements > Authorization and Permissions > Network Access > Authorization Profiles.**

The Authorization Profiles page appears with a list of existing profiles.

Step 2.   Click **Create.**

The Create Authorization Profile page appears.

Step 3.   Enter a name. For this example, use **DACL.**

Step 4.   Click the **Common Tasks** tab.

The page changes to one showing common tasks as shown in Figure 10-10.

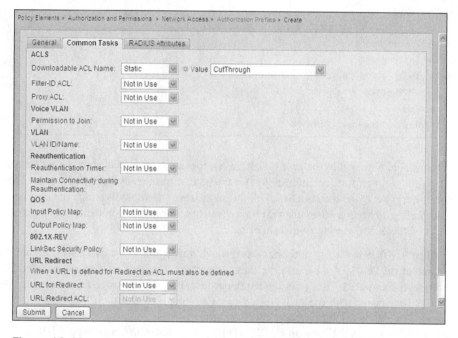

Figure 10-10   *Creating an Authorization Profile with Downloadable ACL*

Step 5.   Select **Static** from the Downloadable ACL Name drop-down list.

Step 6.   Select a Downloadable ACL from the Value drop-down list. For this example, select **CutThrough** as shown in Figure 10-10.

Step 7.   Click **Submit.**

The authorization profile is saved and listed in the Authorization Profiles page.

This authorization profile can now be added in an authorization policy that you create for cut-through proxy authentication.

> **Note**   Chapter 4, "Getting Familiar with ACS 5.1," discusses access services and different policies in detail.

Verifying and Troubleshooting Cut-Through Proxy Authorization

After authorization is successful, ASA will store the authorization information in the uauth cache for later use. Example 10-9 shows the uauth cache after authorization is successful using TACACS+. Notice the authorization information in the cache that shows the destination address and port this user is allowed.

Example 10-9   *uauth Cache After Authorization*

```
ASA# sh uauth
                          Current      Most Seen
Authenticated Users       1            1
Authen In Progress        1            2
user 'vivek' at 10.78.167.235, authorized to:
   port 172.16.26.1/telnet
   absolute    timeout: 0:05:00
   inactivity timeout: 0:00:00
```

You should note that in the case of TACACS+, the uauth cache will show only destination address and protocol information for traffic that has already been authorized. The cache entry is by no means a list of all the addresses and protocols which the user is authorized to access. Assuming that the cache entry shows the complete Command Set can be misleading during troubleshooting.

When RADIUS is used to authorize cut-through traffic, the uauth cache will contain the name of the DACL. You can use the **show access-list** command to view the contents of the ACL. Example 10-10 shows the uauth cache and the ACL. Notice the contents of the ACL. They match with the ACL created on ACS.

Example 10-10   *uauth Cache and ACL Entry After Authorization Using RADIUS*

```
ASA# sh uauth
                          Current      Most Seen
Authenticated Users       1            1
Authen In Progress        0            2
user 'vivek' at 10.78.167.235, authenticated

   access-list #ACSACL#-IP-CutThrough-4b208394 (*)

   absolute    timeout: 0:05:00
```

```
    inactivity timeout: 0:00:00
ASA#
ASA# show access-list #ACSACL#-IP-CutThrough-4b208394

access-list #ACSACL#-IP-CutThrough-4b208394; 1 elements (dynamic)

access-list #ACSACL#-IP-CutThrough-4b208394 line 1 extended permit tcp any host
172.16.26.1 eq telnet (hitcnt=0) 0x277ca4f7
```

In case of cut-through proxy authorization, most complaints are related to users not able to access services they are authorized to access or being able to access services for which they are not authorized. To troubleshoot cut-through proxy authorization, you should verify the following:

- **ASA and ACS Version:** Cisco changed the way DACLs are sent from ACS. This change was made in ACS version 4.0. PIX versions earlier than 7.0 use the old way of downloading the ACLs. Ensure that you are using compatible versions of ASA and ACS.

- **Interface ACL:** In most cases, DACLs override the interface ACL. Ensure that all services that a user is permitted to use are allowed by the DACL.

- **Implicit Deny:** DACLs have an implicit deny at the end just like normal ACLs on ASA. If you want to deny few services and permit the rest, you should add an explicit entry at the end of the ACL to permit all IP traffic.

- **Request Format:** When using TACACS+, ASA sends protocol names in the request for well-known protocols. For other protocols, it sends Protocol and Port number in the request. If authorization fails, check the Failed Attempts logs in ACS 4.2 or TACACS+ Authorization logs in ACS 5.1 to see the request format sent by the ASA.

- **ACL Syntax:** Verify that the ACL sent from ACS is created on ASA. If the syntax of the ACL is incorrect on ACS, ASA will not create it locally. One common mistake is to use wildcard masks in ACL instead of network mask. Wildcard masks are valid on IOS-based devices, but not ASA.

- **Unmatched Arguments:** If you want to permit all destination addresses for a protocol, ensure that Unmatched Args check box is selected for that protocol in the command authorization set in ACS 4.2.

Cut-Through Proxy Accounting

ASA supports accounting for cut-through proxy traffic using both RADIUS and TACACS+. You can configure ASA to send accounting information to a RADIUS or TACACS+ server about any TCP or UDP traffic that passes through the security appliance.

If that traffic is authenticated, the AAA server can maintain accounting information by username. If the traffic is not authenticated, the AAA server can maintain accounting information by IP address.

Accounting information includes session start and stop time, username, service used, duration of each session, destination IP address, and user's IP address and source port.

As with authentication and authorization, ASA provides two commands to configure accounting: the legacy **include** command and the new **match** command. The commands are similar to the authentication and authorization commands:

aaa accounting include service interface_name inside_ip inside_mask [outside_ip outside_mask] server_tag

aaa accounting match acl_name interface_name server_tag

For definition of the command options of the **include** command, see Table 10-1.

Note   It is not a good practice to use cut-through proxy accounting for high traffic protocols such as HTTP, SMTP, POP3 or even all IP traffic because ACS will get overwhelmed and will exhaust its resources. If you need to configure accounting for high traffic protocols, you should restrict it to specific source or destination addresses.

As you already know from previous chapters, accounting does not require any configuration on ACS. You must ensure that TACACS+ accounting logs or RADIUS accounting logs are enabled on ACS and that the device is present in ACS as a client with the correct shared key and protocol.

Note   At presstime, neither ACS 4.2 nor ACS 5.1 can display certain accounting information from ASA correctly when RADIUS is used. This is due to the fact that most information such as user's IP address is sent as cisco-av-pair in the RADIUS packet. Hence such information is visible in the accounting record as cisco-av-pair values instead.

Lab Scenario #13: Cut-Through Proxy Authentication, Authorization, and Accounting

ABC Inc. has a web server and an FTP server in its DMZ network. These servers contain sensitive data. Not all of the company's employees need access to these servers. The employees who need access are divided into three groups: Researchers, Managers, and Administrators. Researchers need access to the FTP server for FTP protocol. Managers need access to the web server for HTTP protocol, and Administrators need access to both the servers for FTP and HTTP protocols, respectively.

ABC Inc. has a CiscoSecure ACS in its internal network. It wants the ASA to authenticate and authorize all access to the servers in DMZ. In addition to that, ASA should send accounting information for HTTP and FTP traffic going to these servers.

The company has added the ASA as a RADIUS client on ACS (shared secret is seckey) and have created the groups. Your task is to configure the ASA and ACS for authentication, authorization, and accounting of the traffic.

Lab Setup

The Lab Scenario requires an ASA device, at least one Layer 2 switch, ACS, and at least one host. Figure 10-11 shows the setup required.

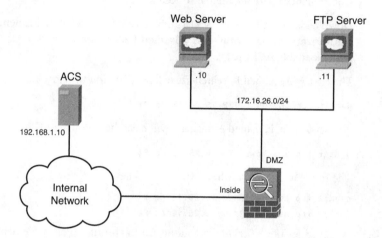

Figure 10-11   *Lab setup for Scenario #13*

Before proceeding with this lab, add the ASA as a client in ACS. If you are using ACS 4.2, rename three groups as Researchers, Managers, and Admins. If you are using ACS 5.1, create three identity groups. You can use the default RADIUS Access Service or create a new one. Identity policy can be left as default (Internal Users). This lab will focus on configuration of ASA and downloadable ACLs.

Lab Solution

The steps that follow outline the solution for this lab for both ACS version 4.2 and 5.1:

Step 1. Create a server group and add the AAA server:

```
ASA(config)#aaa-server myservers protocol radius
ASA(config-aaa-server-group)#exit
ASA(config)#aaa-server myservers host 192.168.1.10
ASA(config-aaa-server-host)#key seckey
ASA(config-aaa-server-host)#exit
```

Step 2. Create an access list for the traffic that needs to be authenticated, authorized, and accounted for:

```
ASA(config)#access-list authlist permit tcp any host 172.16.26.10 eq
http
ASA(config)#access-list authlist permit tcp any host 172.16.26.11 eq
ftp
```

Step 3. Configure ASA to authenticate and account for traffic on the inside interface:

```
ASA(config)#aaa authentication match authlist inside myservers
```

```
ASA(config)#aaa accounting match authlist inside myservers
```

Step 4.   Create three downloadable ACLs on ACS:

Downloadable ACLs on ACS 4.2 can be created at the **Shared Profile Components > Downloadable IP ACLs** page.

Downloadable ACLs on ACS 5.1 can be created at the **Policy Elements > Authorization and Permissions > Named Permission Objects > Downloadable ACLs** page.

The first ACL, named Researchers, will have the following ACE:

```
permit tcp any host 172.16.26.11 eq 21
```

The second ACL, named Managers, will have the following ACE:

```
permit tcp any host 172.16.26.10 eq 80
```

The third ACL, named Administrators, will have the following ACEs:

```
permit tcp any host 172.16.26.11 eq 21
permit tcp any host 172.16.26.10 eq 80
```

Step 5.   (For ACS 5.1 only) Create three authorization profiles (**Policy Elements > Authorization and Permissions > Network Access > Authorization Profiles**). Name the profiles Researchers, Managers, and Administrators, respectively. In each profile, set Downloadable ACL Name to static. From the drop-down box, select the DACL that matches the name of the profile.

Step 6.   Apply the DACL.

In ACS 4.2, go to Group Setup of each group that you renamed before the lab and apply the respective Downloadable ACL. For example, go to the Group Setup page of the Researchers group, scroll to the Downloadable ACLs section, select the Assign IP ACL check box, and then select the DACL that matches the group name.

In ACS 5.1, create three authorization policy rules in the Access Service of your choice. Select identity groups you created before the lab as a condition and match the authorization profile in the results section. For example, select the Researchers identity group as a condition and the Researchers authorization profile as a result.

Lab Verification

To verify the solution, create a user in each group on ACS and initiate an FTP session to 172.16.26.11 or an HTTP session to 172.16.26.10. You will be prompted for authentication.

After authentication, the uauth cache will look similar to the output shown in Example 10-11, 10-12, and 10-13, depending on the group of the user. The examples also show the content of the downloaded ACL.

Example 10-11   *uauth Cache and DACL for the Researchers Group*

```
ciscoasa# show uauth
—output trucated—
user 'researcher' at 10.78.167.235, authenticated
    access-list #ACSACL#-IP-Researcher-4b230bd8 (*)
    absolute    timeout: 0:05:00
    inactivity timeout: 0:00:00


ciscoasa# show access-list #ACSACL#-IP-Researcher-4b230bd8
access-list #ACSACL#-IP-Researcher-4b230bd8; 1 elements; name hash: 0xeebbbbf4
(dynamic)
access-list #ACSACL#-IP-Researcher-4b230bd8 line 1 extended permit tcp any host
172.16.26.11 eq ftp (hitcnt=0) 0x94fbed59
```

Example 10-12   *uauth Cache and DACL for the Managers Group*

```
ciscoasa# show uauth
—output trucated—
user 'manager' at 10.78.167.235, authenticated
    access-list #ACSACL#-IP-Managers-4b230bed (*)
    absolute    timeout: 0:05:00
    inactivity timeout: 0:00:00
ciscoasa# show access-list #ACSACL#-IP-Managers-4b230bed
access-list #ACSACL#-IP-Managers-4b230bed; 1 elements; name hash: 0x5f67bb53
(dynamic)
access-list #ACSACL#-IP-Managers-4b230bed line 1 extended permit tcp any host
172.16.26.10 eq www (hitcnt=0) 0x674bf224
```

Example 10-13   *uauth Cache and DACL for the Administrators Group*

```
ciscoasa# show uauth
—output truncated—
user 'admin' at 10.78.167.235, authenticated
    access-list #ACSACL#-IP-Administrators-4b230c0a (*)
    absolute    timeout: 0:05:00
    inactivity timeout: 0:00:00
ciscoasa# show access-list #ACSACL#-IP-Administrators-4b230c0a
access-list #ACSACL#-IP-Administrators-4b230c0a; 2 elements; name hash: 0xb3fe6f71
(dynamic)
access-list #ACSACL#-IP-Administrators-4b230c0a line 1 extended permit tcp any
host 172.16.26.11 eq ftp (hitcnt=0) 0x16ca663f
access-list #ACSACL#-IP-Administrators-4b230c0a line 2 extended permit tcp any
host 172.16.26.10 eq www (hitcnt=0) 0x0e48e690
```

You should also try to establish an FTP session to 172.16.26.11 after authenticating as a user from the Managers Group. ASA should not allow the session to go through.

Summary

Cut-through proxy AAA is an often neglected part of identity management solutions. Effective use of this feature can strengthen your network security by providing dynamic access policies on a user by user basis.

Before you implement cut-through proxy AAA, it is important to remember the difference in configuration based on the protocol being used. TACACS+ will add more load on ACS because multiple authorization requests will be sent. It is also important to remember where you will need to use Virtual Telnet, Virtual HTTP, or HTTP Redirection.

This chapter also introduced downloadable ACLs, which will be used in authorization of other services discussed in later chapters. You should remember how DACLs are configured and that their syntax depends on the AAA client.

Chapter 11

Router

This chapter covers the following subjects:

- Authentication Proxy on IOS Routers

- Authentication Proxy Authorization

- Configuring Downloadable ACLs for Authentication Proxy

- Authentication Proxy Accounting

Chapter 10, "Cut-Through Proxy AAA on Pix/ASA," covered the limitations of IP address-based restrictions and the need for per-user based access restriction. Similar to the cut-through proxy authentication method on ASA/PIX, IOS-based routers provide the Authentication Proxy feature to restrict access based on user profiles.

When Authentication Proxy is enabled, traffic flowing through the router is intercepted and the authentication cache is checked to see whether the user is already authenticated. If a valid authentication entry exists for the user, the connection is completed with no further intervention by the Authentication Proxy. If no entry exists, the Authentication Proxy responds to the connection with an authentication challenge. The credentials pro-

Note Authentication Proxy can only intercept traffic passing through the router. Traffic destined to the router itself will not be intercepted.

vided by the user are checked with a TACACS+ or RADIUS server. Upon successful authentication, an entry is added to the authentication cache and the session is allowed to go through normally. The session is not allowed to go through unless authentication is successful. Figure 11-1 illustrates how Authentication Proxy works.

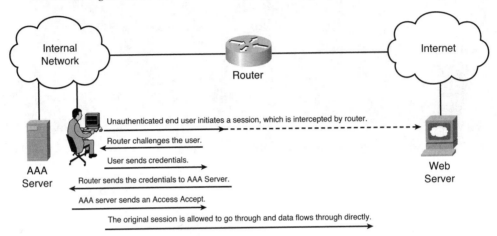

Figure 11-1   *Authentication Proxy*

In addition to authenticating the user, Authentication Proxy can download per-user-based access lists during authorization. This access list serves as a restriction to what services the user can access.

All this sounds familiar? Yes, this is very similar to how cut-through authentication works on ASA/PIX; however, the similarities end here. Recall from Chapter 10 that ASA/PIX can authenticate HTTP(s), FTP, and Telnet directly. For the rest of the services, virtual Telnet, virtual HTTP, and HTTP redirection can be used. Like cut-through authentication, authentication proxy can intercept HTTP, FTP, and Telnet traffic, but does not provide any mechanism to authenticate any other service. So, only these three services can be authenticated using Authentication Proxy. The rest of the services can be denied using an interface access list. After a user authenticates using any of these three services, a per-user access list can be used to allow other services.

Note   Though Authentication Proxy was introduced in Cisco IOS Software Release 12.0(5)T, support for FTP and Telnet services was added in Release 12.3(1).

Prerequisites for Authentication Proxy

Prior to configuring Authentication Proxy, you should ensure the following:

■   If HTTP authentication is required, the HTTP server on the router should be enabled. The server can be enabled using the **ip http server** global configuration command. IOS uses its HTTP server to communicate with the client.

- If FTP authentication is required, the FTP server on the router should be enabled. The server can be enabled using the **ftp-server enable** global configuration command. IOS uses its FTP server to communicate with the client and the destination FTP server.

Note   As per Cisco Security Advisory ID cisco-sa-20070509-iosftp, the FTP server feature was removed from many IOS versions. Authentication proxy for FTP will not work on versions that do not have the FTP server feature. Cisco IOS Software Release 12.3(3i) was used for the FTP Authentication Proxy section of this chapter.

If Telnet authentication is required, at least one virtual telnet (vty) line should allow incoming Telnet connections. These Telnet connections can be allowed by using the **transport input telnet** command in line configuration mode. IOS uses its Telnet server to communicate with the client.

AAA should be enabled on the router using the **aaa new-model** global configuration command.

The default login authentication method should be using the server group for which you want to use Authentication Proxy. Authentication Proxy can use only the default login method for authentication. You can configure the default login authentication list with the **aaa authentication login default group { radius | tacacs+ |** *group-name*} global configuration command.

Note   Chapter 6, "Administrative AAA on IOS," covers the basic AAA configuration on IOS in detail, including enabling AAA and creating method lists.

Authenticating HTTP Sessions

When Authentication Proxy for HTTP is enabled on a router, it will intercept all HTTP sessions going through it. If the source IP address is not found in the authentication cache, the router will reply back with a web page containing an authentication prompt.

Note   For those who are familiar with HTTP, the page returned by the router is not a 401 message but a web page containing a form for the credentials. In other words, IOS spoofs the destination address. This is different from the cut-through authentication behavior seen in PIX/ASA.

Users must enter their username and password in the web page and click OK. When authentication succeeds, the user will see a pop-up window indicating that authentication is successful. On closing the pop-up window, the user will be redirected to the original web server if JavaScript is enabled in the browser. If JavaScript is not enabled, the user will be asked to refresh the page. When the page is refreshed, a new HTTP session is initiated by the browser. This new session is allowed go through the router because an entry exists in the authentication cache.

To configure Authentication Proxy for HTTP, follow these steps:

Step 1.   Create an Authentication Proxy rule using the following command:

> **ip auth-proxy name** *auth-proxy-name* **http** [**list** {*acl* | *acl-name*}]

This command associates connections initiating HTTP protocol traffic with an Authentication Proxy name. If you provide an ACL number or name, only traffic that matches the ACL will be intercepted.

Step 2.   Apply the Authentication Proxy named rule to the interface that will receive the traffic using the following interface configuration mode command:

> **ip auth-proxy** *auth-proxy-name*

Authentication proxy is enabled in the incoming direction only. It will not intercept traffic leaving an interface.

Example 11-1 shows Authentication Proxy configured for HTTP sessions initiated from the 192.168.1.0/24 subnet and received on the FastEthernet0/0 interface.

Example 11-1   *HTTP Authentication Proxy Configuration*

```
Router(config)# access-list 101 permit tcp 192.168.1.0 0.0.0.255 any eq 80
Router(config)# ip auth-proxy name httpauth http list 101
Router(config)# interface FastEthernet 0/0
Router(config-if)# ip auth-proxy httpauth
```

Authenticating FTP Sessions

When Authentication Proxy for FTP is enabled on a router, it will intercept all FTP sessions going through it. If the source IP address is not found in the authentication cache, the router will redirect the FTP sessions to its internal FTP server. This server will prompt users for their credentials.

The client must respond with the username and password in the following format:

> *proxy_username@ftp_username*

and

> *proxy_passwd@ftp_passwd*:

The Authentication Proxy will use the proxy username and password to verify the client's profile against the AAA server's user database. After the client is successfully authenticated with the AAA server, an entry will be added in the cache and the *ftp_username* and *ftp_password* will be sent to the destination server. If the destination server authenticates the user, the session will continue normally between the client and the remote server.

If the user fails authentication with the destination FTP server, an error is sent to the client and the session is disconnected. If the user reinitiates the connection, the router will not challenge the user because an entry exists in the cache. Example 11-2 shows an FTP session in which the user fails FTP server authentication. Example 11-3 shows a session where authentication succeeds.

Example 11-2 *Authentication Proxy Failure on Remote FTP Server*

```
$ ftp 172.16.26.10
Connected to 172.16.26.10 (172.16.26.10).
220 FTP Authentication Proxy.
Name (172.16.26.10:vivek): aaauser@ftpuser
331 Password Required.
Password: [aaapasword@wrongpass]
530 Login incorrect.
Login failed.
```

Example 11-3 *Successful Authentication Through Authentication Proxy*

```
$ ftp 172.16.26.10
Connected to 172.16.26.10 (172.16.26.10).
220 FTP Authentication Proxy.

Name (172.16.26.10:vivek): aaauser@ftpuser
331 Password Required.
Password: [aaapassword@ftppassword]
230 Login successful.

Remote system type is UNIX.
Using binary mode to transfer files.
ftp>
```

To configure Authentication Proxy for FTP, follow these steps:

Step 1. Create an Authentication Proxy rule using the following command:

ip auth-proxy name *auth-proxy-name* **ftp** [**list** {*acl* | *acl-name*}]

This command associates connections initiating FTP protocol traffic with an Authentication Proxy name. If you provide an ACL number or name, only traffic that matches the ACL will be intercepted.

Step 2. Apply the Authentication Proxy named rule to the interface that will receive the traffic using the following interface configuration mode command:

ip auth-proxy *auth-proxy-name*

Authentication proxy is enabled in the incoming direction only. It will not intercept traffic leaving an interface.

Example 11-4 shows Authentication Proxy configured for FTP sessions initiated from the 192.168.1.0/24 subnet and received on the FastEthernet0/0 interface.

Example 11-4   *FTP Authentication Proxy Configuration*

```
Router(config)# access-list 101 permit tcp 192.168.1.0 0.0.0.255 any eq 21
Router(config)# ip auth-proxy name ftpauth ftp list 101
Router(config)# interface FastEthernet 0/0
Router(config-if)# ip auth-proxy ftpauth
```

Note   Authorization is mandatory for FTP Authentication Proxy. If authorization is not configured, then the session will not be allowed through. Authorization is covered later in this chapter.

Authenticating Telnet Sessions

Similar to HTTP and FTP authentication, when Telnet Authentication Proxy is enabled, the router intercepts all Telnet connections going through it. If the source address is not found in the authentication cache, the router redirects the request to its internal Telnet server, which prompts the user for the proxy username and password.

After successful authentication, an entry is added in the cache and the session is allowed to go through normally. At this stage, the remote Telnet server will prompt the user for authentication. This authentication is different from the proxy authentication because its result has no bearing on Authentication Proxy. Even if the user fails the authentication with the Telnet server, the router will allow Telnet sessions to go through if an entry exists in the cache.

To configure Authentication Proxy for Telnet, follow these steps:

Step 1.   Create an Authentication Proxy rule using the following command:

ip auth-proxy name *auth-proxy-name* **telnet** [**list** {*acl* | *acl-name*}]

This command associates connections initiating Telnet protocol traffic with an Authentication Proxy name. If you provide an ACL number or name, only traffic that matches the ACL will be intercepted.

Step 2.   Apply the Authentication Proxy named rule to the interface that will receive the traffic using the following interface configuration mode command:

ip auth-proxy *auth-proxy-name*

Authentication proxy is enabled in the incoming direction only. It will not intercept traffic leaving an interface.

Example 11-5 shows Authentication Proxy configured for Telnet sessions initiated from 192.168.1.0/24 subnet and received on the FastEthernet0/0 interface.

Example 11-5   *Telnet Authentication Proxy Configuration*

```
Router(config)# access-list 101 permit tcp 192.168.1.0 0.0.0.255 any eq 23
Router(config)# ip auth-proxy name telnetauth ftp list 101
Router(config)# interface FastEthernet 0/0
Router(config-if)# ip auth-proxy telnetauth
```

Note   Authorization is mandatory for Telnet Authentication Proxy. If authorization is not configured, then the session will not be allowed through. Authorization is covered later in this chapter.

Configuring ACS for Authentication Proxy

Configuring ACS 4.2 and 5.1 for cut-through authentication requires the steps you followed for configuring administrative authentication on IOS devices. See Chapter 6 to recall the steps you used. A summary of steps required is as follows:

Step 1.   Add router as an AAA client with correct shared key and protocol.

Step 2.   Add a user.

Step 3.   For ease of learning, ensure that you use a new group or access service so that the previous configuration does not cause problems.

Viewing and Maintaining Authentication Proxy Cache

As mentioned earlier, when Authentication Proxy is configured, traffic is intercepted and the user is prompted for authentication if the source address is not present in the Authentication Proxy cache. On successful authentication, an entry is added in this cache. As long as the entry exists in the cache, the user will not be prompted for authentication again.

The Authentication Proxy cache can be viewed using the **show ip auth-proxy cache** command. The Authentication Proxy cache lists the host IP address, the source port number, the timeout value for the Authentication Proxy, and the state of the connection. Example 11-6 shows a sample entry in the Authentication Proxy cache.

Example 11-6   show ip auth-proxy cache *Output*

```
Router#show ip auth-proxy cache
Authentication Proxy Cache
 Client Name vivek, Client IP 192.168.1.54, Port 50390, timeout 60, Time Remaining
47, state ESTAB
```

Note the timeout value shown in the output in Example 11-6. This value, in minutes, denotes the period of inactivity after which the entry will be removed from the cache. After the entry is removed, the user will need to authenticate again.

Authentication proxy enables you to configure an inactivity timer and an absolute timer for the cache entries. These timers can be configured globally for all Authentication Proxy types and rules using the following commands:

```
ip auth-proxy absolute-timer minutes
ip auth-proxy inactivity-timer minutes
```

The default absolute timer is 0 and the maximum is 35,791. The default inactivity timer is 60 and the maximum is 2,147,483,647. You cannot set the inactivity timer to 0.

These timers can also be configured on a per-rule basis by adding the **absolute-timer** and **inactivity-timer** options to the **ip auth-proxy name** command as shown here:

```
ip auth-proxy name auth-proxy-name {http | ftp | telnet} absolute-timer minutes
inactivity-time minutes
```

You can clear the Authentication Proxy cache using the **clear ip auth-proxy cache *** command. To remove a single entry from the cache, use the **clear ip auth-proxy cache** *source-ip-address* command.

Verifying and Troubleshooting Authentication Proxy

The most common problems with Authentication Proxy relate to the communication between the router and the AAA server as discussed in Chapter 6. For the most part, when communication between the router and the AAA server is working, Authentication Proxy works like a charm; however, you might encounter a few problems with Authentication Proxy itself, which relate to the authentication configuration on the router. You should verify that the following are true:

- The **ip auth-proxy** commands are configured correctly for the required protocol.

- The **ip auth-proxy** command is applied to the correct interface(s).

- Ensure that the authentication commands are using the correct server group.

The **show ip auth-proxy cache** command is very important when verifying and troubleshooting cut-through authentication. The state of the connection in the output is of particular interest because it shows the current state of the connection. Table 11-1 describes some important states seen in the cache.

Table 11-1 *Common States in Authentication Proxy Cache*

State	Description
INIT	User is authenticating.
SERVICE_DENIED	User failed authentication.
INTERCEPT	Authentication succeeded. The initial session is currently active between the user and the remote server.
ESTAB	Authentication was successful and timer has not expired. This state is seen after the first session ends.

While troubleshooting, if you encounter the SERVICE_DENIED state, you can use debugs on the router and logs on the AAA server to help troubleshoot the authentication failure.

For troubleshooting Authentication Proxy, the following two **debug** commands are most useful:

- **debug ip auth-proxy detailed**
- **debug {tacacs | radius}**

> **Note** You should remember that **debug** commands can be very CPU intensive. You should try and use them only during periods when the device is less likely to see traffic. **debug ip auth-proxy detailed** gives a lot of output.

Authentication Proxy Authorization

As mentioned in the beginning of the chapter, after a successful authentication, access lists can be downloaded from the AAA server and applied on a per-user basis. In addition to that, Telnet and FTP Authentication Proxy requires the privilege level for the user to be set to 15. If the privilege level is not set, or is lower than 15, the session will not be allowed through.

Downloading an access list and setting the privilege level is done in the authorization phase of Authentication Proxy. As with all previous authorizations, most of the configuration has to be done on the AAA servers. Before configuring the AAA server, you do need execute the following command on the router:

```
aaa authorization auth-proxy default group {tacacs+ | radius | server-group-name}
```

This command tells the router to use the specified group of servers to authorize auth-proxy sessions.

> **Note** Upon successful authorization, the router adds the downloadable ACL to the inbound (input) ACL of an input interface and to the outbound (output) ACL of an output interface. If neither of these interface ACLs is present, the downloadable ACLs are discarded. So you should ensure that one of these interface ACLs are configured, before configuring ACS.

You can use both TACACS+ and RADIUS for Authentication Proxy. There is no distinct advantage of using one protocol over the other because authentication and authorization will be done only if an entry does not exist in the cache. If an entry exists in the cache, the AAA server is not queried.

Configuring ACS 4.2 for Authorization Using TACACS+

Configuring ACS for authorizing proxy authentication using TACACS+ requires you to add a custom Attribute-Value pair. Existing attributes and the downloadable ACL feature in ACS do not work with Authentication Proxy.

To add privilege level and downloadable ACL for Authentication Proxy, using TACACS+, in a group or user profile in ACS 4.2, follow these steps:

Step 1.   Select Interface **Configuration > TACACS+ (Cisco IOS)**.

Step 2.   Under the New Services section, type **auth-proxy** in the Service field and ip in the protocol field.

Step 3.   Select the **Group** and/or **User** check box beside the Service text box used in the previous step. For this example, select just the **Group** check box.

Figure 11-2 shows the configuration mentioned in steps 2 and 3.

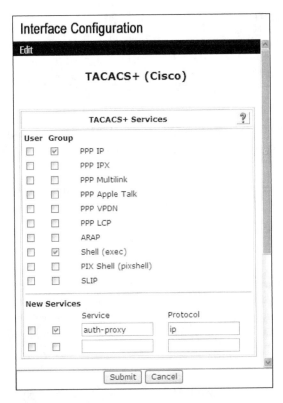

Figure 11-2   *Adding Auth-Proxy service in ACS 4.2*

Step 4.   Click Submit.

Step 5. Go to **User Setup** or **Group Setup** page of the user or group for which you need to add the privilege level and downloadable ACL. For this example, edit **Group 10** from Group Setup.

Step 6. Scroll down to the **auth-proxy ip** option in the **TACACS+ Settings** section.

Step 7. Select the **auth-proxy ip** check box.

Step 8. Select the **Custom attributes** check box below the **auth-proxy ip** check box.

Step 9. You can add the privilege level and downloadable ACL in the text box below the **Custom attributes** check box. To add privilege level, add the following in the text box:

priv-lvl=15

The downloadable ACL can be added in the text box in the following format:

proxyacl#*number*={*standard-acl-entry* | *extended-acl-entry*}

You can add multiple downloadable ACL entries, but each entry should have a different *number*. The ACL entries should follow the format allowed on IOS.

Note You can use only **permit** statements in the downloadable ACL for the Authentication Proxy and the source address on the ACL entry should be kept as **any**.

For the example, enter the following in the **Custom attributes** text box:

priv-lvl=15

proxyacl#1=permit tcp any host 172.16.26.1 eq 23

proxyacl#2=permit tcp any host 172.16.26.10 eq 22

Figure 11-3 shows the configuration done in steps 7, 8, and 9.

Step 10. Click **Submit + Restart**.

Configuring ACS 5.1 for Authorization Using TACACS+

Configuring ACS for authorizing proxy authentication using TACACS+ requires you to add a custom Attribute-Value pair. Existing attributes and the downloadable ACL feature in ACS do not work with Authentication Proxy. To add privilege level and downloadable ACL for Authentication Proxy on ACS 5.1, you will need to create a shell profile containing these attributes. This shell profile can be applied to an authorization rule in the access service used to authenticate the Authentication Proxy request.

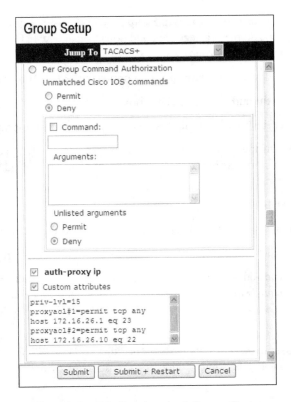

Figure 11-3 *Configuring Auth-Proxy Custom Attributes in ACS 4.2*

Note Chapter 4 covers Access Services, Authorization Rules, and Policy Elements in detail. Chapter 6 covers Shell Profiles in detail.

To create the shell profile with the privilege level and downloadable ACL for Authentication Proxy, follow these steps:

Step 1. Select **Policy Elements > Authorization and Permissions > Device Administration > Shell Profiles**.

Step 2. Click **Create**.

Step 3. Enter a name. For this example, use **Auth-Proxy**.

Step 4. Select the **Custom Attributes** tab as shown in Figure 11-4.

Step 5. In this page, you will need to manually enter the attributes for Privilege level and downloadable ACL.

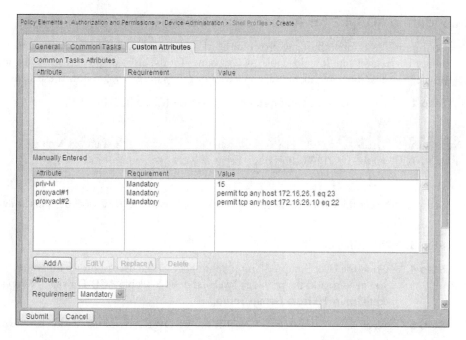

Figure 11-4   *Adding Authentication Proxy Attributes in ACS 5.1*

To add privilege level, follow these steps:

In the **Attribute** text box, enter **priv-lvl**, select **Mandatory** from the **Requirement** drop-down list, and enter **15** in the **Value** text box. Click **Add** to add the attribute.

To add the downloadable ACL entry, follow these steps:

In the **Attribute** box, enter **proxyacl#***number*. The *number* should be different for each entry. Select **Mandatory** from the **Requirement** drop-down list. In the **Value** text box, enter the permit statement in the format allowed on IOS. Click **Add** to add the attribute.

For the example, add the following attributes as shown previously in Figure 11-4:

priv-lvl=15

proxyacl#1=permit tcp any host 172.16.26.1 eq 23

proxyacl#2=permit tcp any host 172.16.26.10 eq 22

Step 6.   Click **Submit**.

The shell profile will be created and available for use in an authorization rule.

Configuring ACS 4.2 for Authorization Using RADIUS

Configuring ACS for authorizing proxy authentication using RADIUS requires you to add privilege level and downloadable ACL as values for the cisco-av-pair attribute. To add privilege level and downloadable ACL in a user or group in ACS 4.2, follow these steps:

Step 1.   Select **Interface Configuration > RADIUS (Cisco IOS/PIX 6.0)**.

Note   The RADIUS (Cisco IOS/PIX 6.0) option will not be available if an AAA client using RAIDUS (Cisco IOS/PIX 6.0) is not present in Network Configuration.

Step 2.   Select the **Group** and/or **User** check box beside the **[026/009/001] cisco-av-pair**.

Step 3.   Click **Submit**.

Step 4.   Go to the User Setup or Group Setup page of the user or group for which you need to add the privilege level and downloadable ACL. For this, example edit **Group 10** from **Group Setup**.

Step 5.   Scroll down to the **Cisco IOS/PIX 6.x RADIUS Attributes** section as shown in Figure 11-5.

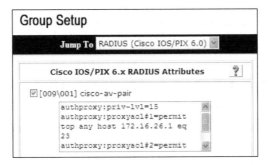

Figure 11-5   *Adding Privilege Level and Downloadable ACL as cisco-av-pair in ACS 4.2*

Step 6.   Select the check box next to **[009\001] cisco-av-pair**.

Step 7.   You can add the privilege level and downloadable ACL in the text box below **[009\001] cisco-av-pair**. To add the privilege level, enter the following in the text box:

authproxy:priv-lvl=15

You can add the downloadable ACL in the following format in the text box:

authproxy:proxyacl#*number*={*standard-acl-entry* | *extended-acl-entry*}

You can add multiple downloadable ACL entries, but each entry should have a different *number*. The ACL entries should follow the format allowed on IOS.

Note   You can use only permit statements in the downloadable ACL for Authentication Proxy and the source address on the ACL entry should be kept as **any**.

For this example, enter the following in the text box as shown in Figure 11-5:

authproxy:priv-lvl=15

authproxy:proxyacl#1=permit tcp any host 172.16.26.1 eq 23

authproxy:proxyacl#2=permit tcp any host 172.16.26.10 eq 22

Step 8.   Click **Submit+Restart**.

Configuring ACS 5.1 for Authorization Using RADIUS

Configuring ACS for authorizing proxy authentication using RADIUS requires you to add privilege level and downloadable ACL as values for cisco-av-pair attribute. On ACS 5.1, you will need to create an authorization profile containing these attributes. This authorization profile can be applied to an authorization rule in the access service used to authenticate the Authentication Proxy request.

Note   Chapter 4 covers access services, authorization rules, and policy elements in detail. Chapter 6 covers authorization profiles in detail.

To create an authorization profile with a privilege level and downloadable ACL for Authentication Proxy, follow these steps:

Step 1.   Select **Policy Elements > Authorization and Permissions > Network Access > Authorization Profiles**.

Step 2.   Click **Create**.

Step 3.   Enter a name. For this example, use **Auth-Proxy**.

Step 4.   Select the **RADIUS Attributes** tab as shown in Figure 11-6.

In this page, you need to manually add the **cisco-av-pair** attributes with the privilege level and downloadable ACLs as values.

Step 5.   Select **RADIUS-Cisco** from the **Dictionary Type** drop-down list.

Step 6.   Click **Select** next to the **RADIUS Attribute** field and select **cisco-av-pair** from the dialog box that opens.

Step 7.   Select **Static** from the **Attribute Value** drop-down box.

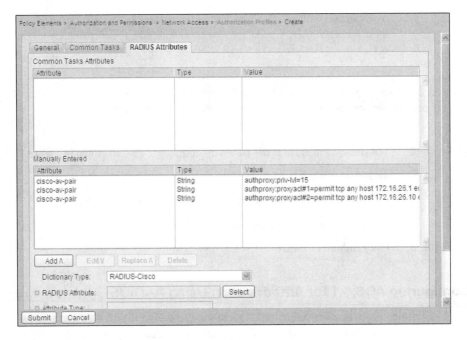

Figure 11-6   *Adding Privilege Level and Downloadable ACLs in ACS 5.1*

Step 8.   In the text box below the **Attribute Value** field, you can add the privilege level and downloadable ACLs. To add privilege level, enter the following in the text box:

authproxy:priv-lvl=15

You can add the downloadable ACL in the following format in the text box:

authproxy:proxyacl#*number=*{*standard-acl-entry* | *extended-acl-entry*}

You can add multiple downloadable ACL entries; however, each entry should have a different number. The ACL entries should follow the format allowed on IOS.

Note   You can use only permit statements in the downloadable ACL for Authentication Proxy.

You will need to repeat steps 6 through 8 after adding the privilege level and for each downloadable ACL entry.

For this example, add the following values for **cisco-av-pair** as shown previously in Figure 11-6:

authproxy:priv-lvl=15

> authproxy:proxyacl#1=permit tcp any host 172.16.26.1 eq 23
>
> authproxy:proxyacl#2=permit tcp any host 172.16.26.10 eq 22

Step 9.   Click **Submit**.

The authorization profile will be created and will be available for use in an authorization rule.

Verifying and Troubleshooting Authentication Proxy Authorization

After authorization is successful, the router will do the following:

■ If a downloadable ACL is present in the authorization packet from the server, the router will append it on top of the inbound ACL of the source interface and outbound ACL of the destination interface. The router will replace the source address on the downloadable ACL with the source IP address of the authentication-triggering packet.

■ Match the authentication-triggering packet to the interface ACL and route it if the traffic is permitted. If the traffic is not permitted by the interface ACL, the packet is dropped. Any further packets from the source IP address will be checked against the new interface ACL.

You can verify the downloaded ACL using the **show access-list** [*number* | *name*] command. The downloaded access control entries will be shown on top of the interface ACL without any numbers, as shown in Example 11-7.

Example 11-7   **show access-list** *Command Output Displaying Downloaded ACL*

```
Router#show access-list 102
Extended IP access list 102
    permit tcp host 192.168.1.54 any eq telnet (33 matches)
   10 permit udp any eq 1645 any (21 matches)
   20 permit udp any eq 1812 any
```

With Authentication Proxy authorization, most issues relate to users not being able to access services they are authorized to access or users being able to access services that they are not authorized to access. To troubleshoot cut-through authorization, you should verify the following:

■ **Interface ACL:** You should verify that an inbound ACL in the ingress interface or outbound ACL in the egress interface exists. If one of these is not present, the downloadable ACL will not be applied and all traffic will be permitted.

■ **Traffic Permitted by Interface ACL:** Downloadable ACL is appended on top of the interface ACL. If the interface ACL permits certain traffic, it will be allowed to go through.

■ **Implicit Deny:** There is an implicit deny at the end of the interface ACL. If neither the downloadable ACL nor the interface ACL permits the traffic, it will be dropped.

- **ACL Syntax:** Verify that the downloadable ACL is appended to the interface ACL. If the syntax of the ACL is incorrect on ACS, the router will not be able to append it to the interface ACL. Also ensure that you do not use a standard ACL on ACS when an extended ACL is applied on the interface of the router or vice versa.

- **Wrong Service or Attribute Name:** In case of TACACS+, you need to add **auth-proxy** service/attribute. In case of RADIUS, privilege level and downloadable ACL should be prefixed with the **authproxy** service name. If the service/attribute name is incorrect, the router will not be able to apply the attributes.

The following debugs are useful for troubleshooting authorization:

- **debug {radius | tacacs }**

- **debug ip auth-proxy detailed**

Authentication Proxy Accounting

IOS routers support accounting for Authentication Proxy using both TACACS+ and RADIUS. Apart from the usual information such as username, source address, and so on, the router also sends the duration of the session, input octets, and input packet count. To enable accounting, use the following global configuration command:

```
aaa accounting auth-proxy default {start-stop | stop-only} group {radius |
tacacs+ |  name}
```

The preceding command will cause accounting information to be sent either at the start and end or only at the end of the Authentication Proxy session to the group mentioned.

As you already know from previous chapters, accounting does not require any configuration on ACS. You must ensure that TACACS+ accounting logs or RADIUS accounting logs are enabled.

Lab Scenario #14: Authentication Proxy

ABC Inc. has two web servers in a network separated from their internal network by a router. These servers contain sensitive data. The company wants access to these servers to be restricted and monitored. The employees who need access to Server1 are members of the Research group on ACS. The employees who need access to Server2 are members of the Engineering group on ACS.

The ACS server is in the internal network. The inbound ACL on the ingress interface of the router denies all traffic to the servers. The company wants the router to authenticate all HTTP sessions and then download ACL from ACS to permit traffic as needed. It also wants the router to send accounting information at the start and end of all authenticated sessions.

The router is added in ACS as a RADIUS client with a shared key of *abckey*. Your task is to configure the router and add downloadable ACLs on ACS.

Lab Setup

The Lab Scenario requires a router, at least one Layer 2 switch, ACS, and at least one host. Figure 11-7 shows the setup required.

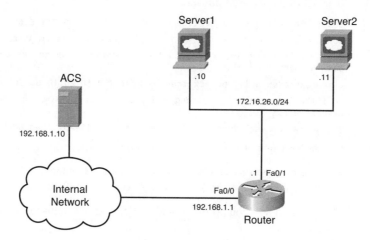

Figure 11-7   *Lab setup for Scenario #14*

Before proceeding with this lab, add the router as a client in ACS. If you are using ACS 4.2, rename two groups as Research and Engineering. If you are using ACS 5.1, create two identity groups: Research and Engineering. You can use the default RADIUS access service or create a new one. The identity policy can be left as default (Internal Users). You also need to create two authorization rules in the access service. The first rule should match the Research identity group and the second rule should match the Engineering identity group.

This lab focuses on configuration of the router and downloadable ACLs.

Lab Solution

The following solution provides the steps for both ACS version 4.2 and 5.1:

Step 1.   Add the ACS server on the router:

```
Router(config)#aaa new-model
Router(config)#radius-server host 192.168.1.10 key abckey
```

Step 2.   Configure the router to authenticate and authorize HTTP traffic on interface fa0/0:

```
Router(config)#aaa authentication login default group radius
Router(config)#aaa authorization auth-proxy default group radius
Router(config)#ip auth-proxy name secure http
Router(config)#interface fa0/0
Router(config-if)#ip auth-proxy secure
```

Step 3.   Configure the router to account for authenticated traffic:

```
Router(config)#aaa accounting auth-proxy default start-stop group
radius
```

Step 4.   (For ACS 4.2 only) Add downloadable ACL in the groups:

```
Select Interface Configuration > RADIUS (Cisco IOS/PIX 6.0).
Select the Group check box next to [026/009/001] cisco-av-pair.
Edit the Research group and add the following value in the cisco-av-
pair attribute:
authproxy:proxyacl#1=permit tcp any host 172.16.26.10 eq 80
Edit the Engineering group and add the following value in the cisco-
av-pair attribute:
authproxy:proxyacl#1=permit tcp any host 172.16.26.11 eq 80
```

Step 5.   (For ACS 5.1 only) Create two authorization profiles.

Authorization profiles can be created from **Policy Elements > Authorization and Permissions > Network Access > Authorization Profiles**.

The first authorization profile should have the following **cisco-av-pair** attribute:

authproxy:proxyacl#1=permit tcp any host 172.16.26.10 eq 80

The second authorization profile should have the following **cisco-av-pair**:

authproxy:proxyacl#1=permit tcp any host 172.16.26.11 eq 80

Step 6.   (For ACS 5.1 only) Apply the authorization profiles to authorization rules.

Apply the first authorization profile to the rule that matches the Research identity group. Apply the second profile to the rule which matches the Engineering identity group.

Lab Verification

To verify the solution, create a user in each group/identity group on ACS and initiate an HTTP session to 172.16.26.10 or 172.16.26.11. You will be redirected to an authentication page.

After authentication, the Authentication Proxy cache and the interface ACL will look similar to the output shown in Example 11-8.

Example 11-8   *Verification of Lab Scenario #14*

```
Router#show ip auth-proxy cache
Authentication Proxy Cache
 Client Name research1, Client IP 192.168.1.31, Port 58452, timeout 60, Time
Remaining 60, state ESTAB

Router#show access-list 101
```

```
Extended IP access list 101
    permit tcp host 192.168.1.31 host 172.16.26.10 eq www (10 matches)

    20 permit udp any eq 1645 any (5 matches)
    30 permit udp any eq 1646 any (2 matches)
```

You should also try to initiate an HTTP session to 172.16.26.11 after authenticating as a user from the Research group. The router should not allow the session to go through.

Summary

Although Authentication Proxy can be used with only three protocols, it is very useful for restricting access based on the user profile.

Very little goes wrong with Authentication Proxy configuration and usually it has to do with the downloadable ACL configuration on ACS. The interface ACL on the router is important because it can provide more access than a user is entitled to.

This chapter concludes Part IV, "Pass Through Traffic." Part V, "Remote Access," looks at authentication, authorization, and accounting of various remote access services.

Chapter 12

AAA of VPN and PPP Sessions on IOS

This chapter covers the following subjects:

- Authenticating, Authorization, and Accounting of IPsec Remote Access VPN (EzVPN) on IOS

- Authentication, Authorization, and Accounting of SSL VPN on IOS

- Authentication, Authorization, and Accounting of PPP Sessions on IOS

Telecommuting has become a very important part of an organization today and the Internet provides the perfect medium for it. With all the benefits associated, there is also a huge security risk involved. Almost anyone with an Internet connection can try to connect to your network. To minimize the risks associated, it is very important to authenticate, authorize, and monitor users connecting to your network remotely.

This chapter discusses authentication, authorization, and accounting (AAA) on IOS in relation to different types of remote access virtual private network (VPN) methods and Point-to-Point Protocol (PPP).

Authenticating VPN Sessions

The two most commonly used Remote Access VPN methods are IPsec (also known as Easy VPN Remote or EzVPN Remote) and Secure Sockets Layer (SSL) VPNs. This section discusses how to configure authentication with each of these VPN methods. You should have some knowledge about the operation and configuration of these VPN technologies before beginning with this section. The VPN configuration shown in this section is minimal.

Authenticating IPsec Remote Access Sessions

IPsec is one of the most widely used methods for connecting to a VPN. It uses Internet Key Exchange (IKE) to handle negotiation of protocols and algorithms based on local policy and to generate the encryption and authentication keys to be used by IPsec. IKE has two phases of key negotiation:

- **Phase 1:** Phase 1 negotiates a security association (a key) between two IKE peers. The key negotiated in Phase 1 enables IKE peers to communicate securely in Phase 2.

- **Phase 2:** During Phase 2 negotiation, IKE establishes keys (security associations) for other applications, such as IPsec.

The IKE standard does not provide for user authentication. It provides only for authentication of the device. The most common implementation is using a preshared key for group authentication. As you might have realized, this raises a huge security risk. If a machine with the VPN group password saved in a profile is compromised or stolen, a malicious user can connect to the network without requiring any user authentication.

To overcome this, the IETF has developed a draft RFC for IKE Extended Authentication (Xauth). The Xauth feature is an enhancement to the existing IKE protocol feature, which allows Cisco IOS Software to perform user authentication using AAA authentication methods. The user authentication is performed after IKE phase 1 and before IKE phase 2. It is commonly referred to as phase 1.5.

Xauth uses a Request/Reply mechanism to get the credentials from the user when the VPN gateway is configured to require user authentication. It then passes the credentials to the AAA mechanism of IOS. Usually, RADIUS is used to authenticate the user with the AAA server. Figure 12-1 shows the steps involved with Xauth.

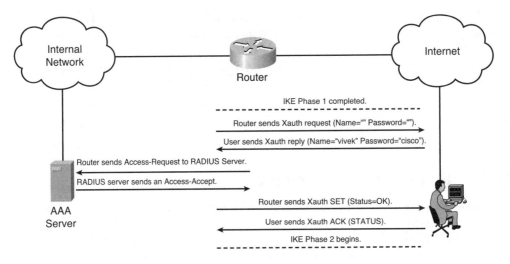

Figure 12-1   *Typical Xauth Session*

Note   You can use both TACACS+ and RADIUS for AAA of IPsec, but RADIUS is better suited due to the various Cisco attributes available for authorization. This section uses RADIUS only.

There are various ways of configuring an IPsec remote access VPN on IOS. Xauth configuration changes according to the method used for IPsec configuration. Before configuring Xauth, you need to define a method list for authentication using the following command:

```
aaa authentication login method-name {group radius | group tacacs+ | local}
```

You can use the default method; however, recommended practice dictates using a named method list for IPsec authentication.

The most common form of remote access IPsec VPN configuration is using dynamic crypto maps, as demonstrated in Example 12-1. Authentication can be configured using the following command when such a configuration is used:

```
crypto map map-name client authentication list method-name
```

This command ties the crypto map to an authentication method list. After this command is added, Xauth will be initiated at the end of Phase 1 and the credentials will be verified using the method specified in the authentication method list. The *method-name* should match the authentication method list created. Example 12-2 expands Example 12-1 to include authentication.

Example 12-1   *Remote Access IPsec VPN Configuration*

```
Router(config)#crypto isakmp policy 1
Router(config-isakmp)#authentication pre-share
Router(config-isakmp)#encryption 3des
Router(config-isakmp)#exit
Router(config)#crypto ipsec transform-set remote esp-3des esp-sha-hmac
Router(config)#crypto dynamic-map rvpn 10
Router(config-crypto-map)#set transform-set remote
Router(config-crypto-map)#exit
Router(config)#crypto map remotevpn client configuration address respond
Router(config)#crypto map remotevpn 10 ipsec-isakmp dynamic rvpn
Router(config)#interface FastEthernet0/0
Router(config-if)#ip address 200.1.1.1 255.255.255.0
Router(config-if)#crypto map remotevpn
```

Example 12-2   *Remote Access IPsec VPN Authentication Including Authentication*

```
Router(config)#aaa authentication login vpnauth group radius
Router(config)#crypto isakmp policy 1
Router(config-isakmp)#authentication pre-share
Router(config-isakmp)#encryption 3des
Router(config-isakmp)#exit
Router(config)#crypto ipsec transform-set remote esp-3des esp-sha-hmac
Router(config)#crypto dynamic-map rvpn 10
Router(config-crypto-map)#set transform-set remote
Router(config-crypto-map)#exit
```

```
Router(config)#crypto map remotevpn client authentication list vpnauth
Router(config)#crypto map remotevpn client configuration address respond
Router(config)#crypto map remotevpn 10 ipsec-isakmp dynamic rvpn
Router(config)#interface FastEthernet0/0
Router(config-if)#ip address 200.1.1.1 255.255.255.0
Router(config-if)#crypto map remotevpn
```

A crypto map set is a collection of crypto map entries, each with a different *seq-num* argument but the same *map-name* argument. The configuration shown in Example 12-2 applies Xauth to all entries in the crypto map (remotevpn in Example 12-2). There might be entries in the crypto map that do not require Xauth. For such entries, you will need to disable Xauth individually.

Note   Xauth can be disabled only if preshared keys are used as the authentication mechanism for the given crypto map. To disable Xauth, use the **no-xauth** keyword when defining the preshared key for a IPsec peer using the following command:

crypto isakmp key *keystring* **address** *peer-address* [**mask**] [**no-xauth**]

To overcome this problem, the ISAKMP profile was introduced in Cisco IOS Software Release 12.2(15)T. The ISAKMP profile is an enhancement to Internet Security Association and Key Management Protocol (ISAKMP) configurations that enables modularity of ISAKMP configuration for Phase 1 negotiations. This modularity allows mapping different ISAKMP parameters to different IPsec tunnels. It also allows different Xauth configurations for different tunnels. Example 12-3 shows a common configuration using dynamic crypto maps and an ISAKMP profile.

Example 12-3   *Remote Access IPsec VPN Configuration Using an ISAKMP Profile*

```
Router(config)#crypto isakmp policy 1
Router(config-isakmp)#encr 3des
Router(config-isakmp)#authentication pre-share
Router(config-isakmp)#exit
Router(config)#crypto isakmp client configuration group Vpngroup
Router(config-isakmp-group)#key cisco123
Router(config-isakmp-group)#pool vpnpool
Router(config-isakmp-group)#exit
Router(config)#crypto isakmp profile remotevpn
Router(conf-isa-prof)#match identity group Vpngroup
Router(conf-isa-prof)#client configuration address respond
Router(conf-isa-prof)#exit
Router(config)#crypto ipsec transform-set remote esp-3des esp-sha-hmac
Router(config)#crypto dynamic-map rvpn 10
Router(config-crypto-map)#set transform-set remote
```

```
Router(config-crypto-map)#set isakmp-profile remotevpn
Router(config-crypto-map)#exit
Router(config)#crypto map remotevpn 10 ipsec-isakmp dynamic rvpn
Router(config)#interface FastEthernet0/0
Router(config-if)#ip address 200.1.1.1 255.255.255.0
Router(config-if)#crypto map remotevpn
```

Where an ISAKMP profile is used, Xauth is configured in the profile instead of the crypto map, using the following commands:

```
crypto isakmp profile profile-name
  client authentication list method-name
```

Similar to the **client authentication** command used with crypto map, this command ties the profile to an authentication method list. The *method-name* should match the authentication method list name. Example 12-4 shows the configuration required to add authentication to the configuration shown in Example 12-3.

Example 12-4   *Authentication Configuration with an ISAKMP Profile*

```
Router(config)#aaa authentication login vpnauth group radius
Router(config)#crypto isakmp profile remotevpn
Router(conf-isa-prof)#client authentication list vpnauth
```

Authenticating SSL VPN Sessions

SSL-based VPNs provide remote-access connectivity from almost any Internet-enabled location using a web browser and its native SSL encryption. Unlike IPsec Remote Access VPNs, SSL-based VPNs do not require client software to be preinstalled on a machine. Any software required for application access across the SSL VPN connection is dynamically downloaded on an as-needed basis.

Cisco IOS supports the following three kinds of SSL VPN:

- Clientless mode

- Thin-Client mode

- Tunnel mode

Discussion on the modes and their configuration is beyond the scope of this book; however, Example 12-5 shows a sample basic configuration of an SSL VPN.

Note   You can find information regarding SSL VPN and its modes at the following URL: http://www.cisco.com/en/US/docs/ios/12_4t/12_4t11/htwebvpn.html

Example 12-5 *Sample SSL VPN Configuration*

```
Router(config)#webvpn gateway test
Router(config-webvpn-gateway)#hostname AAA-Test
Router(config-webvpn-gateway)#ip address 192.168.26.44 port 443
Router(config-webvpn-gateway)#ssl encryption 3des-sha1
Router(config-webvpn-gateway)#ssl trustpoint TP-self-signed-998521732
Router(config-webvpn-gateway)#inservice
Router(config-webvpn-gateway)#exit
Router(config)#webvpn context test
Router#(config-webvpn-context)#title "AAATest"
Router#(config-webvpn-context)#ssl authenticate verify all
Router#(config-webvpn-context)#login-message "Welcome"
Router#(config-webvpn-context)#policy group test
Router(config-webvpn-group)#banner "Welcome to AAATest SSL VPN"
Router(config-webvpn-group)#exit
Router#(config-webvpn-context)#default-group-policy test
Router#(config-webvpn-context)#gateway test
Router#(config-webvpn-context)#inservice
```

IOS supports both local and AAA server–based authentication for SSL VPNs. Before configuring authentication for an SSL VPN, you need to define a method list for authentication using the following command:

`aaa authentication login` *method-name* `{group radius | group tacacs+ | local}`

You can use the default method; however, recommended practice dictates using a named method list for IPsec authentication.

Authentication for SSL VPN is configured in the WebVPN context, using the following command:

`aaa authentication list` *method-name*

This command ties the method list you created earlier to the WebVPN context. For example, you can use the following commands to configure authentication for the *test* context from Example 12-5:

```
Router(config)#aaa authentication login vpnauth group radius
Router(config)#webvpn context test
Router(config-webvpn-context)#aaa authentication list vpnauth
```

Configuring ACS 4.2 and 5.1 for IPsec and SSL VPN Authentication

Configuring ACS 4.2 and 5.1 for VPN authentication requires the steps you followed for configuring administrative authentication on IOS devices. Refer to Chapter 6, "Administrative AAA on IOS," to recall the steps you used. A summary of steps required is as follows:

Step 1.   Add a router as an AAA client with the correct shared key and protocol.

Step 2.   Add a user.

Step 3.   For ease of learning, ensure that you use a new group or access service so
that the previous configuration does not cause problems.

Verifying and Troubleshooting VPN Authentication

Most common problems with VPN authentication are related to the communication
between the router and the AAA server as discussed in Chapter 6. For the most part,
when communication between the router and the AAA server is working, VPN authentication works also. If communication between the router and the AAA server is working
well, but VPN authentication fails, you can verify the following:

■   Ensure that the authentication command is applied correctly on the **crypto map**,
    ISAKMP profile, or **WebVPN context**.

■   Ensure that the authentication commands are using the correct method list and server
    group.

■   Test the local user authentication before configuring Xauth or SSL VPN authentica-
    tion. This rules out problems with VPN configuration itself.

For troubleshooting VPN authentication, the following debug commands are most useful:

■   **debug radius:** This command shows debugs of the RADIUS communication
    between the router and the RADIUS server. If authentication is failing, this is a good
    place to start troubleshooting from.

■   **debug crypto isakmp:** This command shows debugs of Internet Key Exchange (IKE)
    events. Xauth-related events are also part of these debugs. You can use these debugs
    in combination with RADIUS debugs to find out whether Xauth is failing or Phase 1
    of the VPN negotiation is failing.

■   **debug webvpn aaa:** This command shows debugs of events and errors related to
    AAA during WEBVPN negotiation. If authentication is failing for WebVPN, you can
    use these debugs along with RADIUS debugs to identity the cause of failure.

■   **debug aaa authentication:** This command shows information regarding the authenti-
    cation process. The output is especially useful in finding the method list used by an
    authentication event.

Authorizing VPN Sessions

Cisco IOS supports authorization of VPN sessions using a local database as well as external AAA servers. This section looks at authorization of IPsec remote access and SSL VPN
authorization using ACS 4.2 and 5.1.

Authorizing IPsec Remote Access Sessions

In cases where local authorization is configured, when Cisco IOS receives a remote access IPsec connection, it attempts to match the group name contained in the connection to a group configured on the router. This group, called the client configuration group (or the VPN group), contains all the attributes for the session, including the group preshared key (if digital certificates are not used), address pool, and so on.

When Cisco IOS is configured for authorization using RADIUS, the client configuration group is defined on the RADIUS server as a user. This user's profile contains all group configuration options as attributes. In such cases, when IOS receives a remote access IPsec connection, it will do the following:

Step 1. It will attempt to authenticate the group name received in the IPsec connection with the RADIUS server using cisco as a password.

Step 2. On successful authentication, it will look for the group password (also called the preshared key) in the attributes received from the RADIUS server. If the password matches the one received in the IPsec connection, the session will be continued to the next phase.

Step 3. If Xauth is configured, IOS will attempt to authenticate the user with the RADIUS server. On successful authentication, the user attributes received from the server are stored.

Note There is a difference between IPsec group and user attributes. There are only four user attributes that can be defined in the Xauth user profile. These four attributes, if present in the Xauth user profile, will override similar attributes present in the group profile. IOS will apply the user attributes even if authorization is not configured.

Group attributes should not be configured in the user profile. This will cause IOS to ignore all attributes in the group profile. Valid group and user attributes are discussed in the next section.

Step 4. If the user profile received during Xauth contains any group attributes, IOS will not use any group attributes from the group profile itself. You will need to define all group and user attributes in the Xauth user profile. These attributes will be used during the MODECFG phase. If the user profile does not contain any group attributes, IOS will generate another RADIUS request to authenticate the group again to get the group attributes again.

Step 5. IOS will merge the user attributes received during Xauth and the group attributes received in reply to the third RADIUS request. The resulting list of attributes is used in the MODECFG phase to configure the client.

Before configuration authorization for VPN sessions, you must add a **network** authorization method list using the following command:

```
aaa authorization network {list-name | default} group radius
```

You can use the **default** method list; however, recommended practice dictates that you should use a named list to avoid problems between different services on a router that might be using AAA.

As with Xauth configuration, the commands required to configure VPN authorization depend on the VPN configuration method.

If you are *not* using an ISAKMP profile for VPN, the following command is needed for configuring authorization:

```
crypto map map-name isakmp authorization list method-list-name
```

The defined *method-list-name* parameter should match the list you created using the **aaa authorization network** command.

If you *are* using an ISAKMP profile for VPN, the following commands are needed for configuring authorization:

```
Router(config)#crypto isakmp profile profile-name
Router(conf-isa-prof)#match identity group group-name
Router(conf-isa-prof)#isakmp authorization list method-list-name
```

The defined *group-name* parameter in the **match identity** command should match the name of the group created on the RADIUS server and the defined *method-list-name* parameter should match the list you created using the **aaa authorization network** command.

Configuring ACS 4.2 and ACS 5.1 for IPsec Remote Access Authorization

Configuring ACS for authorization of IPsec remote access sessions requires you to create a user in ACS. The username created will be configured on the VPN client as the group name for the connection. You will recall from the previous section that Cisco IOS sends the group name of the connection to ACS for authentication and uses **cisco** as the password. This means that the password for the user should be kept as **cisco** in ACS. The user, or the group to which this user belongs, should have the following attributes configured at the least:

RADIUS IETF Attribute: Service-Type with value set to **Outbound**

RADIUS IETF Attribute: Tunnel-Type with value set to **IP ESP**

cisco-av-pair attribute with the following values:

> **ipsec:tunnel-type=ESP**
>
> **ipsec:key-exchange=IKE**
>
> **ipsec:tunnel-password=**tunnel-pre-shared-key*
>
> **ipsec:addr-pool=**pool-name*

tunnel-pre-shared-key is the group preshared key that will be used by the clients for group authentication. The *pool-name* is the name of the address pool configured on the router and will be used to provide address to the clients.

You can define additional group attributes as values of the **cisco-av-pair** attribute. Some of the valid attributes are given in Example 12-6.

Example 12-6 *Some valid Group Attributes for IPsec Remote VPN*

```
ipsec:default-domain=cisco
ipsec:inacl=101
ipsec:access-restrict=fastethernet 0/0
ipsec:group-lock=1
ipsec:dns-servers=10.1.1.1 10.2.2.2
ipsec:firewall=1
ipsec:include-local-lan=1
ipsec:save-password=1
ipsec:wins-servers=10.3.3.3 10.4.4.4
ipsec:split-dns=example.com
ipsec:ipsec-backup-gateway=10.1.1.1
ipsec:ipsec-backup-gateway=10.1.1.2
ipsec:pfs=1
ipsec:cpp-policy=Enterprise Firewall
ipsec:auto-update=Win http://www.example.com 4.0.1
ipsec:browser-proxy=bproxy_profile_A
ipsec:xauth-banner=Xauth banner text here
```

Apart from the group attributes discussed and shown in Example 12-6, there are four user attributes that can be added in the VPN user profile. Remember that the VPN user profile is the profile of the actual end user, which is used during Xauth. This differs from the group name added as a user previously. You can use these four attributes when a user or group of users need more or less privileges than the rest of the users of the VPN group. Table 12-1 lists and describes these four attributes.

Note   As mentioned in the previous section, you can add group attributes in the end user profile; however, this will cause IOS to expect all group attributes to be present in the user profile. If the user profile does not contain the minimum required group attributes, IOS will not generate the third RADIUS request to get the group attributes and will terminate the VPN negotiation.

This can quickly become unmanageable if there are many groups of user accessing the same VPN (client configuration) group.

You already know how to add users and configure the RADIUS attribute in ACS 4.2 and 5.1 from previous chapters. If you cannot recall the steps, refer to Chapters 3 and 4 to add a user and refer to Chapter 8, "IOS Switches," for the steps to add attributes for users and groups.

Table 12-1   *IPsec User Attributes*

Attribute	Description
Framed-IP-Address	This is a RADIUS IETF attribute that can be used to assign an IP address to the user. This attribute is used when you define an IP pool on ACS and configure the group or user profile to assign an address from the pool or when you configure a static IP address in the user profile. Use this option to assign addresses from the ACS pool instead of the pool created on IOS or to assign a static IP address to a user. These options can be found in the **IP Address Assignment** section in user and group setup in ACS 4.2. IP pools are not available in ACS 5.1 but you can use the **Frame-IP-Address** attribute in an **Authorization Profile** to assign station IP address.
ipsec:user-save-password	This attribute can be used as a value for **cisco-av-pair** attribute. When used, this will allow the user to save the password on the VPN Client. Example: **ipsec:user-save-password=1**
ipsec:user-include-local-lan	This attribute can be used as a value for **cisco-av-pair** attribute. When used, this will allow the end user to access his local LAN while connected to the VPN. Example: **ipsec:user-include-local-lan=1**
ipsec:user-vpn-group	This attribute can be used as a value for **cisco-av-pair** attribute. When used, this will restrict the user to the VPN group specified. If the user tries to connect to any other VPN group, an authentication failure will be sent to the client. Example: **ipsec:user-vpn-group=salesvpn**

Authorizing SSL VPN Sessions

You will recall from the SSL VPN authentication section that user privilege is controlled by a policy group defined on the router. In Example 12-5, policy group **test** is defined for the context. This policy group applies on every user that connects to this context and does not allow a per-user change in the policies.

If you are using RADIUS to authenticate the users, you can define some attributes in the user profile that will override the policies in the group on IOS and provide privileges tailored to a user or a group of users.

You only need to configure the SSL VPN context to authenticate users using a RADIUS server as discussed earlier in the chapter. No additional configuration is required for authorization. IOS will use any attributes received during authentication.

Configuring ACS 4.2 and ACS 5.1 for SSL VPN Authorization

Most of the attributes that can be used for SSL VPN authorization are configured as values for the **cisco-av-pair** attribute. These attributes start with **webvpn:**. A list of all valid attributes can be found at http://www.cisco.com/en/US/docs/ios/sec_secure_connectivity/configuration/guide/sec_ssl_vpn.html#wp1055019.

You already know how to add users and configure RADIUS Attribute in ACS 4.2 and 5.1 from previous chapters. If you cannot recall the steps, refer to Chapters 3 and 4 for steps to add a user and refer to Chapter 8 for the steps to add attributes for users and groups.

Verifying and Troubleshooting VPN Authorization

When troubleshooting VPN authorization, the following problems are most commonly seen:

- **Using group attributes in Xauth user profile:** This leads to IOS ignoring group attributes and causing undesirable results.

- **Attributes incorrectly configured:** IOS will not be able to parse attributes incorrectly spelled. Attributes should be checked if something is not working properly.

- **Attribute value incorrect:** Incorrect value or reference to nonexistent objects, such as address pools, will cause IOS to ignore the attribute. You should ensure that the values are correct and objects are present on the router.

The following commands are useful when troubleshooting VPN authorization:

- **debug radius:** This command shows debug of the RADIUS communication between the router and the RADIUS server, which includes the attributes received from the RADIUS server. If authorization results are not as desired, these debugs will help verify the attributes that were received from the server.

- **debug crypto isakmp:** This command shows debugs of Internet Key Exchange (IKE) events. Xauth- and MODECFG-related events are also part of these debugs. You can use these debugs in combination with RADIUS debugs to find out whether there are problems during MODECFG.

- **debug webvpn aaa:** This command shows debugs of events and errors related to AAA during WEBVPN negotiation. If desired results are not seen, you can use this debug along with RADIUS debugs to verify the attributes received.

- **debug aaa authorization:** This command shows information regarding the authorization process. The output is especially useful in finding the method list used by an authorization event.

Accounting for IPsec Remote Access and SSL VPN

IOS enables you to send accounting information for IPsec remote access and SSL VPN sessions.

Before configuring accounting for these sessions, you need to create an accounting method list using the following command:

```
aaa accounting network method-list-name {start-stop | stop-only} group radius
```

You can use the default method list; however, recommended practice dictates using a named method list.

When accounting is configured for IPsec remote access sessions, IOS sends the following information:

- Session ID
- Session Time
- Input Octets
- Output Octets
- Input packets
- Output Packets
- Framed-IP-Address (Address assigned to the client)

To configure accounting for IPsec remote access sessions, use the following command in an ISAKMP profile:

```
accounting method-list-name
```

If you are not using ISAKMP profiles, use the following command to configure accounting:

```
crypto map map-name client accounting list method-list-name
```

When accounting is configured for SSL VPN sessions, IOS sends the session ID and session time in the accounting packet. To enable accounting for SSL VPN, use the following commands:

```
webvpn context context-name
aaa accounting list method-list-name
```

Lab Scenario #15: VPN AAA

ABC Inc. has IPsec remote access VPN configured on its router. Currently it is using the router's local database to authentication users and assign group policies. It now wants to use its ACS server to authenticate users.

Split-tunneling is disabled for the VPN sessions. For the ACS group named Admins, the company wants to allow the users to have access to their local LAN.

The crypto map used on the router is named **officevpn**. ABC Inc. does not use ISAKMP profiles. Your task is to configure the router and ACS to complete this requirement.

Lab Setup

The Lab Scenario requires a router, at least one Layer 2 switch, ACS, and a host with Cisco VPN client. Figure 12-2 shows the setup required.

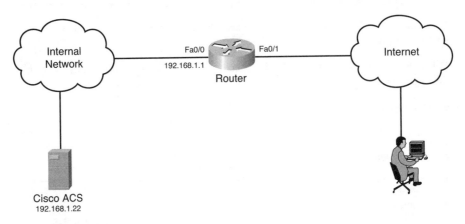

Figure 12-2 *Lab Setup for Scenario #15*

Before proceeding with this lab, add the router as a client in ACS. If you are using ACS 4.2, rename a group as **Admins**. If you are using ACS 5.1, create an identity group name **Admins**. You can use the default RADIUS Access Service or create a new one. The identity policy can be left as default (Internal Users). You also need to create an Authorization rule in the Access Service. This rule should match the Admins identity group.

Apply the following VPN configuration on the router before starting the lab:

```
crypto isakmp policy 1
authentication pre-share
encryption 3des
!
crypto ipsec transform-set vpn esp-3des esp-sha-hmac
!
crypto dynamic-map ovpn 10
set transform-set vpn
!
crypto map officevpn client configuration address respond
crypto map officevpn 10 ipsec-isakmp dynamic ovpn
!
interface FastEthernet0/0
ip address 200.1.1.1 255.255.255.0
crypto map officevpn
```

Lab Solution

The following solution provides steps for both ACS version 4.2 and version 5.1:

Step 1. Add the ACS server on the router:

```
Router(config)#aaa new-model
Router(config)#radius-server host 192.168.1.10 key abckey
```

Step 2. Configure the router for Xauth using ACS:

```
Router(config)#aaa authentication login vpnauth group radius
Router(config)#crypto map officevpn client authentication list vpnauth
```

Step 3. (For ACS 4.2 only) Add the **user-include-local-lan** attribute to the group:

Select Admins group from Group Setup and click Edit Settings.

Scroll down to the RADIUS (IOS/PIX 6.0) section and select cisco-av-pair.

In the text box below cisco-av-pair, enter **ipsec:user-include-local-lan=1**.

Click **Submit+Restart**.

Step 4. (For ACS 5.1 only) Create an authorization profile:

Authorization profiles can be created from **Policy Elements > Authorization and Permissions > Network Access > Authorization Profiles**.

The authorization profile should have the following cisco-av-pair attribute:

ipsec:user-include-local-lan=1

Step 5. (For ACS 5.1 only) Apply the authorization profiles created in step 5 to the authorization rule created during Lab Setup.

Lab Verification

To verify the solution, create a user in the **Admins** Group/Identity Group in ACS. Create a new connection on the VPN Client according to the **client group configuration** on the router and connect. When prompted for Xauth, authenticate with the user you created. The authentication should succeed and you should have access to the local LAN even when connected to the VPN.

Authenticating PPP Sessions

PPP is probably one of the best known and time-tested protocols for transporting IP traffic across point-to-point links. It is commonly used to transport IP traffic across plain old telephone service (POTS) dialup, ISDN, or point-to-point leased lines. This section looks at how to use RADIUS to authenticate PPP dial-in sessions on IOS. The concepts and configuration discussed in this section can be used for authentication of any kind of PPP session, including PPPoE, with little or no change.

Note   You can use both TACACS+ and RADIUS for AAA of IPsec; however, RADIUS is better suited due to the various Cisco attributes available for authorization. Throughout this section, we will use RADIUS only.

There are three phases over which PPP sessions are established:

- **Phase 1:** The two hosts use Link Control Protocol (LCP) to configure and optionally test the data link. Among other things, an authentication protocol is decided on during this phase.

- **Phase 2:** This is an optional authentication phase. The authentication protocol negotiated during the first phase is used to authenticate the client. The authentication is usually one-way with the called party (an IOS router) authenticating the calling party (a remote dial-in user). IOS allows using PAP, CHAP, MS-CHAP, and MS-CHAPv2 as authentication protocols.

- **Phase 3:** Network Control Protocol (NCP) is used to choose and configure a network layer protocol such as IP.

IOS allows using the local database as well as a RADIUS or TACACS+ server for authentication for PPP sessions.

Before configuring PPP for authentication using RADIUS, you need to add an authentication method list using the following command:

`aaa authentication ppp {default | method-list-name} group radius`

You can use the **default** method list and this is one time where you *should* use it unless you want a different authentication method or servers for different type of PPP sessions.

There are different ways of configuring PPP on IOS. Whichever method you use, it will have a **ppp authentication** *protocol* command. If you use the **default** method list for PPP authentication, it will apply to all kinds of PPP configuration and force an authentication using the RADIUS servers. If you use named method lists, you will need to modify the **ppp authentication** *protocol* command to the following:

`ppp authentication protocol method-list-name`

Example 12-7 shows an example of PPP configuration using named method list.

Example 12-7   *PPP Authentication Configuration Using Named Method List*

```
aaa authentication ppp myauth group radius

!
interface Group-Async1
ip unnumbered FastEthernet0/0
```

```
no ip directed-broadcast
encapsulation ppp
no ip route-cache
no ip mroute-cache
dialer in-band
async mode dedicated
peer default ip address pool default
ppp authentication pap myauth

group-range 1 16
!
radius-server host 192.168.1.10 key cisco
```

Configuring ACS for PPP Authentication

Configuring ACS 4.2 and 5.1 for VPN authentication requires the steps you followed for configuring administrative authentication on IOS devices. Refer to Chapter 6 to recall the steps you used, although a summary of the required steps is as follows:

Step 1.   Add Router as an AAA Client with correct shared key and protocol.

Step 2.   Add a user.

Step 3.   For ease of learning, ensure that you use a new group or access service so that previous configuration does not cause problems.

Verifying and Troubleshooting PPP Authentication

Most common problems with PPP authentication are related to the communication between the router and the AAA server as discussed in Chapter 6. For the most part, when communication between the router and the AAA server is working, PPP authentication works as well. If communication between the router and the AAA server is working well but PPP authentication fails, you can verify the following:

■   Authentication command is applied in the correct place.

■   Ensure that the authentication commands are using the correct method list and server group.

■   Test the local user authentication before configuring RADIUS authentication. This rules out problems with the PPP configuration itself.

For troubleshooting PPP authentication, the following debug commands are most useful:

■   **debug ppp negotiation:** This command shows packets sent during PPP startup, where PPP options are negotiated. You can use these debugs to see the authentication negotiation.

- **debug radius:** This command shows debugs of the RADIUS communication between the router and the RADIUS server. If authentication is failing, this is a good place to start troubleshooting from.

- **debug ppp authentication:** This command shows authentication protocol messages, including Challenge Authentication Protocol (CHAP) packet exchanges and Password Authentication Protocol (PAP) exchanges. You can use these debugs along with the previous two debugs to isolate the root cause of authentication failure.

Authorizing PPP Sessions

When authenticating PPP sessions using RADIUS, you can configure authorization to do the following:

Permit or deny PPP sessions for a user or a group of users.

Configure different attributes for a user or a group of users to provide them with different access levels.

To enable authorization using RADIUS, use the following global configuration command:

```
aaa authorization network {default | method-list-name} group radius
```

You can use the **default** method list or create a named method list and apply it to the PPP configuration using the following command:

```
ppp authorization method-list-name
```

Configuring ACS 4.2 and 5.1 for PPP Authorization

Configuring ACS for PPP authorization requires configuring RADIUS IETF and RADIUS (IOS/PIX 6.0) attributes in an ACS 4.1 user or group profile or in an authorization profile applied to an authorization rule in ACS 5.2.

The following attribute and value pairs should be present in the user/group profile or the authorization profile to permit PPP sessions:

RADIUS IETF Attribute: Service-Type = Framed

RADIUS IETF Attribute: Framed-Protocol = PPP

You can set the **Service-Type** attribute to something other than **Framed** if you want to deny PPP access to a user or group of users. Apart from the preceding attributes, there are various attributes that can be used to change various aspects of a PPP session for a user or group of users. Table 12-2 outlines some of the more common attributes.

You already know how to add users and configure RADIUS attributes in ACS 4.2 and 5.1 from previous chapters. If you cannot recall the steps, refer to Chapters 3 and 4 for steps to add a user and refer to Chapter 8 for the steps to add attributes for users and groups.

Table 12-2   *Common RADIUS Attributes for PPP*

Attribute	Description
Framed-IP-Address	This is a RADIUS IETF attribute that can be used to assign an IP address to the user.
	This attribute is used when you define an IP pool on ACS and configure the group or user profile to assign an address from the pool or when you configure a static IP address in the user profile.
	Use this option to assign an address from the ACS pool instead of the pool created on IOS or to assign a static IP address to a user.
	These options can be found in the **IP Address Assignment** section in user and group setup in ACS 4.2. IP pools are not available in ACS 5.1, but you can use the **Frame-IP-Address** attribute in an **authorization profile** to assign station IP address.
ip:addr-pool	This attribute can be used as a value for **cisco-av-pair** attribute. When used, this attributes tells IOS to assign the client an IP address from the specified pool defined on the router. Example:
	ip:addr-pool=clientpool
ip:inacl	This attribute can be used as a value for **cisco-av-pair** attribute. When used, this attribute defines the input access list to be used for the PPP session. The value of this attribute can be the name or number of an access list defined on IOS as follows:
	ip:inacl=101
	The value can also be an Access Control Entry (ACE). Multiple such values can be used to send an access list to IOS as follows:
	ip:inacl#1=deny tcp any any eq 23
	ip:inacl#2=permit ip any any
	The attribute defined here will be used to create a dynamic access list on IOS.
Session-Timeout	This RADIUS IETF attribute can be used to define an absolute timeout for the PPP sessions. IOS will disconnect the session as soon as this timer expires. The value of this attribute has to be in seconds.
Idle-Timeout	This RADIUS IETF attribute can be used to define an inactivity timeout for the PPP session. IOS will disconnect the session if no activity is seen for the defined period of time. The value of this attribute has to be in seconds.

Verifying and Troubleshooting PPP Authorization

When troubleshooting PPP authorization, the following problems are most commonly seen:

- **Attributes incorrectly configured:** IOS will not be able to parse attributes incorrectly spelled. Attributes should be checked if something is not working properly.

■ **Attribute value incorrect:** Incorrect value or reference to nonexistent objects, such as address pools, will cause IOS to ignore the attribute. You should ensure that the values are correct and objects are present on the router.

■ **User attributes override group attributes:** Remember that user attributes will override group attributes. Ensure that you do not have conflicting attributes in user and group profiles.

The following commands are useful when troubleshooting PPP authorization:

■ **debug ppp negotiation:** This command shows packets sent during PPP startup, where PPP options are negotiated. You can use these debugs to see the authorization negotiation.

■ **debug radius:** This command shows debugs of the RADIUS communication between the router and the RADIUS server, which includes the attributes received from the RADIUS server. If authorization results are not as desired, these debugs will help verify the attributes that were received from the server.

Accounting for PPP Sessions

IOS enables you to send accounting information for PPP sessions to a RADIUS server.

Before configuring accounting for these sessions, you need to create an accounting method list using the following command:

`aaa accounting network` *method-list-name* `{start-stop | stop-only} group radius`

You can use the default method list; however, recommended practice dictates that you use a named method list.

When accounting is configured for PPP sessions, IOS sends the following information:

■ Session ID

■ Session Time

■ Input Octets

■ Output Octets

■ Input packets

■ Output Packets

■ Framed-IP-Address (address assigned to the client)

■ Session Terminate Cause

If you use a named method list, you can apply it to the PPP configuration using the following command:

`ppp accounting` *method-list-name*

Summary

In this chapter you learned about authentication, authorization and accounting of IPsec Remote Access VPN (EzVPN), SSL VPN, and PPP sessions.

This is the right place to stress of the importance of RADIUS attributes because this chapter exhibits the difference these attributes can make when properly used. The attributes can be used extensively to design your security policies and exceptions on per-user or per-group basis.

This chapter also forms the basis for the next chapter, which looks at AAA of IPsec remote access VPN on ASA.

Chapter 13

AAA of VPN on ASA

This chapter covers the following subjects:

- Authentication, Authorization, and Accounting of Remote Access IPsec VPN on ASA

- Authentication, Authorization, and Accounting of SSL VPN on ASA

- Authenticating and Authorizing IPsec and SSL VPN Using LDAP

In Chapter 12, "AAA of VPN and PPP Sessions on IOS," you learned about authenticating, authorizing, and accounting (AAA) for IPsec Remote Access VPN (EzVPN Remote) and SSL VPN on IOS. In this chapter, you will learn about AAA for EzVPN and SSL VPN on ASA.

If you have not done so already, you should read the previous chapter to ensure that you have a firm grasp of the different phases of IPsec, Xauth, and the role of RADIUS attributes during authorization. This chapter will not rehash this content, but will focus on the difference in configuration and RADIUS attributes. In addition, this chapter looks at authentication and authorization of VPN sessions using LDAP because it is very commonly used today. This chapter again focuses on RADIUS as a protocol of choice for VPN authentication due to the extensive list of attributes available for authorization.

Authenticating Remote Access IPsec VPN (EzVPN Remote) and SSL VPN Using RADIUS

ASA was not only the successor for Cisco PIX but also for the Cisco VPN 3000 series Concentrators. It inherited and eventually built on the concepts from the 3000 series devices to evolve into a very powerful VPN platform.

There is no difference between the way IPsec is implemented between Cisco IOS and Cisco ASA including the support for Xauth. Similar to IPsec VPN, there is very little difference in SSL VPN implementation between IOS and ASA. Again, make sure you read about the mechanics of IKE, Xauth, and SSL VPN in Chapter 12.

It is also important that you familiarize yourself with the VPN configuration on ASA because it is very different from the VPN configuration on IOS.

Before enabling Xauth for IPsec or User authentication for SSL VPN, you have to configure an AAA server group using the following commands:

aaa-server *group-tag* **protocol radius**

aaa-server *group-tag* [*if-name*] **host** *server-ip-address shared-key*

You can add multiple servers to a single group for fallback. These commands are discussed in detail in Chapter 7, "Administrative AAA on ASA/PIX."

When a new IPsec Remote Access or SSL VPN connection is initiated to an ASA, it matches the group name presented to a configured Tunnel-Group. Example 13-1 shows a Tunnel-Group configured on ASA. The tunnel-group configuration is divided into **general attributes** and **ipsec attributes**.

Example 13-1   *Tunnel-Group Configuration on ASA*

```
ASA(config)#tunnel-group remvpn type remote-access
ASA(config)#tunnel-group remvpn general-attributes
ASA(config-tunnel-general)#address-pool myvpn
ASA(config-tunnel-general)#default-group-policy remvpn
ASA(config-tunnel-general)#exit
ASA(config)#tunnel-group remvpn ipsec-attributes
ASA(config-tunnel-ipsec)#pre-shared-key *****
```

To enable Xauth or user authentication for SSL VPN, add the following command to the tunnel-group general attributes section:

authentication-server-group [*if_name*] *group-tag*

This command ties the AAA server group to the tunnel-group and enables Xauth or user authentication. The *if_name* parameter defines the interface through which the AAA servers can be reached. If you configure an *if_name* in this command, it will override the *if_name* configured in the aaa-server command. The wrong *if_name* will cause all RADIUS requests to be sent out the wrong interface in some ASA versions. Example 13-2 shows the tunnel-group configuration with Xauth enabled.

Example 13-2   *Tunnel-Group Configuration with Xauth Enabled*

```
ASA(config)#aaa-server vpnauth protocol radius
ASA(config)#aaa-server vpnauth (inside) host 192.168.1.10
ASA(config)#tunnel-group remvpn type remote-access
ASA(config)#tunnel-group remvpn general-attributes
ASA(config-tunnel-general)#address-pool myvpn
ASA(config-tunnel-general)#authentication-server-group vpnauth
ASA(config-tunnel-general)#default-group-policy remvpn
```

```
ASA(config-tunnel-general)#exit
ASA(config)#tunnel-group remvpn ipsec-attributes
ASA(config-tunnel-ipsec)#pre-shared-key *****
```

Configuring ACS for IPsec Remote Access and SSL VPN Authentication

Configuring ACS 4.2 and 5.1 for VPN authentication requires the steps you followed for configuring administrative authentication on IOS devices. Refer to Chapter 6, "Administrative AAA on IOS," to recall the steps you used. A summary of steps required is as follows:

Step 1.   Add the ASA as an AAA Client with the correct shared key and protocol.

Step 2.   Add a user.

Step 3.   For ease of learning, ensure that you use a new group or access service so that previous configuration does not cause problems.

Verifying and Troubleshooting VPN RADIUS Authentication

The most common problems with VPN authentication relate to the communication between the ASA and the AAA server as discussed in Chapter 7. For the most part, when the communication between the ASA and the AAA server is working, VPN authentication works as well. If communication between the ASA and the AAA server is working well, but VPN authentication fails, you should verify the following:

■   Authentication command is applied to the correct tunnel-group.

■   Ensure that the authentication commands are using the correct group tag.

■   Ensure that the server entry in the AAA server group is pointing to the correct interface.

■   Test the local user authentication before configuring Xauth or SSL VPN authentication. This rules out problems with VPN configuration itself.

For troubleshooting VPN authentication, the following debug commands are most useful:

■   **debug radius:** This command shows debugs of the RADIUS communication between the ASA and the RADIUS server. If authentication is failing, this is a good place to start troubleshooting.

■   **debug crypto isakmp:** This command shows debugs of Internet Key Exchange (IKE) events. Xauth-related events are also part of these debugs. You can use these debugs in combination with RADIUS debugs to find out whether Xauth is failing or Phase 1 of the VPN negotiation is failing.

■   **debug webvpn:** This command shows debugs of events and errors related to WebVPN. You can use these debugs along with RADIUS debugs to find out whether authentication is failing or WebVPN configuration is incorrect.

■ **debug aaa authentication:** This command shows information regarding the authentication process. You can use this debug along with RADIUS and crypto/webvpn debugs to see the entire sequence of events starting from session establishment to authentication failure.

Authorizing IPsec Remote Access and SSL VPN Using RADIUS

You already know that when a new IPsec and SSL VPN connection is received by ASA, it looks for a tunnel-group matching the request. The tunnel-group has, among other configuration, a group-policy name configured in it. This group-policy contains all the authorization attributes required for connection. This group-policy can be configured on ASA for local authorization or on an external RADIUS server.

In Chapter 12, you learned that the group-policy (called **client configuration group** on IOS) can be added in the RADIUS server as a user with all the required attributes. VPN authorization on ASA works almost the same way. One difference between IOS and ASA VPN authentication is that you need to define the group as external on ASA and can use any password for group authentication (IOS allows using **cisco** as a password only). The following command is used to define the external group on ASA:

```
group-policy group-policy-name external server-group group-tag password group-
password
```

group-policy-name is the name of the group-policy. This is added as a user in the RADIUS server with password set to *group-password. group-tag* is the RADIUS server group to be used for group authentication.

Another important difference between ASA and IOS is that the tunnel password used between the ASA and the VPN client is always defined on ASA. This means that ASA will generate only two RADIUS requests—the first one for Xauth and the second one to get the group attributes using the group-policy name as the username.

After you have defined the group as external on ASA, it can be associated to a tunnel-group using the following command:

```
tunnel-group group-name general-attributes
    default-group-policy group-policy-name
```

If you do not want to define the entire group-policy on the RADIUS server, you can use a local group-policy and configure a few attributes in the VPN user profile. These attributes will override the conflicting attributes in the group-policy. This can provide an increased or decreased privilege level on a per-use basis. Unlike on IOS, you can define any attribute in the VPN user profile. The remaining attributes are taken from the group profile.

> **Note** User attributes will override conflicting group attributes irrespective of where the group-policy is configured.

Before moving onto ACS configuration, you should be aware of the fact that ASA has a local group-policy called **DfltGrpPolicy** defined by default. Any attributes not present in a VPN user profile and the group-policy will be picked up from **DfltGrpPolicy.** You can view this group-policy using the **show run all group-policy DfltGrpPolicy** command.

Configuring ACS 4.2 and 5.1 for IPsec and SSL VPN Authorization

When ASA is configured to use an external group-policy, the group is added in ACS as a user. The password of this user has to match the password specified in the group-policy on ASA.

Unlike VPN authorization on IOS, authorization on ASA requires you to use the Cisco VPN 3000/ASA 7.x RADIUS attributes, which have a vendor ID of 3076. These are an extensive list of attributes specifically created for IPsec and SSL VPN on VPN 3000 series Concentrators and ASA 7.x.

If you haven't changed anything in the **DfltGrpPolicy** on ASA, the group-policy (added as a user) on ACS should have at least the following attribute—RADIUS (CVPN3000/ASA 7.x) **Group-Based-Address-Pools** (Attribute number 217), with the value set to a pool name configured on ASA for IPsec Remote Access VPN to work. For SSL VPN (WebVPN), there is no minimum requirement in terms of attributes.

There are many attributes in the Cisco VPN 3000/ASA 7.x RADIUS dictionary, owing to which you can create a comprehensive group or user profile on ACS. It is not possible to discuss each and every attribute in the dictionary but a few of the most commonly used attributes are as follows:

- **IPSec-Split-Tunneling-Policy (3076/55):** Used to specify the split tunnel policy of the group. Acceptable values are 0 (No Split Tunneling), 1 (Split Tunneling), and 2 (Local LAN permitted).

- **IPSec-Split-Tunnel-List (3076/27):** Used to specify the split tunnel access list name/number. The access list has to be present in the ASA configuration.

- **Tunnel-Group-Lock (3076/85):** Used to specify which tunnel-group the user is allowed to log in to. If the user tries to log in to a different group, the session will be disconnect after Xauth. This attribute works for both IPsec and SSL VPN.

- **Class (RADIUS IETF Attribute 25):** Used to specify the group-policy name to apply to the user. This is another form of group lock but, unlike the Tunnel-Group-Lock attribute, it does not disconnect the user if the user tries to log in to a different group. This attribute will simply apply the correct group-policy irrespective of the tunnel-group the user connects to. This attribute works for both IPsec and SSL VPN. The value of this attribute has to be in the following format:

OU=*group-policy-name*;

- **Downloadable Access List:** You can use the Downloadable IP ACLs feature in ACS for VPN. When configured for a user or group of users, these ACLs will be downloaded on ASA and applied on a per-connection basis as VPN filters. This will restrict the traffic that can be initiated by the client to the network. See Chapter 10, "Cut-Through Proxy AAA on PIX/ASA," for more details on configuring downloadable ACLs.

Note   Although the ip:incl# attribute can also be used in Cisco-Av-Pair to push downloadable ACL to the ASA but it I strongly recommend using the Downloadable IP ACLs feature on ACS.

A complete list of supported Cisco VPN 3000/ASA 7.x attributes for VPN on ASA can be found at http://www.cisco.com/en/US/docs/security/asa/asa82/configuration/guide/ref_extserver.html#wp1605508.

A complete list of supported RADIUS IETF attributes for VPN on ASA can be found at http://www.cisco.com/en/US/docs/security/asa/asa82/configuration/guide/ref_extserver.html#wp1773486.

You already know how to add users and configure RADIUS attributes in ACS 4.2 and 5.1 from previous chapters. If you cannot recall the steps, see Chapter 6 for the steps to add a user and Chapter 8 for the steps to add attributes for users and groups.

Verifying and Troubleshooting VPN Authorization

When troubleshooting VPN authorization, the following problems are most commonly seen:

- **Attribute value incorrect:** An incorrect value or reference to nonexistent objects, such as address pools, will cause ASA to ignore the attribute. You should ensure that the values are correct and objects are present on the ASA.

- **Downloadable ACLs on ASA will only work with ACS 4.0 and later:** If you are using an earlier version, ASA will not be able to download the ACL from ACS. You will need to use Cisco-av-pair to define the ACL. Use the **show access-list** command on ASA to verify that the downloaded ACL is present in the configuration.

- **Attribute not supported by VPN type:** Certain attributes are meant for certain types of VPNs. Ensure that the VPN type supports the attribute you are configuring.

The following commands are useful when troubleshooting VPN authorization:

- **debug radius:** This command shows debugs of the RADIUS communication between the ASA and the RADIUS server that includes the attributes received from the RADIUS server. If authorization results are not as desired, these debugs will help verify the attributes that were received from the server.

- **debug crypto isakmp:** This command shows debugs of Internet Key Exchange (IKE) events. Xauth- and MODECFG-related events are also part of these debugs. You can use these debugs in combination with RADIUS debugs to find out whether there are problems during MODECFG.

- **debug webvpn:** This command shows debugs of events and errors related to WebVPN. You can use these debugs along with RADIUS debugs to find out whether authorization is failing or WebVPN configuration is incorrect.

- **debug aaa authorization:** This commands shows information regarding the authorization process. You can use this debug along with RADIUS and crypto/webvpn debugs to see the entire sequence of events starting from session establishment.

Accounting for IPsec and SSL VPN Using RADIUS

ASA enables you to send accounting information for IPsec Remote Access and SSL VPN sessions. When accounting is configured, ASA sends the following information for both IPsec and SSL VPN:

- Session ID
- Session Time
- Input Octets
- Output Octets
- Input packets
- Output Packets
- Framed-IP-Address (sends the address assigned to the client, where relevant)

To configure accounting, add the following command in the **tunnel-group general-attributes** section:

```
accounting-server-group group-tag
```

ASA sends start and stop accounting packets by default. This behavior cannot be changed.

Lab Scenario # 16: VPN AAA Using RADIUS

ABC Inc. has IPsec Remote Access VPN configured on its ASA. Currently it is using the ASA's local database to authenticate users and assign group policies. It now wants to use its ACS server to authenticate users.

Split-tunneling is disabled for the VPN sessions. For the ACS group named **Admins**, the company wants to allow the users to have access to their local LAN.

The tunnel-group used on the ASA is named **officevpn**.

Lab Setup

The lab scenario requires an ASA, at least one Layer 2 switch, ACS, and a host with Cisco VPN client. Figure 13-1 shows the setup required.

Before proceeding with this lab, add the ASA as a client in ACS with the key set to **cisco123**. If you are using ACS 4.2, rename a group as **Admins**. If you are using ACS 5.1,

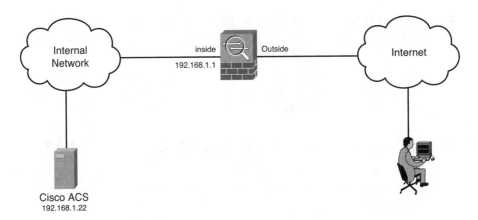

Figure 13-1 *Setup for Lab Scenario #16*

create an identity group named **Admins.** You can use the default RADIUS Access Service or create a new one. The Identity policy can be left as default (Internal Users). You also need to create an authorization rule in the Access Service. This rule should match the **Admins** identity group. You should also apply the following initial configuration on the ASA:

```
ip local pool officepool 192.168.10.1-192.168.10.100 mask 255.255.255.0
crypto ipsec transform-set esp-3des-sha esp-3des esp-sha-hmac
crypto dynamic-map officemap 10 set transform-set esp-3des-sha
crypto map vpn 10 ipsec-isakmp dynamic officemap
crypto map vpn interface outside
crypto isakmp enable outside
crypto isakmp policy 10
  authentication pre-share
  encryption 3des
  hash sha
  group 2
  lifetime 86400
group-policy officevpn internal
group-policy officevpn attributes
split-tunnel-policy tunnelall
tunnel-group officevpn type remote-access
tunnel-group officevpn general-attributes
address-pool officepool
default-group-policy officevpn
tunnel-group officevpn ipsec-attributes
pre-shared-key officevpnkey
```

Lab Solution

The following solution provides steps for both ACS version 4.2 and version 5.1:

Step 1.   Add the ACS server on the ASA:

```
ASA(config)#aaa-server labserver protocol radius
ASA(config-aaa-server-group)#exit
ASA(config)#aaa-server labserver host 192.168.1.22 cisco123
```

Step 2.   Configure the ASA for Xauth using ACS:

```
ASA(config)#tunnel-group officevpn general-attributes
ASA(config-tunnel-general)#authentication-server-group labservers
```

Step 3.   (For ACS 4.2 only) Add the **IPSec-Split-Tunneling-Policy** attribute to the group:

Enable the **IPsec-Split-Tunneling-Policy** attribute from **Interface Configuration > RADIUS (Cisco VPN 3000/ASA/PIX 7.x+)** for the Group level.

Select Admins group from Group Setup and click **Edit Settings.**

Scroll down to **RADIUS (Cisco VPN 3000/ASA/PIX 7.x+)** section and select **IPsec-Split-Tunneling-Policy.** In the drop-down list, select **Tunnel Everything except Local-LAN.**

Click **Submit+Restart.**

Step 4.   (For ACS 5.1 only) Create an authorization profile:

Authorization profiles can be created from **Policy Elements > Authorization and Permissions > Network Access > Authorization Profiles.**

The authorization profile should have the following **RADIUS-Cisco VPN 3000/ASA/PIX 7.x attribute:**

CVPN3000/ASA/PIX7.x-IPSec-Split-Tunneling-Policy with Static value set to **Local LAN permitted.**

Step 5.   (For ACS 5.1 only) Apply the authorization profile created in step 4 to the authorization rule created during Lab Setup.

Lab Verification

To verify the solution, create a user in the **Admins** Group/Identity Group in ACS. Create a new connection on the VPN Client according to the **tunnel-group** on the ASA and connect. When prompted for Xauth, authenticate with the user you created. The authentication should succeed and you should have access to the local LAN even when connected to the VPN.

Authenticating IPsec and SSL VPN Using LDAP

Most enterprises today use some kind of directory services, such as Microsoft Active Directory, for centralized account management. These directory services can be used for authentication and authorization of various services and usually support Lightweight Directory Access Protocol (LDAP) for access. Cisco ACS supports such directory services as external databases for user accounts. ASA supports authentication with such directory services using LDAP in case you do not have a RADIUS server or your RADIUS server does not support external databases.

This section looks at authenticating VPN sessions using LDAP. Microsoft Active directory is used as the LDAP server for this section and the next; however, the concepts and configuration discussed here can be applied to any LDAP server.

The first and most important step in configuring authentication with LDAP is to define the server. To define the server, you create a server group and then add the server in the group using the following commands:

```
aaa-server group-tag protocol ldap
aaa-server group-tag [if_name] host {server_ip_address | server_name}
```

The second command will bring you to the aaa-server-host configuration mode. In this mode, you need to define the parameters that ASA will use to communicate with the LDAP server. You will need to configure the following parameters at the least:

- **ldap-login-dn:** The Distinguished Name (DN) for the admin account or any account in the directory that can log in, search, and retrieve account information from the directory. ASA will log in to the directory using this account to search for the user. For most LDAP servers, this should be the complete DN of the account.

- **ldap-login-password:** The password of the account configured as the **ldap-login-dn.**

- **ldap-base-dn:** This specifies the starting point for the user search. This can be the base DN of the directory itself.

- **ldap-naming-attribute:** This is the relative DN attribute that uniquely identifies a user account in the directory. Microsoft Active Directory uses **sAMAccountName.** Other common naming attributes are **CN** and **UID.**

- **ldap-scope:** This defines whether ASA will look at the base DN level or go below the base DN level to search for the user accounts.

- **server-port:** This defines the port the server is listening on. By default, port 389 is used.

Example 13-3 shows an LDAP host configuration.

Example 13-3   *LDAP Host Configuration*

```
ASA(config)#aaa-server myservers protocol ldap
ASA(config)#aaa-server myservers (inside) host 192.168.1.10
```

```
ASA(config-aaa-server-host)#ldap-base-dn dc=testaaa,dc=com
ASA(config-aaa-server-host)#ldap-scope subtree
ASA(config-aaa-server-host)#ldap-naming-attribute sAMAccountName
ASA(config-aaa-server-host)#ldap-login-password *
ASA(config-aaa-server-host)#ldap-login-dn cn=vivek,cn=Users,dc=testaaa,dc=com
```

After the LDAP server group is configured, it can be used as an authentication server group in a tunnel-group using the following commands:

```
tunnel-group group-name general-attributes
authentication-server-group group-tag
```

Verifying and Troubleshooting VPN Authentication Using LDAP

If VPN authentication fails with LDAP, but works with local users, you can use the **debug ldap 255** command to troubleshoot the communication between ASA and LDAP. In an attempt to authenticate the user, ASA tries to bind to the LDAP server twice. The first time, it tries to bind as the user specified by the **ldap-login-dn** command. If this bind is not successful, debug output will be similar to that shown in Example 13-4. This shows that either the login DN is invalid or a wrong password has been configured. One thing you should be certain about is the complete DN of the login account.

Example 13-4   debug *Output for a Failed LDAP Admin Bind*

```
ASA#debug ldap 255
[943] Session Start
[943] New request Session, context 0xd7bcc9a0, reqType = Authentication
[943] Fiber started
[943] Creating LDAP context with uri=ldap://192.168.1.10:389
[943] Connect to LDAP server: ldap://192.168.1.10:389, status = Successful
[943] supportedLDAPVersion: value = 3
[943] supportedLDAPVersion: value = 2
[943] Binding as vivek

[943] Performing Simple authentication for vivek to 192.168.1.10

[943] Simple authentication for vivek returned code (49) Invalid credentials

[943] Failed to bind as administrator returned code (-1) Can't contact LDAP
server
```

After the first bind is successful, ASA will attempt to search the LDAP server for the user as per the configuration. The debug output in Example 13-5 shows an unsuccessful search. If authentication is failing at this stage, ensure that the base DN, naming attribute, and the scope are correct.

Example 13-5 debug *Output for an Unsuccessful LDAP Search*

```
ASA#debug ldap 255
! output omitted for brevity
[947] Creating LDAP context with uri=ldap://192.168.1.10:389
[947] Connect to LDAP server: ldap://192.168.26.1:10, status = Successful
[947] supportedLDAPVersion: value = 3
[947] supportedLDAPVersion: value = 2
[947] Binding as vivek
[947] Performing Simple authentication for vivek to 192.168.1.10
[947] LDAP Search:

        Base DN = [dc=testaaa,dc=com]

        Filter  = [sAMAccountName=vpnuser]

        Scope   = [ONE LEVEL]

[947] User vpnuser not found
```

If this search is successful, ASA retrieves the complete DN of the user and attempts to bind to the LDAP server again, using the user's DN and the password provided by the user. If the authentication fails at this stage, the password provided by the user is incorrect. Upon successful authentication, ASA will retrieve all the attributes from the user profile that can be used for authorization.

Authorizing IPsec and SSL VPN Using LDAP

After a successful LDAP authentication, ASA queries the server for the user profile that contains various attributes. These attributes vary from server to server and are not understood by ASA. To use them for authorization, you need to map them to RADIUS attributes that can be used for VPN authorization.

LDAP attributes are mapped to RADIUS attributes using LDAP attribute maps. These maps are a list of mapping between LDAP and RADIUS attributes and values.

To better understand how LDAP attribute-maps work, consider the output in Example 13-6. This output, from the **debug ldap 255** command, shows some of the attributes received from an LDAP server on successful authentication.

Example 13-6 *LDAP Attributes Received After Authentication*

```
ASA#debug ldap 255
! output omitted for brevity
[1000] Authentication successful for vpnuser to 192.168.1.10
```

```
[1000] Retrieved User Attributes:

[1000]  objectClass: value = top
[1000]  objectClass: value = person
[1000]  objectClass: value = organizationalPerson
[1000]  objectClass: value = user
[1000]  cn: value = VPNUser
[1000]  givenName: value = VPNUser
[1000]  distinguishedName: value = CN=VPNUser,CN=Users,DC=testaaa,DC=com
[1000]  memberOf: value = CN=AllVpnUsers,CN=Users,DC=testaaa,DC=com

[1000]  sAMAccountName: value = vpnuser
```

Earlier in the chapter you learned that based on group membership in ACS you can restrict the tunnel-group that can be used by the user. This is done by using **Cisco VPN 3000/ASA 7.x attribute 85 (Tunnel-Group-Lock)**. Similarly, to restrict an LDAP user to a tunnel-group, you can map any LDAP attribute, such as the **memberOf** attribute shown in Example 13-6, to the RADIUS **Tunnel-Group-Lock** attribute. Based on the value of the LDAP attribute, a value can be assigned to the mapped RADIUS attribute and applied to the VPN session.

You can create an LDAP attribute-map using the following command:

ldap attribute-map *map-name*

This command will put you in the **ldap-attribute-map** configuration mode. You can create a new mapping here using the following command:

map-name *LDAP-attribute RADIUS-attribute*

After you have created a map, you also need to map the values between the LDAP and RADIUS attributes. This can be done using the following command:

map-value *LDAP-attribute LDAP-value RADIUS-value*

The **map-value** command tells the ASA to assign *RADIUS-value* to the *RADIUS-attribute*, defined in the **map-name** command, if the value of the *LDAP-attribute* is equal to *LDAP-value* in the user profile.

Example 13-7 shows an LDAP attribute-map that maps the LDAP **memberOf** attribute to the RADIUS **Tunnel-Group-Lock**. In this example, if the value of the **memberOf** attribute is equal to the specified value, the user will be locked to the **remvpn** tunnel-group.

Example 13-7 *LDAP attribute-map*

```
ASA(config)#ldap attribute-map myldapmap
ASA(config-ldap-attribute-map)#map-name  memberOf Tunnel-Group-Lock
ASA(config-ldap-attribute-map)#map-value memberOf CN=AllVpnUsers,CN=Users,DC=tes-
taaa,DC=com rempvpn
```

After creating the LDAP attribute-map, you need to apply the map to the AAA server group that is being used by the tunnel-group for authentication using the following commands:

```
aaa-server group-tag host {server-ip-address | server-name}
ldap-attribute-map map-name
```

Almost any RADIUS attribute can be used in an LDAP attribute map. A list of all the RADIUS attributes supported for LDAP mapping can be found at the following link: http://www.cisco.com/en/US/docs/security/asa/asa82/configuration/guide/ref_extserver.html#wp1773708.

Verifying and Troubleshooting VPN Authorization with LDAP

When troubleshooting VPN authorization with LDAP, the most useful command is **debug ldap 255**. Of particular interest in the debug are the lines where the mapped LDAP attributes are shown. The debug will show whether the attribute received from the server was successfully mapped to a RADIUS attribute, as shown in Example 13-8.

Example 13-8 *debug LDAP Showing Mapped Attributes*

```
ASA#debug ldap 255
! output omitted for brevity
[1012] Retrieved User Attributes:
[1012]  cn: value = VPNUser
[1012]  givenName: value = VPNUser
[1012]  distinguishedName: value = CN=VPNUser,CN=Users,DC=testaaa,DC=com
[1012]  displayName: value = VPNUser
[1012]  memberOf: value = CN=AllVPNUsers,CN=Users,DC=testaaa,DC=com

[1012]          mapped to Tunnel-Group-Lock: value = remvpn
```

If the debug output does not show a successful mapping, the LDAP attribute-map is not properly configured. The attribute names are case sensitive; so you should consider copying and pasting the attribute name and value from the debug itself. Apart from this potential for error, ensure that the following items are true:

■ The RADIUS attribute that you are trying to use is supported by the VPN type.

■ The objects referenced in the RADIUS value, such as IP pool names, exist on the ASA.

Lab Scenario # 17: VPN Authentication and Authorization Using LDAP

ABC Inc. has IPsec Remote Access VPN configured on its ASA. Currently the company is using the ASA's local database to authenticate users and assign group policies. It now wants to use Active Directory to authenticate users using LDAP.

Split-tunneling is disabled for the VPN sessions. For users belonging to LDAP group **CN=Domain Admins,CN=Users,DC=abc,DC=com**, the company wants to allow the users to have access to their local LAN. The group membership is defined by the **memberOf** attribute.

The tunnel-group used on the ASA is named **officevpn**. The base DN of the LDAP server is **DC=abc,DC=com**. The login DN to be used is **cn=admin,cn=Users,dc=abc,dc=com** with a password of **ldappass**. The user accounts are defined by the naming attribute of **sAMAccountName**.

Lab Setup

The Lab Scenario requires an ASA, at least one Layer 2 switch, an LDAP server (preferably a Microsoft Active Directory domain controller), and a host with a Cisco VPN Client. Figure 13-2 shows the setup required.

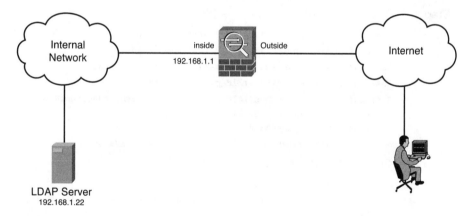

Figure 13-2 *Setup for Lab Scenario #17*

If you are not using an Active Directory domain controller as an LDAP server, use any group from your LDAP server instead of the group given in the Objective. You will also need to use your own LDAP parameters.

You should also apply the following initial configuration on ASA:

```
ip local pool officepool 192.168.10.1-192.168.10.100 mask 255.255.255.0
crypto ipsec transform-set esp-3des-sha esp-3des esp-sha-hmac
```

```
crypto dynamic-map officemap 10 set transform-set esp-3des-sha
crypto map vpn 10 ipsec-isakmp dynamic officemap
crypto map vpn interface outside
crypto isakmp enable outside
crypto isakmp policy 10
  authentication pre-share
  encryption 3des
  hash sha
  group 2
  lifetime 86400
group-policy officevpn internal
group-policy officevpn attributes
split-tunnel-policy tunnelall
tunnel-group officevpn type remote-access
tunnel-group officevpn general-attributes
address-pool officepool
default-group-policy officevpn
tunnel-group officevpn ipsec-attributes
pre-shared-key officevpnkey
```

Lab Solution

Step 1. Add the LDAP server on ASA:

```
ASA(config)#aaa-server labserver protocol ldap
ASA(config)#aaa-server labserver host 192.168.1.22
ASA(config-aaa-server-host)#ldap-base-dn dc=abc,dc=com
ASA(config-aaa-server-host)#ldap-scope subtree
ASA(config-aaa-server-host)#ldap-naming-attribute sAMAccountName
ASA(config-aaa-server-host)#ldap-login-dn
cn=admin,cn=Users,dc=aaa,dc=com
ASA(config-aaa-server-host)#ldap-login-password ldappass
```

Step 2. Create an LDAP attribute-map for authorization:

```
ASA(config)#ldap attribute-map vpnmap
ASA(config-ldap-attribute-map)#map-name memberOf IPSec-Split-Tunneling-
Policy
ASA(config-ldap-attribute-map)#map-value memberOf CN=Domain
Admins,CN=Users,DC=abc,DC=com 2
```

Step 3. Apply the attribute-map to the server group:

```
ASA(config)#aaa-server labserver host 192.168.1.22
ASA(config-aaa-server-host)#ldap-attribute-map vpnmap
```

Step 4. Enable Xauth on the tunnel-group:

```
ASA(config)#tunnel-group officevpn general-attributes
ASA(config-tunnel-general)#authentication-server-group labserver
```

Lab Verification

To verify the solution, create a user in the **Domain Admins** group in LDAP Server. Create a new connection on the VPN Client according to the **tunnel-group** on the ASA and connect. When prompted for Xauth, authenticate with the user you created. The authentication should succeed and you should have access to the local LAN even when connected to the VPN.

Summary

This chapter covered AAA in regard to IPsec and SSL VPN on ASA. You must have noticed that, as in the previous chapter, this chapter also shows the importance of attributes in VPN authorization.

ASA has more options for authorization compared to IOS that can be used to design your security policies and exceptions on per-user or per-group basis. You should look at the various attributes available in the links provided throughout the chapter because this will help you decide the kind of user or group policy you want for VPN connections.

Chapter 14

ACS 4.2 Advanced Configuration

This chapter covers the following subjects:

- Understanding Network Access Restrictions (NAR) on Access Control Server (ACS) 4.2

- Backup and Restore Feature on ACS 4.2

- Replication of Database Among ACS 4.2 Servers

- Understanding Relational Database Management System (RDBMS) Synchronization

- Understanding Network Access Profiles (NAP)

- Local Password Management on ACS 4.2

- Remote Logging Feature on ACS 4.2

- Log File Management on ACS 4.2

- CSUtil Database Utility for ACS 4.2

This chapter looks at advanced configuration components involved in ACS 4.2. The chapter provides detail on the components involved in replication and the options available for backup and restoring an ACS database. The chapter also covers bulk import of network resources and users. Finally, the chapter also examines features such as NAP and NAR.

Network Access Restrictions

Network Access Restrictions (NARs) provides an authorization condition that must be met before a user is allowed to access the network resources. On ACS, these conditions are applied based on information sent in attributes by AAA clients. Throughout this section you will gain a better understanding of NAR.

NAR on ACS can be configured either one of the following ways:

- **On user or group:** This option is available under the **Advanced Settings** and **Access Restrictions** sections, respectively as **Network Access Restrictions (NAR)**. If the

NAR option is not available, it can be enabled from the **Interface Configuration > Advanced Options** section. To enable NAR, you need to check **User-Level Network Access Restrictions** for user-level configuration and **Group-Level Network Access Restrictions** for group-level configuration.

■ **Using Shared Profile Components (SPC):** Because NAR can also be configured from SPC, to enable it you need to again navigate to **Interface Configuration** and enable the **User-Level Shared Network Access Restrictions** and/or the **Group-Level Shared Network Access Restrictions** option.

When you first look at NAR, you will find two sections, **Define IP-based access restrictions** and **Define CLI/DNIS-based access restrictions,** as shown in Figure 14-1.

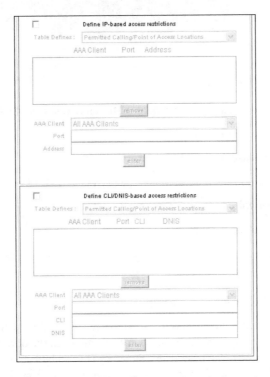

Figure 14-1   *Network Access Restrictions*

As you can see, there are two types of NARs available:

IP-based

CLI/DNIS (Non-IP) -based

Under both NARs, you have a set of conditions: **AAA client, Port, Address** (for IP-based) and **AAA client, Port, CLI, DNIS** (for CLI/DNIS-based). These parameters/attributes are ANDed to evaluate the condition.

Table 14-1 *NAR Permit and Deny Conditions*

	Match	No Match	Insufficient Information
Permit	Access Granted	Access Denied	Access Denied
Deny	Access Denied	Access Granted	Access Denied

At first glance, it is very clear what the attribute fields are and how to set them, but that does not end the story. Using the drop-down option available for each condition, you also need to define what action should be taken after a condition is matched. So, you must also choose whether the filter/condition operates positively or negatively as outlined in Table 14-1.

Although you now know the basics of how NAR works, there are still few unanswered questions. When does ACS decide to choose IP-based NAR or CLI/DNIS-based NAR? Or how does ACS retrieve attributes to build the filter/condition?

ACS selects IP-based or CLI/DNIS-based NAR depending on a simple condition that is protocol-dependent (TACACS+ or RADIUS).

A TACACS+/RADIUS session can be matched against IP-based NAR or CLI/DNIS-based NAR. Depending on the user session information, Cisco Secure ACS selects the following:

IP-based NAR when the rem_addr field in the TACACS+ start packet body or the calling-station-id (RADIUS attribute 31) in the RADIUS Access-Request packet contains a valid IP address

CLI/DNIS-based NAR in all other cases.

This answers the first question as to how ACS selects IP-based NAR or CLI/DNIS-based NAR. To answer the second question (how does ACS retrieve attributes to build the filter/condition?), look at Table 14-2 and Table 14-3.

Table 14-2 *Fields Used When Evaluating NAR for TACACS+ Session*

NAR Field	TACACS+ Fields
AAA client	NAS IP address (taken from the source address in the socket between ACS and the TACACS+ client).
Port	Taken from port field in the TACACS+ start packet body.
Address / CLI	Taken from the rem_addr field in TACACS+ start packet body.
DNIS	Taken from the rem_addr field in TACACS+ start packet body. In cases in which the rem_addr data begins with "/", the DNIS field will contain the rem_addr data without the "/" character.

Table 14-3 *Fields Used When Evaluating NAR for RADIUS Session*

NAR Field	RADIUS Fields
AAA client	NAS-IP-Address (RADIUS attribute 4) or, if NAS-IP-Address does not exist, NAS-Identifier (RADIUS attribute 32)
Port	NAS-Port (RADIUS attribute 5) or, if NAS-Port does not exist, NAS-Port-Id (RADIUS attribute 87)
Address / CLI	Calling-Station-Id (RADIUS attribute 31)
DNIS	Called-Station-Id (RADIUS attribute 30)

You should now have everything sorted out, but do you need to dig into every packet while configuring NAR? No. ACS reports make it very simple to understand which information means what. If you navigate to the Reports and Activity section and check the passed or failed logs, you can check the required detailed as shown as Table 14-4 and Figure 14-2.

Date ↓	Time	Message-Type	User-Name	NAS-IP-Address	NAS-Port	Caller-ID	Called-Station-Id	Group-Name
08/16/2010	18:34:38	Authen OK	prem	192.168.26.189	prem	00-50-56-C0-00-08	00-15-C5-48-11-C8	Group 499

Date ↓	Time	Message-Type	User-Name	NAS-IP-Address	NAS-Port	Caller-ID	Called-Station-Id	Group-Name	Authen-Failure-Code	Author-Failure-Code	Author-Data
08/16/2010	18:42:30	Authen failed	prem	192.168.26.189	prem	00-50-56-C0-00-08	00-15-C5-48-11-C8	Group 499	ACS password invalid	..	..

Figure 14-2 *NAR Fields and Passed and Failed Authentication Reports*

Based on the preceding information, let's redefine the rule on selecting IP-based or CLI/DNIS-based NAR. A TACACS+/RADIUS session can be matched against IP-based NAR or CLI/DNIS-based NAR. Depending on the user session information, Cisco Secure ACS chooses:

IP-based NAR when the Caller-ID attribute in ACS reports contains a valid IP address

CLI/DNIS-based NAR in all other cases

Table 14-4 *NAR Fields and Reports*

NAR Field/Attribute	Passed/Failed Report Attribute
AAA client	NAS-IP-Address
Port	NAS-Port
Address / CLI	Caller-ID
DNIS	Called-Station-Id

Note The **Called-Station-Id** attribute does not appear in ACS passed/failed user reports because it is not under **Logged Attributes** by default. It can be enabled under Logged Attributes from the **System Configuration > Logging** section.

To use the NAR feature based on the information so far, consider the following configuration scenario to restrict WLAN access based on the Cisco Wireless LAN Controller (WLC) Service Set Identifier (SSID). The knowledge that you are going to use to restrict access to SSID is as follows: During RADIUS authentication, when a client tries to connect to an SSID on a Cisco WLC, it sends RADIUS Access-request with RADIUS attribute 30 (Called-Station-Id) in a special format.

   WLC-MAC-Address:SSID

For example:

   00-AA-BB-F8-C6-40:ABC-Wireless

where 00-AA-BB-F8-C6-40 is the MAC address of WLC and ABC-Wireless is the SSID.

When authenticating wireless clients with WLC, the Caller-ID is the MAC address of the client machine, which is not a valid IP address. Therefore ACS evaluates CLI/DNIS-based NAR.

So, if you want to restrict any particular group's access to SSID ABC-Wireless, you will configure NAR as shown in Figure 14-3.

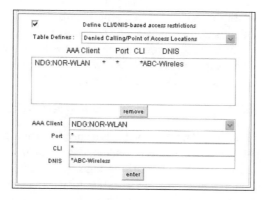

Figure 14-3 *NAR: Restricting Access to SSID*

In Figure 14-3, **Denied Calling/Point of Access Locations** has been selected from **Table Defines**, the AAA client defined as **NDG:NOR-WLAN,** which has WLC for a location, Port as any (*), CLI as any (*), and DNIS as *ABC-Wireless. If applied on a group, this configuration will restrict users in that group from being able to connect to SSID **ABC-Wireless** for the WLC configured under **NDG:NOR-WLAN.**

> **Note**   For more detail on NAR refer to the "Network Access Restrictions White Paper" on Cisco.com:
>
> http://www.cisco.com/en/US/products/sw/secursw/ps2086/products_white_paper09186a0 0801a8fd0.shtml.

Backup and Restore

Another important aspect of maintaining your ACS configuration is to perform frequent database backups of the ACS database. This section covers the steps needed to perform manual backups, schedule backups, cancel scheduled backups, and recover ACS from a backup.

Under the umbrella of database backup, you have the following options:

■ Perform a manual backup

■ Schedule a backup to take place at periodic intervals, or at a given time

■ Cancel a scheduled backup

■ Recover from a backup file

Database backups are performed from the System Configuration subsection, **ACS System Backup Setup.** From this subsection, you can configure manual backups, which requires an administrator to force the backup process into effect or schedule a backup. If you decide to schedule a backup, you have a few options. You can back up based on an interval (the default is 60 minutes) or you can specify times to perform the database backup. To perform a backup, you must tell ACS where to store the backup file. The default location to store backup files in the directory is

    C:\Program Files\CiscoSecure ACS v4.2\CSAuth\System Backups

This backup file is stored as a .dmp file. The file is named by date. For example, the file 11-May-2010 02-48-00.dmp was created at 2:48 on May 11 2010. Consider managing this directory if you have ACS perform automatic backups. This directory might get full quickly. For this reason, you might want to keep files for a certain period of time using the available **Manage Directory** option or frequently back up this directory to external media.

> **Note**   You also have the option **Add hostname** to prepend the hostname of the ACS to the backup. This option is available under **System Configuration > ACS Backup > Backup Name.**

Note   Backup and restore features between different versions of ACS are not supported. The only exception is version 4.2, on which you can restore database backups of version 4.1 using a special option available under the **ACS Restore** section **Restore from 4.1 backup file to ACS 4.2.** On ACS 4.2.1, a similar option is available to restore database backup from 4.2.0: **Restore from 4.2.0 backup file to ACS 4.2.1.**

Manual Backups

To perform a manual backup on ACS, go to **System Configuration > ACS Backup.** From here, you simply need to select the button **Backup Now** to perform a manual backup (see Figure 14-4 in the next section).

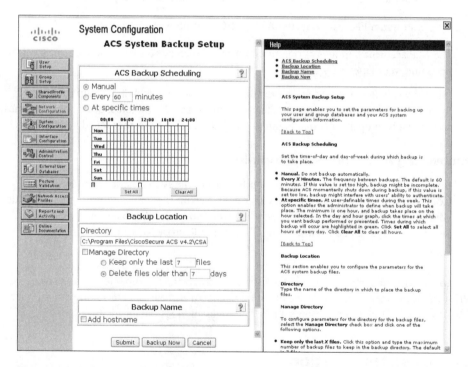

Figure 14-4   *ACS Backup Option*

Note   On ACS SE, the backup files are stored on an FTP server. You need to provide the FTP server details in the ACS Backup/Restore section.

Scheduled Backups

To schedule a backup, go to **System Configuration > ACS Backup**. Choose one of the following options:

■   Every _X_ minutes

■   At specific times

If you select to back up at a given time interval, enter an interval or accept the default of 60 minutes. If you choose to back up at specific times, use the time grid provided to select those times. Complete the configuration by selecting **Submit**.

You can manage the directory that backups are performed in by manipulating those options in the ACS interface. The default directory used for backup is

C:\Program Files\CiscoSecure ACSv4.2\CSAuth\System Backups

The Management option is also in place for this directory so that it can be managed from becoming very large, very quickly.

It is fairly simple to cancel a scheduled backup. Simply access **ACS backup** from the **System Configuration** section and change from **Every _X_ minutes**, or **At specific times**, to **Manual backup** as shown in Figure 4-4.. This cancels any further scheduled backups.

Recovering ACS from a Backup file

If you want to recover ACS from a .dmp file, select the **ACS Restore** from **System Configuration**, choose the directory that your backup files are stored in, choose the file you want to restore from, opt for restoring **user and group database** and/or **Cisco Secure ACS system configuration**, and select the **Restore Now** button as shown in Figure 14-5.

Note   ACS is momentarily shut down during backup. If the backup interval is too frequent (that is, the setting is too low), users might be unable to authenticate. In addition, using the ACS System Restore feature restarts all ACS services and logs out all administrators.

Database Replication

Database replication is a means of providing a more fault-tolerant network design. This section explains the process of database replication as well as the steps to configure database replication.

Understanding Database Replication

Database replication is a way for you to create a copy of the ACS database on one or more mirror systems. This process allows for the processing of authentication requests if the primary ACS goes down. You can schedule database replication or you can perform

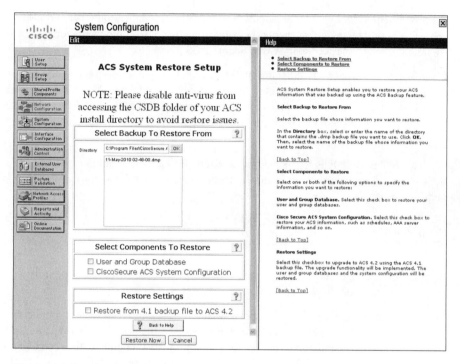

Figure 14-5 *ACS Restore Option*

immediate database replications. Another benefit to database replication is that the database is actually compressed before it is sent, and the secondary server has the capability to decompress the information after it has been received.

The replication process in the text that follows is taken from the user guide for ACS and details the communication between the primary and secondary ACS.

The database replication process begins when the primary Cisco Secure ACS server compares the list of database components it is configured to replicate with the list of database components each secondary Cisco Secure ACS is configured to replicate. The primary Cisco Secure ACS replicates only those database components that it is configured to send and that the secondary Cisco Secure ACS is configured to receive. If the secondary Cisco Secure ACS is not configured to receive any of the components that the primary Cisco Secure ACS is configured to send, the database replication is aborted.

After the primary Cisco Secure ACS has determined which components to send to the secondary Cisco Secure ACS, the replication process continues on the primary Cisco Secure ACS as follows:

Step 1.   The primary Cisco Secure ACS stops its authentication and creates a copy of the Cisco Secure database components that it is configured to replicate. During this step, if AAA clients are configured properly, those that normally use the primary Cisco Secure ACS failover to another Cisco Secure ACS.

Step 2.   The primary Cisco Secure ACS resumes its authentication service. It also compresses and encrypts the copy of its database components for transmission to the secondary Cisco Secure ACS.

Step 3.   The primary Cisco Secure ACS transmits the compressed, encrypted copy of its database components to the secondary Cisco Secure ACS. *This transmission occurs over a TCP connection, using port 2000.* The TCP session uses an encrypted, Cisco-proprietary protocol.

Note   The TCP port 2000 is for the Skinny protocol. If Skinny inspection is enabled on Cisco ASA, it will break replication if the replication data needs to flow through it. For more information, please refer to the following URL:

http://www.cisco.com/en/US/products/hw/vpndevc/ps2030/products_configuration_example09186a0080742f60.shtml.

After the preceding events on the primary Cisco Secure ACS, the database replication process continues on the secondary Cisco Secure ACS as follows:

Step 1.   The secondary Cisco Secure ACS receives the compressed, encrypted copy of the Cisco Secure database components on the primary Cisco Secure ACS. After transmission of the database components is complete, the secondary Cisco Secure ACS uncompresses the database components.

Step 2.   The secondary Cisco Secure ACS stops its authentication service and replaces its database components with the database components it received from the primary Cisco Secure ACS. During this step, if AAA clients are configured properly, those that normally use the secondary Cisco Secure ACS failover to another Cisco Secure ACS.

Step 3.   The secondary Cisco Secure ACS resumes its authentication service.

To clarify a few items for you, it is important to understand that only those components that the primary is configured to send and the secondary is configured to receive are replicated. The secondary can be configured to receive other components; however, if the primary isn't configured to send them, it won't do so. The primary can be configured to send other components; however, the secondary won't receive them if it isn't configured to do so. So, all that is actually replicated is what the primary is configured to send and what the secondary is configured to receive. This replication occurs as long as both the primary and secondary Cisco Secure ACS agree on at least one component. If they do not agree, the replication process is aborted. Additionally, if nothing has changed on the primary server since the last replication, no reason to replicate exists.

Replication Versus Backup

The major difference between database replication and database backup is that database backup creates a backup file on the local drive. This can be copied to other forms of media, or to network shares, and can be used to recover a system that has failed. What database backup does not do is copy the database or portions of the database to other ACSs, known as *secondary servers*. By using replication, you can provide a redundant server configuration. In database backup, you back up the complete ACS configuration. With database replication, the following items cannot be replicated:

- IP pool definitions

- ACS certificate and private key files

- Unknown user group mapping configuration

- Dynamically-mapped users

- Settings on the ACS Service Management page in the System Configuration section

- RDBMS synchronization settings

Configuring the Primary Server for Replication

Database replication is found in the System Configuration section of ACS. To configure the server for database replication, follow these steps:

Step 1.   Under the **Network Configuration** section, configure secondary server as an **AAA Server** with a shared secret key that will be used in secondary server configuration.

Step 2.   Select **System Configuration**.

Step 3.   Select **ACS Internal Database Replication**.

Step 4.   In the resulting screen, shown in Figure 14-6, select **Send** for any of or all the replication components:

- User and group database

- Network configuration device tables

- Distribution table

- Interface configuration

- Interface security settings

- Password validation settings

- Network Access Profiles

- Logging Configuration (Enable/Disable Settings)

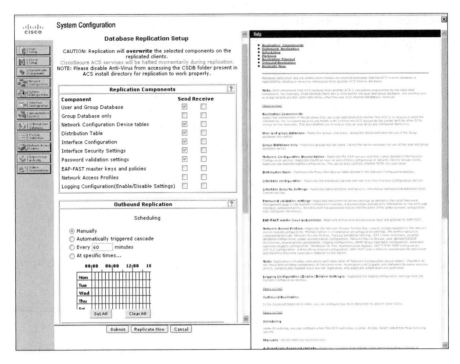

Figure 14-6   *ACS Internal Database Replication*

Step 5.   Next, for outbound replication, select the **Scheduling of Outbound Replication** options that you want to employ. Choose **Manually, Automatically Triggered Cascade** (meaning when the master receives information it is automatically copied to the others), **Every _X_ minutes,** or select a specific time using the grid provided.

Step 6.   Choose the **Partner server(s)** from the list of AAA servers in the left column of the **Partners** section, and use the right arrow button to place them in the replication list to the right.

Step 7.   Because this is the primary server, you should not need to configure the Inbound Replication settings; however, a server in a cascade can accept incoming replication, as well as perform outbound replication. If you choose a specific time, select the times from the grid provided.

Step 8.   Select the **Submit** button or, to perform immediate replication, select the **Replicate Now** button.

Configuring a Secondary Server

The secondary server must be configured to receive the exact configuration that the primary server is sending.

To configure the secondary server for database replication, follow these steps:

Step 1.   Under **Network Configuration**, create an **AAA Server** entry for the primary ACS server with the same shared secret key that was used in the primary ACS server to create an AAA Server entry for the secondary ACS server.

Step 2.   From the System Configuration menu, select the **ACS Internal Database Replication** option.

Step 3.   Select the **Receive** check box for each item you want to receive (refer back to Figure 14-6). These include user and group database, AAA servers and AAA clients tables, distribution table, interface configuration, interface security settings, and password validation settings. These should match the options that the primary ACS is sending.

Step 4.   Next, from the Inbound Replication section (see Figure 14-7), choose to receive replication from any known Cisco Secure ACS or use the drop-down list to select a trusted server.

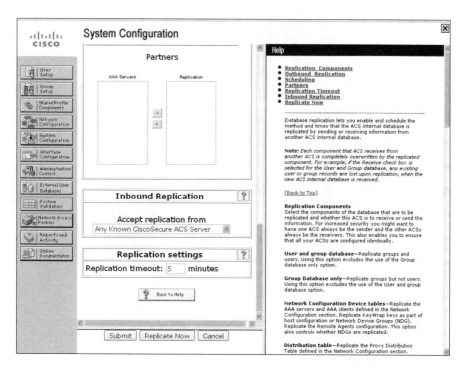

Figure 14-7   *ACS Internal Database Replication*

Step 5.   Select **Submit.**

Tip   When configuring a secondary server for replication; ensure that you do not include the primary server in the **Replication list** under **Partners.** This is one of the common reasons for replication failure.

Note   Load sharing is not supported in ACS and works only as failover. If the primary fails, the secondary takes over.

RDBMS Synchronization

The RDBMS Synchronization feature supports creation, addition, modification, and deletion of ACS database objects. RDBMS synchronization can be done manually or configured to occur on a regular schedule.

The following lists outline the different kinds of configuration that can be done using RDBMS synchronization.

For users, you can configure the following attributes:

■   Adding a user

■   Deleting a user

■   Setting passwords

■   Setting user group membership

■   Setting max sessions parameters

■   Setting network usage quota parameters

■   Configuring command authorization

■   Configuring network access restrictions

■   Configuring time-of-day/day-of-week access restrictions

■   Assigning IP addresses

■   Specifying outbound RADIUS attribute values

■   Specifying outbound TACACS+ attribute values

For user groups, you can configure the following parameters:

■   Setting max sessions parameters

■   Setting network usage quota parameters

■   Configuring command authorization

■   Configuring network access restrictions

■   Configuring time-of-day/day-of-week access restrictions

- Specifying outbound RADIUS attribute values

- Specifying outbound TACACS+ attribute values

For network configuration, you can configure the following:

- Adding an AAA client

- Deleting an AAA client

- Setting AAA client configuration details

- Adding an AAA server

- Deleting an AAA server

- Setting AAA server configuration details

- Adding and configuring proxy distribution table entries

For custom RADIUS vendors and vendor-specific attributes (VSAs), ACS enables you to create up to 10 IETF-compliant RADIUS vendors. All VSAs that you add for those servers must be subattributes of IETF RADIUS attribute number 26.

ACSs listen on TCP port 2000 for synchronization data. RDBMS synchronization communication between ACSs is encrypted using a 128-bit encrypted, proprietary algorithm.

Most of the configuration that can be done through the ACS web interface can be alternatively maintained through this feature, so in some cases this feature speeds up the process. For instance, if you are required to add, say, 100 users on ACS internal database, doing so through the ACS web interface will surely take some time. Using this feature, you can create a list of users with passwords and other information in a CSV file, or pick users from an already configured Open Database Connectivity (ODBC) database into ACS internal database in one go.

The feature of interacting with an ODBC database is available only on ACS for Windows, along with CSV. On ACS SE, you can use this feature only via a CSV file.

The CSV file and/or the ODBC input table is called accountActions. The accountActions that you create, be it a CSV file or some ODBC table, must adhere to a specification; otherwise, RDBMS synchronization might import incorrect information or fail.

accountActions Format

Table 14-5 lists the fields that compose accountActions. There are 14 fields/columns in accountActions, where each row reflects an action or input to be processed. The order is of importance as accountActions must have 14 fields/column in the same order as shown in Table 14-5.

Out of 14 fields, the following fields are mandatory, cannot be empty, and must have a valid value:

- SequenceID

- Action

- Status

Table 14-5   *accountActions Fields*

Field Name	Mnemonic	Type	Size (Max. Length)	Comments
SequenceId	SI	AutoNumber	32	The unique action ID.
Priority	P	Integer	1	The priority with which this update is to be treated. Zero (0) is the lowest priority.
UserName	UN	String	32	The name of the user to which the transaction applies.
GroupName	GN	String	32	The name of the group to which the transaction applies.
Action	A	Number	$0–2^{16}$	The action required.
ValueName	VN	String	255	The name of the parameter to change.
Value1	V1	String	255	The new value (for numeric parameters, this is a decimal string).
Value2	V2	String	255	The name of a TACACS+ protocol; for example, IP or RADIUS VSA Vendor ID.
Value3	V3	String	255	The name of a TACACS+ service; for example, ppp or the RADIUS VSA attribute number.
DateTime	DT	DateTime	-	The date and time the action was created.
MessageNo	MN	Integer	-	Used to number related transactions for audit purposes.
ComputerNames	CN	String	32	Reserved by CSDBSync.
AppId	AI	String	255	The type of configuration parameter to change.
Status	S	Number	32	TRI-STATE:0=not processed, 1=done, 2=failed. This value should normally be set to 0.

There are different action codes available for the addition, creation, deletion, modification of different ACS objects. For more information on different action codes, refer to the "RDBMS" section of the "User Guide for Cisco Secure Access Control Server":

http://www.cisco.com/en/US/docs/net_mgmt/cisco_secure_access_control_server_ for_windows/4.2.1/User_Guide/A_RDBMS.html#wp77962

As an example, Figure 14-8 looks at action code 100, which is used for user addition. Every action code has required field(s) that must not be left empty. As in case of adding a user, action code 100 has UN|GN and V1 as the mandatory fields (apart from SequenceID, Action, and Status). UN|GN means that while creating a user, it is optional to assign a user to a desired group. If a group is not defined, the user created will be assigned to the default group on ACS. Figure 14-8 shows a CSV file with action code 100 to add a user.

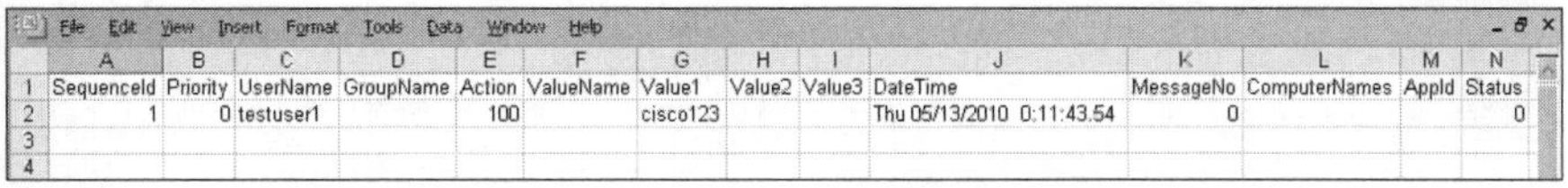

	A	B	C	D	E	F	G	H	I	J	K	L	M	N
1	SequenceId	Priority	UserName	GroupName	Action	ValueName	Value1	Value2	Value3	DateTime	MessageNo	ComputerNames	AppId	Status
2	1	0	testuser1		100		cisco123			Thu 05/13/2010 0:11:43.54	0			0
3														
4														

Figure 14-8 *RDBMS Synchronization: Adding User*

On ACS 4.2, you can use RDBMS synchronization in different ways. One of the easiest ones available (on ACS for Windows and ACS SE) is to import the CSV file with the data. On ACS SE, this file needs to be placed on a FTP server; on ACS for Windows, it can be placed on a local drive. The section that follows outlines how to import the CSV file in Figure 14-8 on ACS for Windows.

Performing RDBMS Synchronization

RDBMS synchronization is found under the System Configuration section. If it is not available, this feature can be made visible from **Interface Configuration > Advanced Options** and by checking the **RDBMS Synchronization** option to display the screen shown in Figure 14-9.

Step 1. Create your accountActions table/file.

Step 2. Choose how you want to synchronize data into ACS—using ODBC databases or using local CSV file. If using an ODBC database, set up a system DSN as instructed in "User Guide for Cisco Secure Access Control Server" under the "System Configuration Advanced" section:

http://www.cisco.com/en/US/docs/net_mgmt/cisco_secure_access_control_se rver_for_windows/4.2.1/User_Guide/SCAdv.html#wp757441

Step 3. Choose the **Synchronization Scheduling** option if you want to schedule the synchronization; otherwise, leave it on the default for manual synchronization.

Step 4. Choose the AAA server(s) from the **AAA Servers** column and move it to the **Synchronize** column on which you want to do the RDBMS synchronization.

Step 5. Save the changes by choosing **Submit**. If required to do synchronization manually, choose the **Synchronize Now** button.

Step 6. Finally, check the RDBMS Synchronization reports from Reports & Activity to ensure that synchronization went properly.

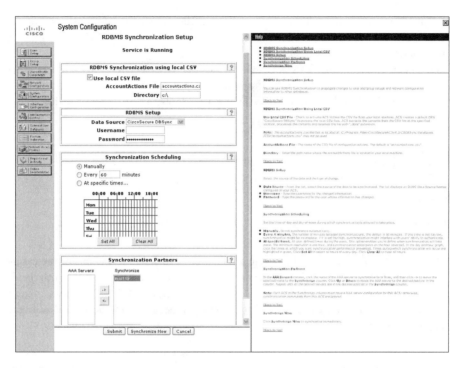

Figure 14-9 *RDBMS Synchronization*

Network Access Profiles

Before the Network Access Profile (NAP) feature was introduced in ACS, there was no clear classification on different security policies that could be applied to different use cases. For instance, suppose that you have a wired and wireless network and have secured them using 802.1 x frameworks. The security policy needs to be more limiting when access is through wireless as compared to wired. Suppose that you are required to assign users to VLAN 200 (which is a restricted VLAN) when they access the network through wireless, and assign users to VLAN 300 when they access the network through a wired connection. On ACS, you can configure attributes on either the user or group level. Only one configuration will take effect, but that will not satisfy the security need. Without NAP, you can either have VLAN 200 or VLAN 300, always.

Now, with NAP, you can classify access requests and depending upon conditions, you can apply different policies.

So, a NAP, also known as a *profile*, is a classification of network access request for applying a common policy.

Note Profiles are not supported for TACACS+ protocol. They only work with the RADIUS protocol.

There are two main components of profiles:

■ Classification of network request

■ Policies

The sections that follow describe these in more detail.

Classification of Network Request

The following are the classification methods available:

■ **NAFs:** *Network Access Filter* (NAF) is configured under **Shared Profile Components** and is used for grouping AAA clients. If a NAF is created and selected in NAP, access requests from only those devices are examined by the NAPs that are under NAF.

■ **Protocol Types:** This option is used to further classify access requests based on type of protocol.

■ **Advanced Filtering:** This option enables you to further classify access requests based on RADIUS attributes and values included in access requests. You can create multiple conditions/rules in this section; the final result is derived by a Boolean AND of all the rules created in this section.

Finally, a profile is selected when all the selected conditions (NAFs, Protocol Types, and Advanced Filtering) match or are true.

Policies

Until now, you have only classified a network access request, but you have still not applied any security policy, as in what needs to be done when you have identified the section that needs to be taken care of according to the security policy. This action or application of security policy is handled by profile-based policies.

The following options are available for creating a profile-based policy (see Figure 14-10):

■ **Protocols:** In this section, you create a rule that defines which password protocol and/or EAP configuration is allowed.

■ **Authentication:** In this section, you have a configuration related to authentication. For example, from which database does the user need to be authenticated?

■ **Posture validation:** In this section, you create rules on how a posture validation will be performed. This option is configured only if you plan to deploy NAC in your network.

■ **Authorization:** In this section, you configure authorization rules and can define System Posture Token, RADIUS Authorization Components (RAC), and Downloadable ACL as the authorization result.

Using NAP and NAP policies, you can now classify an access request and apply the desired security policy. An access request that does not match any profile is also controlled from the **Network Access Profiles** section, as shown in Figure 14-10. By default,

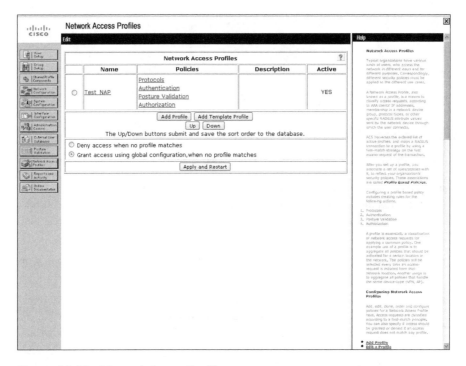

Figure 14-10 *Network Access Profile*

if no profile is matched, access is granted based on global configuration on ACS. If you want to configure a stricter security policy, you can choose the option **Deny access when no profile matches** to make it mandatory for any RADIUS access request to first match a NAP in order to gain network access.

Now suppose that in your network you have a LAN and a WLAN, and the requirement is that if a user successfully authenticated on the LAN he or she should be assigned VLAN 50. Furthermore, if a user successfully authenticates on the WLAN, he or she should be assigned VLAN 60. Without the NAP feature, this would not be possible.

To achieve your objective, you would be required to create two NAP profiles. A NAP profile for the LAN will have a classification of request based on a NAF. You will create a NAF from the shared profile components that will contain all the LAN switches.

After you have selected a NAF in the LAN NAP profile, you need to choose the appropriate protocol that needs to be allowed. Because VLAN assignment will involve EAP protocols, you can choose the EAP protocol of your choice that needs to be allowed.

After deciding which protocol to allow, you need to choose the database where the user identity is held. This is done from the **Authentication** section of the NAP. In this section, you can choose which database to check directly for user account verification.

If posture validation is required in your network, you can configure it from the **Posture Validation** section in NAP according to your security policy.

The final requirement for this example is to define the authorization components for the requests matching the criteria defined in NAP through the **Authorization** section in NAP. Before you configure this section, all the required authorization components must first be configured under **Shared Profile Components' RADIUS Authorization Component** and/or **Downloadable IP ACLs.** These are the two authorization components returned if all the conditions are met successfully.

For this example, you need to create a RAC as follows:

- [64] Tunnel-Type = VLAN

- [65] Tunnel-Medium-Type = 802

- [81] Tunnel-Private-Group-ID = 50

Under the LAN NAP, you can then select this RAC for any/specific user with any/specific system posture.

Similarly, a WLAN NAP needs to be created to assign VLAN 60.

Local Password Management

The Local Password Management section is available under the **System Configuration** section as **Local Password Management.** As shown in Figure 14-11, under this section, you can configure validation parameters/complexity for user passwords. In this section, you can also configure whether a Telnet password change is allowed. If the change is allowed, you can further configure whether ACS sends updated password information to replication partners.

Note   The password policy configured in this section applies only on ACS internal users and is not linked to administrator account created in the **Administration Control** section on ACS.

Remote Logging

By default, ACS audit logs are stored locally, be it ACS for Windows or ACS SE. In the case of ACS for Windows, audit logs are stored at a default location:

- C:\Program Files\CiscoSecure ACS v4.2\Logs\Failed Attempts

- C:\Program Files\CiscoSecure ACS v4.2\Logs\Passed Authentications

- C:\Program Files\CiscoSecure ACS v4.2\Logs\RADIUS Accounting

- C:\Program Files\CiscoSecure ACS v4.2\Logs\TACACS+ Accounting

- C:\Program Files\CiscoSecure ACS v4.2\Logs\TACACS+ Administration

- C:\Program Files\CiscoSecure ACS v4.2\Logs\VoIP Accounting

- C:\Program Files\CiscoSecure ACS v4.2\Logs\Backup and Restore

- C:\Program Files\CiscoSecure ACS v4.2\Logs\DBReplicate

- C:\Program Files\CiscoSecure ACS v4.2\Logs\AdminAudit

- C:\Program Files\CiscoSecure ACS v4.2\CSAuth\PasswordLogs

- C:\Program Files\CiscoSecure ACS v4.2\Logs\ServiceMonitoring

- C:\Program Files\CiscoSecure ACS v4.2\Logs\DbSync

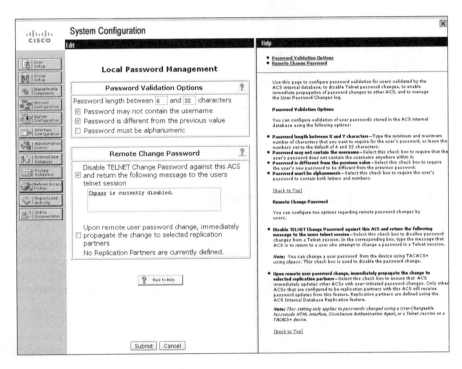

Figure 14-11   *Local Password Management*

For ACS SE, logs are by default stored on a local drive with a retention policy. For each CSV log, ACS SE writes a separate log file. When a log file size reaches 10 MB, ACS SE starts a new log file. ACS SE retains the seven most recent log files for each CSV log.

On ACS for Windows, you have the flexibility to change the default audit log location, which you will see in next section. On ACS SE, you do not have that flexibility. For auditing purposes, if you want to send logs from ACS for Windows and/or ACS SE to a remote location, that can be done. There are two ways to achieve this:

- Remote Agent

- Syslog

Remote Agent is software that needs to be installed on the Windows server, which will act as a log collector. On ACS for Windows, you need to create an AAA server entry for Remote Agent; on ACS SE, you have to create it as Remote Agent under the **Network**

Configuration section. You can have multiple remote agents added on the ACS server. Specifying which remote agent gets the log and how is configured from the following:

■ **System Configuration > Logging > Remote Logging Servers Configuration** (see Figure 14-12)

■ **System Configuration > Logging > Remote Agent Reports Configuration**

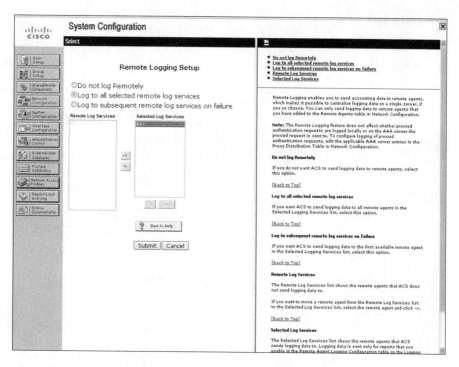

Figure 14-12 *Remote Logging Servers Configuration*

> **Note**   For detail on Remote Agent software, consult Cisco Secure Access Control Server documentation.

Syslog is another option available to send logs on a remote server. This configuration option is very easy to configure; you need only have a syslog server configured, and on ACS you need to configure Syslog server settings on ACS from **System Configuration > Logging**.

Every individual log has a section for Syslog logging that can be configured.

Log File Management

The Log File Management feature (see Figure 14-13) is available for audit and service logs on ACS for Windows and for Remote Agent Reports on ACS SE. This feature enables you to manage logs that get generated on the ACS server or on the Remote Agent directory. This feature provides you with options on how log files needs to be generated, including

- Every day

- Every week

- Every month

- When size is greater than _X_ KB

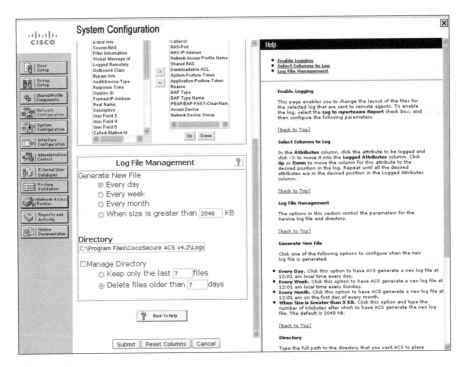

Figure 14-13   *Log File Management: Passed Authentication Logs*

In this section you can also change the default log location to a different log location on the disk drive, under the **Directory** option.

The **Manage Directory** section has two options on how the directory needs to be maintained. To use this feature you need to enable **Manage Directory** by checking the check box. The two rules by which a directory can be maintained are

- Keep only the last _X_ files

- Delete files older than _X_ days

These options are configurable from **System Configuration > Logging**. Each audit log can be configured as per need under CSV column. This option is available under **System Configuration > Service Control** for service logs. For Remote Agent, it is available on ACS SE under **System Configuration > Logging > Remote Agent Reports Configuration**.

Tip   Log file management for service logs must be turned on and the **Manage directory** option should be checked too, as shown in Figure 14-14, because space on disk is limited. A huge accumulation of logs might cause ACS services disruption and/or issues while upgrading ACS to a newer version.

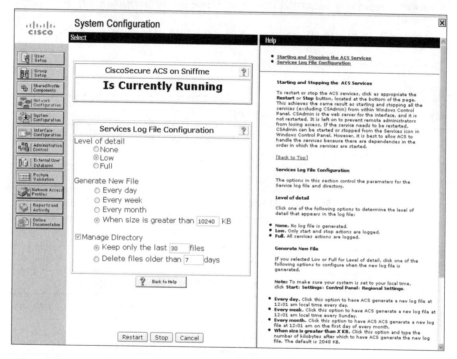

Figure 14-14   *Log File Management: Service Control*

CSUtil Database Utility

CSUtil is a command-line utility/tool for ACS for Windows only. This utility/tool can be used to add, edit, and delete users and AAA client configuration from a colon-delimited text file, along with many other functions. This can be seen as a utility with functions similar to RDBMS synchronization.

The CSUtil.exe is located under the bin subdirectory of the ACS installation directory. For ACS 4.2, if installed on the C: drive, bin will be under:

    C:\Program Files\CiscoSecure ACS v4.2\bin

The files that are generated or are accessed by CSUtil.exe are located under the bin directory.

The CSUtil command syntax is as follows:

```
csutil [-q] [-b backup_filename] [-e number] [-g group_number] [-i file]
[-d [-p secret_key] dump_filename] [-l filename [-passwd secret_key]] [-n]
[-r all|users|config backup_file ] [-u] [-listUDV] [-addUDV slot filename.ini]
[-delUDV slot] [-dumpUDV database_dump_filename]
[-t] [-filepath full_filepath] [-passwd password] [-machine]
(-a | -g group_number | -u user_name | -f user_list_filepath)
[-addAVP filepath] [-delAVP vendor_id application_id attribute_id] [-dumpAVP
filename]
[-delPropHPP attribute_ID property_ID] [-delEntHPP attribute_ID entity_name]
```

Table 14-6 describes the CSUtil options in greater detail.

Table 14-6   *CSUtil Options*

Syntax	Meaning
-q	Use Quiet mode. Does not prompt, use before other options.
-b *backup_filename*	Create a system backup.
-d [-p *secret_key*] *dump_filename*	Dump users and groups database to dump.txt or a named file. You should provide a secret key to encrypt user passwords in the dump file.
-e *number*	Decode error number to ASCII message.
-g *group_number*	Dump group information only to group.txt.
-i *file*	Import users or NASs from import.txt or named file.
-p *secret_key*	Reset password-aging counters during users' and groups' database dump (-d).
-l *filename* [-passwd *secret_key*]	Empty the user table, initialize profiles, and load users and groups database from dump.txt or named file. If you used an encrypt key when dumping the information, you must provide a key to decrypt user passwords and other sensitive information in the dump file.
-n	Empty the user table and shared profile components table, initialize user, group, and network access profiles, and create a new database.
-r all|users|config *backup_file*	Restore a system backup.
-u	List users by group to users.txt.

Table 14-6 *CSUtil Options*

Syntax	Meaning
-listUDV	List currently installed user-defined vendors (UDVs).
-addUDV *slot filename.ini*	Install user-defined vendor or vendor-specific-attribute (VSA) data from the .ini file.
-delUDV *slot*	Remove a vendor or VSA.
-dumpUDV *database_dump_file*	Dump currently installed vendors to the System UDVs folder.
-t -filepath *full_filepath* **-passwd** *password* **-machine** (**-a** | **-g** *group_number* | **-u** *user_name* | **-f** *user_list_filepath*)	Generate protected access credentials (PAC) files for use with Extensible Authentication Protocol-Flexible Authentication via Secure Tunneling (EAP-FAST) clients. You can generate a user PAC or a machine PAC.
-addAVP *filename*	Add attributes from *filename*.
-delAVP *vendor_id application_id attribute_id*	Remove an AVP attribute.
-dumpAVP *filename*	Dump AVP attributes into *filename*.
-delPropHPP *attribute_ID property_ID*	Remove specific property from an extended attribute under Cisco:Host.
-delEntHPP *attribute_ID entity_name*	Remove specific entity from an extended attribute under Cisco:Host.

Although it's clear from Table 14-6 what the CSUtil utility can do, here is a list of CSutil functions:

- Backup ACS database
- Restore ACS database
- Initialize ACS database
- Clean ACS internal database
- Add, update, delete User and AAA client
- Export user list
- Export group information
- Decode error numbers
- Add, delete, list, export user-defined RADIUS VSA
- PAC file generation
- Import, export, delete posture-validation attributes
- Adding external audit device type attributes

As an example, Example 14-1 shows the CSutil option to backup the ACS database.

Example 14-1   *CSUtil Backup*

```
C:\Program Files\CiscoSecure ACS v4.2\bin>CSUtil.exe -b backup.dmp
CSUtil v4.2(0.124), Copyright 1997-2008, Cisco Systems Inc
All running services will be stopped and re-started automatically.
Are you sure you want to proceed? (Y or N)(Y)
Done

C:\Program Files\CiscoSecure ACS v4.2\bin>dir backup.dmp
 Volume in drive C has no label.
 Volume Serial Number is 84E7-28DE

 Directory of C:\Program Files\CiscoSecure ACS v4.2\bin

05/17/2010  07:56 PM          1,557,582 backup.dmp
               1 File(s)      1,557,582 bytes
               0 Dir(s)  36,175,253,504 bytes free

C:\Program Files\CiscoSecure ACS v4.2\bin>
```

Note   Different operations with the CSUtil utility might require precise steps to be followed. Please refer to the "CSUtil Database Utility" section of "User Guide for Cisco Secure Access Control Server" for complete instructions:

http://www.cisco.com/en/US/docs/net_mgmt/cisco_secure_access_control_server_for_windows/4.2.1/User_Guide/A_CSUtil.html.

In most options, it is required to stop the CSAuth service, which will stop authentication until CSAuth is restarted.

The text that follows demonstrates another instance of importing a RADIUS vendor-specific attribute. This example takes an imaginary vendor (NewVendor) whose RADIUS attributes for a device need to be added in ACS. Example 14-2 shows the VSA file to be used.

Example 14-2   *VSA File Content*

```
[User Defined Vendor]

Name=NewVendor
IETF Code=32767
VSA 101=NewVendor-Role

[NewVendor-Role]

Type=STRING
Profile=OUT
```

To import the new VSA into ACS, you first need to check the free slots that can be used on ACS to fit the new VSA as done in Example 14-3.

Example 14-3   *Listing Unassigned Slots Using csutil.exe*

```
C:\Program Files\CiscoSecure ACS v4.2\bin>csutil.exe -listudv
CSUtil v4.2(1.15), Copyright 1997-2009, Cisco Systems Inc
UDV 0 - Unassigned
UDV 1 - Unassigned
UDV 2 - Unassigned
UDV 3 - Unassigned
UDV 4 - Unassigned
UDV 5 - Unassigned
UDV 6 - Unassigned
UDV 7 - Unassigned
UDV 8 - Unassigned
UDV 9 - Unassigned
```

As you can see, there are 10 slots available and you can choose any free slot. In this example, slot 0 was chosen. The next step is to import the VSA file as shown in Example 14-2.

Example 14-4   *RADIUS VSA Import Using csutil.exe*

```
C:\Program Files\CiscoSecure ACS v4.2\bin>csutil.exe   -addUDV 0 c:\newvendor.ini

CSUtil v4.2(0.124), Copyright 1997-2008, Cisco Systems Inc

Adding or removing vendors requires ACS services to be re-started.
Please make sure regedit is not running as it can prevent registry
backup/restore operations

Are you sure you want to proceed? (Y or N)Y
Parsing [c:\newvendor.ini] for addition at UDV slot [0]
Stopping any running services
Creating backup of current config
Adding Vendor [NewVendor] added as [RADIUS (NewVendor)]
Adding VSA [NewVendor-Role]
Done
Checking new configuration...
New configuration OK
Re-starting stopped services
```

In Example 14-4, the newvendor.ini file has the contents shown previously in Example 14-2.

Now go to **Network Configuration** on ACS and add an entry for the NewVendor device using **RADIUS (NewVendor)**. Then select **Submit+Apply.**

Then go to **Interface Configuration > RADIUS (NewVendor)** and check the attributes that you need to be available for configuration on user/group configuration.

Summary

This chapter went through a few of the advanced features available in ACS 4.2. The key concepts covered in the chapter are as follows:

- The Network Access Restriction (NAR) feature as a means for providing authorization based on user access request.

- The features and options available for backing up and restoring an ACS database.

- Replication as a means for creating redundant ACS database, along with differences in ACS backup and ACS replication.

- RDBMS synchronization as a tool (more of an API) to achieve bulk operation in a single go.

- Network Access Profiles (NAPs) as a means for classifying access request and applying common security policy on a network.

- Options available for local password policy.

- Remote logging options with Remote Agent and syslog server.

- Managing and customizing log files on ACS using the Log File Management option.

- The CSUtil database utility for performing various operations from the command line (DOS) on ACS for Windows.

Chapter 15

ACS 5.1

This chapter covers the following subjects:

- Replication Among ACS 5.1 Servers in a Distributed Environment

- Understanding Dictionaries

- Remote Logging on ACS 5.1

- Importing Network Resources and Users

- Managing System Administration

- Backup and Restore Options Available on ACS

This chapter looks at some of the advanced configuration components involved in ACS 5.1. The chapter provides details about components involved in replication as well as the options available for backing up and restoring an ACS database. The chapter also covers bulk import of network resources and users. System administration is also a part of advanced configuration, so you will familiarize yourself with the configuration part pertaining to system administrators.

Replication

In a deployment, you can have multiple ACS servers with one server designated as the primary server and all other servers as secondary servers. For the purpose of centralized management, configuration changes are made only on a primary server, and the changes are propagated to all secondary servers.

In a distributed deployment of ACS, communication happens only between the primary server and the secondary servers. There is no communication between the secondary servers and they are not aware of other secondary server status in a deployment.

Distributed deployment ensures that all instances in a system will have an identical configuration. The primary instance centralizes the configuration of the registered secondary instances. Configuration changes made in the primary instance are automatically replicated to the secondary instances.

Secondary instances in a deployment can view the configuration data only as read-only data. A small number of configuration changes can be performed on a secondary instance in a deployment, including configuration of the server certificate, and these changes remain local to the server.

If there is a firewall between the primary instance and the secondary instances in a deployment, you must ensure that communication over port 2638 and port 61616 is allowed.

In a distributed deployment, the changes made on the primary instance are automatically replicated to secondary instances. If configuration changes do not replicate to the secondary instances, you can force a *full replication*.

Note   Replication on ACS 5.1 happens immediately when the change is made, as opposed to ACS 4.2 where changes get replicated only during configured replication time.

After the distributed deployment is working well, there might be times when you want to test some configuration on a single ACS server while not affecting other ACS servers in the deployment. This can be done using a mode called *local mode*.

You can use the local mode option in following scenarios:

■   If the primary server is unreachable from a secondary server and a configuration change must be made to a secondary server, you can specify that the secondary server go into local mode.

■   If you want to perform some configuration changes on a trial basis that would apply to only one server and not impact all the servers in your deployment, you can specify that one of the secondary servers go into local mode.

In local mode, you can make changes to a single ACS instance through the local web interface, and the changes take effect on that instance only. When the connection to the primary server resumes, you can reconnect the disconnected secondary instance in local mode to the primary server. All configuration changes made while the secondary server was in local mode are lost.

Registration of a server to the primary server and local mode operation on ACS 5.1 are controlled from **System Administration > Operations > Local Operations > Deployment Operations**.

Activating Secondary Servers

To add a server to a deployment, you must perform the following steps:

Step 1.   From the secondary server, issue a request to register on the primary server/instance from **System Administration > Operations > Local Operations > Deployment Operations**.

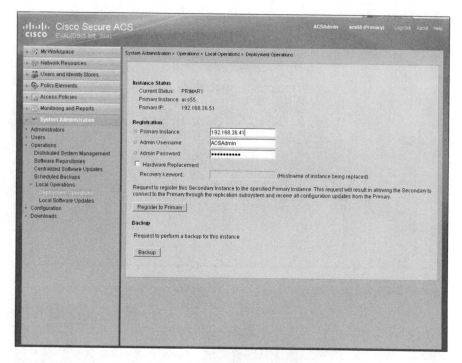

Figure 15-1 *Registering Secondary Server to Primary*

In the Registration section, specify the primary server details as illustrated in Figure 15-1.

After choosing the option **Register to Primary**, the ACS instance will provide you with information regarding the next step to follow as shown in Figure 15-2.

Step 2.   Activate the secondary instance on the primary server. You must activate the secondary instance on the primary instance for the secondary instance to receive configuration information; this provides a mechanism of admission control. However, there is an option to automatically activate newly added secondary instances, rather than performing a manual activation request as shown in Figure 15-3—check the radio button for **Enable Auto Activation for Newly Registered Instances**.

After the secondary instance has been registered successfully and the services are up, the status can be viewed from either instance (primary or secondary) from **System Administration > Operations > Distributed System Management** as shown in Figure 15-4.

Note   Unlike ACS 4.2 where full replication was performed, in ACS 5.1, only the specific changes are propagated.

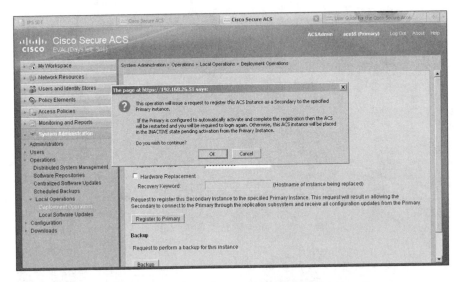

Figure 15-2   *Registering the Secondary Instance to the Primary Instance*

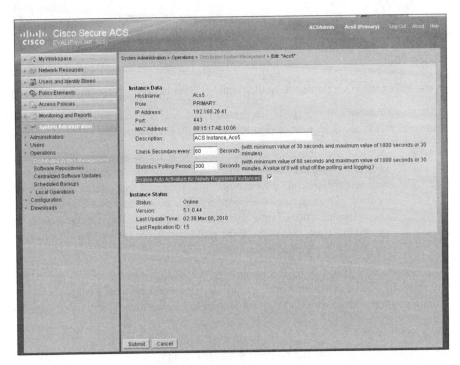

Figure 15-3   *Auto Activation Setting on Primary Server*

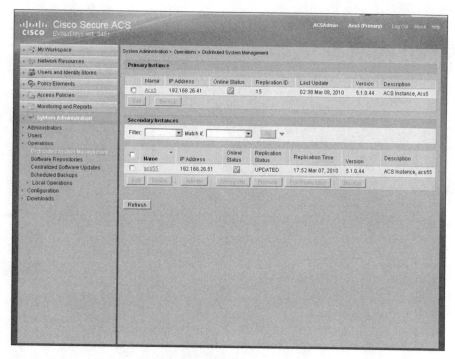

Figure 15-4 *Distributed System Management*

Recall the previously discussed information about local mode on an instance. On a secondary server, you can find this option at **System Administration > Operations > Local Operations > Deployment Operations.**

Figure 15-5 shows the Request Local Mode option available on the secondary instance.

A full replication can be initiated from either instance (primary server or secondary server). As an example, Figure 15-6 provides an example of full replication initiated from the primary server from **System Administration > Operations > Distributed System Management.**

During full replication, the full set of configuration data is transferred to the secondary server to ensure the configuration data on the secondary server is resynchronized.

Dictionaries

As the name suggests, dictionaries on ACS 5.1 are a place to hold all RADIUS- and TACACS+-related dictionaries. This section displays available protocol attributes in the respective dictionary.

To view and choose attributes from a protocol dictionary, select **System Administration > Configuration > Dictionaries > Protocols;** then choose a RADIUS or TACACS+ dictionary.

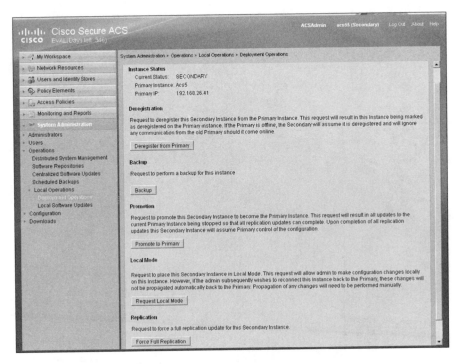

Figure 15-5 *Options Under Deployment Operation on Secondary Instance*

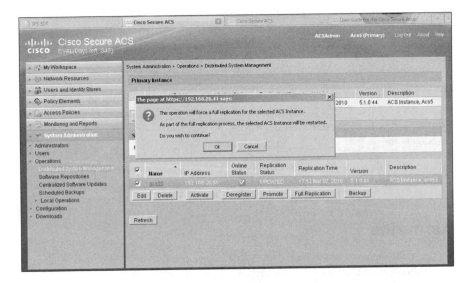

Figure 15-6 *Full Replication from Primary Server*

ACS 5.1 supports RADIUS Vendor Specific Attributes (VSAs). A set of predefined RADIUS VSAs pre-exists on ACS. You can also create, edit, or delete RADIUS VSAs from the ACS web interface.

Note Some of the internally used attributes cannot be modified. You cannot modify an attribute's type if the attribute is used by any policy or policy element.

On ACS 5.1, you can only *view* TACACS+ attributes; you cannot create, edit, or delete them.

To view or edit RADIUS IETF attributes, go to **System Administration > Configuration > Dictionaries > Protocols > RADIUS > RADIUS IETF**.

To view, edit, create or delete RADIUS VSA attributes, go to **System Administration > Configuration > Dictionaries > Protocols > RADIUS > RADIUS VSA** as shown in Figure 15-7.

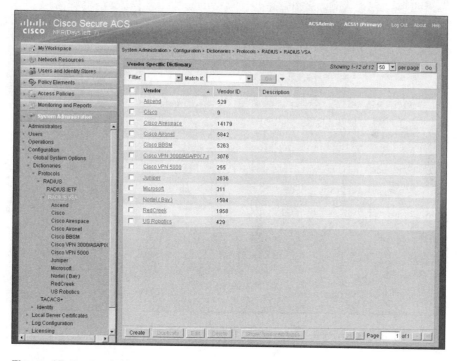

Figure 15-7 *Predefined RADIUS VSAs on ACS*

To create a RADIUS VSA for a vendor, perform the following steps:

> **Note**   The IETF specifies VSAs as a method for communicating vendor-specific informa-
> tion between network access servers and RADIUS servers. Attribute 26 encapsulates ven-
> dor-specific attributes, thereby allowing vendors to support their own extended attributes
> otherwise not suitable for general use.

Step 1.   Go to **System Administration > Configuration > Dictionaries > Protocols > RADIUS > RADIUS VSA.**

Step 2.   Choose the **Create** option to create a RADIUS VSA for a vendor.

Step 3.   Fill in the name and vendor ID as the minimum information, as shown in Figure 15-8, and press **Submit.**

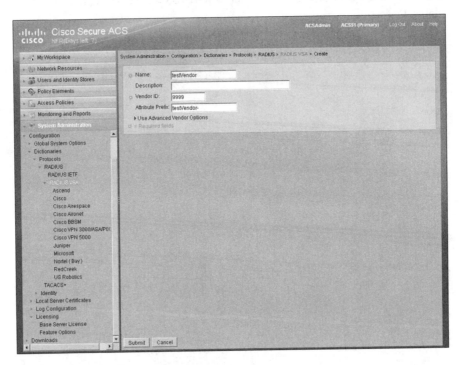

Figure 15-8   *Creating RADIUS VSA*

Step 4.   To create attributes for the new vendor VSA, navigate to the newly created vendor VSA under the RADIUS VSA section. Go to **System Administration > Configuration > Dictionaries > Protocols > RADIUS > RADIUS VSA > testVendor.**

Choose the **Create** option to create a new attribute for the vendor VSA. Specify the attribute name and vendor attribute ID as minimum and press **Submit**. Configure additional options based on information provided by the vendor about its attributes.

Figure 15-9 illustrates a sample configuration of a new vendor VSA attribute.

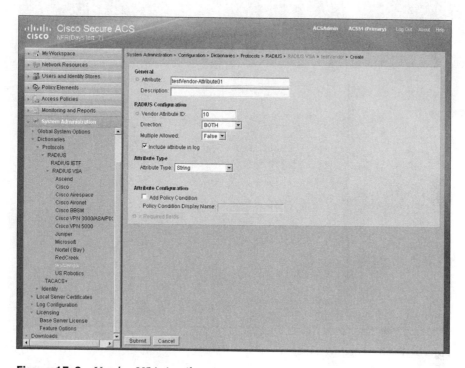

Figure 15-9   *Vendor VSA Attribute*

After a RADIUS VSA is created, it can be used in policies, authorization profiles, and RADIUS token servers in the same way as predefined VSAs.

Remote Logging

On ACS, log records are generated for the following types of messages:

- Accounting

- AAA audit and diagnostics

- System diagnostics

- Administrative and operational audits

As shown in Figure 15-10, these log messages are arranged in a tree hierarchy structure, which you can view by going to **System Administration > Configuration > Log Configuration > Logging Categories > Global.**

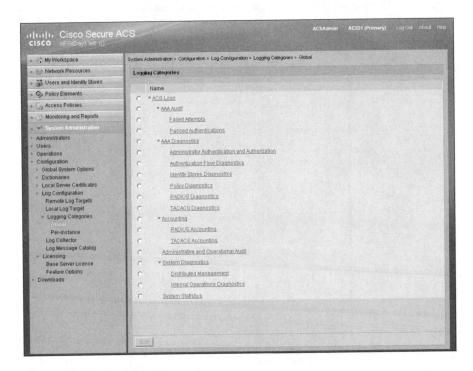

Figure 15-10   *Logging Categories*

Log messages can be stored locally or remotely based on the logging categories and maintenance parameters.

This section looks at how to configure remote logging on ACS 5.1 for log records.

On ACS 5.1, you can configure specific remote log targets to receive the logging messages for a specific logging category. The remote log targets first need to be defined, which you can do only on a syslog server. After you define a remote log target, you can specify it under a specific logging category.

Defining a Remote Log Target

To define a remote log target, follow these steps:

Step 1.   Go to, System Administration > Configuration > Log Configuration > Remote Log Targets.

Step 2.   Choose the **Create** option to create a new remote log target. Provide name, IP address, port, and maximum length for the syslog server as shown in Figure 15-11 and press **Submit**.

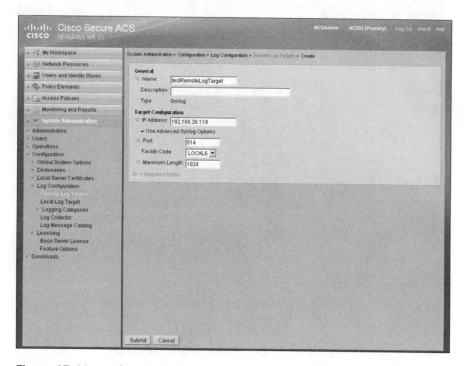

Figure 15-11 *Defining a Remote Log Target*

Specifying a Remote Log Target Under a Logging Category

If you want to change the log target globally for all instances, go to the **Global** option under **Logging Categories**; otherwise, if you want to change the log target for only a particular instance of ACS, choose **Per-Instance** under **Logging Categories** for the particular ACS.

The list that follows shows how to change the log target using the **Global** option.

Step 1.   Go to **System Administration > Configuration > Log Configuration > Logging Categories > Global**.

Step 2.   Select any log for which you want to change the remote log target and click **Edit**.

Step 3.   Select the **Remote Syslog Target** tab and choose the remote log target that you created previously under Selected Targets.

For example, go to **System Administration > Configuration > Log Configuration > Logging Categories > Global > Edit: "Passed Authentications"** as shown in Figure 15-12.

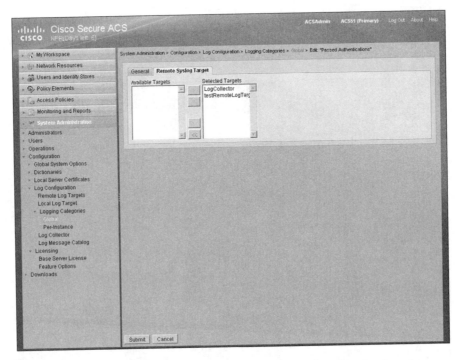

Figure 15-12 *Specifying Remote Log Target for Passed Authentications Log*

Importing Network Resources and Users

You can perform bulk operations for network resources and users on ACS 5.1. You can achieve this using the **File Operations** function, which enables you to add, update, or delete internal users, internal hosts, or network devices on the database.

The File Operations function is accessible from the following sections for network devices, internal users, and internal hosts, respectively:

- **Network Resources > Network Devices and AAA Clients**
- **Users and Identity Stores > Internal Identity Stores > Users**
- **Users and Identity Stores > Internal Identity Stores > Hosts**

Bulk import on ACS is done using a comma-separated values (CSV) file. There are certain guidelines that you must to follow to bulk-import information into a ACS database.

Because the .csv templates for users, internal hosts, and network devices are specific to their individual type, you must download the .csv file template from ACS. You can then add the records that you want to add, update, or delete to the .csv file and save it to your local disk.

While updating the template .csv file, you must adhere to these requirements:

- Do not alter the contents of the first record (the first line, or row, of the .csv file).

- Use only one line for each record.

- Do not embed new line characters in any fields.

- For non-English languages, encode the .csv file in utf-8 encoding or save it with a font that supports Unicode.

For demonstration purposes, consider the following procedure of importing a user using File Operations.

Step 1.   Go to **Users and Identity Stores > Internal Identity Stores > Users** and select the option **File Operations** as shown in Figure 5-13.

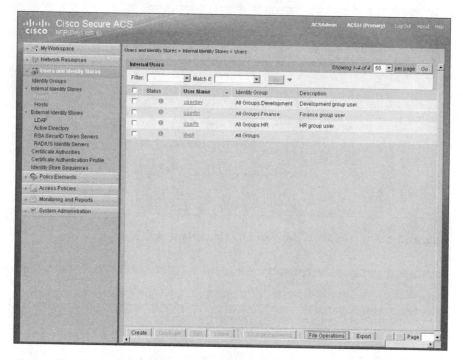

Figure 15-13   *Choosing File Operations Function*

Step 2.   From the screen in Figure 15-14, select the **Add** option select **Next**.

Step 3.   Click **Download "Add" Template** options and save the template on your PC as shown in Figure 15-15.

Step 4.   Open the CSV file and add the user record as shown in Figure 15-16. All fields are not mandatory. Mandatory fields have the **Required** keyword in their column header. After the information has been filled, save the file.

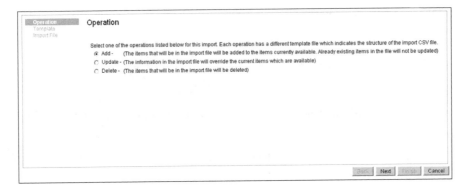

Figure 15-14 *Add Option: File Operations*

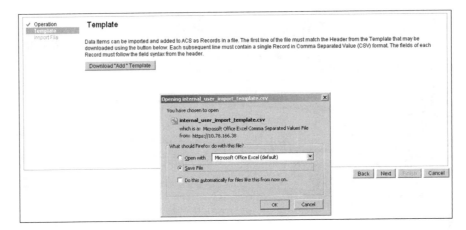

Figure 15-15 *Download Template: File Operations Add User*

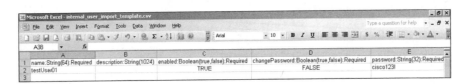

Figure 15-16 *Editing Template File: File Operations Add User*

Step 5.   After you have a file ready to import, you can either restart the process from step 1 until step 3, skipping the option to download the template if you have closed or canceled the operation; otherwise, click **Finish** to proceed to upload the file as shown in Figure 15-17.

ACS will show you the import progress and will log the success/failure messages on the progress windows as shown in Figure 5-18.

You can adopt a similar process to update or delete user, host, or network resources.

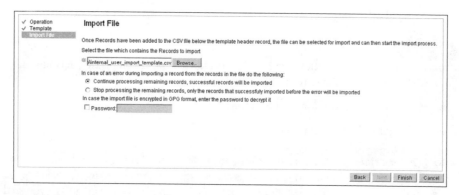

Figure 15-17 *Import File: File Operations Add User*

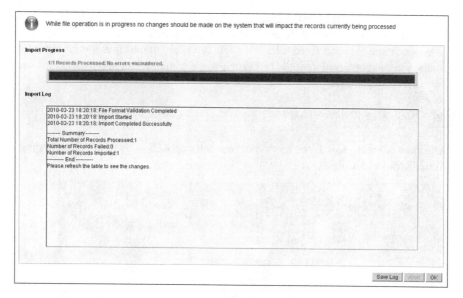

Figure 15-18 *Import Progress: File Operation Add User*

Managing System Administrators

As with any application or system, system administrators on ACS are responsible for deploying, configuring, maintaining, and monitoring. The administrators are controlled through the ACS administrative interface on ACS, available at **System Administration > Administrators**.

This section enables you to perform various system administration–related operations, including the following:

■ Create, edit, duplicate, or delete administrator accounts

■ Change the password of other administrators

- View predefined roles

- Associate roles to administrators

- Configure authentication settings that include password complexity, account lifetime, and account inactivity

- Configure administrator session setting

- Configure administrator access setting

Note The first time you log in to ACS 5.1, you are prompted for the predefined administrator username (ACSAdmin) and required to change the predefined password (default). This administrator has super administrator permissions—Create, Read, Update, Delete, and Execute to all ACS resources.

To control what an administrator can do, ACS provides *roles*, which consist of typical administrator tasks, each with an associated set of permissions. Each administrator can have more than one predefined role, and a role can apply to multiple administrators. As a result, you can configure multiple tasks for a single administrator and multiple administrators for a single task.

Note On ACS, by design, all roles are predefined and cannot be changed.

As shown in Figure 15-19, you can view these roles on ACS at **System Administration > Administrators > Roles.**

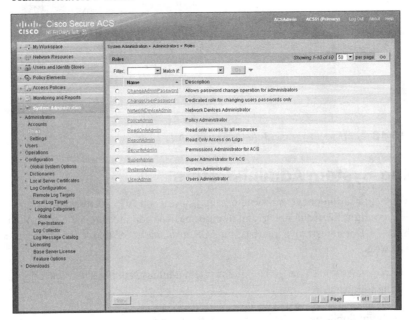

Figure 15-19 *Administrator Roles*

Table 15-1 describes the predefined administrator roles in greater detail.

Table 15-1   *Predefined Role Descriptions*

Role	Privileges
ChangeAdminPassword	This role is intended for ACS administrators who manage other administrator accounts. This role entitles the administrator to change the password of other administrators.
ChangeUserPassword	This role is intended for ACS administrators who manage internal user accounts. This role entitles the administrator to change the password of internal users.
NetworkDeviceAdmin	This role is intended for ACS administrators who need to manage the ACS network device repository only, such as adding, updating, or deleting devices. This role has the following permissions: • Read and write permissions on network devices • Read and write permissions on Network Device Groups (NDGs) and all object types in the Network Resources drawer
PolicyAdmin	This role is intended for the ACS policy administrator responsible for creating and managing ACS access services and access policy rules, and the policy elements referenced by the policy rules. This role has the following permissions: • Read and write permissions on all the elements used in policies, such as authorization profile, NDGs, IDGs, conditions, and so on • Read and write permissions on services policy
ReadOnlyAdmin	This role is intended for ACS administrators who need read-only access to all parts of the ACS user interface. This role has read-only access to all resources.
ReportAdmin	This role is intended for administrators who need access to the ACS Monitoring & Report Viewer to generate and view reports or monitoring data only. This role has read-only access on logs.
SecurityAdmin	This role is required in order to create, update, or delete ACS administrator accounts, to assign administrative roles, and to change the ACS password policy. This role has the following permissions: • Read and write permissions on internal protocol users and administrator password policies • Read and write permissions on administrator account settings • Read and write permissions on administrator access settings

Table 15-1   *Predefined Role Descriptions*

Role	Privileges
SuperAdmin	The Super Admin role has complete access to every ACS administrative function. If you do not need granular access control, this role is most convenient, and this is the role assigned to the predefined ACSAdmin account. This role has Create, Read, Update, Delete, and eXecute (CRUDX) permissions on all resources.
SystemAdmin	This role is intended for administrators responsible for ACS system configuration and operations. This role has the following permissions: • Read and write permissions on all system administration activities except for account definition • Read and write permissions on ACS instances
UserAdmin	This role is intended for administrators who are responsible for adding, updating, or deleting entries in the internal ACS identity stores, which includes internal users and internal hosts. This role has the following permissions: • Read and write permissions on users and hosts • Read permission on IDGs

Note   Administrators are authenticated against the internal database only.

The most important task is to create an administrator account and assign it the required role. You can do this from **System Administration > Administrators > Accounts > Create**, as shown in Figure 15-20.

Administrator account definitions consist of a name, status, description, e-mail address, password, and role assignment.

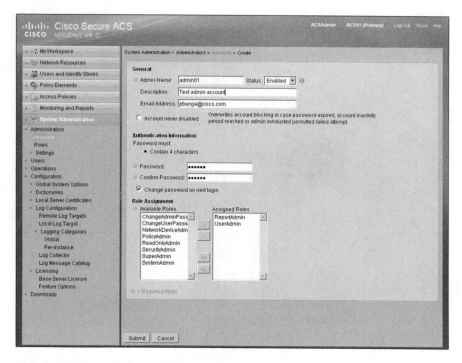

Figure 15-20 *Administrator Accounts*

ACS provides the following configurable options to manage administrator passwords:

■ **Password Complexity:** Required length and character types for passwords

■ **Password History:** Prevents repeated use of same passwords

■ **Password Lifetime:** Forces the administrators to change passwords after a specified time period

■ **Account Inactivity:** Disables the administrator account if it has not been in use for a specified time period

■ **Password Failures:** Disables the administrator account after a specified number of consecutive failed login attempts

You can find these configurable options under the **Password Complexity** and **Advanced** tabs available from **System Administration > Administrators > Settings > Authentication** as shown in Figure 15-21 and Figure 15-22.

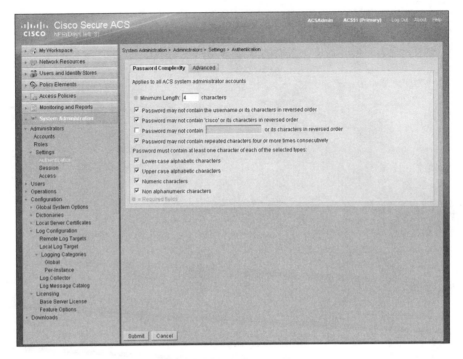

Figure 15-21 *Administrator: Password Complexity*

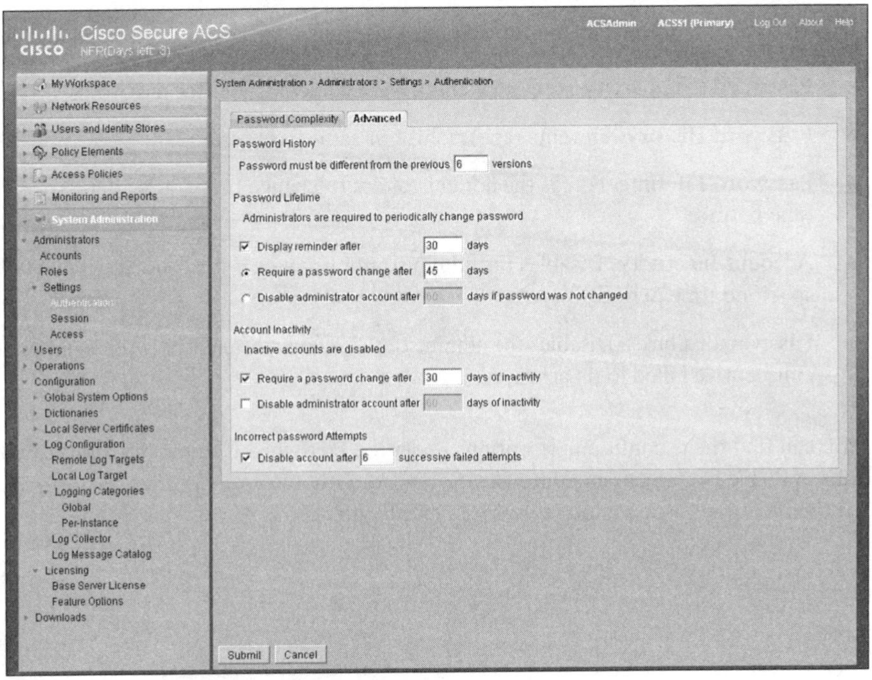

Figure 15-22 *Administrator: Advanced*

To make administration to ACS more secure, you have configurable options that determine the IP addresses from which administrators can access the ACS administrative web interface and the session duration after which idle sessions are logged out from the system.

These options are available at

- **System Administration > Administrators > Settings > Access** (see Figure 15-23)

- **System Administration > Administrators > Settings > Session** (see Figure 15-24)

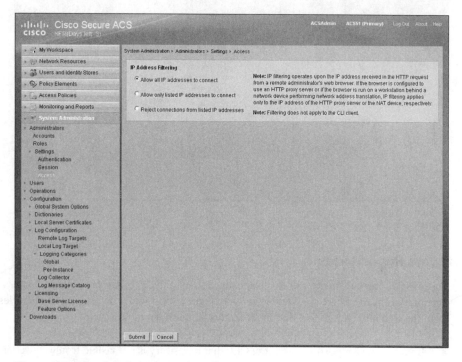

Figure 15-23   *Administrator: Access*

Backup and Restore

Backup is an essential process; in a data loss event, the database backed up using the backup process can be restored using the restore process. ACS provides various options to back up a database.

Before you can perform any backup or restore operation on ACS 5.1, you must have a software repository to do so.

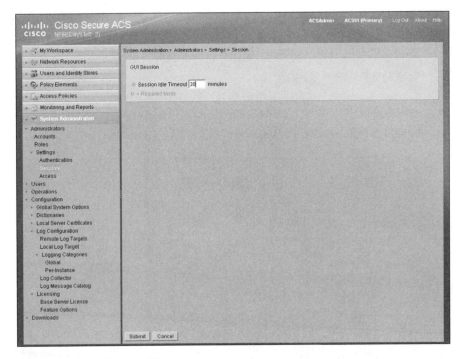

Figure 15-24   *Administrator: Session*

Software Repositories

On ACS 5.1, you can create software repositories using the web interface or command-line interface (CLI). There are a few rules associated with creating or deleting repositories from the web interface or CLI that must always be considered, however:

■ If you create a repository from the CLI, that repository is not visible from the web interface and can be deleted only from the CLI.

■ If you create a repository from the web interface, it can be deleted from the CLI; however, that repository still exists in the web interface. If you use the web interface to create a repository for a software update, the repository is automatically created in the CLI.

■ If you delete a repository using the web interface, it is also deleted in the CLI.

As an example, Figure 15-25 shows how to create a software repository from the web interface from **System Administration > Operations > Software Repositories > Create**.

After you click **Submit**, the software repository **FTPRepository** is visible in the web interface. In addition, you can view the corresponding configuration from the CLI as shown in Example 15-1.

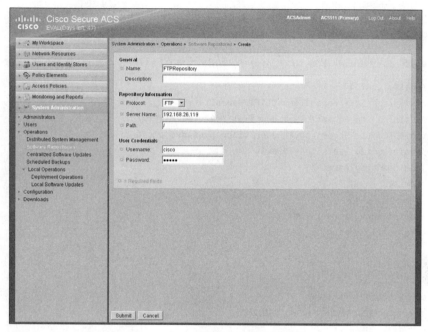

Figure 15-25 *Software Repository from Web Interface*

Example 15-1 *Software Repository Configuration: CLI and Web Interface*

```
ACS511/admin# show running-config
Generating configuration...
!
hostname ACS511
!
interface GigabitEthernet 0
  ip address 192.168.26.51 255.255.255.0
!
<snip>
!
service sshd
!
repository FTPRepository

  url ftp://192.168.26.119/

  user cisco password hash cc14bc179d2708cc31cbc21ee6a679cd22c095ae

!
<snip>
!
icmp echo on
!
ACS511/admin#
```

If you create a software repository from the CLI as shown in Example 15-2, it will not be visible in the web interface.

Example 15-2   *Software Repository Configuration in CLI Only*

```
ACS511/admin# conf t
ACS511/admin(config)# repository CLIFTPRepository
ACS511/admin(config-Repository)# url ftp://192.168.26.119/
ACS511/admin(config-Repository)# user cisco password plain cisco
ACS511/admin(config-Repository)# exit
ACS511/admin(config)#exit
ACS511/admin#


ACS511/admin# show running-config
Generating configuration...
!
hostname ACS511
!
interface GigabitEthernet 0
   ip address 192.168.26.51 255.255.255.0
!
<snip>
!
service sshd
  !
repository CLIFTPRepository

  url ftp://192.168.26.119/

  user cisco password hash cc14bc179d2708cc31cbc21ee6a679cd22c095ae

  repository FTPRepository
  url ftp://192.168.26.119/
  user cisco password hash cc14bc179d2708cc31cbc21ee6a679cd22c095ae
!
<snip>
!
icmp echo on
!
ACS511/admin#
```

After a software repository is created, you are ready to back up or restore a database.

Backing Up a Database

ACS 5.1 provides you with the option to back up data from primary and secondary instances at any time along with the option of regular scheduled backups.

There are two types of configuration available on ACS 5.1:

- ACS configuration data backup
- ADE-OS configuration data backup

For a primary instance, the following backup options are available:

- ACS configuration data only
- ACS configuration data and ADE-OS configuration data

For a secondary instance, you can only back up ADE-OS configuration data. This actually makes sense, as in replication ACS configuration on both instances primary and secondary are identical.

To perform a backup operation from the web interface, go to **System Administration > Operations > Distributed System Management**.

Choose an instance from the Primary Instance table or the Secondary Instances table and use the Backup function as demonstrated in Figure 15-26.

The next step is to provide a name for the backup file, choose the repository, and finally choose the configuration that you need to back up, as shown in Figure 15-27.

Note You can select only one primary instance, but many secondary instances for a backup.

The backup file that gets created on the repository has a predefined format:

<Filename Prefix>-YYMMDD-HHMM.tar.gpg

For example, if you specified the Filename Prefix as **testBackup** and the current date and time on ACS clock is Mar 3 22:25:28 EST 2010. The filename would be

testBackup-100303-2051.tar.gpg

Another method to backing up data is to use the CLI as outlined in the steps that follow.

Step 1.   **Back up the ACS configuration:** To back up an ACS configuration only, use the **acs backup** command in the EXEC mode:

acs backup *backup-filename* **repository** *repository-name*

Example 15-3 demonstrates this configuration.

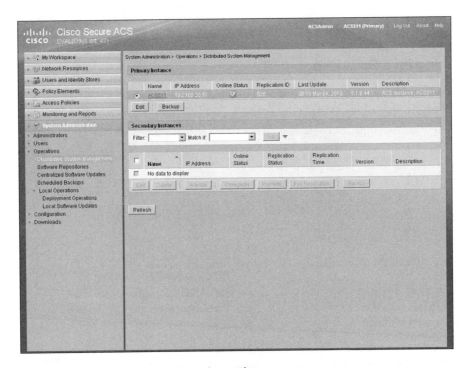

Figure 15-26   *Choosing Instance for Backup*

Example 15-3   CLI ACS Configuration Backup

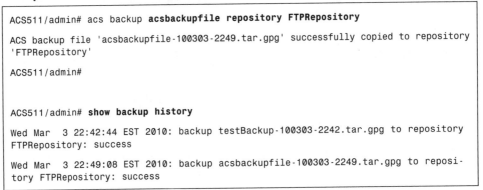

```
ACS511/admin# acs backup acsbackupfile repository FTPRepository

ACS backup file 'acsbackupfile-100303-2249.tar.gpg' successfully copied to repository
'FTPRepository'

ACS511/admin#


ACS511/admin# show backup history

Wed Mar  3 22:42:44 EST 2010: backup testBackup-100303-2242.tar.gpg to repository
FTPRepository: success

Wed Mar  3 22:49:08 EST 2010: backup acsbackupfile-100303-2249.tar.gpg to reposi-
tory FTPRepository: success
```

Step 2.   Backup ACS and ADE-OS configuration: To perform ACS and ADE-OS configuration data backup and place the backup in a repository, use the **backup**
command in the EXEC mode:

backup *backup-name* **repository** *repository-name*

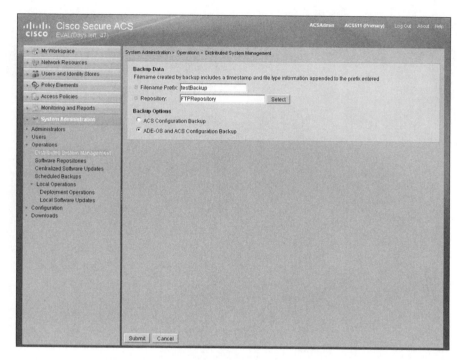

Figure 15-27   *Primary Instance ADE-OS and ACS Configuration Backup*

Example 15-4 demonstrates this configuration.

Example 15-4   *CLI ACS and ADE-OS Configuration Backup*

```
ACS511/admin# backup testBackup repository FTPRepository
% Creating backup with timestamped filename: testBackup-100303-2242.tar.gpg
ACS511/admin#


ACS511/admin# show backup history
Wed Mar  3 22:42:44 EST 2010: backup testBackup-100303-2242.tar.gpg to repository
FTPRepository: success
```

Scheduled Backups

You can schedule ACS backup to run at periodic intervals. You can schedule ACS backup from the primary web interface or through the CLI. One important point to note is that the scheduled backup feature only backs up ACS configuration data.

From the web interface, you can create scheduled backups from **System Administration > Operations > Scheduled Backups > Create** as shown in Figure 15-28.

Example 15-5 shows the resulting CLI configuration for the backup scheduled in the web interface in Figure 15-28.

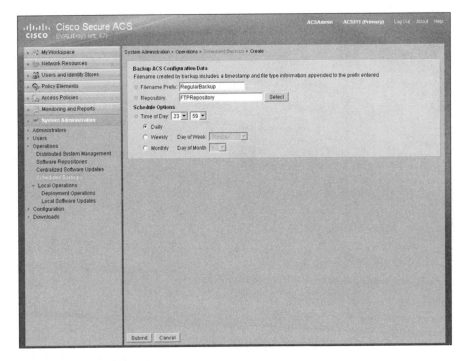

Figure 15-28   *Scheduling Backup from the Web Interface*

Example 15-5   *CLI Schedule Backup Configuration*

```
ACS511/admin# show running-config
Generating configuration...
!
hostname ACS511
!
interface GigabitEthernet 0
  ip address 192.168.26.51 255.255.255.0
!
<snip>
!
service sshd
!
repository CLIFTPRepository
  url ftp://192.168.26.119/
  user cisco password hash cc14bc179d2708cc31cbc21ee6a679cd22c095ae
repository FTPRepository
  url ftp://192.168.26.119/
  user cisco password hash cc14bc179d2708cc31cbc21ee6a679cd22c095ae
!
```

```
<snip>
!
kron policy-list policyList_RegularBackup

   cli acs scheduled_backup RegularBackup repository FTPRepository

!

kron occurrence occurrence_RegularBackup

   at 23:59

   recurring

   policy-list policyList_RegularBackup

!
icmp echo on
!
ACS511/admin#
```

Restoring Databases

As in the case of the backup where you can back up the ACS configuration only or both the ACS and ADE-OS configuration; similarly, you can restore ACS configuration only on ACS 5.1 or you can restore ACS and ADE-OS configuration.

Restoration on ACS 5.1 can be performed only through the CLI. At presstime, the option to restore from the web interface was not available.

To restore an ACS configuration only from one ACS node to another, use the following command in EXEC mode:

acs restore *backup-file-name* **repository** *repository-name*

Example 15-6 demonstrates restoring ACS only.

Example 15-6   *CLI ACS Configuration Restore*

```
ACS511/admin# acs restore acsbackupfile-100303-2249.tar.gpg repository
FTPRepository
Restore requires a restart of ACS services. Continue?  (yes/no) yes
Stopping ACS.
Stopping Management and View................
Stopping Runtime.........................
Stopping Database....
Cleanup.....
Starting ACS ....
```

```
To verify that ACS processes are running, use the
'show application status acs' command.
ACS511/admin#


ACS511/admin# show restore history
Wed Mar  3 22:25:28 EST 2010: restore testBackup01-100303-2051.tar.gpg from repos-
itory FTPRepository: success
Thu Mar  4 17:09:08 EST 2010: restore acsbackupfile-100303-2249.tar.gpg from
repository FTPRepository: success
```

To perform a restore of a previous backup for both ACS and ADE-OS, use the following command in EXEC mode:

restore *filename* repository *repository-name*

This restore operation restores data related to ACS as well as the ADE OS.

When you use this command for ACS, the ACS server restarts automatically.

Example 15-7 demonstrates restoring ACS and ADE-OS.

Example 15-7   *CLI ACS and ADE-OS Configuration Restore*

```
ACS511/admin# restore testBackup01-100303-2051.tar.gpg repository FTPRepository
Restore requires a reboot to successfully complete. Continue? (yes/no) [yes] ?
Stopping ACS.
Stopping Management and View.................
Stopping Runtime.........................
Stopping Database....
Cleanup....

Broadcast message from root (pts/0) (Wed Mar  3 22:25:28 2010):

The system is going down for reboot NOW!
ACS511/admin#


ACS511/admin# show restore history
Wed Mar  3 22:25:28 EST 2010: restore testBackup01-100303-2051.tar.gpg from repos-
itory FTPRepository: success
```

Note   You cannot back up data from an earlier version of ACS and restore it to a later version. Backup and restore must be performed on the same version of ACS. If you need the data on a different version of the ACS, you can perform an upgrade after you restore the data.

Summary

This chapter covered a few of the advanced features available in ACS 5.1. The key concepts and takeaways from the chapter can be summarized as follows:

- Distributed deployment on ACS 5.1 has two components: primary server/instance and secondary server(s)/instance(s).

- In a distributed deployment, replication happens automatically from primary instance to secondary instance(s) only.

- In distributed deployment, to make changes on the secondary instance, you need to use the local mode option. When a secondary instance is registered back to primary, all changes on secondary instance are lost.

- ACS 5.1 provides an option to create a dictionary for RADIUS VSAs.

- Only syslog option is available for remote logging on ACS 5.1.

- ACS 5.1 provides File Operation function to facilitate bulk operation for network resources and users.

- System administrator creation with predefined roles along with session and access restriction settings for ACS 5.1 access.

- Two type of backups are available on ACS 5.1: ACS configuration and ADE-OS configuration.

- You can back up a database from both the CLI and web interface.

- You can restore a database only through the CLI in ACS 5.1.

INDEX

Numerics

A

V

W

CISCO

ciscopress.com: Your Cisco Certification and Networking Learning Resource

Subscribe to the monthly Cisco Press newsletter to be the first to learn about new releases and special promotions.

Visit **ciscopress.com/newsletters.**

While you are visiting, check out the offerings available at your finger tips.

—Free Podcasts from experts:
  • OnNetworking
  • OnCertification
  • OnSecurity

Podcasts

View them at **ciscopress.com/podcasts.**

—Read the latest author **articles** and **sample chapters** at **ciscopress.com/articles.**

—Bookmark the Certification Reference Guide available through our partner site at **informit.com/certguide.**

Connect with Cisco Press authors and editors via Facebook and Twitter, visit **informit.com/socialconnect.**

Try Safari Books Online FREE
Get online access to 5,000+ Books and Videos

FREE TRIAL—GET STARTED TODAY!
www.informit.com/safaritrial

> ### Find trusted answers, fast
> Only Safari lets you search across thousands of best-selling books from the top technology publishers, including Addison-Wesley Professional, Cisco Press, O'Reilly, Prentice Hall, Que, and Sams.

> ### Master the latest tools and techniques
> In addition to gaining access to an incredible inventory of technical books, Safari's extensive collection of video tutorials lets you learn from the leading video training experts.

WAIT, THERE'S MORE!

> ### Keep your competitive edge
> With Rough Cuts, get access to the developing manuscript and be among the first to learn the newest technologies.

> ### Stay current with emerging technologies
> Short Cuts and Quick Reference Sheets are short, concise, focused content created to get you up-to-speed quickly on new and cutting-edge technologies.

FREE Online Edition

Your purchase of **AAA Identity Management Security** includes access to a free online edition for 45 days through the Safari Books Online subscription service. Nearly every CIsco Press book is available online through Safari Books Online, along with more than 5,000 other technical books and videos from publishers such as Addison-Wesley Professional, Exam Cram, IBM Press, O'Reilly, Prentice Hall, Que, and Sams.

SAFARI BOOKS ONLINE allows you to search for a specific answer, cut and paste code, download chapters, and stay current with emerging technologies.

Activate your FREE Online Edition at
www.informit.com/safarifree

> **STEP 1:** Enter the coupon code: XRTJZAA.

> **STEP 2:** New Safari users, complete the brief registration form.
> Safari subscribers, just log in.

If you have difficulty registering on Safari or accessing the online edition,
please e-mail customer-service@safaribooksonline.com